To: John Vogt

John,

Please enjoy my book, courtesy of Dave Bego!

God Bless,

Praise for
THE ULTIMATE OBAMA SURVIVAL GUIDE

"Wayne Root is one libertarian I like! (Because he's left his childish games behind and become a full-fledged conservative.) In *The Ultimate Obama Survival Guide* Wayne dissects the coming economic collapse under his old Columbia college classmate Obama and shows you how to capitalize and prosper through hell."

—Ann Coulter, bestselling author of
High Crimes and Misdemeanors, Slander, and *Mugged*

"At a time of suffocating political correctness and damaging crackpot economic theories, particularly at the Federal Reserve, Wayne Allyn Root comes out with both guns blazing! He 'gets it' on preserving freedom and enhancing the opportunity to better oneself and to get ahead."

—Steve Forbes, Chairman and Editor-in-Chief of Forbes Media

"Wayne Allyn Root hits Obama with both barrels, no holds barred. Then he provides solutions that anyone can use to protect themselves and profit during the next four years. That's why they call Wayne the Capitalist Evangelist!"

—Peter Schiff, CEO, Euro Pacific Capital, and bestselling author
of *Crash Proof 2.0* and *The Real Crash*

"President Obama, look out. There's a new sheriff in town and he's not afraid to speak his mind LOUDLY. Wayne Allyn Root is a living, breathing Capitalist Evangelist. Wayne shows you how to beat Obama at his own game, how to protect your assets, and prosper during the next four years. Bravo Wayne!"

—Mike Huckabee, 44th governor of Arkansas, former Republican
presidential candidate, and host of Fox News's *Huckabee*
and *The Mike Huckabee Show*

"Wayne Allyn Root is one of the great conservative thinkers in America. His opinions and commentaries are in the Conservative Hall of Fame with greats like Sean Hannity, Mark Levin, Charles Krauthammer, and Thomas Sowell. Instead of simply cursing the darkness, damage, and decline caused by President Obama, Wayne has lit a candle brighter than a ten-fold beacon shining into a dark night. Follow him."

—Bill Cunningham, host of *The Bill Cunningham Show*, nationally syndicated on Premiere Radio

"We all know that it is dangerous to be right when the government is wrong. Wayne Allyn Root has the courage to be right and to make it public."

—Marc Faber, founder of Marc Faber Limited, Hong Kong, and editor of the *Gloom Boom & Doom Report*

"How did Wayne Allyn Root assemble eighteen financial heavyweights in one book to give their brilliant advice, financial insights, and priceless wisdom? That took magic. Thank you, Wayne!"

—Eric Singer, portfolio manager, Congressional Effect Fund

"The Conservative movement desperately needs someone like Wayne Allyn Root. Dynamic, charismatic, fearless. Wayne's book boldly charts a new direction for you and your family—to transform your thinking, to give you the confidence to take action, to protect your assets and prosper. Sheer genius. Wayne is the new conservative media powerhouse."

—Rita Cosby, three-time Emmy-winner, CBS special correspondent, and host of *The Rita Cosby Show* on WOR radio, New York

"The modern-day conservative movement needs a Ronald Reagan. Wayne Allyn Root is charismatic, dynamic, passionate, a great communicator, and presents economic ideas in a simple, easy-to-understand way. Read Wayne's book and discover how to survive and thrive no matter what Obama throws at us!"

—Mark Skousen, founder and producer of FreedomFest and editor of *Forecasts & Strategies*

THE
ULTIMATE
OBAMA
SURVIVAL GUIDE

THE
ULTIMATE
OBAMA
SURVIVAL GUIDE

HOW TO SURVIVE, THRIVE, AND PROSPER DURING OBAMAGEDDON

WAYNE ALLYN ROOT

Since 1947
**REGNERY
PUBLISHING, INC.**
An Eagle Publishing Company • Washington, DC

Cataloging-in-Publication data on file with the Library of Congress

ISBN 978-1-62157-091-2

Published in the United States by
Regnery Publishing, Inc.
One Massachusetts Avenue NW
Washington, DC 20001
www.Regnery.com

Manufactured in the United States of America

10 9 8 7 6 5 4 3 2 1

Books are available in quantity for promotional or premium use. Write to Director of Special Sales, Regnery Publishing, Inc., One Massachusetts Avenue NW, Washington, DC 20001, for information on discounts and terms, or call (202) 216-0600.

Distributed to the trade by
Perseus Distribution
250 West 57th Street
New York, NY 10107

Nothing in this book should be considered personalized investment advice. Any investments recommended in this book should be made only after consulting with your investment advisor and only after reviewing the prospectus or financial statements of the company.

Dedicated to

*My parents in heaven David and Stella Root—
who gave me my foundation and values in life*

*My grandparents Meta and Simon Reis—who taught me the meaning of
courage, chutzpah, and entrepreneurship*

*My wife Debra and four wonderful children Dakota, Hudson, Remington
Reagan, and Contessa—the loves of my life*

*My political heroes and role models—Barry Goldwater, Ronald Reagan,
Jack Kemp, and Ron Paul*

*America—"a shining city upon a hill whose beacon light guides freedom-
loving people everywhere"*

*Patriots across this great country who fight for God, country, family, capital-
ism, and American exceptionalism*

CONTENTS

PART ONE

OBAMAGEDDON: THE DISASTER WE ARE FACING

"The whole aim of practical politics is to keep the populace alarmed... by an endless series of hobgoblins, most of them imaginary."[1]

—H. L. Mencken

Poker players understand, it's not the hand you are dealt, it's how you play the hand! I'm going to show you how to play the hand Obama is dealing. But first, I have to show you exactly what you're facing. You can't play the hand blind. You need to look carefully at the cards and know the rules before you can draw up a winning game plan.

Let's get started.

CHAPTER ONE

HOW TO SURVIVE OBAMAGEDDON—AND PROSPER IN THE OBAMA GREAT DEPRESSION TO COME

DID YOU KNOW?

- Obama promised to cut the deficit in half by the end of his first term; instead, he increased our debt by 50 percent, adding nearly $6 trillion to what we owe
- Obama promised to cut healthcare premiums $2,500 per family, but they've gone *up* by $3,065 instead
- The work force participation rate for men is at its lowest point since that statistic was first recorded—in 1948
- More Americans became millionaires during the Great Depression than during any other period of history

W elcome to *The Ultimate Obama Survival Guide*. You're reading this book because you know something is very wrong...spectacularly wrong...disastrously wrong...*Apocalypse Now* wrong.

President Obama says the economic picture is improving.[1] Yet in 2013 Americans' disposable income dropped by 4 percent—the biggest collapse in fifty-four years (since record-keeping began in 1959).[2] And the labor participation rate—the percentage of working-age Americans who are working or even looking for work—is the lowest in three decades. For men, it's the lowest ever measured (the statistics start in 1948). Millions of Americans not only aren't working, they've dropped out of the workforce *forever*.[3] Something is very wrong.

THE BIGGEST SPENDER

Obama told us his administration would "cut the deficit we inherited by half by the end of my first term in office."[4] Instead he increased our debt by 50 percent.[5] In his first four years alone, Obama added nearly $6 trillion to the debt we owe. By the time his eight years are up, Obama will have added $12 trillion in debt.[6] Obama is the biggest-spending politician in world history. Something is very wrong.

Obama denies he's a socialist.[7] Apparently he just wants to move America toward the European model of social capitalism. Then you realize Europe is a basket of bankrupt welfare states,[8] with record 11.8 percent unemployment and 24.4 percent youth unemployment across the Eurozone. Twenty-six million Europeans are unemployed. Greece and Spain both have 26 percent unemployment and over 50 percent youth unemployment.[9] Something is very wrong.

Obama says he is working hard to improve the economy. Yet the United States has joined Ireland as the only advanced economies in the world to have lost economic freedom five years in a row.[10] Something is very wrong.

Obama warns the country about the so-called "fiscal cliff"—practically pushing the panic button.[11] Then he "solves" the problem by adding $4 trillion *more* in deficits.[12] Something is very wrong.

The government tells us 847,000 jobs were created in the U.S. from June to November of 2012. Guess what? Over 70 percent were government jobs. The only one hiring is government. We're living in a one-company town.[13] Something is very wrong.

IS THIS REALLY "THE RIGHT DIRECTION"?

Obama says, "We're moving in the right direction."[14] The food stamp rolls are growing seventy-five times faster than the job rolls,[15] disability benefits have hit all-time highs (more on that later), and unemployment benefits are apparently going to be extended to infinity. Does that sound like "the right direction" to you? Something is very wrong.

Obama takes credit for the "recovery" in the housing market.[16] Meanwhile, in one city, in one month, $120 million of commercial real estate went into default.[17] This isn't an isolated instance, it's happening across America. Does this sound like a "recovery" to you? Something is very wrong.

President Obama acts like our economy is doing better, like America is a solvent nation. Yet Apple Inc. has more cash than the federal government.[18] Then you realize it's not just Apple. Twenty-nine different companies have more cash on hand than the U.S. government. How sad, embarrassing, and pathetic. Something is very wrong.[19]

THE BIGGEST TAX INCREASE IN HISTORY

Obama says, "Taxes are lower on families than they've been probably in the last fifty years."[20] Yet somehow high taxes are sucking the life out of you. Obamacare alone is the biggest tax hike ever.[21] You know your president is lying to you. Something is very wrong.

Your government reports there is virtually no inflation, yet gas prices have doubled under Obama, and food prices are up over 44 percent since 2004.[22] You know your government is lying to you. Something is very wrong.

The banks were supposedly fixed by the massive government bailout. Yet Bank of America has over $64 billion worth of delinquent mortgages (with payments more than six months late). None of these have even entered foreclosure yet.[23] That's more than half of the bank's *market capitalization*. Something is very wrong.

Social Security is supposed to be safe. The money is safely in a "lockbox." The fact is there is not one penny in a lockbox. Social Security has unfunded liabilities of $18 trillion and had negative cash flow of $47.8 billion in 2012, after $48 billion negative cash flow the prior year.[24] Does that sound safe to you? Something is very wrong.

Obama says the "rich" can afford a tax increase.[25] Meanwhile, in the "fiscal cliff" deal, taxes were hiked on small businesses, but $40 billion in corporate welfare was redistributed to the biggest corporations in America, NASCAR owners and Hollywood film producers.[26] Something is very wrong.

Obama said, "You didn't build that."[27] Yet you risked your life savings on your business and work sixteen-hour days, weekends, and holidays. You personally guaranteed every loan, every bill, every rent payment. Where was the government when you were taking all this risk, and working all those long hours? *You did build it.* Something is very wrong.

IF YOU BUILD IT, THEY WILL COME ... TAKE IT AWAY

You're being hit from all angles. While government is taxing you to death, your revenues and income are dramatically down. Prices are way up. You are being forced to cut back on your spending ... yet government spends more, hires more government employees, gives out more corporate welfare, hands out more food stamp and welfare bribes, and adds $150 million to the debt every hour of every day.[28] Something is very wrong.

According to the White House website, Obama is "working to build a country and an economy where we reward hard work."[29] Yet Obama's Environmental Protection Agency (EPA) keeps issuing more devastating rules and regulations that will first drive energy producers out of business and then drive costs—which will be passed directly to you—through the roof. Your gasoline, utility, and food bills are all going up dramatically because of government policies.[30] Something is very wrong.

Obama's Food and Drug Administration (FDA) announces new rules and regulations, claiming they'll make us safer. Yet the cost to comply will be half a billion dollars—passed directly through to you in even higher food costs.[31] Mr. Obama, please stop helping us. We can't take any more of your kind of help. Something is very wrong.

Obama promised to cut healthcare premiums by $2,500 per family in his first term. Instead premiums *increased* by $3,065 per family under Obama.[32] This should have come as no surprise. Government intrusion always increases costs. The U.S. Postal Service lost $15.9 billion last year—*with no competition.*[33] How could Obamacare "save" money? Something is very wrong.

It's happening all around us.

And it's no mistake. It's no coincidence. It's a consciously thought out, well executed plan.

Stop listening to what Obama says. Instead watch what he does. Our assets are melting away. Our incomes are in decline. Our job prospects are disappearing. Our bills are rising. Our options are shrinking. Our rights are being violated. The middle class is being squeezed out of existence. Small business is being regulated and taxed to death. Our children's future is being destroyed by debt. We are living a never-ending nightmare. Under Obama it gets worse hour by hour.

Obama's attack on the "rich"—pitting "Wall Street" against "Main Street"—is a con game … Three-card Monte. It's one of Obama's WMDs (Weapons of Mass Distraction). Obama's big-government socialist agenda isn't aimed at the super-rich. That's just a head fake to cover the truth. That's just the propaganda he uses to sell his con game to the masses. Obama's destructive agenda is aimed squarely at *you*: middle class Americans, entrepreneurs, small business owners, the upper middle class. It is aimed at those with ambition. His tactic is to confiscate your money. But his goal is to kill the American Dream.

WEAPONS OF MASS DISTRACTION

Obama's real aim is to create two classes of Americans, 1) the super-rich, who support and contribute to Obama and are rewarded with bribes, stimulus, bailouts, and government contracts, and 2) the poor, who loyally vote for Obama and in return receive the handouts they need to survive. In Obama's America, the middle class, upper middle class, and small business must be sacrificed; and the poor must be kept in their place. (That place is hopeless, helpless, and dependent on him.) The super-rich help fund his plans to accomplish all that.

That's how you take control of an entire economy. The super-rich and the corporations are bribed into cooperation with the government, and the poor are dependent on government to survive. There is no in-between.

Why do the mega-wealthy, the big corporations, and big unions benefit the most from Obama's big socialist government? Because the higher taxes go, and the more regulations are put in place, the better off the ultra-rich, the connected, and the Fortune 500 are. Their armies of lobbyists and lawyers guarantee them special tax credits, exemptions, and write-offs. They'll find ways around the draconian new financial laws, healthcare mandates, environmental regulations, and labor laws.

At the same time the middle class and small businesses who are the engines of American job creation (but have no lobbyists, connected lawyers, or big contributions to give) will bear the brunt of Obama's Nanny State plans. They'll be regulated, intimidated, and taxed to death. That's Obama's plan—so you can't compete, you can't start up new businesses, you can't expand your business, you can't invest in great opportunities. You can't live the American Dream. Wealth gives you independence. Obama wants you dependent on government. That is Obama's Grand Plan for America.

That's why I wrote *The Ultimate Obama Survival Guide* ...for *you*. For the middle class ...for small business owners ...for the little guy struggling to survive in the socialist Nanny State that America has become under Obama. So that you can even the score, and level the playing field.

HOW YOU CAN SURVIVE, THRIVE, AND PROSPER

I will show you ways to turn Obama's economic model—a miserable food-stamps-and-unemployment-benefits economy—into opportunity. I will show you ways to turn the pain Obama is inflicting on America into gain. I will show you ways to turn his misery into money. With this book as a guide we can turn Obama's dependence society into independence. And turn this national nightmare back into the American Dream.

We are in the midst of an Obama Great Depression that could very well surpass what America experienced in the 1930s. It really doesn't matter why this is happening. It doesn't matter whether Obama is a Marxist ideologue hell-bent on destroying America …or if he's just a progressive, politically correct, liberal do-gooder with the best of intentions, looking to model America after "socialist lite" Europe. Either way, we are in deep trouble. America is being pushed into disaster. Without the knowledge of how this is being done and the tools to overcome it—we all lose.

Later I'll explain the economic catastrophe that is happening in Detroit right now, and why it should be a warning to the whole country. Detroit is the ultimate "Obama experiment"—a one-party city under 100 percent Democrat rule for decades, and now a Third World city in the center of America. Detroit is a look at the future of America if Obama gets his way. The results are frightening. That's why I've dedicated an entire chapter to Detroit.

TURN "DEPRESSED" INTO "SUCCESS"

But as bad as the future looks, all is not lost. To the contrary, history proves there is more opportunity during crisis and bad times than when times are good. You just have to be prepared. You must be ready to strike quickly, with the audacity of a riverboat gambler and the knowledge and patience to capitalize on the crisis while others are weak, confused, struggling, and fearful.

Did you know that more self-made millionaires were created during the Great Depression than any other epoch in our history?[34] We are living through a repeat of that miserable episode in American history. Bush and Obama have repeated the same mistakes as Hoover and FDR (as I'll explain in detail later in this book).

During that first tragic Great Depression, there were both winners and losers. We experienced the greatest wealth transfer in history (until now). For most Americans it was a terrible time. But for the smart and savvy few, it was a once-in-a-lifetime opportunity. It's all about to happen again. In this book I'm going to teach you how to be one of the winners, how to be ready for your opportunity of a lifetime.

The advice and strategies you will learn in this book aren't just my ideas. As a national media personality, well-known entrepreneur, and former vice presidential nominee, I am blessed to have an incredible circle of friends. Most are small business owners, just like me. But a handful of my friends are members of a special group—very wealthy and mega-successful self-made millionaires. I'm lucky to count a few friends close to billionaire status. I asked them to give you, my readers, their best advice. So along with my own insights into how to survive and thrive in the crisis we face, this book features their wisdom and advice on how you can make it through, and even capitalize on, the next four years under Obama.

YOUR OWN BOOMING PERSONAL ECONOMY

The key lesson of the first Great Depression—and of other challenging times—is that during periods of great crisis and economic decline, opportunities abound for people with the right mindset and vision (and I do mean RIGHT).

This is one of those times!

The Ultimate Obama Survival Guide is dedicated to showing you how you can build your own Booming Personal Economy in the midst of the Obama misery, malaise, despair, and disaster. As one of my heroes, Ronald Reagan, once said, "A recession is when your neighbor loses his job. A depression is when you lose yours." Well, a Booming Personal Economy is what you create by seeing opportunity where others see only misery and challenge. It's what happens when you are dedicated to making lemons out of lemonade.

And the opportunity of a lifetime is what you create when you keep your wits, confidence, and courage … and make the right moves … when everyone around you is fearful, depressed, losing their faith, unable to think clearly, and unwilling to take financial risk. To the bold, tenacious, relentless visionaries go the spoils.

If "lemons to lemonade" is the single most important mindset for success, then you're in luck. Because Obama is a *lemon*—a socialist lemon who wants to make us all dependent on big government. We've got no choice but to make lemonade—there is no other option. Not only for our own sake, but for future generations. We cannot afford to give up on America, the greatest country in the history of the world. Or on capitalism, the economic force that has made America the Shining City on a Hill that Ronald Reagan used to speak about.

Opportunity is a three-step process: seeing, creating, and seizing.

The saying goes, "Opportunity only knocks once."

I disagree. My experience has been that opportunity doesn't knock at all. *Ever.* The seeds of opportunity may be there, but it takes a person with vision, courage, and tenacity even to see them. And only then does the truly difficult part begin—taking bold action to seize that opportunity, to turn it into gain for you and your family.

This is a crucial moment in your life, as well as the lives of your children, grandchildren, and future descendents yet unborn. Americans *generations* from now will thank you—or curse you—for the decisions you make now. You don't want to look back later and say, "I would have, could have, should have." The successful survivors and thrivers in this Obama economy will be those who take action. It is my goal to point you toward areas of opportunity, provide you with the tools to take advantage of them, and motivate you to take action.

YOUR LIFE RAFT

Let *The Ultimate Obama Survival Guide* be your life raft. You are going to need a life raft. You will see people around you quietly accept their fate, foolishly waiting for government to save them, before they eventually drown. Or perhaps worse than drown—willingly drift into lives of mediocrity, misery, and desperation, silently accepting Obama's dependence economy.

You can swim over the next four years, while others are drifting and drowning, IF ...

- You have the right mindset, attitude, and tools for success
- You have the ability to see the glass as half full, rather than half empty

- You have the confidence to move in the opposite direction from the masses who are all headed in lockstep toward the edge of the cliff
- You have the clarity to trust what you see with your own eyes, rather than the fairy tales and lies painted by Obama's propaganda
- You have the vision to see opportunity where others see only disaster and despair
- You have the confidence and chutzpah (an old Yiddish word for boldness combined with a dash of cockiness) to take action and go after your dreams when others say it cannot be done
- You continue to value self-reliance, rugged individualism, and personal responsibility (the traits of our Founding Fathers), and are willing to use them to take control of and responsibility for your life

The Ultimate Obama Survival Guide is about empowering and motivating you to higher levels of success than you've ever imagined possible—even under the pall Obama is casting over America.

On a daily basis, you'll have to ignore the media propaganda telling you that the Obama agenda is making America a better place, and helping create a better economy, when all you have to do is open your eyes to see the destruction Obama is inflicting.

On a daily basis, you'll have to fight the temptation to take the easy way out—allowing Big Brother to take care of all your needs. It will not be easy to turn down the "Obama money."

"IF IT IS TO BE, IT IS UP TO ME"

But in this book you'll learn that "Obama money" is cursed. It's like taking a bribe from the mafia. Once you touch that dirty money, you are enslaved. They've got you. *They own you.* Your independence is a thing of the past. Taking government's money is falling into the same trap as taking money from the Gambino crime family. Except the Gambinos are much nicer!

The common trap in both cases is that it looks "easy" in the short run, in the moment. But your life will never be the same. You are now compromised. Your life is no longer yours. You are dependent. And of course, that's exactly what Obama wants. That's how he keeps you hooked on big government and loyally voting for it forever more.

The purpose of this book is to teach you to be *independent*. To teach you to live by those great words, *"If it is to be, it is up to me."*

To teach you to remain self-reliant, ambitious, and *hungry*. That hunger is what lifts people out of poverty into the life of their dreams. It is what creates mobility, opportunity, and financial freedom. It is the ambition that inspires entrepreneurs to invent things that make all our lives better, whether it's the internet, the iPhone, or a cure for cancer or Alzheimer's. That ambition to do well for yourself and your family is what creates the wealth that funds charity. The restless hunger of capitalists is what pays for all the government programs for the needy, and all the salaries and pensions for government employees. It's still alive today—but it's found in places like China, India, Singapore, Hong Kong, Cambodia, Thailand, Laos, Vietnam. How sad is that? My goal is to awaken it again here in America.

So stay hungry, my friends. Stay ambitious. Stay independent and self-reliant. Don't give in to Obama's enticing offers. Learn to say "NO" while those around you are saying "YES" to gifts from Santa Claus (a.k.a. Obama). You'll be thankful you did. What they think is manna from heaven is nothing more than "fool's gold."

Obama & Co. will try to make you feel guilty about wanting to keep more of your own money, about objecting when the money you worked so hard to earn is redistributed to others who did nothing to earn it. I'm here to snap you out of it. Obama and his socialist cabal—politicians, media, government bureaucrats, and educators—want to brainwash you into accepting a welfare state and a government-dependent mentality.

They'll tell you it's "greedy" to want to keep more of your own money that you worked hard for, that you *earned*. But working hard (and smart) to support yourself and the people you love isn't greedy. The very definition of greed is for government to confiscate money and assets from those who earned it, to redistribute it to those that didn't. That is real greed. No amount of Obama propaganda can ever change that.

The Ultimate Obama Survival Guide is here to empower you, to enrich your life … to educate you about the right investments and opportunities to protect your family, career, and assets … to get you thinking like a chess master (always two moves ahead of Obama)…to get you motivated and enthusiastic about the great opportunities Obama's economic destruction is creating just for you…to teach you to be *relentless* in pursuing your success.

And to unlock within you the uniquely American values of Faith, Family, and Freedom that Obama can never take away. That DNA has been in us since 1776, passed down from generation to generation. It's not just our guns that Obama will have to pry from our cold dead fingers. It's our faith in God, capitalism, individualism, independence, and American exceptionalism.

The goal of this book is to turn you into the very thing Obama despises … the ultimate Capitalist Evangelist.

But the advice in this book isn't just about financial opportunities. It's about successful living. To be successful in the face of these disastrous Obama economic headwinds, you need a healthy foundation of body, mind, and spirit. You need to protect your family. Mentally, you need to be the sharpest of your life. Physically, you need to be the healthiest of your life. You need to become a finely tuned fighting machine in a world of pain, distress, depression, and decline.

The Ultimate Obama Survival Guide is about:

- *Supercharging* all areas of your life, by teaching you the mindset to attack each day with *an enthusiasm unknown to mankind*!
- *Standing up* to the Obama Axis of Evil—taxation, regulation, unionization, litigation, and government strangulation. More details to come!

- *Harking back* to the Founding Fathers—to independence from Big Brother, government intrusion, intervention, and confiscation
- *Turning* tragedy into opportunity, disaster into destiny, dependence into independence
- *Creating* your own Booming Personal Economy

Let the journey begin. Your life raft has arrived.

CHAPTER TWO

DEPENDENCE DAY

DID YOU KNOW?

- Obama learned at Columbia University how to pave the way for socialism by creating a financial crisis with government overspending
- Obama's deal purporting to solve the "fiscal cliff" actually adds $4 trillion to the deficit
- The fiscal cliff deal raises taxes on 77 percent of Americans—while giving $40 billion in tax *credits* to "green energy" companies, Hollywood, and other Obama cronies

F our years ago I made three public predictions, all the while hoping and praying that I was wrong.[1]

Sadly, I wasn't.

My first prediction: Obama's goal is not to "save" the U.S. economy, it is to *transform* the economy from capitalism to Nanny State socialism, the system that has bankrupted Europe. His ambition is not to save you or me. It is to save his favored voting groups—big business, the poor, the unions—those who are willingly dependent on big government.

To curry their favor Obama needs to keep the entitlements and bailouts coming. So he needs gigantic new sources of revenue—that is, taxes. That's what Obama has to do in this second term: find ways to tax us to death to pay the bills for Obama's hugely expanded government.

My second prediction was that Obama is not interested in debt reduction. Quite the opposite, his plan is to *increase* the debt…both to reward and bribe his voters and to destroy capitalism. The exploding debt creates a fiscal emergency—a debt crisis. It's only during times of fear and panic, under the guise of a national emergency, that wealth redistribution and confiscation get passed.

Don't believe me? Obama promised to cut the deficit in half.[2] Instead, he increased the debt by 50 percent.[3] *Coincidence?*

This strategy to overwhelm the system with crisis and debt is a well-planned, conscious, purposeful strategy by Obama. Does that sound like a crazy conspiracy theory to you? It's actually something Obama learned in college. I should know. I was Obama's classmate at Columbia University in the class of '83.

THE CLOWARD-PIVEN STRATEGY

The strategy Obama is implementing today was originally devised by two Columbia University professors, the husband-and-wife team of Richard Cloward and Frances Piven. Anyone who majored in political science at Columbia University in the years we were both there would have been exposed to this Cloward-Piven plan. It was discussed in class, among students outside class, and at political meetings. It was literally impossible to avoid. It was part of the Columbia political science experience. The students I met were all proud that it was two Columbia professors who had created this plan.

The Cloward-Piven plan is brutal in its simplicity: to kill capitalism by overwhelming the U.S. economic system with debt and dependency.[4] And look around! *It's*

MEET THE REAL OBAMA

Now that he's been re-elected and never has to face voters again, President Obama can finally take off his business suit and show the cape underneath with the great big "S"—for socialist.

happening just as they, and Obama, planned.

My third prediction was that Obama would be moderate and reasonable in his first term (at least by his standards) in order to convince middle class voters that he was on their side and could be trusted. Although Obama's definition of "moderate" is more than a little different from mine, his re-election proved this prediction to be correct as well.

FAKE SPENDING CUTS

Obama's "fiscal cliff" deal is even worse than it looks. The CBO reported that most of the measly $25 billion in spending cuts (versus $4 trillion in new debt) came from money never expected to be spent in the first place. In other words, they were totally bogus.[5]

It has already started. Even before his second term inauguration, the REAL Obama had begun to emerge. Obama's offer in the so-called "fiscal cliff" negotiations was the most radical "compromise" in U.S. history—a mind-boggling, unimaginable $1.6 trillion in increased taxes (double what he asked for only a year before), coupled with virtually nothing resembling a spending cut, and lots of additional spending.[6]

The final fiscal cliff deal raised taxes in a big way, not only on the upper 2 percent of income earners, but also, despite Obama's assurances (a.k.a. lies), on 77 percent of all Americans.[7]

Yet before the "compromise" was even signed...Obama was promising even more tax increases in 2013. This is the game for him. It's always about new taxes.[8]

The real clue to Obama's radical agenda is the massive new spending in the fiscal cliff compromise. Obama headed us toward the cliff with his irresponsible policies—almost $6 trillion in new debt with no serious plan to get the deficit under control, no willingness to agree to reasonable spending cuts in exchange for debt ceiling increases, no plan for tax reform beyond more taxes on "the rich." Then he screamed about the "fiscal cliff" day and night in order to panic the American people. Then we found out that the deal that was supposed to get our financial house in order actually *added* $4 trillion to the national deficit.[9]

The spending cuts in the deal totaled a pitiful $25 billion. Even worse, of the $25 billion in spending cuts, only $2 billion take effect in 2013.

Obama ballooned the deficit…encouraged a panic…then used the crisis to increase the debt by $4 trillion. And the Republican cowards in Congress let him get away with it, because they were so frightened of being blamed.

Then we found out—after the fact—that the "fiscal cliff" deal gave $40 billion in tax *credits* to big corporations and Obama's allies—including "green energy" companies and Hollywood film producers.[10]

Then it got even worse. The *Wall Street Journal* pointed out that the bill included massive new "phase-outs" and limits on deductions and exemptions that will affect far more American taxpayers than the tax increases. Why was this never mentioned anywhere by the media until after the bill passed?[11]

Do you need to know any more than this, to realize why you need the advice in this book? Your president and representatives in Congress certainly aren't looking out for you. I wrote this book to look out for *you*.

Trust me. You'll need help and guidance to survive the next four years.

Let me ask a few questions. Does any of this make sense? Are these the actions of a president who wants to reduce the debt—or of one purposely creating a debt crisis? Are these the actions of a president trying to save the economy, or send us over the cliff?

Obama isn't so stupid as to believe that the way to solve a spending and debt crisis is with more spending and debt. But hyping the crisis ultimately created by the debt is a great way to frighten

THEY'RE DOING JUST FINE, THANKS

New taxes and higher government debt may bother you, but your Congressional representatives will have nothing to worry about. Someone is always looking out for them. During the same week that the fiscal cliff deal was agreed to, Obama issued an executive order raising the pay of all federal employees—including members of the Senate and House of Representatives.[12] I don't know what you call that. I call it "bought and paid for."

voters into supporting higher taxes (on the other guy). The fact we borrow forty cents of every dollar we spend just makes it more of a crisis.[13] How will the higher taxes be used? To spend more. And for every dollar spent, we'll borrow forty cents more. Rinse, spin, then start again. It's the Obama Spend and Tax Cycle.

Notice who the tax increases are always aimed at? Obama's favorite boogie-man: the "rich." Obama figured out he could never pass tax increases on everyone and still win re-election. So he produced a public-relations plan to demonize one group. He pits the 99 percent against the 1 percent. George Bernard Shaw had this con game figured out a hundred years ago: "A government with the policy to rob Peter to pay Paul, can be assured of the support of Paul."[14]

Don't be deceived by the "tax the rich" mantra. The rich, the truly wealthy (big business, Hollywood, inherited wealth, billionaires) are not Obama's real targets. They are, in fact, his biggest supporters and contributors.

The president's real target is the middle class, especially small business owners. They don't support Obama and his socialist policies, and they are exactly the people he has targeted to destroy with confiscatory taxes. "Tax the rich" is a Weapon of Mass Distraction. (It's also a much more effective campaign slogan than "Screw the middle class.")

Higher taxes are only a small part of Obama's second-term agenda. Obama has also made it clear that he wants full control over the debt ceiling, billions more in stimulus (to hand out to his biggest contributors), "cap-and-trade" (to take control of the economy), immigration reform (code words for amnesty), and draconian new gun restrictions. And only days after the election, the man who claimed in the presidential debates to be a friend of oil drilling excluded 1.6 million acres west of the Mississippi from oil exploration—land that could contain a trillion barrels of oil.[15]

All these things happened in only the first sixty days after Obama's re-election. Before he was even sworn in for his second term. I promise you this is just a small start.

As I predicted, this was always the plan. First act "moderate" until re-election. Then hammer home the real radical leftist agenda. Overwhelm

Americans with Weapons of Mass Distraction. Make our heads spin with so many proposals to defend against at once, that we can't keep track, or eventually grow so overwhelmed that we give up.

The American public saw it coming with Jimmy Carter in 1980 and voted to stop him. But since then several generations of voters have been indoctrinated and dumbed down by ultra-liberal teachers' union members inside public schools. So this time, with the blind assistance of the mainstream media, the majority of voters either never saw it coming—or didn't mind.

OBAMA'S BRILLIANT PLAN, UNFOLDING RIGHT IN FRONT OF OUR EYES

Obamacare is the centerpiece. It sounded innocent enough—it was positioned as "free healthcare." In reality it was about unionizing 21 million healthcare workers. That will produce $21 billion in new union dues to support and elect big government Democrat politicians.[16] *Brilliant.*

Another effect of Obamacare is massive new taxation in the name of "fairness." The government gets billions of new dollars, while the taxes fall primarily on the backs of small business (the group that writes checks to Republican candidates and conservative causes).[17] Who could say no to new taxes and government expansion in the name of sick kids? *Brilliant.*

And the bonus Obama gets from national healthcare is that people become comfortable being dependent on government. Now government takes care of your sick children. They pay for your cancer treatment. They even pay for you to see the doctor when you get the sniffles. Wow, that Uncle Sam is some generous benefactor. Isn't government nice? *Brilliant.*

And finally, thousands of new IRS agents are being hired to police Obamacare.[18] That's thousands of new government employees with bloated salaries and obscene pensions to protect, and therefore more loyal Democrat voters. Obama also achieves more government oversight and control over your life, now that the IRS oversees your healthcare—giving them even more reasons to intrude, inspect every inch of your life, and snoop around your bank accounts. *Brilliant.*

Then there's the deficit, and the national debt. Remember when Obama promised that healthcare reform was going to "bend the cost curve" downward?[19] Of course in reality, Obamacare won't save money. It isn't even "deficit neutral"—it's going to add more than a trillion dollars in deficit spending in the next decade. That's *on top of* Obamacare's half a trillion dollars in new taxes.[20] And Obamacare is just one example of the runaway deficit spending that is causing our national debt to skyrocket under Obama. He has put the debt on a course to *double*.[21] Why would Obama want to double our debt? He needs the debt to explode in order to create a crisis, giving him an excuse to raise yet *more* taxes. Higher taxes give Obama more revenues to redistribute to his voters, while also making the baseline for government spending bigger forever.

For decades to come (long after Obama is gone), taxes will need to be increased just to pay the exploding interest on the debt. This is how you hook people on dependency. This is how you enslave future generations. This is how you win the debate, decide the conversation, and explode the size of government—all in one.

As a bonus, it's also how Obama starves his political opposition. Democrats call the GOP "the party of the rich."[22] Why do you think every tax increase is aimed at "the rich"? It's part of the plan. Where will "the rich" and the business owners get the money to contribute to Republican candidates and conservative causes, if they're taxed to death? The answer is, they won't. *Brilliant.*

But raising tax rates alone isn't enough to bankrupt small business owners. Their deductions need to be taken away, too.[23] That's how you skyrocket tax rates and bankrupt the middle class (excuse me—"the rich"). Take away deductions, and taxes are doubled overnight. In Obama's ideal world it's not fair for some people to have big homes, big cars, and their own businesses. Take them away and you achieve equality and "fairness."

Except it's not equality, and it's certainly not fair. It's shared misery…shared misery that destroys incentive and kills the American Dream. The only dream it fulfills is the socialist dream of Obama and his cohorts—

tax the middle class so they have neither the will nor the ability to achieve independence, then use those taxes to bribe your voters and pay off your key contributors. *Brilliant.*

By eliminating the mortgage deduction for "the rich," Obama hits the Daily Double. First, the so-called rich are forced to pay higher taxes. Second, the value of homes plummets, robbing middle and upper middle class Americans of their biggest asset. No assets, no way to support conservative causes. *Brilliant.*

Capping the charitable deduction would be an even bigger coup for Obama.[24] This is how you starve churches. Churches are among the biggest opponents of big government and socialism. Limit the charitable deduction—that results in more money going to government, and less to churches. Eliminate *both* the mortgage and charitable deductions and the greatest opposition to Big Brother is out of business. *Brilliant.*

Now, add in "card check," a promise Obama made to unions, his biggest financial backers.[25] This will be the final straw that breaks the camel's back for business owners. Obama has raised their taxes and added huge new burdens with Obamacare. Now he takes away their profits. Card check allows easy unionization of even small businesses, making them hostage to unions demanding higher wages. In a terrible economy, the only way to pay higher wages is to cut profit or go out of business. You can't possibly raise prices, so there goes your profit. *Brilliant.*

But wait, we've still got the biggest Trojan horse of them all—"climate change." Convince Americans that we are doomed unless we give massive new powers to government. This is just another crisis (like the debt crisis) that demands an emergency response—which always just happens to include sweeping new government powers.

Obama will use either "cap-and-trade" or radical EPA regulations (through executive order) to strangle business. To regulate the coal industry out of existence. To dramatically reduce oil drilling. Either way, rates for electricity and natural gas are about to skyrocket. The super-rich like Warren Buffett don't have to worry. The poor (Obama's voters) have their expenses paid by government. But the rest of us, the middle class and small businesses, will have our earnings reduced even further. Life becomes more and more of a struggle to survive and pay the bills. There's no money left to contribute to conservative causes. *Brilliant.*

Even those who survive without losing their homes and businesses will be forced to downscale their lifestyle. Motivation to achieve will be destroyed. Equality will be achieved by making everyone poorer (there's the shared misery, again). Obama will succeed in his goal to kill "the American Dream." But, no worry, the number of poor will increase, and they'll receive bigger government checks than ever before. That's how he'll create more loyal voters. And, what's left of the middle class—well he can always blame their problems on "the rich." *Brilliant.*

This is the Obama plan. He has to demonize, punish, and bankrupt the middle class, upper middle class, and small business ("the rich"), all in pursuit of "fairness"—in reality, misery for everyone. And it's all happening right in front of our eyes.

Just remember, if you are an independent thinker, if you distrust government, if you are a capitalist, if you own a business, if you are an independent contractor, if you earn a high income … it's not your equality that Obama cares about. "Fairness" and "social justice" have nothing to do with you. In Obama's agenda you are the oppressor, the enemy.

Obama's game plan is to create class warfare and division. It's about dividing America: rich versus poor; the makers versus the takers; the self-made and self-reliant versus those dependent on government checks; blue collar versus white collar; taxpayers versus public employees; black versus white; those who trust in God versus those who trust in big government; small business versus big business; women versus men (remember "the war on women"?); married couples versus single women; straight versus gay. It's ugly. It's brutal. I've never seen such division, anger, and envy in America. This is the new normal in Obama's second term. But make no mistake—the final goal is simple: dependence on big government.

Get ready to celebrate Obama's new national holiday: *DEPENDENCE DAY.*

CHAPTER THREE

THE ZOMBIE ECONOMY

DID YOU KNOW?

- Since Obama was elected, over 8.5 million Americans have dropped out of the workforce
- The average American's net worth is down a whopping 40 percent
- Under Obama, unemployment stayed at over 8 percent for forty-three months straight—more months than under all presidents from Truman to Bush *combined*

Whenever I talk to delusional liberals or members of the media (I know, I repeat myself), they say, "Wayne, the economy isn't that bad. It's on the mend—haven't you seen the unemployment numbers? Things are getting better under Obama."

But I'm about to prove to you that "Yes, it is *that* bad"...and "No, things are *not* getting better under Obama."

Despite what the Obama-adoring, Kool-Aid-drinking liberal mainstream media tells you, this economy is bad and getting worse. I call it "the Zombie Economy" because the typical business owner today is a walking zombie. Our businesses (and sales revenues) are in a coma under Obama.

The key to understanding is to study the REAL facts and statistics—not the ones manufactured out of thin air, lied about, or manipulated by Obama, government, or the media. Facts are facts. Unfortunately the ones

I'm about to report don't often make it to (or should I say through?) the mainstream media. *I wonder why?*

This may be the first time you've ever seen these remarkable statistics. We are in the midst of an economic Armageddon that can only be called "the Obama Great Depression." The facts below clearly show the economic collapse is far worse than most Americans understand…*yet.* Read through them, and you'll see. The Obama economy is actually a Zombie Economy, right out of *Night of the Living Dead.*

Judge for yourself:

- Obama is the biggest spender in world history.[1]
- The debt ceiling was raised on August 11, 2011, from $14.299 trillion to $16.394 trillion. As of January 1, 2013, we reached the limit of the ceiling again. That means in only sixteen months the Obama administration added another $2.1 trillion to the national debt.[2]
- Under Obama the national debt has increased by 50 percent. Obama is on track to add $12 trillion to the national debt in his eight years in office—a staggering three times more than George W. Bush.[3]
- Under Obama the national debt now exceeds the entire output of the U.S. economy.[4]
- Obama is not only the first president in history to produce four consecutive years of deficits over $1 trillion, but in his

THE ZOMBIE ECONOMY: CHECK OUT THE FACTS FOR YOURSELF

For mountains of revealing statistics on Obama's Zombie Economy, check out a few of my favorite websites—ZeroHedge.com, ShadowStats.com, TheEconomicCollapseBlog.com, CNSnews.com, KickThemAllOut.com, and EndoftheAmericanDream.com. Facts like these aren't going to leap out at you from the reports of the mainstream media. You have to dig down deeper.

first term he racked up more debt than all the presidents from George Washington through Bill Clinton—COMBINED.[5]

- How far out of control is the debt? During Obama's reign the national debt grew more in *one day* than the deficit for the *entire year* of 2007.[6]
- The national debt is increasing by a mind-boggling $3 million dollars per minute.[7]

But as bad as Obama's out-of-control government spending and debt are, the damage he has done to the private sector economy is even more shocking. The repeated attempts at "stimulus" have nearly bankrupted the government, but they haven't managed to "stimulate" anything but Obama's biggest contributors.

What exactly did we get for all that spending and massive debt?

- The U.S. credit rating has been downgraded for the first time in history. With Obama's re-election, get ready for more credit downgrades to come.[8]
- The net worth of the average American is down a whopping 40 percent.[9]
- According to the U.S. Census Bureau, household income has fallen for all four years under Obama. It's down $4,000.[10]
- The housing collapse is worse than at the peak of the Great Depression.[11]
- Unemployment was over 8 percent for an unimaginable forty-three consecutive months. That's more months of unemployment over the 8 percent level than all the presidents from Harry Truman to George W. Bush COMBINED.[12]
- According to economist John Williams of ShadowStats. com, if you factor in all the short- and long-term discouraged workers, and all those working part time because they cannot find full-time employment, the real unemployment

rate is over 20 percent—higher than most years during the Great Depression.[13]

- The employment rate under Obama has been under 59 percent for thirty-nine months in a row. That means more than 41 percent of those capable of working are not employed. (It makes you wonder how the jobless rate reported by the government—and mainstream media—can be improving.)[14]

- Since Obama has been president, over 8.5 million Americans have dropped out of the workforce.[15]

- The Labor Force Participation Rate among men is the lowest since the government began measuring it, in 1948. In 1950, 80 percent of all working-age men had a job versus today, when only 65 percent are working.[16]

- Over 100 million working-age Americans don't have jobs. About 12.5 million are "officially" listed as unemployed, added to almost 88 million of working age listed simply as "not working."[17]

- The average unemployed worker has been out of a job for forty weeks. At the peak of the early 1980's deep recession, with unemployment close to 11 percent, the highest average length of unemployment was only twenty-one weeks.[18]

- If you gathered all the unemployed people in America in one place, they would constitute the sixty-eighth largest country in the world.[19]

- The U.S. has roughly the same number of jobs today as it had in 2000, but the population is well over 30 million larger. To get back to the civilian-employment-to-population ratio we had in 2000, we would have to gain 18 MILLION jobs.[20]

- According to a report released in February by the National Employment Law Project, higher-wage industries are accounting for 40 percent of the job losses in America, but only 14 percent of the job growth. Lower-wage industries are accounting for 49 percent of the job growth.[21]

- Back in 1980, less than 30 percent of all jobs in the United States were low-income jobs. Today, more than 40 percent of all jobs in the United States are low-income jobs.[22]
- Fifty-three percent of all college graduates in America under age twenty-five are either unemployed or under-employed.[23]
- Black unemployment is at 14 percent. When did you hear that trumpeted in the media during the presidential election? Obama received over 99 percent of the votes of black women, despite the fact that overall unemployment improved during his first term while African American unemployment remained high.[24]
- In 1965 one out of every fifty Americans was on Medicaid. Today, approximately one out of every six Americans is on Medicaid.[25]
- Medicare faces an unfunded liability of almost $40 trillion dollars. That's over $328,000 per U.S. household.[26]
- Over 100 million Americans are getting some form of welfare. That's almost one out of every three Americans. And that does not include Social Security or Medicare.[27]
- One sixth of all personal income in the U.S. is now provided by government.[28]
- About 57 percent of all children in the United States are living in poverty or defined as low-income.[29]
- According to the National Center for Children in Poverty, 36.4 percent of all children that live in Philadelphia are living in poverty, 40.1 percent of all children in Atlanta are living in poverty, 52.6 percent of all children in Cleveland are living in poverty and 53.6 percent of all children in Detroit are living in poverty.[30]
- For the first time in history, over one million public school students are HOMELESS.[31]
- "Free" meals at school now cost taxpayers $11.1 billion per year.[32]

- Total student loan debt is now over $1 trillion, with defaults at record levels.[33]
- According to the Mortgage Bankers Association, in the third quarter of 1980 under the failed presidency of Jimmy Carter, there were 76,885 delinquent mortgages. Shockingly, in the second quarter of 2012 under President Obama, there were 3,107,247 delinquent mortgages.[34]
- Almost half of all Americans don't have even $500 in savings.[35]
- New business start-ups are at the lowest level in thirty years.[36]
- In the World Economic Forum's rank of global competitiveness, the U.S. has fallen four years in a row under Obama.[37]
- And with the reality of Obamacare now upon us, polls show 83 percent of all doctors are thinking of retiring—at just the same time as we are adding 30 million new patients.[38]

I could go on for another twenty pages, but I think you've gotten the message by now. Yes, the facts prove it: the economy under Obama really is *that* bad—and getting worse.

We are experiencing UNIMAGINABLE economic wreckage, crisis, and collapse from coast to coast. The joke is, there are only three industries enjoying a boom in this Obama economy…gun shops, foreclosure specialists, and print shops—now working twenty-four hours a day to keep up with demand for "**Going Out of Business**" signs.

None of this is a coincidence. This is a cold, calculated plan to collapse the U.S. economy under the weight of debt and entitlements, to bankrupt business owners (particularly small business), and to destroy capitalism.

And it's all working according to plan.

BACK TO THE FUTURE

Simon Black of SovereignMan.com is an international investor, financial advisor, and world-class entrepreneur. Black (not his real name) is also a financial historian who wanted to measure precisely just how bad our economy is right now in historical terms. So he priced the entire U.S. economy since 1791 in terms of gold.[39]

Black calls his standard measurement gold per capita, or GPC. Using GPC, Black measured our economy's Gross Domestic Product (GDP), denominated in ounces of gold, for every year since 1791. His one standard GPC measurement allows for an "apples to apples" comparison of our economy today with the U.S. economy at various times in our past—taking into account population growth and inflation. You may be shocked at the findings (although you really shouldn't be, after reading the Zombie Economy statistics above).

Black found that, measured in gold, the post-World War II average of GPC is 72.83 ounces. Today we are at 28.40.

That means our economy is an astounding 61 percent off our historical *average*.

The U.S. economy is now producing about as much actual value per capita, taking into account inflation and population growth, as it did in 1931—in the Great Depression. (Or maybe we should start calling it the *first* Great Depression.)

Even taking into account all our technological advances, efficiency, productivity, computers, the Internet, email, cell phones, and the much higher percentage of Americans with college and graduate degrees—despite all those marvelous improvements—our economy has fallen backward about *eight decades*!

And the economy is still getting worse. The figure of 28.40 gold per capita (as we enter 2013) is worse than last year. Which was also worse than the previous year. We are in a serious, long-term decline.

Black points out something ominous. As measured by GPC, our economy has been contracting since 2001—the exact same period as government spending and our national debt exploded under both Bush and Obama, and the Federal Reserve went on the greatest money-printing spree in world history. Coincidence? I think not.

Throughout history high taxes, big-spending government, and huge debt have always combined to cause economic crisis and collapse.

CHAPTER FOUR

WHY WE ARE FACING THE GREATEST DEPRESSION OF ALL TIME

DID YOU KNOW?

- The structural, economic, and societal problems we have today could make the Obama Great Depression worse than the original Great Depression
- Under Obama, the food stamp rolls have grown seventy-five times faster than employment
- Unfunded government liabilities amount to a debt of $360,000 per American citizen
- One out of five government employees is now paid more than $100,000 a year
- More than 5 million Americans have filed for disability since Obama was elected

As we enter 2013, we are already beginning to experience what can only be described as the Obama Great Depression. The only question is, just how bad can Obama's policies make the Zombie Economy over the next four years?

Pretty darn bad.

As in Apocalypse. As in Armageddon. As in the end of America.

But don't get depressed on me. Don't get scared. You can survive and even thrive in the Obama Great Depression. But first you need to face the cold, hard truth before you can take action. You can't make proper decisions without knowing exactly what you are facing. The good news: once you face the awful truth, your decisions can make you wealthy, even as all hell breaks loose around you. By the end of this book you will be in possession of the knowledge to capitalize on and actually profit from the Obama Great Depression—no matter how bad things get.

THIS TIME, THE GLASS IS NOT HALF FULL

What we're facing is not pretty.

I am a successful entrepreneur, small businessman, Capitalist Evangelist, and patriot who loves America and always sees its greatness. I'm also an optimistic, positive thinker who always sees the glass half full.

Not this time.

As a small business owner with boots on the ground (on Main Street, not Wall Street), I have been publicly warning of economic collapse and a new Great Depression for over three years. In *Time* magazine back in 2010, I called Obama "the Great Jobs Killer" and recommended the FBI add him to the top of their "Most Wanted List" because of all the jobs he was responsible for killing. That was *before* things got really bad.

Even three years ago, it wasn't hard to see where things were going. Not if you just looked closely, took your blinders off, and stopped listening to the mainstream media.

This time there is no "glass half full."

This time the results are going to be dramatically worse than in 1929. This time we are facing the Greatest Depression *ever.*

Why? Because in the original Great Depression America had NONE of the structural, economic, and societal problems we have today—nor the massive obligations we are now facing.

Read the facts below. But again, a reminder: please don't get depressed. Later in this book I'm going to show you how to not only survive, but to thrive and prosper despite all of this bad news.

Buckle up, and here we go.

In 1929, America was not $16 trillion in debt, plus responsible for over $100 trillion in unfunded liabilities. That's an unbelievable $360,000 in debt per citizen.[1]

In 1929, most of our states were not bankrupt, insolvent, and dependent on federal government handouts to survive. (Today, a single county—Cook County, the site of Chicago, Illinois—now owes over $108 billion in debt, most of it in unfunded government employee pensions.)[2]

In 1929, we did not have 22 million government employees with bloated salaries, obscene pensions, and free healthcare for life. Today one out of five federal employees is paid over $100,000 a year.[3]

And staggering numbers of federal government employees retire at a young age with pensions for life.[4]

Unfortunately on the state and local levels it's even worse. There is now nearly $4 trillion in unfunded pension liabilities for state government employees.[5]

Protected by their unions and the politicians they elect, government employees are bankrupting America. In Illinois there are retired government employees getting over $425,000 per year.[6]

No one could have imagined any of this in 1929. **There is no possible way to pay these bills—ever.**

In 1929, Social Security, Medicare, and Medicaid didn't exist. The federal government had no such "entitlements" threatening to consume the entire federal budget. We didn't face unfunded obligations of $18 trillion (for Social Security alone) in 1929.[7]

Boy we've come a long way, haven't we? This is what big government proponents call "progress."

In 1929, there was no such thing as welfare, food stamps, SSDI (Social Security Disability Income), or ESL (English as a second language) programs. Americans didn't consider it the responsibility of government to pay for students' breakfasts and lunches—*let alone for the meals of illegal immigrant students.* Only government could call something that costs $11.1 billion per year "free."[8]

Who could have imagined back in 1929 that one seventh of the U.S. population would be on food stamps ... and the federal government would ADVERTISE to encourage even more Americans to sign up for welfare?[9]

Who could have imagined back in 1929 that the food stamp rolls could ever grow seventy-five times faster than the employment rolls—as they have under Obama?[10]

Who could imagine, back in the original Great Depression, that the federal government would team up with the president of Mexico to encourage Mexicans living illegally in America to sign up for food stamps?[11]

In 1929, who could have imagined the president would offer not just welfare, but waivers to allow states to opt out of requiring recipients to work to receive their welfare?[12]

Back in 1929, who could have imagined eighty-six teenage girls would be pregnant in *one* Memphis high school?[13]

In 1929 we had families, moral codes, and churches to prevent this kind of tragedy. Do you actually believe this is just one abnormal high school? Unmarried teenagers are pregnant in high schools all across America. They have figured out that the choice is to either work a drab, depressing job paying minimum wage for the rest of their lives, or pump out babies and have government pay their bills for decades to come. But where will the money come from?

In 1929, legal immigrants wanted only to work. My grandparents from Russia and Germany received no government benefits. They worked day and night to provide for their family and become American citizens. It was sink or swim. My grandmother Anna Root never took a penny in welfare, even when my grandfather died and left her with no job, no money, and seven young children.

Today's illegal immigrants demand welfare for life. Forty-three percent of all immigrants who have been in the United States for twenty years or longer are on welfare.[14] Fifty-seven percent of households headed by an immigrant (legal or illegal) with children under eighteen used at least one welfare program, compared with 39 percent of native households with children.[15]

Today we have millions of illegal immigrants and their children collecting billions of dollars in entitlements from U.S. taxpayers. In California alone, illegal immigrants cost taxpayers over $10.5 billion annually just for education, healthcare, and incarceration. Do you now understand why California suffers from massive annual deficits and record-setting unfunded liabilities? This is spreading across the country.[16]

WELFARE STATE EXPLOSION

We're also suffering from health-related dysfunctions that would have astonished the Americans of 1929. Studies show that almost 20 percent of American children under age eighteen are obese, and thus more prone to develop diabetes and cardiovascular disease.[17] Experts predict that by 2020, 52 percent of adult Americans will have either diabetes or pre-diabetes.[18] Do you understand the astronomically high cost of caring for patients with diabetes?[19] The coming epidemic of this single costly disease alone will overwhelm America's healthcare system.

In 1929, we had no federal disability program. Today over 11 million Americans are on disability. There are more citizens on the disabled rolls than in thirty-nine of our fifty states.[20] Even more amazingly, about half of them (5.5 million) joined the disability rolls during Obama's first term.[21]

Do you really believe 5.5 million Americans suddenly became disabled in the past four years? Once someone is on disability, especially if they claim mental illness, it's almost impossible to get him off. Ninety percent of people on disability rolls never get off. Why would they? It guarantees them health insurance and an income for life.[22] But who will pay for all of this?

Have the disability claims simply risen with our rising population? Absolutely not. The ratio of able-bodied workers to disabled in 1967 was forty-one to one. As of June 2012 it is sixteen to one. An appalling 4.5 percent of the working age population is on Social Security Disability.[23] This is quite simply and clearly a change in the American work ethic and

OUT OF THE ARMY, ONTO THE DOLE

American soldiers are doing their part—for the explosive growth of the welfare state. An astonishing 45 percent of returning veterans are claiming "disability."[24] That number dwarfs all prior records in the history of warfare. No nation can afford this.

the whole mindset of the American people. It is impossible to pay this bill long term.

In 1929, we had an education system that was the envy of the world. Today our public schools are in shambles. We spend the most money in the world and get among the worst results. A report recently published by Harvard University's Program on Education Policy and Governance showed the disaster that U.S. education has become. Students in Latvia, Chile, and Brazil are making academic gains three times faster than American students. Those in Portugal, Hong Kong, Germany, Poland, Liechtenstein, Slovenia, Colombia, and Lithuania are improving at twice the rate of our students. Can you spell NATIONAL DISGRACE?[25]

The difference today? Teachers' unions are in charge, instead of parents. So our students graduate with few skills, qualified only for blue-collar jobs that no longer exist in the U.S.—they've been shipped to China and India. What will this workforce do for the rest of their lives? Live on the government dole? Who will pay for it?

In 1929, taxes were much lower. Forget the tax rates, they're meaningless. In those days we had a cash economy, so most businesses paid little or no taxes. Sales taxes and FICA taxes didn't exist. Today the combined taxes we pay—local and state property, gas, and sales taxes, plus federal FICA, gas, and income taxes—are enormously higher than the taxes Americans paid in 1929. Unconvinced? When income taxes started in 1913, the average American was untouched. Only the richest 350,000 Americans paid a 2 percent income tax.[26] Today the average American works until April 12 just to pay his or her taxes. In some high-tax states the date is early May.[27]

These higher taxes stifle entrepreneurship and discourage the financial risk-taking necessary to create the jobs that could get us out of a new Great

Depression. If government takes more of our money, how can we start or expand our businesses? How can we spend more? Buy more homes? Buy more stocks? Taxes are killing our chances of recovery.

Do you now get the picture? America is staring at the Greatest Depression *ever*—unless we change paths and policy quickly. Sadly, Obama's re-election has thrown a wrench into that hope.

The economy is crumbling. And the more government gets involved, the worse it gets. Remember, this is Obama's plan. His "solutions" are *planned* to explode the debt and overwhelm the system. *And it's working.*

Unfortunately most liberal/progressive politicians are cheering him on while too many so-called "moderates" and conservatives are simply wimps or cowards. The whole while, the liberal media spreads the propaganda that things are getting better.

WHY DOESN'T IT SEEM LIKE 1929?

People ask me, "If we are really on the verge of a second Great Depression, why is the stock market doing well? Why are auto sales doing well? Why are there no bread lines or tent cities like in the 1930s?"

The answer is big government. What you're seeing is a fraud—the biggest Ponzi scheme in world history. There would be bread lines and tent cities if government weren't handing out billions in checks, paid for by the Fed printing trillions in fake dollars.

You've seen the numbers. Obama is the biggest spender in world history, adding almost $6 trillion to the debt in only four years. Where do you think the money is going? Among other runaway spending, food stamps, disability, welfare, and unemployment benefits are all at record highs.

We're borrowing from China to pay entitlement checks to Americans—and hand out billions in foreign aid to countries that hate us and support terrorism. The Fed is running the printing presses day and night to pump trillions of dollars into the system to artificially prop up banks and Wall Street.

Obama hands out billions of stimulus dollars and government contracts like candy to publicly traded multi-national companies like GE,

KEEP BAILING (THEM OUT)

You've probably heard that car sales are up and the auto industry is recovering. But who's buying the cars? Government purchases of GM vehicles were up 79 percent in the past year.[31]

so the stock market can stay in positive territory.[28] He gives out hundreds of billions to green energy companies run by Democratic contributors—all without a hope of ever making a profit.[29] He hands billions in government money to unions to save overpaid jobs that are bankrupting their companies in the first place.[30]

There are no bread lines or tent cities because we're living in a fantasyland. It's fraud on a massive scale. A Ponzi scheme. Government is paying for *everything*.

Housing allowances and food stamps prevent bread lines and tent cities.

Free breakfasts and lunches at school make it seem like children aren't going hungry.

Earned income "tax credits" are handed out to millions of lower income Americans, who pay no taxes in the first place. How long would they survive without those checks?

Government buys cars to keep GM in business, so union workers keep getting their checks.

Take away the government handouts, government entitlements, government stimulus, Fed printing, government jobs, government contracts, government pensions, government car purchases, earned income tax credits, housing allowances, assistance for needy families, food stamps, Medicaid (free healthcare), free breakfasts and lunches at school, and America would look exactly like 1929.

Our entire economy is being propped up by government spending and debt that didn't exist in 1929.

Don't kid yourself. We are in an Obama Great Depression. It's being hidden, disguised, and propped up with government spending and government printing presses adding trillions in debt.

Everything *seems* normal. But it's not real. Look around . . . you already see abandoned homes, empty buildings, empty parking lots outside office parks, vacant storefronts, and homelessness from coast to coast. Take that spending away and the whole country would very quickly look like Detroit.

But doesn't that just prove that government programs are the answer? If Obama's trillions of dollars in spending are saving us from bread lines and tent cities, shouldn't we be grateful?

The problem is, this fake economy can't go on like this forever— any more than you can personally live a wonderful life on credit cards forever. You can live on debt for a while, but eventually it catches up with you. America is already running out of suckers to loan us money. That's why the Fed printing presses are now running day and night. The reality is that all this debt has to be paid back eventually. Then the party is over.

THEY DON'T EVEN HAVE TO PRINT IT

In this day and age the Federal Reserve doesn't need to literally, physically print dollar bills to inflate the currency—or, as we say now, "to increase the money supply." Now they just buy U.S. Treasury bonds—which is essentially just one part of the federal government borrowing from another part of the federal government. The *Wall Street Journal* recently reported on the Federal Reserve buying *over 61 percent* of our debt issued by the Treasury Department.[32]

Worse, the debt won't destroy just *your* life. It will destroy the lives of your children and grandchildren. They will be ensnared and enslaved by that debt. We are ruining the lives of future generations—before they are even born. No wonder babies cry and scream at the moment they are born!

If we don't act fast, America will be just another story in the history books . . . just like Rome and the empire of Alexander the Great. We're not the first people who ever believed their reign of power would never end.

Have I got your attention?

CHAPTER FIVE

OBAMA AND BUSH CHANNEL FDR AND HOOVER

DID YOU KNOW?

- Hoover was a Republican who abandoned free market principles (not unlike George W. Bush) and plunged America into the original Great Depression
- Obama has promised to emulate FDR's "bold, persistent experimentation," which prolonged the Great Depression for years
- With Hoover and FDR retreads following each other in the White House, you'd better start planning how to survive the new Obama Great Depression

To know what we're up against and plot a course of action to salvation we need to look at history. The place to start is the tragedy of the combined policies of Hoover and FDR.

Keep in mind that FDR is Obama's hero. Few Americans understood the significance of the most important line in his acceptance speech at the 2012 Democratic National Convention. Obama promised he'd pursue "the kind of bold, persistent experimentation that Franklin Roosevelt (FDR) pursued during the only crisis worse than this one."

The implications of that promise are truly frightening—because history has already *proven* that these policies lead to economic disaster.

Unfortunately, the wheels are in motion. Bush and Obama are channeling the disastrous mistakes of Hoover and FDR. And the results are eerily similar—economic decline, disaster, and tragedy for average American families. Going through events since the financial collapse blow by blow, it becomes apparent that Bush and Obama have responded to a deep recession in a way that's disturbingly familiar to anyone who knows what Hoover and FDR did in the original Great Depression. And once again, a recession is being turned into a long-term Great Depression through government "help."

Sadly, the honest truth about Hoover and FDR's disastrous failure has never been taught to us, or our children, by the ultra-liberal teachers' union clones in charge of education in America today. What is taught in our failing, dumbed-down public schools is the myth that the Republican Hoover did nothing about the Depression because of his laissez-faire capitalist principles, and then Democrat FDR saved America from the Great Depression with his "bold, persistent" experimentation (in other words, relentless government meddling in the economy). The reality is that big government intrusion and intervention by Hoover *caused* the Great Depression, and even more government meddling by FDR made it last many years *longer.*[1]

Obama's plans to emulate FDR and get government even more involved in the economy today—following up on Bush's unfortunate decision to try to rescue the economy in the first place—is creating a similar tragedy for America. Those who don't study or understand history are doomed to repeat the exact same mistakes that have caused the disasters of the past. Obama is Exhibit A. He doesn't understand, or refuses to accept, that there was no Great Depression (either I or II) *until government got involved to "save" us.* It's no coincidence that whenever government comes to the rescue, calamity ensues.

Here's the real story of the Great Depression. The stock market crashed in 1929. But the natural business cycle is boom and bust—the market had collapsed many times before without causing a Great Depression. There was no reason for politicians to panic and over-react. There was no reason for politicians to get involved at all. The less they do, the better. The 1929 stock market crash by itself may have turned many high flying investors and speculators into bankrupt losers, but it did not create massive unemployment, bread lines, and a Great Depression. It took panicked politicians and disastrous government action to cause the original Great Depression—

> # WORDS OF WISDOM FROM A PRESIDENT WE *SHOULD* BE EMULATING
>
> "The nine most terrifying words in the English language are 'I'm from the government and I'm here to help.'"
>
> —Ronald Reagan

"bold, persistent" government action just like the meddling being implemented by Obama today, which is creating our modern day economic tragedy.

Want proof? Just look at the history. In the early 1920s America had installed high tax rates to pay for World War I. The result was a recession. In a brilliant move, President Calvin Coolidge—a Republican who actually did believe in free market laissez-faire economics—responded by cutting taxes, cutting spending, cutting government programs, and paying off debt. Not only did tax rates go down dramatically—top rates were brought down from 73 to 24 percent—but by the end of Coolidge's presidency, only 2 percent of Americans were paying any income tax at all.[2] Coolidge reduced the national debt by approximately one-third, even while also cutting taxes.[3] The result: the bust quickly ended and turned into the boom known as "the Roaring Twenties."

When the government spends less and lets business owners and job creators keep more, the result is always prosperity. Ironically, in school we are taught Coolidge was blamed for being a "do nothing President." (You've got to love those biased, ultra-liberal educators who don't have even a rudimentary knowledge of economics.)

Herbert Hoover was Coolidge's successor. And if only Hoover had followed Coolidge's "do nothing" example, there would never have been a Great Depression. But Hoover was a different kind of Republican; he couldn't keep his hands off the economy; he had to try to fix it. As Coolidge remarked, "That man has given me unsolicited advice for six years—*all of it bad.*" Coolidge could have been looking into a crystal ball.

When the 1929 stock market crash occurred, just as Coolidge predicted, Hoover's instincts were all bad. President Hoover panicked, abandoned the laissez-faire principles that had worked so well under Coolidge, and got government heavily involved in trying to resolve the financial crisis. (Remind anyone of George W. Bush?) Big mistake. He didn't have to do anything. The 1929 crash wasn't actually all that bad. For one month unemployment went to 9 percent. Just a year later it was back down to 6 percent.

But that wasn't good enough for Hoover and Congress. They soon passed a tariff bill (Smoot-Hawley) that was the largest tax increase on traded U.S. goods in history. They passed a massive income tax increase—from 24 percent to over 60 percent. They started passing a never-ending stream of new government rules and regulations.[4] And the government spent and spent and spent, frantically trying to rescue the American economy from collapse.[5] (Remind anyone of the $700 billion TARP under George W. Bush?)

GEORGE W. BUSH CHANNELS HERBERT HOOVER

"Well, I have obviously made a decision to make sure the economy doesn't collapse. **I've abandoned free market principles to save the free market system.** I think when people review what's taken place in the last six months, and put it all in one package, they'll realize how significantly we have moved."[6]

The result? *Disaster.* Businesses failed, jobs were killed, and the economy tanked. Unemployment hit double digits. Because of government intervention, America now went into a full-blown depression.

Enter Obama's hero, FDR. Roosevelt demanded even more government help, promising government would save America. Roosevelt began "helping" with even higher taxes, more rules and regulations, nonstop demonization of business, and massive spending on public works projects and new entitlement programs—resulting in more debt and deficits. FDR was Obama, before Obama was Obama.

On January 1, 1936, income taxes were raised to 79 percent...and a year later to 83 percent. *Madness.* But FDR was just getting warmed up. He also increased most other taxes, from estate to corporate and gift taxes. State and local taxes were also raised. Like Obama, FDR never met a tax he didn't like.[7]

The results were devastating. Six years after Hoover was gone... SIX YEARS into FDR's presidency... unemployment was at 20 percent.

WHY SHOULD IT BE ANY DIFFERENT THIS TIME AROUND?

"We have tried spending money. We are spending more than we have ever spent before and it does not work . . . After eight years of this administration we have just as much unemployment as when we started . . . and an enormous debt to boot!"—Henry Morgenthau, FDR's Treasury Secretary

Even FDR's own Treasury Secretary, Henry Morgenthau, bemoaned the fact that FDR spent a record amount of federal money and amassed a record amount of debt *without* creating jobs or stimulating the economy.[8]

Sound familiar? Remember, FDR is Obama's hero.

Still Obama got one thing right. He said, "I won't predict the path I'm offering is quick or easy." Correct—with Obama in charge, this mess will take years to heal, maybe a decade or longer—just as it did under his hero FDR. It took World War II to get FDR out of the original Great Depression...let us all pray we can get out of the new Obama Great Depression without a calamity of that magnitude.

History proves that when Bush and Obama, just like Hoover and FDR, spent too much, piled up debt, raised taxes, and grew government bigger, the economy declined and jobs disappeared. History always repeats.

The solution is so simple. Milton Friedman once said, "You can't spend or tax an economy into prosperity. Only RESTRAINING government spending stimulates the economy by freeing up money for private sector."

We need to get this FDR retread out of office and set about cleaning up this Obama Great Depression he's creating (just as his hero helped prolong the original Great Depression). But first, we all have to survive the next four years. That's what this book is all about—showing you how to survive, thrive, and prosper in Obama's second term.

CHAPTER SIX

DETROIT—THE MODEL FOR OBAMA'S AMERICA

DID YOU KNOW?

- Detroit, under 100-percent Democrat control for decades, is a preview of Obama's America
- Detroit is America's most dangerous city
- Almost a third of Detroit's housing stock is vacant

etroit was just ranked "America's Most Dangerous City" for the fourth year in a row—with a rate of violent crime five times higher than the national average.[1]

Two-thirds of Detroit's street lamps are broken. But why fix them? No one lives there any more. Of the 363,281 housing units in Detroit, almost one-third are vacant.[2]

You don't have to look far to see how bad it could get. We already have the perfect preview of what Obama's vision will do to America—right here in America. We need look no further than the once great city of Detroit.

Detroit is a hell-hole, a war zone, a Third World country smack dab in the middle of America. Detroit is the canary in the coal mine. Look at Detroit to see the future results of the Obama Axis of Evil—taxation, regulation, unionization, litigation, and government strangulation. Look at Detroit to preview the after-effects of the Obama Great Depression.

Detroit has been under 100-percent Democrat Party rule for decades.[3] The result? Detroit is now dysfunctional, insolvent, and teetering on the verge of bankruptcy. Actually, it has been bankrupt for years, but the state of Michigan has kept the city running with smoke and mirrors, band-aids, spit, and glue. The bad news is that time and money have finally run out. Detroit is about to become officially bankrupt.[4] The good news is that there are valuable lessons to be learned from the one-party experiment that is the city of Detroit. But first we have to get the facts straight—after the Obama campaign and the mainstream media have done their best to cover them up.

Detroit Fact #1: Obama did *not* save Detroit, or the auto industry. President Obama got re-elected in part based on his claim to have rescued Detroit and American auto manufacturing. His opponent, Mitt Romney, was demonized by Obama as the man who would have "let Detroit go bankrupt."[5] But the voters were scammed. Obama was lying. He didn't save Detroit or the automakers. He just dumped billions of our money down a rathole, to buy votes. Obama let GM go bankrupt—and rigged the process to stiff bondholders so he could reward his union cronies with billions in bailout money from us, the taxpayers.[6] And Detroit was never going to be saved. Obama only postponed the inevitable and bought votes by spending your children's and grandchildren's money. Your heirs will be paying the interest on this debt fifty years from now—and they won't even get a car in the bargain!

AN INTERESTING CHOICE OF WORDS

When Detroit city council member JoAnn Watson said Detroit residents deserved a bailout as a "quid pro quo" for voting for Obama, did she realize that that phrase is typically used to describe the crime of bribery?

Detroit Fact #2: President Obama *did* bribe voters with public money. Mitt Romney was criticized *harshly* for saying Obama bought the election with "gifts" to certain voters.[7] But the auto bailout was just that— federal money to the auto unions.

And did you see the Detroit councilwoman saying that her city voted overwhelmingly for Obama, so now he owes them "some bacon"—in other words, a federal bailout? She wants a bailout for Detroit as a "quid pro quo" for all the votes Obama got from the city.[8] Sounds like Romney hit the nail on the head. Obama's voters did indeed vote for the candidate they thought would provide them with the most freebies—bailouts, free contraception, food stamps, free healthcare, entitlements, and handouts. The irony is that this freeloader mentality is *exactly* what has made Detroit the disaster it is in the first place.

DETROIT'S DEMISE IS AMERICA'S FUTURE UNDER OBAMA

Look at the facts. Detroit is a one-party town. It has been run 100 percent lock, stock, and barrel by liberal progressive Democrats for decades—politicians with the exact same agenda and policies as Obama. There is no opposition party, no checks and balances. Republican sightings in Detroit are just a rumor. So Detroit is the perfect test case for finding out what happens when you allow Democrats (like Obama) to run things 100 percent their way. Detroit has been following Obama's policies of big government always knows best, massive taxing and spending, and entitlements galore *for decades*. There is no argument or debate. There is no Republican opposition. Detroit is the Obama dream come true. Detroit is the rock-solid proof of what happens when Democrats get to run things exactly the way they want.

So let's look at the results. Detroit is not only $2.5 billion in debt, the debt has been downgraded to junk status.[9] Obama's America is $16 TRIL-LION in debt. (If you add our unfunded liabilities, it's over $100 TRIL-LION.)[10]

Because of too many government employees paid way too much and allowed to retire way too young, with obscene pensions and unaffordable health care paid for life, Detroit has $11 billion in government employee retirement obligations. $11 billion in a single city.[11]

Obama's America, for exactly the same reason, has several TRILLION in unfunded liabilities for government employees.[12]

A CITY ADDICTED TO SPENDING

Like a crack addict, Detroit is a dysfunctional, self-destructive, out-of-control spending addict headed for a tragic ending.

Detroit's unemployment rate is sky-high, just like in Obama's America—only more so. The mayor of Detroit actually admitted recently that true unemployment in his city tops 50 percent.[13] Is that where America is headed under Obama?

Unemployment in the city of Detroit is twice as high as in the metropolitan area around Detroit.[14] Why? I'd hazard an educated guess that many of the suburbs are run by Republican mayors with discipline, fiscal responsibility, lower taxes, and lower spending.

Unemployment and bankruptcy aren't the only results of progressive liberal policies—in Detroit, or in Obama's plans for America.

Seventy-five percent of the children born in Detroit in the past twelve months were born to unmarried mothers.[15]

Out of 264,209 households in Detroit, 34.5 percent (91,204 households) get food stamps.[16]

Detroit was just ranked "America's Most Dangerous City" for the fourth year in a row—with a rate of violent crime five times higher than the national average.[17]

Detroit is the murder capital of America.[18]

All of that is happening with strict gun control.[19] Which just proves once again that gun control only disarms the law-abiding citizens and shop owners. It leaves them defenseless—to be murdered, robbed, raped, or car-jacked by the armed-to-the-teeth criminals.

Homes in Detroit sell for $1,000 or less—some for less than $100—some for $1.[20] This should come as no surprise. Would you live in the city I've been describing even if your house only cost you one dollar?

Detroit used to be known as "the Paris of the West" for its architecture. Now Detroit's abandoned lots cover more area than all of Paris, France.[21]

In the 1950s Detroit was the fifth-largest city in America, with a population of about 2 million residents. Today the population is about 700,000.

During the past decade a quarter of Detroit's population has escaped, leaving a largely vacant town. Between 2000 and 2010, Detroit lost another resident every twenty-two minutes.[22]

In a recent poll commissioned by the *Detroit News*, forty percent of respondents said they planned to move away within the next five years. And if they could, the poll reported, more than half of Detroiters said they'd pick up and leave the city today.[23]

The mayor's plan to save Detroit is to bulldoze one quarter of the city. He will leave entire neighborhoods without police, fire, or garbage services. Detroit will close about half its schools. The mayor's plan abandons major portions of the city to gangs and the homeless.[24]

Detroit is home to America's most disgraceful public schools. Think of what an inferior education means for the future of Detroit's children? No need to guess—the facts are in. Almost 50 percent of the adults in Detroit are "functionally illiterate"—meaning they can't read, or fill out basic forms necessary to get a job, or read the instructions on their prescription medicine.[25]

Aren't Democrats supposed to be the ones who care about education? So how come half the adults in a city controlled by Democrats and their teachers' unions are illiterate? Doesn't this prove spending huge sums of money "for the kids" is a failure? But of course, the money doesn't go to the kids, it goes to teachers' unions. And those unions refuse to allow teachers to be graded for performance, or fired for incompetence.

If children living in poverty bothers you (and it should), take a look at this statistic: 54 percent of all children in Detroit live in poverty.[26] Aren't Democrats the ones who talk about "the children" all day? Aren't Democrats the ones who say Republicans don't care about "the children?" So why does Detroit, under 100 percent Democrat rule for decades, lead the nation in childhood poverty?

Folks, this is what Armageddon looks like. Vast swaths of Detroit look like a war zone in Baghdad or Libya. But even more frightening, Detroit is the test case for what America will look like if Obama's plan succeeds.

Detroit's policies are Obama's dream come true: big government, big taxes, big spending, powerful unions, out-of-control entitlements, big deficit and debt, too many government employees, early retirement, obscene pensions, public schools run by all-powerful teachers' unions with no competition, and free healthcare provided by government.

What is at the center of this tragic American nightmare? *Unions.* You know, Obama's staunchest supporters and contributors. The same ones that now own him and most progressive leftist politicians. The *Wall Street Journal* points out that Detroit will spend $160 million this year and $135 million next year on just the retirement benefits of government union employees. That's *after* factoring in the mayor's recent labor reform victory.[27] Unions have looted and bankrupted Detroit.

Government employees in Detroit have "defined benefit" pensions that let them retire in their forties and then get paid a fortune until they die—almost twice as long as they worked.[28] This exact same insanity is bankrupting cities, counties, states, and even our federal government—from sea to shining sea. Keep in mind there are over 22 million government employees in America.[29] They're aiming to retire with big pensions in their forties, to live forty more years of leisure—playing golf, taking cruises, enjoying early bird dinners, and of course voting Democrat on election day, so they can keep this fleecing of taxpayers going.

Detroit is the future of Obama's America. This is what happens when an economy is run based on "fairness," "equality," and "social justice." This is what happens when politicians and government bureaucrats get together with unions, entitlement addicts, and class action lawyers to rig up the system targeting "the rich" and business owners to pay for it all.

In Detroit, this targeted class…simply left. They moved out. Left town. Oh, it took a few years, but it became clear there was absolutely no reason to stay in misery and be mugged by thieves. Smart people eventually figure these things out.

The very same thing is happening all around the world. Think France, Italy, Spain, Greece, Argentina, and other socialist or socialist-lite countries. The exodus of productive people from places governed by parasitic government has begun. Gerard Depardieu is leaving France![30] Is there any reason to think the same thing won't happen to America?

The rich and business owners leave as fast as they can. They run for their lives to protect themselves and their families. Look around. The proof

DETROIT FINALLY GOES BROKE

As if on cue, just as I was finishing this book, a Michigan state-appointed review team of financial experts who had spent weeks digging into the finances of Detroit declared Detroit officially in a financial emergency, with no realistic plan to save it. Their findings: Detroit's deficit last year was just under $1 billion—with long-term liabilities of $14 billion.[31]

The week before, the Michigan Department of Transportation had reported that one-fifth of the lights along Metro-Detroit's freeways are no longer working because copper thieves have stripped the metal from the transformers.[32]

Third World hell hole indeed. Oh, by the way, Detroit hasn't had a Republican mayor since 1961. This is *Obamageddon.*

is Detroit, a vacant, abandoned, bankrupt city. Read the list of states leading the country in moving vans leaving—a good measure of outbound migration. They are all big-taxing, big-spending, big-government, Democrat-ruled states. Michigan is always right at or near the top.[33]

And this is the Obama blueprint. This is how Democrats run things when they have no Republican opposition. In other words, it's what they would do everywhere, if they could get away with it. Detroit is our future. Its miserable, poor, helpless, illiterate residents are the canaries in the coal mine.

By re-electing Obama, a majority of Americans—after decades of being dumbed down and indoctrinated by members of the public school teachers' unions—voted for... *Detroit.*

Be scared. Be very scared.

It's truly *that* bad.

CHAPTER SEVEN

WILD WEST COWBOY CAPITALISM

DID YOU KNOW?

- From 2000 to 2010, more than half a million people moved to Texas—from California alone
- New Yorkers relocating to the Lone Star State in the same decade brought almost $1 trillion in assets and income with them
- Eight of the fifteen fastest-growing cities in the U.S. are in Texas
- More jobs were created in Texas in the past decade than in the other forty-nine states *combined*

You know what's the opposite of Detroit? The Great State of Texas. Texas is an upbeat, real-life example of how government can be good and actually work for, not against its citizens.

But only if it does exactly the opposite of everything Obama is doing to America.

If you want to see how a country *should* be run; if you're interested in seeing your citizens succeed...and if you're interested in opportunity, mobility, and the pursuit of happiness, all you need to do is look at Texas.

Facts don't lie. It seems like everyone is moving to Texas—the land of Wild West Cowboy Capitalism. Especially residents of high-tax-and-spend states such as California, New York, New Jersey, Pennsylvania, Connecticut, Illinois, and Michigan.

From 2000 to 2010 a staggering 3.4 million people moved out of New York resulting in a net loss of 1.3 million residents. California was a close second with a net population loss of 1.2 million during the same decade.

During that same time Texas led the nation in net population growth. A remarkable 551,914 new Texans came from a single state—California. They brought with them $14.3 billion in income. In just one short period from 2009 to 2010, 48,877 Californians moved to Texas, bringing with them $1.2 billion.[1]

But even that paled in comparison to the almost $1 trillion in assets and income that re-located New Yorkers brought to the Lone Star State. *WOW!*

THE GREAT ESCAPE

So why is everyone running for their lives from New York and California? And why are so many of them heading to Texas? The answer is taxes, regulations, and quality of life. In other words, government interference in their lives…or in the case of Texas…minimal interference.

It's no coincidence that New York has ranked first or second in the nation for tax burden every year since 1977.[2]

In addition to state income taxes, property taxes, and sales taxes, New York has a whopping 49-cents-per-gallon gas tax and the highest estate and gift taxes in the nation. After grabbing more of your money than any state while you're alive, New York also steals more of your money after you're dead (with estate taxes). I should know—*I left New York twenty-five years ago and never looked back.*

But California couldn't stand to be number two. Those Hollywood liberals are so competitive. Not to be outdone by New York, last November California passed the highest state income taxes in America.[3] You can almost hear the liberals shouting, "We're Number One!" Yes, number one in taxes, but also number one in people running for the exit—especially high earners and high-net-worth individuals. Be careful what you wish for.

California not only leads the nation in taxes, it is also a leader in excessive rules and regulations.[4] It's no wonder so many people are escaping California. I should know—*I left California too.*

Lest you think this is some kind of fluke, or that taxes are not a determining factor in the trend to escape from New York and California, it isn't just Texas that is gaining residents who have fled from high-tax states. The U.S. Census reported that all of the top fifteen states with population growth during the past decade are no-tax or low-tax states including Nevada, Florida, Arizona, Utah, Georgia, North Carolina, and South Carolina.[5]

Since the 2010 Census, Texas dominates the list of fastest-growing cities, with eight of the top fifteen.[6]

It seems Americans are smarter than politicians give them credit for— they are voting with their feet for lower taxes, pro-business attitude, and more economic freedom.

Because no state in the union has a better economy, let's look up close and personal at the Texas miracle. What **exactly** is Wild West Cowboy Capitalism and why does it work?

COWBOY CAPITALIST MAGIC

Texas has zero state income tax, zero capital gains tax, and zero death tax. It is a "right to work" state where employees may choose to join a union, but are never forced to. It is a pro-business and anti-lawyer state— having passed both landmark medical lawsuit reform and America's first "loser pays" tort reform. The results of the medical reforms? Lawsuits dropped by 70 percent. Twenty-five thousand doctors moved to Texas. Medical liability insurance rates dropped by as much as 50 percent.[7]

Texas is also one of the most difficult states to file class action lawsuits in.[8]

Quite simply, Texas treats businesspeople and taxpayers nicely. The state offers more business incentives ($19 billion) than any other state.[9]

On the other hand, Texas is tight-fisted with taxpayer money. It pays among the least generous welfare and entitlement benefits. California is the exact opposite. They are the welfare capital of America. California has one third of the nation's welfare recipients versus 12 percent of the nation's population. Why? Because California pays the most generous welfare benefits in the nation—$179 per citizen compared to $32 per citizen in Texas.[10]

Texas is also tight-fisted with its government employees—benefits there are last in the nation.[11] California has the highest-paid teachers in America, while Texas pays its teachers far less. Yet the high school graduation rate is higher in Texas than California.[12]

Texas runs its government far more efficiently. Texas has a balanced budget amendment. By contrast California owes an astounding $167 billion.[13]

The result is people with high incomes, assets, and ambition are moving into Texas, while those who lack work ethic, and feel entitled to handouts are moving out. Good luck to New York and California—we'll see you in bankruptcy court.

LESS GOVERNMENT = MORE PROSPERITY

Why does Texas have such prosperity-friendly government—in contrast to, say, Detroit? The Texas state constitution limits the time politicians can meet to ninety days *every other* year. That explains everything. Texas, like my adopted home state of Nevada, has low taxes and a fast-growing population because politicians aren't allowed to sit in their seats all year long thinking of new ways to re-distribute income, impede business, and destroy jobs.

Just look at the remarkable results of favoring hard-working business owners and job-creators over entitlement addicts and lawyers. The annual Texas economy has passed $1 trillion, and now accounts for 8.3 percent of the entire U.S. economy. Texas has passed New York to become the second-largest economy in America and the fourteenth-largest in the world, equivalent to Russia's.[14]

How about jobs? Feast your eyes on these statistics: Since 2007 one third of all jobs in America were created in Texas, and in the past decade, more jobs were created in Texas than in the other forty-nine states *COMBINED*. Texas has three out of every five jobs created in America since 2007.[15]

Even more amazing is the *kind* of jobs Texas has been creating. They have created the most private sector jobs in the nation—the ones that pay taxes and cost taxpayers nothing. At the same time Texas has eliminated government jobs—the kind that cost taxpayers big money.[16]

And they didn't do it by spending the federal government's money. Texas receives the second lowest stimulus funding per capita out of all fifty states. That's what you call bang for the buck.[17]

According to CNN Money, Texas now has more Fortune 500 headquarters than New York.[18]

Texas is also home to six of the top fifty Fortune 500 companies.[19]

Texas's economy had the most explosive growth in all of America for the past fifty years, while California's economy peaked in 1990, and showed the fourth-biggest decline of all the states from 2000 to 2010.[20]

Texas flourishes while California, New York, Illinois, and all these other high-tax-and-spend states career from crisis to crisis, always on the verge of bankruptcy.

Business is booming in Texas. Here's an example showing why. California-based CKE Restaurants has over three thousand restaurants, including Carl's Jr. and Hardee's. Its president, quoted in the *Wall Street Journal*, called his home state of California business-unfriendly and noted that opening a restaurant in California takes two years and costs $200,000 more than opening one in Texas, where it takes only six *weeks*. Is it a surprise that CKE has stopped opening new restaurants in California, but plans to open three hundred in Texas?[21]

Chevron must have gotten the same memo. They just announced they are moving eight hundred high-paying employees (one quarter of their workforce) from California to Houston, Texas.[22]

Still unconvinced? Ask the CEOs of America. In *Chief Executive* magazine's annual poll . . . the one that ranked California dead last in America for business for eight consecutive years . . .Texas has been ranked number one for those same eight straight years.[23]

And CNBC just ranked Texas as the top state in America for business for 2012—the third time they've been ranked number one in six years![24]

So there you have it. Now you know why businesses, as well as people, choose states that treat them better, give them more economic freedom, and allow them to keep more of their own money. *Can you imagine that?*

The results of smaller government, restrained politicians, and lower taxes are dramatically increased wealth, job creation, and citizens with a higher quality of life. Long live Wild West Cowboy Capitalism!

The solution to saving America is so simple—It's to do the opposite of everything Obama does. *Texas proves it works!*

By the way, while I was writing this book, Texas passed its 2013 budget. Texas cut taxes and spending and wound up with a record-setting $8 billion budget surplus. Congratulations to Governor Rick Perry. Gosh I love Texas![25]

P.S. My Texas friends want everyone to know, "Come on down, y'all are welcome. Just leave your socialist politics at home."

CHAPTER EIGHT

OBAMA'S TARGET #1: SMALL BUSINESS

DID YOU KNOW?

- Obama's Department of Labor is unleashing a swarm of frivolous lawsuits on small business
- Texas has made it harder to harass businesses with lawsuits—and their economy is booming
- If Obama succeeds in removing the cap on income that's subject to FICA taxes, small business owners could see those taxes go up by $59,104 *a year*

How is President Obama moving America away from the Texas model and toward the Detroit horror story? By attacking and destroying businesses—especially small businesses.

Obama's number one target is small business. Why? As you'll soon see, small businessmen and women are his most dangerous opponents. In the kind of Marxist-fascist combination economy Obama is thrusting upon us, small business owners have the most to lose and therefore are undoubtedly the most motivated to lead the fight against him to save capitalism and this great country.

Don't be deceived by listening to what Obama says; look at what he does. Some smart business owners that I know and respect admit while Obama was running for office (the first time) they felt like they had at least some common ground with him. They actually liked him—at least a bit. They certainly did not fear him. But since he was elected, they have agreed with him less—and feared him more—than any other president. I am repeatedly stunned at Obama's ability to say one thing and then do exactly the opposite. It's a rare talent—I'll give him that. But that's cold comfort for the people whose lives he is damaging or destroying.

THE ENGINE OF JOB CREATION

I've started more than a dozen businesses. Over $20 million was raised from investors (including me) for one of them. Small businesspeople have all risked our hard-earned money on an idea that at the time was just a dream. That's called entrepreneurship. That's what fuels capitalism. The willingness to risk is what fuels the U.S. economy. It's not driven by big business, or multi-national conglomerates. The economy's driving force is small businessmen and women with ideas and enough faith in those ideas to risk their own time and money and convince others to do the same.

Small business creates about two-thirds of the new jobs in America and accounts for 54 percent of all U.S. sales.[1]

Even more importantly, studies prove that "start-ups" (new small businesses) are responsible for virtually 100 percent of our job growth.[2]

Since 1990, while big business was eliminating 4 million jobs, small business was adding over 8 million. Without small business, America's economy would be up the proverbial creek without a paddle.[3]

It's no wonder. As a small businessman, I've paid payrolls, health insurance, payroll taxes, workers' comp, and unemployment insurance for hundreds of employees at a time (for *thousands* of employees over the last thirty years).

Because of what they were paid from those small businesses, my employees were able to pay their mortgages or rent, buy groceries, buy gas, send their kids to college, and provide for their families. As consumers they fueled the economy with the money they were paid by my small businesses.

The multiplier effect of a small business is remarkable. The small business I mentioned above, the one I raised $20 million for, had only about a hundred employees. After a decade-long run it closed. Yet during that decade we spent over $60 million dollars on advertising, marketing, promotion, rent, lawyers, and accountants. That money enriched and employed thousands of others. And, that's just *one* small business. All of this GDP came from one idea that I thought up on a walk in the park with my dog.

If that's what a single small business can do, think of the impact almost 30 million small business owners have on the U.S. economy. Small business employs 57 million Americans. The economic impact, according to the U.S. Small Business Administration, is $11 trillion annually.[4] We create about two-thirds of America's new jobs. Almost 30 million small businessmen and women are a far more powerful economic force than Exxon, Microsoft, GE, or Walmart.[5]

IN HIS SIGHTS

So why do Obama and his socialist cabal hate us? Why do small businessmen and women feel demonized and punished? Why does Obama target us for all his tax increases?

First, we're an easy target. We may be the economic engine of America, but we can't fight back like big business. Individually we can't afford big law firms, Big Four accounting firms, lobbyists, or tax shelter experts. In the eyes of a socialist like Obama, we're the perfect target: helpless sitting ducks with no pull in Washington, D.C., or in the mainstream media.

But the primary reason Obama is targeting us is because we are his most dangerous opponents. Small business owners believe in capitalism and personal responsibility. We believe in faith, family, and the American Dream. And we are vehemently opposed to Big Brother controlling our lives and telling us how to live them. Small business owners define "independent." That's why we are the biggest contributors to conservative politicians.

Is Obama really targeting us? Mug or rob me once—maybe it's coincidence or a mistake. Twice? It's a pattern. But, when you rob, denigrate, and punish me on a weekly basis...I get the message. Without a doubt, Obama and the progressive left are the enemy of small business.

Obama's war on small business is being fought on two fronts. He attacks the very existence of small business itself. And he also attacks the small business owner.

The attack on small business itself is multi-pronged. Let's take a look at just a few of the ways Obama is making life impossible for those who would employ Americans and get the economy moving again.

PUTTING CAPITAL OUT OF REACH

For the entire length of my career in business, small business owners (like me) have been able to raise capital without government permission. An entrepreneur didn't need the government's permission to raise $100,000 or $1,000,000 or even $20,000,000 for a private business deal with "accredited investors" (individuals with high incomes or high net worth). Obama and his socialist friends in Congress tried to change that. With Obama's full support, Democratic Senator Chris Dodd tried to pass a so-called "financial reform" bill that included a provision dramatically increasing the amount of assets one would have to have to be considered an "accredited investor"[6]—making it much more difficult for entrepreneurs to raise money privately. If that provision had passed, I estimate that the investor pool for small businesses would have been reduced by about 70 percent.

Some of the most onerous restrictions were stripped out of the final bill. But one thing is clear—it was never meant to help small business. It was meant (as usual) to make raising money more complex, more difficult, more confusing. Once again, small business would be forced to spend far more money—to hire lawyers, consultants, and accountants to deal with a complicated legal quagmire.[7]

This would have damaged entrepreneurship, venture capital, and new business start-ups. Only the super-rich could ever raise money to start a business. Thank heavens, the worst provisions didn't make it into the final version of the Dodd-Frank financial "reform" bill that became law. But there's absolutely nothing to stop Obama from trying again.

Who came up with an idea like this in the first place? There are three possibilities: First, a Marxist ideologue looking to destroy the American economy by wiping out small business. Second, a cabal of extortionist lawyers, looking for a government mandate forcing businessmen to pay obscene legal fees. Third, a cabal of *big* businesses and billionaire titans looking to fix the system, so only *they* can compete. In any case, it was designed to put small business out of business. And in any case, Obama's friends win.

HARASSING SMALL BUSINESSES WITH LAWSUITS

Did you know the White House has gone into partnership with the American Bar Association? Obama has found a way to encourage every lawsuit junkie and disgruntled employee to make up a story and sue his or her employer (with no financial outlay). Every caller to the Labor Department

WHY TEXAS IS BOOMING

Compared to the Zombie Economy in the rest of the country, Texas is booming. We've seen that the Lone Star State leads the nation in job creation and that record numbers of citizens of states like California and New York are moving to Texas, bringing their assets with them.[8] Why? On top of being low-tax, low-regulation, and anti-union, Texas is the least friendly state to lawyers and lawsuits. Texas just passed a "loser pays" law making it difficult and expensive to file frivolous lawsuits.[9] Texas is also one of the most difficult states in which to file class action lawsuits.[10] If Obama were interested in creating jobs, why would he be moving in the exact *opposite* direction from Texas?

alleging his boss has broken the law now gets assigned a lawyer willing to work on contingency—no fees up front.[11] No fees from the complaining employee, that is. Do you know the astronomical cost to a small business to defend even a frivolous lawsuit? You can't make this stuff up.

Do socialists like Obama stay awake at night thinking of ways to destroy business? Do they dream about lawyers, taxes, and IRS agents? What sweet dreams. Think about this for a moment.

Lawsuits are job-killers second only to taxes. This White House partnership with the Bar Association will kill jobs. The only question is why would Obama want to kill jobs, when he says he wants to create jobs? After reading this book you will know the answer to that question.

DESTROYING SMALL BUSINESSES WITH TAXES

A law requiring payment of state sales tax for online purchases is a top Democrat priority.[12] After all, it's only fair. My definition of "fair" is very different from the Democrats'. Today every American can buy goods online and save the sales tax. If you don't think that's fair, you can choose to buy from a land-based retailer and pay the extra 5 to 10 percent. .

An online sales tax is just more taxes to feed Obama's entitlement society, more money taken from us, more money not in your pocket. And what do you get for that extra 5 to 10 percent? *Nothing.*

But the implications for small business are far worse than what the consumer will have to pay. Think about the compliance costs associated with collecting the different sales taxes for the fifty separate states. Small businesses (including individuals running online businesses from their homes) will have to keep track of fifty separate sales tax rates from hundreds or thousands of separate transactions, then compile, report, and pay them to fifty different states. Mindboggling. Without doubling their prices so they can afford to hire new bookkeepers, controllers, and accountants, few small online businesses will survive. But that's the point. The Democrats and their cronies in big business are trying to make small business extinct. They don't want competition from you or me. Big business wants to drive us out of business, so that they are the only game in town.

DRIVING SMALL BUSINESSES OUT OF BUSINESS WITH ONEROUS REPORTING REQUIREMENTS

One little-known provision of Obamacare was a clause demanding every business in America report virtually every dollar they spent to the IRS on a 1099 form—a separate form for every vendor from whom we purchased more than $600 of goods or services during the year. If the mandate to collect online sales tax for fifty different states didn't put you out of business, this new IRS requirement surely would. The blizzard of paperwork it would require was unfathomable.[13]

Coincidence? Obama didn't know this clause was in his Obamacare bill? Well, then who put it in? Why did they include it? They knew small business could not possibly comply. This was no mistake or coincidence. There is a reason for everything Obama does.

I'm proud to report that I was one of the first commentators to report on this stealth clause, due to go into effect in January of 2013.[14] I sounded the alarm in hundreds of media appearances and commentaries reaching millions of Americans. So many small business owners complained to their Congressmen that the clause was stripped out of Obamacare after the fact—something almost unheard of in Washington.[15] This time the outcry was so loud, even our politicians listened.

But it's the intent that matters. You can go to jail for "attempted murder" or "attempted armed robbery"—even if you don't finish the act, or you run out of the store with nothing. Obama and his socialist cabal tried to wipe out small business. This wasn't just a "suggestion" they dreamed up. This provision actually passed into law. Never forget that fact. They got caught and claimed they knew nothing about it. But it was the "attempted murder" of small business. *Think about that.*

ATTACKING THE SMALL BUSINESS OWNER

Now let's look at what Obama is doing to destroy the small business owner as an individual. You need to be prepared to fight Obama's plans and tactics, so you'll find them explained in more detail below. But first you need to get an overview of the threat.

For thirty years, I've been able to deduct mortgage interest from my taxable income. We've already seen that Obama wants to cap the mortgage deduction.[16] If his plan goes into effect, how many so-called "wealthy" taxpayers (small business owners, that is) will no longer be able to pay their mortgage? How many homes will go into foreclosure? What will happen to the housing market? Overnight every home in America will lose more of its already decimated value.

Make no mistake about it—any plan to end or limit the mortgage deduction is aimed squarely at the middle class and the small business owner. The truly rich will be unaffected. If you make $5 million or $20 million per year, what does it matter if you lose a $75,000 mortgage deduction? That's peanuts to the super-rich. But it could mean life or death for a small businessman in the $250,000-to-$500,000 income range. That's exactly what Obama intends.

Losing the mortgage deduction will be even more damaging than tax rate increases. Many, if not most, small business owners use their homes as collateral for business loans. They use their homes as a piggy bank to start and expand their businesses. They use the equity in their home to buy equipment and make payroll during tough times. Small business owners do this because we're *not* super wealthy. Our home is our number one investment. Unlike big corporations, we can't go to banks for business loans. Banks only loan us money if we put our homes up as collateral.[17]

What will happen to our businesses, job creation, and the economy if home values decline even more because the mortgage deduction is capped, or abolished altogether? *Think about it.*

Unfortunately that's just the start of a barrage Obama has aimed specifically at small business owners.

The earnings on which FICA taxes for Social Security are paid have always been capped, currently at $113,700 per year. Obama desperately wants to remove the cap. There's talk of leaving a "doughnut hole" for income up to $250,000, but if the cap is simply lifted, middle class earners and small business owners could face an almost unimaginable and certainly unaffordable tax increase.[18] Overnight a small business owner whose business has a profit of $500,000 per year could see his or her FICA taxes go from $17,396 per year (15.3 percent of $113,700 for the self-employed) to $76,500 (15.3 percent of all $500,000).

That's $76,500 in FICA taxes *before* federal or state income taxes. That's a $59,104 tax increase PER YEAR for a small business owner. Thousands of small business owners will be driven out of business. It will force massive layoffs and dramatically lower consumer spending. The IRS reports that 24 percent of small businesses with employees are run by owners who are being hit by the new Obama tax increase on "the rich."[19] That adds up to just under 1 million small businesses. Can you imagine what will happen to the U.S. economy if 923,000 small business owners each have tens of thousands of dollars less to spend and invest in their businesses . . . PER YEAR! How many jobs will be lost?

Now, add in the new Obamacare taxes. We face new taxes on medical devices, stock sales, home sales, even on tanning beds![20] That's on top of increased income taxes, the loss of deductions, and the potential lifting of the FICA cap that Obama wants. Folks, taken together . . . this is the obliteration of small business. It's a great example of Boiling the Frog Slowly (more about that strategy later). Obama just keeps repeating the socialist propaganda: It's "the height of unfairness" that the wealthy don't pay more in taxes.[21] The rich "can afford to pay a little bit more."[22] Then pass it all, bit by bit, until we have nothing left.

It's all part of the Obama plan. He doesn't want independent thinkers with money and assets. Remember, Obama aims to create a nation with only two classes: the super-rich who support him in return for bribes (government contracts, stimulus, bailouts), and the hopeless, helplessly dependent poor who also support him in return for bribes (the handouts, entitlements, and food stamps they need to survive). The class in the middle must be destroyed.

Keep in mind that all these new taxes and regulations will hit hardest the people who risk their own money to start businesses. Collectively small business owners risk trillions of dollars. Our courage and capitalism fuel the economy and create two-thirds of new jobs.[23] Our taxes pay for government (and all those government employees with their obscene pensions). Running a business often requires working sixteen-hour days. It's the hardest thing you'll ever do. If our reward for all this risk, sacrifice, work ethic, and job creation is to be punished, why would we keep doing it? Why indeed.

The attack on small business is no mistake or coincidence. This is a purposeful plan to destroy capitalism. Obama and his socialist friends know the best way to destroy capitalism is to destroy small business. Obama's goal is to redistribute our wealth and create a jobs crisis. He can't stand that small business owners don't need or want government to bail us out. He can't stand that we think we can survive just fine without government anywhere in our lives. So he's out to ruin our businesses and bring us to our knees, begging for government to help. He revealed his hostility toward small business—and especially toward the stubborn independence of small business owners—with his outrageous claim that we "didn't build" what we have created.[24] As a bonus, he gets to wipe out the biggest contributors to conservative causes. In other words, killing small business wipes out Obama's political opposition.

Yes, ladies and gentleman, we have met the enemy of small business…and he resides in the White House.

CHAPTER NINE

PITTING BIG BUSINESS AGAINST SMALL BUSINESS

DID YOU KNOW?

- Small businesses are responsible for virtually 100% of all job growth
- Big business no longer sides with small business in defense of capitalism—they've become crony capitalists aiding and abetting Obama, the crony socialist
- The "fiscal cliff" deal was a huge win for big, government-subsidized businesses—at the expense of mom-and-pop America
- The "fiscal cliff" deal raised taxes on small businesses while giving $40 billion in tax credits and other benefits to Hollywood, GE, and other businesses favored by Obama

We've seen how President Obama has *small* businesses and independent Americans in his sights. But we'll never thoroughly understand how he plans to implement his socialist program until we understand the role of his cronies in the *big* businesses that increasingly depend on the government.

THE CRONY SOCIALIST

President Obama is a unique breed of socialist. As we'll see, he is a hybrid socialist-Marxist-fascist, a new breed we might call the *crony socialist*. Obama understands he needs cover for his plans to destroy America. Americans are not ready to give up on capitalism and embrace socialism. We'll go along only if we're fooled. So Obama needs famous billionaires and credible, rich, fat cat CEOs from corporate America to support him, to convince middle America that nothing is really changing, that we're still a capitalist country. Only then will we go along with the con.

So Obama has made friends, campaign donors, and political allies— cronies—of the super-rich.

What does Obama care about a small restaurant owner making $250,000 per year? That person is insignificant to him. But a CEO of a billion-dollar multi-national conglomerate is very significant. That company can write the big checks to bankroll Obama's campaign, or his inauguration, or the DNC (Democratic National Committee). And that Fortune 500 company also has teams of lawyers and lobbyists—all willing to write more big fat checks.

CRONY CAPITALISTS BETRAY SMALL BUSINESSES— AND FREE MARKET PRINCIPLES

The ground has shifted in America. Big business, Wall Street, banks, and most of corporate America used to be on the same side as small business. American business was on one team, supporting capitalism and conservative financial principles. That's no longer the case. Big business and corporate America have sold out to big government and cronyism. They aren't capitalists any more. They're crony capitalists—they've sold out their values for a tax cut, or credit, or government contract, or stimulus money, or bailout. They're in bed with Obama, the ultimate crony socialist.

It started with the bailouts and the stimulus. Big business begged, lobbied . . . and received billions of taxpayer dollars. Small business got nothing but the bill. It's our kids and grandkids that will be paying the interest on these bailouts and wasted stimulus, generations from now. Under Obama, the only recovery has been among the biggest public companies listed on the stock exchanges. They received bailouts, stimulus money, government loans, and government contracts worth billions. On Main Street, Obama's policies are creating a Great Depression. Small business is dying.[1]

The irony is that small business creates most of the jobs. Since the first day of the Reagan presidency, about 40 million new jobs have been created in America. Virtually all 40 million were created by small business. Of course big business also created a few million jobs along the way, but they also laid off and off-shored a few million jobs—for a net job creation total of ZERO over the past thirty years. The entire 40 million new jobs since the 1980s were created by small business start-ups.[2]

How important are new business start-ups to the U.S. economy? The Kauffman Foundation reports that new businesses add 3 million jobs in their first year, but established firms lose 1 million jobs annually.[3]

So why aren't politicians more appreciative? Simply because politicians only understand money and power. Small businesses can't afford expensive lawyers and lobbyists. We can't afford glitzy public relations firms. We have no media megaphones. We can't get into the White House to see the president like Jeffrey Immelt, the CEO of GE, and buy his support with campaign donations. So we are ignored, disrespected, and fleeced every step of the way.

But now big business has gone a step further—they've become our adversary. Big business and small business no longer play for the same team. After the bailouts and stimulus came Obamacare. I never imagined big business would support this socialist scheme. Back in the 1990s big business teamed with small business to stop the Clintons' attempt to socialize medicine and put government in charge of the entire healthcare system. Not this time. Just two decades later, big business took Obama's side. The big health insurance and pharmaceutical companies were bribed with billions in new revenues aimed their way.[4] The rest of big business went along with Obamacare, too—probably because he was making noises about dramatically reducing the corporate tax rate.[5] They supported

Obamacare, but they never got their tax cuts. Every once in a while Obama's deceptions actually make me happy. Big business got the shaft from Obama. They were left holding an empty bag—which was exactly what they deserved.

Then came the coup de grace—the fiscal cliff negotiations in December 2012. At that point, the split between big business and small business widened into an outright divorce—an ugly one. This time Obama did reward big business to get his way.

Most small business owners pay their taxes as individuals—in subchapter S and LLC corporations the business income is passed down to the individual small business owner and taxed as individual income. That's where big business lawyers and lobbyists saw an opening.

The *Wall Street Journal* reported on groups like the Business Roundtable (made up of 150 corporate titans) and the RATE Coalition (AT&T, Ford, Lockheed Martin, Home Depot) publicly endorsing and blessing big tax hikes on mom-and-pop America.[6]

The $625 billion tax increase passed. Big business still didn't get their corporate tax cut...*yet*. But boy did they get goodies—$40 billion in crony capitalism (really crony socialism) payoffs.[7]

Mom-and-pop small businesses just had their income redistributed to big business? That's right; billion-dollar companies ripped off small busi-

OBAMA REWARDS HIS CRONIES

The fiscal cliff deal gives away $78 million in tax breaks to benefit NASCAR; $62 million in tax credits for companies operating in American Samoa; $222 million in tax rebates to rum companies; $430 million in tax rebates for Hollywood film producers; $12 billion (with a "b") in tax credits for wind power companies like GE; $2.2 billion to renewable diesel companies; $650 million to manufacturers of energy-efficient appliances; and $222 million in accelerated tax depreciation for businesses located on Indian reservations. Many of these companies could wind up paying no taxes *at all* because of these rebates and credits.[8]

nesses on Main Street under the guise of avoiding the "fiscal cliff." But if we were really on *the edge of a fiscal cliff*, how could we afford to give $430 million to Hollywood film producers? This was the biggest swindle since Bernie Madoff.

I predict this is only the start of Obama's payoff to corporate America. I bet you Obama told the corporate lobbyists that he'd give them $40 billion in tax credit gifts now...if they would support his tax hikes on middle America, including their rivals in small businesses...and be patient and wait until Obama can implement *real* "tax reform" later (code words for fleecing small business and middle America, *again*). My bet is we'll be seeing even more elimination of tax deductions for individuals, in return for "tax reform" that dramatically cuts corporate tax rates. Anyone want to bet me?

It's all part of Obama's plan. Build an alliance with big business and use their money to overwhelm the capitalist system and socialize America.

Obama's big government agenda isn't aimed at the super-rich. The really rich, and the big corporations, are Obama's partners in crony socialism. His attacks on the rich are just a head fake to conceal the truth. That's just the propaganda he uses to sell his con game to the masses. Obama's destructive agenda is aimed squarely at *you*: the middle class, entrepreneurs, and small business owners.

The split between big business and small business is Obama's dream come true. Big business has abandoned small business.[9] Obama has broken the coalition that had worked for decades to defend American capitalism against the socialist threat. Now Obama has the big boys on his side, funding his plans for big government. They will let him have it, as long as he keeps funneling billions in bribes their way.

The cat is out of the bag. The crony capitalists are in bed with the greatest fraud of all time—Obama, the world's biggest crony socialist.

And he's well on his way to replacing the American dream with his crony socialist dream: an America with only two classes, the poor and the super-rich—both dependent on government. The class in the middle must be destroyed to make this possible.

Your goal is to survive Obama's middle class destruction, now well under way, with your independence intact. Later in this book I'll show you how. But you need to be aware—big business is no longer the ally of middle America and small business in the fight for freedom from government dependence.

It's now every man for himself.

CHAPTER TEN

HOW DID AMERICA BECOME A BANANA REPUBLIC?

DID YOU KNOW?

- Days before the 2012 election, out of nowhere, the Obama Labor Department reported that an inconceivable 873,000 jobs had been created in one month
- Those purported new jobs allowed unemployment to unexpectedly dip below 8 percent for the first time in forty-four months
- In stark contrast to George Bush and Katrina, President Obama got such great media coverage for his administration's handling of Hurricane Sandy that it helped him win the election

By this point it should be clear that our current government is a failure ...and bigger government will be an even bigger failure. It's even clearer that Obama represents big government *to the nth power*. He is the greatest threat to America and capitalism since King George.

How the heck did this happen? How did we let government take over our lives? How did a man this dangerous get elected president of the

United States—let alone, re-elected? Why didn't the American people see this coming? The answer is a five-letter word: MEDIA.

First, let me tell you why the media is so biased, prejudiced, and adoring toward Barack Obama. It's quite a story, so strap on your seat belt.

I am NOT your typical conservative Republican—actually my credentials make me sound quite liberal. I am a Jewish New Yorker with an Ivy League degree from Columbia University (one of America's most ultraliberal institutions of higher learning) who has achieved most of my wealth and success in the television business. I've spent the last fifteen years on television—as a network anchor, host, producer, and non-stop cable talk show guest. I've gotten to know and understand the media and their agenda. *And the picture is NOT pretty.*

THE INTOLERANCE OF THE TOLERANT

How pathetically liberal is Columbia University? Well the students and faculty had no problem inviting the evil, anti-Semitic, anti-American, Holocaust-denying president of Iran to speak.[1] But the same students shouted and cursed at the founder of the Minuteman Project, pelted him with objects, and drove him off the stage at Columbia.[2] (To liberals, the right to free speech is only granted to those that agree with them.)

What I've seen in the media recently has brought back a flood of memories from my college days at Columbia. The mean-spirited and intolerant way Columbia University students treated several *invited* conservative speakers over the years was really appalling. I was witness to shocking displays of liberal bias, intolerance, and hatred that many in the heartland of America could never imagine.

One of these incidents at Columbia literally defines America's liberal elite as a group so radical, so extreme, with an agenda so out of the mainstream, and a prejudice versus conservative Republicans (and religious Christians) so strong and so vicious, that it borders on *hate crime.* This event, which I witnessed more than thirty years ago, was so revolting that for decades I shared it with only a few close friends. But now that I've seen the horrible way the biased media treated Mitt Romney in the past election,

I feel the incident must be publicly told. It goes a long way to explain the "why" and "how" of the media's blind adoration and support of Obama.

This incident from almost thirty-two years ago at Columbia University debunks the myth that liberals are compassionate do-gooders out to save the world, that they are somehow better, nicer, and fairer to those less fortunate (you know, the Michael Moore, Hillary Clinton, Al Gore, Rosie O'Donnell, and George Clooney version of the facts). In reality liberals possess a hate toward those with opposing viewpoints—Christians and Republicans, in particular—so strong that it evokes memories of *McCarthyism*.

The roots of that hate and moral superiority can be seen in the event I witnessed in 1981. At the time I was a sophomore majoring in political science at Columbia University. Most if not all of my professors were radical leftists filled with outright contempt for America and capitalism. (And yes, this is still who is teaching our best and brightest children at Ivy League universities.) My fellow students were almost all extreme liberals and socialists—many openly admitted an affinity for communism. I was sickened by the political views I heard day and night, views so left-wing they would make typical Americans cringe in horror.

Many of the people I was in school with were brilliant students, but a lot of them were simply spoiled brats from America's upper class who had been handed everything on a silver platter. And yet they hated America and everything it stood for. As a student at one of America's finest academic institutions, I was subjected to a nonstop verbal tirade against America, its values, and even the idea of God. This was the very definition of "education" and "higher learning" at Ivy League institutions at the time. (Unfortunately it still is.)

As a naïve blue collar S.O.B. (son of a butcher) from a small, dead-end town on the Bronx borderline, I was in awe of these blue-blooded trust fund intellectual debutantes. I had never met people like this. I laughed and shook my head at their radical, anti-American, anti-capitalism beliefs and thought they were just young and misguided but well-meaning people—that none of this was "personal." I'd never held a person's political beliefs against them, and surely they felt the same way—right? I was very wrong.

What I learned at Columbia is that liberals believe they are morally superior. It is their mission to save the world from prejudice, patriotism, racism, greed, intolerance, and inequality. The success America has achieved is a sign of everything these radical leftists despise. Worse, it is living, breathing proof that everything they believe in is pathetically WRONG!

So they resent this country, and especially anyone who has achieved self-made success through American values, and anyone who disagrees with their "morally superior" intellectual point of view. Anyone not on board with their agenda is labeled ignorant, racist, intolerant, greedy, closed-minded, or dangerous. That person must be slashed, burned, slandered, and destroyed (see Mitt Romney, Sarah Palin, George W. Bush, Dick Cheney, Ronald Reagan, Newt Gingrich, and an endless list of conservative leaders). To liberals, *everything* is personal.

We, as conservatives, are seen as "the enemy." We aren't espousing tax cuts out of sound economic principles, for the good of the whole economy—we're throwing single mothers, welfare mothers, children, and the elderly into the streets to benefit "the rich." In the eyes of liberals, we're always acting out of ignorance, greed, and their favorite—"racism."

SHUTTING UP ANYONE WHO DISAGREES WITH THEM

Do you know the new definition of a racist? "A conservative winning an argument with a liberal."
—Thomas Sowell[3]

In this new McCarthy era, there can be no dissent—certainly not among the liberal elite media in New York, Washington, D.C., and Hollywood. There is only one truth—the liberal version. Any other viewpoint is classified as repugnant and "out of the mainstream" (only the liberals' definition of "mainstream" is relevant).

It is hard to comprehend how this all works, until you realize that all these same intolerant, biased, prejudiced, radical liberals started out at the same fancy prep schools and universities, like Columbia. These are the people I attended college with, thirty years later, all grown up with fancy titles. Four times a year I receive our alumni magazine, *Columbia College Today*. It's filled with stories of where our classmates work nowadays. Guess what my classmates do? A majority of them are in *the media*. They are journalists, authors, producers, directors, reporters, anchors, and hosts on the biggest news shows in the country, the ones the masses of Americans watch every day.

So the incident I witnessed at Columbia all those years ago explains a lot about the thinking of the mainstream media. Back in 1981 I was sitting in a political science class in a large theater-style classroom seating a hundred or more students. The president at the time was Ronald Reagan, a man reviled by the left just as viciously as any Republican like Bush, Cheney, Palin, or Romney is today. Suddenly our lecture was interrupted by a door swinging open violently—whereupon a breathless fellow student raced into the room screaming, *"The president has been shot! They've just assassinated President Reagan."*

Ronald Reagan was my hero. The news hit me like a ton of bricks. I instantly felt sick to my stomach, and tears flowed down my cheeks.

But it was the response of the rest of the class that I will remember for the rest of my life. **They cheered.** They clapped, they yelled, they high-fived, and whooped in sheer unadulterated joy. My fellow classmates, the ones I was naively trying so hard to befriend despite their radical leftist views, were HAPPY that my hero President Ronald Reagan was dead (or so they thought). They were celebrating what they thought was the assassination of America's president.

Why? What could possibly cause the brightest young adults in this great country to cheer for the murder of their own country's leader? The answer was simple—he had the audacity to be a Republican conservative. That's how deep the hatred of liberals goes.

That's the dirty little secret liberals don't want you to know. They claim to be "compassionate," to love others less fortunate, and to abhor hate and prejudice. They declare any war inhumane and unjustified. They are full of non-violence, compassion, and goodness. And yet this same liberal elite despises anyone "ignorant" enough to disagree with their definition of what is "right"—with a deep, unbridled prejudice. To liberals, *that* form of hate, *that* form of prejudice, *that* form of intolerance toward others with different views is acceptable.

That intolerance was on display at Columbia when socialist, communist, and Hispanic student groups were allowed to shout down the founder of the Minuteman Project, thereby violating his right to free speech. To radical liberals, it's justified to hate conservatives, to hate Republicans, to hate those who support any war, to hate those greedy individuals who actually have the audacity to want to lower taxes (God forbid anyone should think the taxpayers actually have a right to their own money—how ignorant, greedy, and selfish), to hate those so ignorant that they support the death penalty, gun ownership, or securing the border.

To liberals, *that* kind of hate, prejudice, and intolerance are completely justified. Heck, they're encouraged. To want to see "those kinds" of people dead is okay. After all, it would make the world a better place! To liberals, rooting for the death of a Republican conservative president is morally acceptable—in fact it's "compassionate" because the death of a Reagan, Bush, or Romney would make the world a better place, safe from prejudice, racism, inequality, intolerance, corporate greed, and pollution.

That day at Columbia University over thirty years ago, I became physically sick. I ran out of class—the CHEERS of my classmates reverberating in the halls behind me. I felt sick for America, knowing the people I'd just watched cheer and celebrate the shooting of our president were undoubtedly the future leaders of America. What I did not realize at the time was that I was actually looking at the future *media* elite.

THE MOTIVATION BEHIND THE MEDIA BIAS

Today, my classmates are fifty-one years old. Many have brilliant and well-paid careers. They would not dare cheer out loud for the death of a Republican conservative politician. (Their children on the other hand—now attending Columbia or Harvard or Princeton—would undoubtedly cheer and whoop loudly and passionately at the death of an "ignorant," intolerant, politically incorrect political leader.)

The death of a spotted owl, a rat, a fox, or a radical Islamic or Palestinian terrorist is to be mourned by liberals. But the death of a conservative

Republican, a capitalist, or (today add to the hate list) an Israeli is a reason for celebration. So much for the "compassion" of radical socialists who call themselves "progressive liberals."

Now, my fellow readers, you have some insight into the true mindset and agenda of America's liberal elites, who completely dominate our media. You understand how they were raised—as spoiled brats burdened with terrible guilt for all they were handed on a platter. You grasp how they were educated—by teachers and professors who shared a radical leftist agenda. You see the roots of the bias that's so obvious in all they report on today, as the keepers of the news.

Now you understand them as I do, as an "insider" with a front row seat for two decades. So now I will ask you one simple question: Is it possible for a Republican ever to get a fair shake from the media?

I'm sure the elites in Hollywood and the news business would tell you that what they believed as college students has no impact on their views as adults and professionals today. But let me ask you another simple question: What would liberals say if they found out that a Fox News Channel host or executive, back in his college days, had cheered and high-fived over the death of Martin Luther King? Or even simply attended the meeting of an ultra-right organization? Would those errors of youth be forgiven and forgotten? Of course not!

When Rush Limbaugh made controversial political statements during Monday Night Football a few years back, his short career with ESPN was ended the very next day. But when Bob Costas made controversial leftist comments about guns during Sunday Night Football last year, his job was never threatened, not for a second. The media bias and double standard are alive and well for all to see.

I hope the story from Columbia gives you insight into what I have known for a quarter of a century. The liberal elite are intolerant hypocrites. They now control our media, and they're dangerous to America, American values, capitalism, Christianity, and the very existence of Israel as well. I've known the truth about liberals all these years—and now you do too. That's the reason that every time I watch CNN or PBS, or any anchor on the evening news, I think back to that day in 1981 at Columbia when the future media of America celebrated the death of Reagan. Then I watch and listen for the one-sided reporting. Then I pinpoint the moment facts end...and biased liberal propaganda begins.

The media has given up on the quaint idea of unbiased reporting. They don't even try to hide their love and adoration for Obama and his socialist policies. They've literally run a 24/7/365 public relations campaign on his behalf. It's so obvious, so over-the-top, that it's ridiculous, embarrassing, and scandalous. But who watches the watchers? Who reports on the media? There's no one to report on this massive scam.

A TALE OF TWO HURRICANES

The fraud and dereliction of duty by the mainstream media are turning America into a banana republic. You know, one of those places where leaders control the media. Where is the mainstream media that used to question the actions and motives of our political leaders (that is, the liberal ones as well as the conservative ones)? Sadly, the mainstream media has become nothing more than a propaganda tool, following orders handed down on high from Obama, David Axelrod, Valerie Jarrett, and the progressive political machine. Let's look at just a couple of obvious and glaring examples.

Hurricane Sandy decimated New York and New Jersey the week before the 2012 presidential election. The Federal Emergency Management Agency's response was pathetic, embarrassing, close to criminal. No food or water for days. No power for weeks. FEMA did not pre-position the most basic of supplies, such as bottled water. FEMA was completely unprepared, incompetent, invisible. This was Obama's Hurricane Katrina. Remember how President George W. Bush was vilified and blamed for Katrina. Obama himself, a senator at the time, suggested that the Bush administration's response to Katrina was racist.[4]

Yet the same media portrayed Obama as competent and caring in the wake of the hurricane. They never blamed him. The media coverage was an astonishing contrast with the way Bush was vilified after Katrina. In this case, the media never mentioned government incompetence, or racism, or assigned blame to the president. With that kind of media bias,

WHAT A DIFFERENCE IT MAKES, HAVING THE MEDIA ON YOUR SIDE

"Exit polls by CBS News reveal that Superstorm Sandy, and President Obama's response, was a crucial factor for two in five voters nationwide. . . . Twenty-six percent of those polled said Obama's broadly praised response was an important factor, and 15 percent—about one in six voters—said it was the most important factor in their vote."

—Brad Johnson, *ThinkProgress*[5]

no wonder the Obama administration's shameful response to Hurricane Sandy actually *helped* him in the election.

BIAS ON BENGHAZI

Then there's the U.S. consulate disaster in Benghazi, Libya. President Obama knew that our Libyan consulate could face an attack on 9/11. He did nothing. The consulate asked for beefed up security.[6] Again, he did nothing. Forty-eight hours before the attack, the State Department had credible information that U.S. missions might be targeted. Yet again, Obama did nothing.[7]

When our consulate was attacked, the former SEALs on the ground begged for permission to rescue our diplomats. They were ordered to "stand down." Obama not only left them behind, he refused to help them.[8] Why? Does any of this make sense?

If we had a real media, wouldn't they at least ask a few questions? It is possible that Obama was providing arms to the Libya rebels, and some of the weapons ended up in the hands of Islamists.[9] Were those rebels in partnership with al Qaeda? Did the terrorists then use weapons we supplied to attack the U.S. Embassy and murder four Americans? Did Obama order our Navy SEALs to "stand down" rather than save our own citizens, because he couldn't risk the rescuers finding American weapons, supplied by Obama, in the hands of terrorists, thereby damaging his re-election campaign? *Yet no one in the mainstream media seemed interested—then or now—in these questions.*

Obama proceeded to cover it all up—just long enough to win the election. CIA Chief General Petraeus testified under oath (only *after* the election) that he had made it clear all along that Benghazi was a terrorist attack.[10] But Obama, Hillary Clinton, and UN Ambassador Susan Rice had spent two weeks falsely blaming a YouTube video in a cover-up obviously intended to save Obama's re-election.[11] In football we call this a "Prevent Defense": stall just long enough to run the clock out. This is Obama's Watergate with one difference—four dead Americans. *Still, the media says nothing.*

THE PRE-ELECTION EMPLOYMENT MIRACLE

Days before the election, out of nowhere, the Obama Labor Department reported that 873,000 new jobs had been created in one month.[12] This "miracle" allowed unemployment to unexpectedly dip below 8 percent for the first time in forty-four consecutive months.[13] Perfect timing for a politician trained in Chicago fraud politics. *The media said nothing.*

As soon as the election was over, the Department of Labor reported that new jobless claims rose a staggering 78,000 in just the first week after the election.[14] And the *Wall Street Journal* reported capital spending by America's corporations had collapsed.[15] I guess the perfectly timed one-month recovery was officially over.

Any investigative reporter who reported on this fraud could win journalism awards—if those weren't reserved for compliant members of our banana republic media. *Yet no one in the mainstream media said a thing. Not a creature was stirring—not even a mouse.*

Did you hear from the media that food stamp growth was *seventy-five times* faster in Obama's first term than job growth?[16] The media was completely AWOL when it came to reporting statistics that might be bad for Obama in the months leading up to the election. Obama's forty-three consecutive months of unemployment above 8 percent were more than all the months over 8 percent from President Truman's term through George W. Bush's term, *combined.*[17]

Did you ever hear the media mention facts like that during the election campaign?

OBAMA WINS THE NEWS COVERAGE, 13–1

How about the tape that caught Obama admitting, "I actually believe in redistribution" (the central tenet of socialism)?[18] The media repeatedly pounded Romney's "47 percent" tape into every voter's subconscious, but essentially ignored Obama's tape for the entire campaign. The president's endorsement of the central tenet of Karl Marx and communism wasn't a campaign issue?

Lest you think I'm exaggerating, the Media Research Center compared the media coverage of both tapes. They proved that the media reported on Romney's "47 percent" video versus Obama's "redistribution" video by a margin of thirteen to one.[19]

Do you ever hear in the mainstream media that under Obama 37,000 Americans are now committing suicide annually? Did you know this is an all-time high?[20] Or that suicides have passed car accidents as a cause of death?[21]

Have you ever heard the media connect the dots between the record-high suicides and the terrible economy? Just picture what the media would be saying if suicides were at all-time highs under a Republican president at the same time the economy was in crisis. They'd be trumpeting this tragedy in bold headlines twenty-four hours a day. They wouldn't just blame the suicides on the poor economy. They'd blame them on capitalism. They'd blame them on the spending cuts and the Republican president's lack of compassion. (If you're old enough to remember the constant drumbeat of reporting on the homeless during Ronald Reagan's presidency, you know exactly what the wall-to-wall coverage would look like.)[22]

Yet with Obama as president, *the mainstream media says nothing.*

You think *maybe* after four years of propaganda, shameless cover-ups, and repetitive subliminal brainwashing, the public might start to favor Obama?

With a banana republic media, is it any surprise that we get banana republic election results?

THE REAL OBAMA—REVEALED *AFTER* THE ELECTION

Obama lied outrageously and repeatedly during the presidential debates. The biggest whopper was when he posed as a big supporter of oil drilling, a phenomenal lie. Facts proved that drilling permits were down more than 30 percent under Obama.[23] *Yet the mainstream media said nothing.*

Two days *after* the election, Obama, the supposed fan of oil drilling, issued a plan to close 1.6 million acres of Federal land in the West originally to oil shale extraction.[24] Don't believe what he says. Watch what he does. *But not a peep from the mainstream media.*

Obama also poses as a big supporter of small business—while he raises our taxes, demonizes us with his "You didn't build that" speech, and adds layers of new rules and regulations.[25] *Not a peep from the media.*

Obama also claims to support the Second Amendment right to bear arms.[26] The media never mentions that Obama's two appointments to the Supreme Court are both anti-gun zealots who have long held that the Second Amendment doesn't guarantee individuals the right to guns.[27] *Not a peep from the mainstream media.*

Mysteriously, not one of these blatant lies *ever* attracted the attention of the mainstream media.

As a senator, Obama declared Bush's $4 trillion in new debt over eight years to be "irresponsible" and even "unpatriotic."[28] Yet as president he added nearly $6 trillion in only four years.[29] But that's not irresponsible or unpatriotic? Or hypocritical? The mainstream media never pointed that out to voters. *Strange.*

The media never seems to mention Obama's schedule. We are in the midst of an Obama Great Depression. Our economy is in freefall. Yet Obama's 2012 was filled with golf, basketball, fundraising, campaign rallies, and "morning zoo" media appearances.[30]

How did Obama have time left to deal with the economy?

Well, the fact is, he didn't. In the middle of a jobs crisis of epic proportions, Obama's vaunted "Council on Jobs and Competitiveness" could not find the time to meet *for more than a year.* The week after the inauguration, he let it close up shop altogether.[31]

This is an insult to the millions of jobless Americans. This is an insult to millions of struggling small businesses. *Still, the mainstream media said nothing.*

There's nothing to see here, folks. There is no story. Just move along—and support our wonderful President Obama.

At this point, nothing would shock me. If two-thirds of America's population were wiped out by bubonic plague escaped from an experiment directly ordered by Obama, or starved in a famine caused by Obama's agricultural policies, I would not be surprised to see the mainstream media credit him with "saving" the other third. They'd find absurd reasons to call him "brilliant," "compassionate," and a "hero," while blaming global warming, the fiscal cliff, racism, inequality, and of course George W. Bush for the deaths.

The stories I've just told you are merely the tip of the iceberg. I could write an entire book on the glaring bias of the media. This is expected in Cuba, Venezuela, North Korea, or Zimbabwe. I just never imagined the media in the United States of America would take their marching orders from the president and his campaign team.

This is how Obama and big government are slowly taking over our lives…and no one notices. Most Americans are just too nice, too naïve, too trusting, and too busy earning a living to notice. They rely on the mainstream media for their information about what is happening in Washington. Their understanding of the news is shaped by their morning newspaper, what they happen to see on the Internet, and the evening TV news. The media they rely on never told them what they needed to hear.

It appears we are now officially living in a banana republic.

CHAPTER ELEVEN

THE OBAMA PLAN:
BOIL THE FROG *SLOWLY*

DID YOU KNOW?

- The Cloward-Piven plan to overburden and overwhelm the American system with unaffordable welfare spending was dreamed up by two professors from Columbia, Barack Obama's alma mater
- Saul Alinsky's *Rules for Radicals* was actually dedicated to Lucifer
- Under Obama-style socialism, the government won't actually *own* the whole private economy—but government will *control* it, nonetheless

The U.S. economy is in ruins, the country in crisis from sea to shining sea, and the Middle East is in chaos too. Some say Obama is an inexperienced, incompetent, bumbling Inspector Clouseau in the White House. I say he has been executing a purposeful plan from day one.

Obama is a brilliant chess master who understood that to succeed he had to first bribe the masses with free goodies, never-ending handouts, and a promise of never-ending government checks, all at the expense of his archenemies—"the rich" (really middle America, and especially small business owners).

The bad news is America is in deep trouble. But the good news is there is a ray of hope (and even profit) if you understand exactly what Obama is doing. My goal in this book is to help you stay a couple chess moves ahead, protect your assets, and react (and invest) in a way that turns that knowledge into power and profits.

What we're doing here in the pages of *The Ultimate Obama Survival Guide* is to expose the raw truth without sugar-coating or delusion, dissect and analyze it, then give you the solutions that empower you to capitalize on it. We're going to empower you to turn this Obamageddon tragedy into opportunity.

To be able to do that, it is critical you face the facts head-on, with brutal honesty. From the first day of Obama's election, many concerned patriots have warned about Obama's goals. As Obama's college classmate, Columbia University class of '83, I was among the first to sound the warning. Obama is a follower of radical Marxist strategy—including Saul Alinsky's *Rules for Radicals* and Cloward and Piven's strategy of overwhelming the system to create economic crisis and chaos.

But Obama's radical education wasn't limited to his college years. During his entire upbringing, Obama was surrounded by radicals, Marxists, communists, and even terrorists. Obama's mother attended communist party meetings. His father went on to become an ultra-leftist political leader in Kenya, where he defended the idea of government taking 100 percent of a person's income. His "uncle" and father figure, Frank Marshall, was a leader of the Hawaii communist party. Obama's friend and mentor Bill Ayers was a terrorist. His minister Jeremiah Wright preached racism toward whites and Jews, as well as outright hatred toward America. The list is long (and factual).

For Obama's entire life, he has been immersed in the teachings of and inspired by radical Marxist Saul Alinsky.[1]

Nothing now happening to America is happening by mistake. It is all part of a detailed, coordinated plan, many years in the making. That plan came straight from the minds of radical Columbia University (and later

NYU) professors Richard Cloward and Frances Pivens. That husband-and-wife team believed you could never turn America into a socialist nation overnight. Nor could you do it by admitting you were a socialist (let alone a Marxist). You had to do it slowly—like boiling a frog. Turn the heat up just a little at a time, so the frog is unaware of what is happening. Before you know it, the water is boiling—and the frog is cooked.

Cloward and Piven argued that to make America socialist you had to slowly overwhelm the system with crisis and chaos. You had to overburden the welfare system and crash it.[2]

Does that sound familiar? Who's making sure the economy gets so bad that record numbers of citizens desperately need welfare, food stamps, unemployment benefits, disability (as soon as unemployment runs out), free healthcare, free *everything*? Who's extending unemployment benefits and signing up record numbers of Americans for food stamps and disability? And who's figuring that once they grow accustomed to receiving all this free stuff, they'll never allow the handouts to stop? Obama.

Americans will grow to feel *entitled* to government support from cradle to grave. Deep down they'll be terrified of ever again trying to live without government's support. Then they'll show up loyally to vote for the politicians who promised to keep the government checks coming—as they did in November 2012.

It's all been happening slowly. So slowly that no one notices it happening—just like boiling the frog.

Obama learned all of this from Professors Cloward and Piven. Their teachings revolved around one overriding concept: overwhelm and swamp government programs.

And that's exactly what Obama is doing. Debt is how you slowly, methodically destroy capitalism and introduce socialism. Debt is easy to institute. With the cooperation of voters, even the opposition party (the GOP) will support it. It's easy and fun to spend and spend and spend. Debt is how you make voters dependent. Then once the debt reaches crisis levels (that you purposely caused), you point to the people (with the cooperation of a liberal biased media) and warn, "This is an emergency. We must act now. We must raise taxes to pay for it all before it destroys us." At that point, other politicians (even your Republican opposition) will see little choice but to support massive taxes to pay for the income redistribution and retribution you wanted all along. It's a vicious cycle. The more you spend, the higher the debt, the worse the economy, the more people become frightened, the more they depend on government, the more they demand government intervention to "save" them, the more necessary it becomes to raise taxes.

This is how dependence is created by stealth. This is how you slowly make citizens doubt their own ability to succeed and doubt whether capitalism works for them. This loss of confidence, self-reliance, personal responsibility, and independence sets the stage for a Nanny State, where everyone expects and eventually demands government take care of them from cradle to grave. But the key is, it all has to happen SLOWLY. Obama is not your ordinary garden-variety Marxist. He's a brilliant stealth Marxist.

LOOK AROUND. IT'S HAPPENING *EXACTLY* ACCORDING TO PLAN.

I warned America that Obama would follow the Cloward-Piven game plan he learned about at Columbia. I warned that Obama's goals were to overwhelm the country with deficit, debt, entitlements, government employee pensions, government intrusions, onerous regulations, and tax hikes designed to target, demonize, intimidate, confiscate, and punish wealthy business owners—*class warfare.*

Add it all up. It's a radical recipe to force change upon America and the U.S. economy slowly, without most citizens realizing what is happening—just like boiling the frog.

You already know the truth about the damage Obama is doing to the U.S. economy. (Turn back and read about the Zombie Economy if you've managed to block these facts out of your mind.) Is there any doubt that Obama's goal from the start has been to force Americans to their knees to beg for help from big government and then, in response to those pleas of dependent and addicted Americans, slowly and methodically put

THE DEDICATION OF SAUL ALINSKY'S
RULES FOR RADICALS

"Lest we forget at least an over-the-shoulder acknowledgment to the very first radical: from all our legends, mythology, and history...the first radical known to man who rebelled against the establishment and did it so effectively that he at least won his own kingdom—Lucifer."

—Saul Alinsky, *Rules for Radicals*

government in control over every aspect of our lives? This plan was designed by Cloward and Piven, and it is being executed right out of the pages of the Saul Alinsky playbook.

Now you can understand why Alinsky's book was literally dedicated to the Devil.[3]

Examine the state of the union under President Obama. Judge for yourselves whether we are in a state of *Obamageddon*. Judge whether Lucifer himself could have come up with a better plan.

UNFORTUNATELY, THE FROG IS YOU

The fact is the United States is broke. Bankrupt. Insolvent. We've spent and increased the debt more during the past four years under Obama than any time in history.

Yes, Obama's "solution" to a crisis caused by $6 trillion in debt was to add $4 trillion more, while piling on taxes that instantly went toward more spending. Just think about that. *Let it soak in awhile.*

In four years he racked up more debt than all previous presidents from George Washington through Bill Clinton *combined.*[4] He is on track to triple the debt created by Bush in his eight years. *Triple.*[5] **Obamageddon.**

To pay off this massive unsustainable debt, taxes will have to be raised to levels that leave our children and grandchildren enslaved to big government for decades to come. Obama has put in place factors that are guaranteed to ruin our economy *permanently.* This was always the plan—straight out of the Cloward-Piven playbook. **Obamageddon.**

Who will bail out the bankrupt banks, big corporations, and entire states when the federal government is insolvent itself? But that's just part of our problem. Student loan defaults are at crisis levels—reminiscent of the subprime mortgage crisis.[6]

For the first time in history, student loan delinquencies are now higher than credit card delinquencies. Another massive taxpayer bailout is on the way. The only question is what day will it be announced.[7]

But wait…just like in a Ginsu knife infomercial…there's more! The entire accounting structure of the FHA (Federal Housing Administration) is in question. The government agency has guaranteed over $1 trillion in housing loans, but has only $3.5 billion in reserves.[8]

More debt. More bailouts. More government failures. More taxes needed to pay for it all. **Obamageddon.**

Government claims they have inflation under control.[9] Really? Real inflation—including food and energy prices—has skyrocketed.[10]

The Fed is printing hundreds of billions of dollars to buy America's own bonds.[11] Since America owes a $16 trillion debt compounded with an annual $1 trillion deficit, interest on the debt will soon cost more than our entire defense budget and crowd out all other government spending including Social Security and Medicare.[12] **Obamageddon.**

Small business historically is the engine of job creation. Yet Obama aims every tax increase at small business. Does that make any sense?

LEAVING A SINKING SHIP?

Did you know that Bill Gross, CEO of the biggest bond fund in the world, sold all his U.S. municipal bond holdings during Obama's first term, and invested in emerging country bond funds? The world's biggest and smartest bond expert was quietly telling Wall Street insiders that he trusted the bonds of Russia, Brazil, and African nations more than U.S. bonds. If this isn't frightening to you, it should be.[13]

Only if the plan is to boil the frog slowly. It's all about redistribution and retribution. Call it fairness, equality, and social justice. Label the massive tax increases "small." Call them "fair." Keep proposing so many taxes, rules, regulations, and mandates that our heads spin just trying to keep track of all of them. Hide the details in small print never reported by the media. Keep demonizing small business owners to the masses. Little by little, Obama takes away our businesses—and America's jobs. **Obamageddon.**

In one week during Obama's first term, in my adopted hometown of Las Vegas, two celebrated business institutions closed their doors. Robb & Stucky, an upscale furniture chain in business for ninety-five years, filed for bankruptcy and announced it was closing all stores immediately.[14] Then just days later, the famous Sahara Hotel also closed its doors after fifty-nine years.[15] As I was writing this book, the world famous Stage Deli also closed after a seventy-five year run as a Manhattan fixture.[16] These are frightening signs. Ninety-five years, fifty-nine years, seventy-five years...a combined 229 years of business success could not survive four years under Obama. It's happening all across the U.S.A.

You can't get around the laws of economics. Higher taxes, bigger government, more debt, a government takeover of healthcare—these will all combine to kill *more* jobs. Small businesses will lay off *more* employees so they never have to deal with Obamacare (which kicks in at fifty employees). Big business will lay off *more* employees to deal with higher taxes, more mandates, and of course to pay for Obamacare. Jobs will be shipped overseas to places where taxes are lower and health insurance isn't mandatory. These are the certain consequences of Obama's socialist policies. If I'm wrong it will only be because the books are cooked—because Americans dropping out of the job market by the millions aren't counted as "unemployed" by our honest and ethical government. Any CEO who lied, cheated, and misrepresented like our government would be convicted of fraud and put in prison for decades.

We have a growing union crisis in this country with Obama's best friends and biggest campaign contributors—government employee unions—pitted against private sector taxpayers. Obama has appointed new members to the National Labor Relations Board (NLRB) who are so radical that it's clear Obama's goal is to empower unions to take over the private sector—they're so radical, in fact, that in order to avoid the Senate confirmation process Obama made recess appointments when the Senate wasn't really in recess—appointments that have now been declared unconstitutional by a federal court.[17]

WHAT *CAN'T* UNIONS DESTROY?

Unions have already bankrupted the auto industry and destroyed our public schools. And now they've even killed Twinkies! Hostess, the parent company of Twinkies, went out of business because of union demands. Now it will be sold off piece by piece. Perhaps that is the future fate of America.[18]

Obama has obviously sold the country to his union buddies. Still not convinced? Did you pay attention to how Obama handled the U.S. automaker crisis? He "saved" GM and Chrysler by taking them from their rightful owners, the shareholders and secured creditors, and handing ownership to his biggest contributors, the auto unions, the very groups whose outrageous salaries and obscene pensions bankrupted the companies in the first place.[19]

Obama "saved" the auto industry by losing $26 billion (and counting) of your taxpayer dollars. The losses could eventually reach $70 billion.[20] That's losing tens of billions of dollars in order to save the bloated pensions of auto union members that vote Democrat.

And for good measure, Obama let the private sector autoworkers lose all or most of their pensions (they didn't contribute to his campaign, after all). He also closed hundreds of auto dealerships. The list of closures was dominated by dealers making Republican campaign contributions. Once again, Obama punishes small business.[21] **Obamageddon.**

Still, the cronyism practiced by Obama toward unions is mild compared to the greatest scam of all time: "green energy." Obama has handed out hundreds of billions to his biggest campaign contributors, all in the name of green energy. Think Solyndra. That one company cost taxpayers $500 million.[22]

You've heard of Solyndra, but there are hundreds of these so-called government "investments" (with your money) handed to green energy companies you've never heard of. At least fifty are bankrupt or close to out of business.[23]

Obama's contributors (the CEOs and investors in these companies) will walk away with hundreds of millions of your taxpayer dollars. It would make us all absolutely sick if we could ever find out how many Obama supporters became multimillionaires from the stimulus.

None of this should surprise us. The green economy is a trillion dollar "Bridge to Nowhere." Ask Spain, with the greenest economy in Europe, and over 25 percent unemployment. Youth unemployment in Spain is over 50 percent. Spain is completely bankrupt and begging European central banks to bail them out. Socialist rulers, green energy, and high-speed rail lines have gutted Europe's fifth-largest economy and destroyed its future.[24] *But isn't that the Obama plan?*

Green energy is the scam to allow Obama and his socialist cabal to take control over vast swaths of U.S. industry and manufacturing, waste taxpayer dollars enriching his cronies and contributors, and redistribute income from business owners and homeowners to Obama's voters— because of course, the energy bills of the poor will be subsidized by government. **Obamageddon.**

The housing collapse is now worse than at the peak of the Great Depression.[25] Foreclosures are a tsunami sweeping the nation. What is Obama's solution? He wants to eliminate the home mortgage interest deduction for upper income homeowners.[26] Come again? In the middle of a housing collapse, Obama wants to eliminate the support the tax code offers to home prices? *Just think about that.*

This is all par for the course—at least a course taught by Cloward and Piven. You can't really be interested in saving the housing market if you want to take away the mortgage interest deduction, any more than you can be interested in saving the U.S. economy by rejecting the Keystone Pipeline, rejecting oil drilling permits, and trying to make coal extinct.[27] Obama is boiling the frog slowly. **Obamageddon.**

Don't forget that Obama has for all intents and purposes had the government take control of the auto industry, student loan industry, healthcare industry, and banking. You don't need to actually own these industries to control them. If you bail them out, or lend them billions, they are beholden to you. They'll have to build "green cars" that no one wants, because you've told them to.[28] That's the Obama plan. It's just like the mafia. The key to success is to apprentice under the best. Do you think Obama must have worked as an assistant to the Gambino Crime Family?

Under Obama, government is slowly, gradually, quietly, taking control of the economy. Not ownership, just control—a much smarter plan. Brilliant. Obama gets the same outcome with none of the risk and no blame when the businesses fail.

If Obama had gotten his way in his first term, Cap and Trade would have passed, giving government complete control of every industry in America, with the power to double or triple electric bills. It didn't happen, so Obama merely ordered new EPA rules to accomplish the exact same thing. But, he was devious and smart enough to wait until after the election to impose the rules that will kill industry, kill jobs, and slow down our economy. Always boil the frog slowly.[29] **Obamageddon.**

EPA rules are making it impossible for coal companies to stay in business. The overall picture is a tragedy. The Sierra Club gleefully reports that under Obama, America's 522 coal plants have dwindled down to only 395. They're closing every week.[30]

As I was finishing up this book, EPA chief Lisa Jackson suddenly resigned. Why? It appears she wrote emails under an alias. I'm betting she put her plans to put the coal industry out of business in writing. Those damning emails will be released soon under a Freedom of Information Act request. It looks like we'll soon get a chance to see the Obama plan to destroy traditional energy companies.[31]

Considering that we desperately needed those jobs, and that the U.S. economy runs on oil and coal, does Obama seem like a reasonable man, with America's best interests in mind? Or does he seem like someone bringing about a crisis to purposely bring the U.S. economy to its knees? **Obamageddon.**

Of course Obama needs super-rich and powerful titans on his side. Who benefited from Obama's rejection of the Keystone Pipeline? Warren Buffett, one of Obama's biggest supporters. Buffett just happened to buy up railways in anticipation of Keystone being rejected—so he could make a killing shipping oil by train.[32] **Obamageddon.**

Our southern border is in crisis with drug wars, violence, and murders spilling into the United States. Border agents are out-manned and out-gunned—including by drug dealers carrying guns sold to them by the Obama administration in the "Fast and Furious" scandal. Obama's reaction? Join with Mexico to sue the state of Arizona for defending its own border.[33] Is this a man on America's side? **Obamageddon.**

Are we building a future for our children to be productive and competitive in this world? Obama's own Education Secretary announced recently that 82 percent of all public schools are in danger of failing.[34] SAT scores were the worst in history during Obama's first term.[35]

We spend far more on education than any country in the world, only to get some of the worst results.[36] What would you expect from a president owned by the teachers' unions? I can only think Obama's goal is to dumb down future Democratic voters. Teach them obedience to big government. Teach them to think of cradle-to-grave handouts as a civil right. It's all about fairness and equality. **Obamageddon.**

The dumbing down of America is working—Obama was re-elected. Young voters were his biggest supporters. A recent Pew Research poll found that young people see socialism more favorably than capitalism.[37]

Worse, 42 percent of Americans now believe the words *"From each according to his ability, to each according to his needs,"* are contained in the U.S. Constitution. Of course they aren't. You might recognize them as the words of Karl Marx, author of the *Communist Manifesto*.[38] **Obamageddon.**

Let's set America aside for the moment. Is the *world* better off with Obama as president? Obama supported and encouraged the "Arab Spring." As a result, we got Islamic extremist regimes bent on the destruction of America and our good friend and ally Israel.[39]

Obama's foreign policy strategy was to treat our enemies with respect, apology, and appeasement. How'd that work out? Radical nations like Iran and North Korea have responded well to Obama's respect, don't you think? The more respect we show nations like Iran, the more they see our niceness as a sign of weakness, laugh in our face, and threaten us with disruption to our oil shipping lanes.[40] The more they threaten Israel with annihilation.[41] Enemies around the world are emboldened by our weakness.

Obama supported the Libyan rebels. They repaid us by attacking our U.S. Embassy in Benghazi and killing four Americans—including our ambassador. Things are just hunky dory under Obama's foreign policy, don't you think? **Obamageddon.**

Can it get worse? It's *guaranteed* to get worse in this second Obama term. Obama was actually careful in his first term—quite subtle about handing the country over to entitlement addicts, environmentalists, lawyers, illegal immigrants, and unions. But now that he's been re-elected, it's pedal to the metal, throw caution to the wind. Obama will no longer have anyone to answer to. He will never face voters again. He is free to accelerate the damage and destruction of the U.S. economy. Our entire economy will be run 24 hours a day, 7 days a week to create "social justice."

The country formerly known as the United States of America is now the Crisis States of America. We have a new crisis on a weekly basis—a debt ceiling crisis, a fiscal cliff crisis, a gun crisis, a climate change crisis. Everything becomes a crisis and the flames are fanned until we respond with panic. That's what Obama learned from Cloward and Piven. He's slowly, carefully, quietly changing America, without anyone noticing what is happening.

As of now all we can say to Obama is congratulations: "MISSION ACCOMPLISHED."

Your game plan is brilliant: *Boil the frog slowly.*

CHAPTER TWELVE

THE WORLD'S MOST BRILLIANT STEALTH MARXIST (AND CRONY SOCIALIST)

DID YOU KNOW?

- Obama bailed out GM, stiffed bondholders to pay off his union cronies, fired the CEO, and told the company to make more electric cars (that the public doesn't want)
- Obamacare requires private companies to provide contraceptives without charging anything
- Forty-nine percent of Americans now live in a household receiving some type of government benefit

Make no mistake about it—Obama is brilliant. His plan is brilliant. His execution of the plan is brilliant. He was a much better campaigner than Mitt Romney. He ran circles around House Speaker John Boehner in the "fiscal cliff" negotiations. Never underestimate Obama. He is, in my opinion, the most brilliant stealth Marxist ever. Stealth is the key word.

He is brilliant because he has figured out how to make something work that no one else ever could. How to slowly collapse the formerly great

U.S. economy. How to slowly hook a majority of Americans on government dependence. How to use crisis to turn America into a socialist economy—without a big fight. How to use Weapons of Mass Distraction to spin our heads—to propose so many radical policy changes that conservatives are left distracted, demoralized, and exhausted. How to boil the frog—without the frog even noticing it's happening. It's all breathtakingly brilliant.

I appeared on the *Daily Show* on Comedy Central last spring to answer one simple question: "Is Obama a socialist?" The producers seemed eager to prove that Obama is not a socialist and just as importantly, to prove me an idiot for believing (actually, knowing) that he is.

To get to the bottom of this mystery, the *Daily Show* interviewed a bunch of socialists and Marxists…plus a New York college professor (even worse)…who all agreed that Obama is not a socialist. Obama just doesn't go far enough for them. He hasn't made America into a communist dictatorship like Cuba overnight, so to them he's a moderate.

OBAMA'S SOCIALISM BY STEALTH

I had a unique position on this topic. I told the *Daily Show* something they'd never heard before. I told them Obama plays the game in a new way. A creative way. A brilliant way. He's like a Marxist combined with a CIA agent, combined with a chess master. He plays the game with subtlety and subterfuge. That's what makes him the most dangerous Marxist this country has ever seen. A *stealth Marxist*.

Let's examine the central tenets of socialism and Marxism:

One of Marx's central tenets is demonization of the wealthy. *Sound familiar?* Obama does it every day, in every speech. He plays the game of class warfare like no politician in history. For Obama hunting the rich is a sport. It's like shooting rich people in a barrel.

And it's the perfect way to pass massive tax and spending increases—by always aiming the taxes at the supposed rich, the people Obama is always saying "can afford" to pay more. That way everyone thinks the tax hike is aimed at the *other* guy. Everybody who is getting a government check will certainly never complain—as long as the checks keep coming.

Already 49 percent of Americans live in a household receiving some transfer payment from the government.[1] When it's 51 percent, Obama can convince American voters to change the game, violate the Constitution, and destroy capitalism.

Another central tenet of Socialism and Marxism is redistribution of wealth, accomplished in several ways. First, raise taxes. A socialist thinks what's yours, belongs to the state. If Obama has his way we'd be paying tax rates in the range of 70 percent or higher (federal, state, local, property and sales taxes combined), while losing most of our deductions. Don't laugh—if you live in California or New York, the marginal rates are approaching that range now.[2] Obama's answer for every problem is taxes. Obama plays a lot of golf, but his real hobby is raising taxes. Karl Marx would be proud.

But if a Marxist president is blocked by a Republican Congress from raising taxes to the draconian levels he'd like, there are other ways to skin the taxpayer. The Federal Reserve can print trillions of dollars of fake money. Inflation is a stealth way to bankrupt anyone with income and assets—without ever raising a tax. *Sound familiar?*

Just as effective is spending the country into bankruptcy. Obama has added almost $6 trillion to the national debt in only three years. I've already explained how debt overwhelms the system and cripples the economy. That debt has to be paid some time. That debt will eventually cause a crisis. When it does, a panic will ensue, and taxes will have to be raised. So Obama is enslaving our children and grandchildren to big government and big taxes for years to come.

A socialist economic system is assured when a majority of citizens become dependent on big government and are bribed to keep voting for the candidates that promise to keep the goodies and bribes coming. *Sound familiar?*

But it's not just the actual dollars and cents that make up socialism. It's the propaganda.

Obama repeats the same lie over and over again—the rich "can afford" to pay more.[3] That is a play on "From each according to his ability, to each according to his need." *Sound familiar?* Those are the words of Karl Marx.

The stealth Marxist Obama changed the words to sound less harsh and hide the true intent.

Then there's Obama's famous statement, "You didn't build that."[4] Once again he was demeaning and discrediting the life's work of almost 30 million American business owners.[5] By the way, if building a business is so easy because of government's help, how come most businesses fail in the first five years?[6] If building a business is so easy with government's help, how come everyone doesn't do it? Why don't 22 million government employees all quit their jobs and go build a business this afternoon?

The reason of course is because government doesn't help at all. Government only hinders the odds of success in the business world. Government gets in the way. Government taxes away the money a business owner would have used to create more jobs, or expand the business, or make the payroll. But Obama can't say that. If he admitted that business owners have special skills and take big risks, he'd have to reward us—instead of demeaning and punishing us. *Do you see the pattern?*

By the way, Obama's argument with "You didn't build that" is that small business owners benefited from government spending on roads, bridges, schools, airports, hospitals, and so forth. Well guess who paid for all of that, Comrade Obama? **We did.** The business owners through all the income and payroll taxes we pay, all the economic growth we create, paid for every last cent. You see, government has no money of its own. The government gets it all from us—the taxpayers.

When Obama says "You didn't build that"…he leaves no doubt about who he is. Only a socialist or Marxist would have the audacity and hypocrisy to even think something so demeaning—let alone say it out loud to small business owners, the hardest working and most courageous people in America. That's why I call them "Financial First Responders."

Socialism and Marxism are about government control. But with *stealth* socialism, it doesn't have to be a direct takeover. Government can bail out Wall Street, banks, mortgage providers, insurance giants like AIG, and automakers like GM and Chrysler—and then call the shots, deciding what kind of products these companies offer (even if the public doesn't want to buy them—for example, electric cars), who is hired and fired, and what they're paid.[7] When government "invests" in companies, it gets to tell them what to do.

First government bribes the private sector, then they resort to intimidation and coercion. Government control of private businesses comes to be taken for granted. It becomes routine for government to treat any business entity as a branch of the government. Soon the government is demanding that student loans be forgiven, and that people who don't pay their mortgages be allowed to stay in their homes.[8] At first government pays the tab for all these goodies. But soon they start just requiring that private businesses provide goods and services to the public at their own expense. Already under Obama, health insurance companies have to cover preventive care without a co-pay, and private employers are required to provide contraceptives at no charge to the employee.[9] *Sound familiar?*

Government can just pass so many new rules, regulations, and mandates that it's impossible to do business any more. Federal regulation cost private businesses $518 *billion* just in Obama's first four years.[10] And he's only getting warmed up.[11] When businesses fail because of all this over-regulation, more Americans become dependent on government jobs or entitlements to put food on the table. *Sound familiar?*

NOT YOUR FATHER'S SOCIALISM

Marxists have always aimed for public "ownership of the means of production." What Obama has figured out is that the government doesn't have to literally hold the title to factories and other private businesses—as long as government controls them. It amounts to the same thing in the end. They can do it all by regulation. So Obama's National Labor Relations Board simply told Boeing, a private company, that it couldn't open a plant in South Carolina because it's a "right to work" state.[12] Isn't that government control of the economy? Of course it is, but Obama's fingerprints aren't on the ownership of the business. He's not the CEO or owner, but he's calling the shots. It's a brilliant new twist on Marxism.

If government passes so many rules, regulations, and taxes that every business is forced to pay half or more of what they make to government— or go out of business—still Obama's fingerprints aren't on their bankruptcy. Unlike the old Soviet Union, government doesn't actually own the businesses. So if the businesses succeed, Obama gets half their profits in taxes. If they fail, he blames capitalism. A brilliant new twist on the Marxist game.

And not only is it subtle, it's gradual. Remember: boil the frog...slowly. Are you starting to see a pattern?

Obama is following to a T the main tenets of socialism and Marxism: redistribute wealth, overwhelm the system, destroy assets, increase debt, make everyone dependent on big government and big labor, and control the economy. But he's doing it slowly, carefully, and with moderate language that allows him to pull it all off without anyone even realizing what is happening. *Boil the frog slowly.* He doesn't ever say "We are stealing your money, or your business." He just talks about fairness, equality, social justice, and "You didn't build that." These are all code words for *I'm going to confiscate your earnings and your property.* Just gradually enough to not alarm anyone.

Marxists always violate private property rights. Obama did just that when he stole GM and Chrysler from its investors and shareholders and awarded ownership to his auto union buddies.[13] He's taking similar action by demanding private companies (employers and health insurers) to provide a product (contraceptives), while banning them from charging for it.[14] *Sound familiar?*

Marxists discredit and demonize the opposition. In Obama's America, government agencies have identified libertarians, conservatives, Tea Partiers, Ron Paul fans, and veterans as possible domestic terrorists. The Department of Homeland Security funded a study that characterizes Americans who are "reverent of individual liberty" as "extreme right-wing" and suggests they pose a terrorist threat.[15]

Marxists also violate civil rights. Obama extended and expanded the Patriot Act to listen to our calls without warrants.[16] He signed legislation to allow for indefinite detention of U.S. citizens.[17] His Justice Department found a legal basis for why Obama has a right to assassinate U.S. citizens on foreign soil, without due process. And, his Obamacare bill allows for the creation of a civilian defense force on U.S. soil.[18]

Marxists control and censor the media. Many of Obama's Democrat political friends support the "Fairness Doctrine," which would cripple conservative talk radio. Meanwhile his $16 billion bailout of GE, parent of NBC, CNBC and MSNBC, allows government to manipulate and intimidate the media.[19] Five hundred thousand dollars of "stimulus" spending went directly for advertisements on MSNBC. Don't you think they understood that they needed to be friendly to Obama to keep the money coming?[20]

Obama even publicly talked of bailing out newspapers.[21]

And of course Obama has always had Hollywood under his thumb.

Yes, Obama is definitely a Marxist. But he's a stealth Marxist. He believes in achieving his goals slowly, subtly. He believes in hiding and disguising his intentions. He believes in incremental success. But incremental or not, eventually the frog dies. Don't look now, but you're the frog.

We've already seen one crucial difference between a classic Marxist and a hybrid stealth Marxist like Obama. Marxists are supposed to hate the rich. But Obama figured out that he needs a few key billionaires and high profile CEOs to support his agenda and give him cover as he implements his socialist agenda. So he pals around with Warren Buffett, CEO Jeffrey Immelt of GE, and of course every filthy-rich big shot actor, producer, and studio chief in Hollywood.[22]

By accepting support and money from billionaires and powerful CEOs, Obama destroys the narrative that he hates the rich. Well of course, he doesn't hate all the rich. He just hates the ones who don't give him million dollar contributions and bow down to him like a god—the ones who don't go along with his crony socialism.

Jon Stewart and the *Daily Show* were right about one thing. Obama is no ordinary socialist or Marxist. Obama is a hybrid. He is a socialist-Marxist-fascist-corporatist all rolled into one. He is brilliant—for realizing there was never any other way to destroy America. His way is the breakthrough that Marxists have been waiting for. Where radical leftists have failed in the past, Obama is succeeding by stealth with his "Axis of Evil"—taxation, regulation, unionization, litigation, and government strangulation. Obama is the most brilliant and deadliest breed of stealth Marxist and crony socialist that America has ever seen.

CHAPTER THIRTEEN

THE TAX FRAUD

DID YOU KNOW?

- The top 1 percent of earners pay 39 percent of all income taxes—though they only have 13 percent of all income
- The top 20 percent—the "rich"—*already* pay 94.1 percent of income taxes
- The bottom 60 percent pay on net *less than zero* income taxes, once the tax credits the government pays them are taken into account
- Europeans used to work longer hours than Americans—until their tax rates skyrocketed

L et's take a close look at a key part of Obama's "Axis of Evil"—taxes. Obama seems to have some challenges when it comes to this subject. The first you might blame on "new math"—Obama's tax plans just don't add up. But the other really ought to be called "tax fraud." Obama simply lies about taxes. In the private sector, if a CEO on Wall Street lies or distorts the truth, that's called fraud. When Obama, the CEO of America, does the same thing, let's call that fraud, too.

PAYING THEIR FAIR SHARE

First of all, Obama and the Democrats argue that the wealthy don't pay their fair share. Really? The top 1 percent of income earners in America pay 39 percent of all the taxes. That's actually three times more than their share of income (13 percent).[1] That's not fair?

According to the *New York Times*, the 1 percent also account for 33 percent of consumer spending and 30 percent of all charitable giving.[2]

By the way, the top 5 percent pay 64 percent of all income taxes.[3]

The top 20 percent pay 94.1 percent of all income taxes. And that figure was from 2009, when Obama was just getting started.[4]

In fact all these figures are from before the "fiscal cliff" deal that ended the Bush tax cuts for "the rich."[5]

Speaking of "fair," the middle class earned 15 percent of America's income, yet paid only 2.7 percent of the taxes. So as *Forbes* recently pointed out, the top 1 percent paid fifteen times as much in federal income taxes as the middle class—even though the middle class earned more as a group. The rich aren't paying their fair share? They can "afford" to pay more?[6] Sounds like propaganda to me.

According to IRS data, the bottom 40 percent not only pay virtually zero in income taxes, they get massive tax credits paid back to *them*. They are handed checks by the IRS because of their low income. The government calls it a "tax credit"—but that's simply a nice way of saying "welfare check." Taking into account these "tax credits," the bottom 60 percent combined pay a net of less than *zero* in income taxes. Is that fair?[7]

So let's throw the idea of "fairness" out the window. Only a socialist or Marxist would find the numbers above unfair. Well, actually they are unfair—*unfair to "the rich."*

RAISING TAXES ON "THE RICH" HURTS THE WHOLE ECONOMY

Now to the idea that raising taxes on the rich is a good idea—because, as Obama says, they "can afford to pay" more.[8] Well everyone, including even Obama, seems to agree that allowing a tax increase on the middle class in the middle of an economic crisis is very bad for the economy. Obama even visited middle class families at their homes to ask what a $2,000 tax increase would do to their lives…and their spending habits.[9]

So why would it be okay to raise taxes on "the rich"—the 1 percent that make 33 percent of all purchases in the economy?[10] You mean high-income taxpayers won't cut back on spending, buying homes, starting businesses, and creating jobs if they have less disposable income? Wow, if that's true, monkeys can fly, hell is freezing over, and Democrats can defy the force of gravity.

Only those totally ignorant about the economy believe the fairy tale that taking money away from the top spenders, investors, and job creators isn't going to further damage the economy.

If the rich are taxed more, will they continue to give to charity? In my adopted home state of Nevada a recent study by Nevada State Bank shows that the top 0.2 percent (not the top 2 percent, but rather the top 2/10 of 1 percent) of wealthy Nevadans account for 27 percent of all charitable giving. The average Nevada family donates $957 to charity, while the average

THE REAL FACE OF THE TOP 2 PERCENT

Why isn't the GOP playing the same public relations battle as Obama? The real face of the top 2 percent of income earners in the U.S. is not a billionaire like the top-hatted plutocrat in Monopoly. Once again, the portrait Obama is painting is a fraud. The top 2 percent is actually made up mostly of small business owners, professionals, and family farmers.[11] The GOP needs to win over the American public by showing them the faces of small business owners who will be affected by higher taxes: farmers who will lose their farms because of higher taxes on "the rich"; doctors who will lay off nurses; homeowners who will no longer be able to pay the mortgage on their underwater home if they get hit with higher taxes or loss of deductions; small business owners who, because of a tax increase, will lay off employees or postpone an expansion of their business. Show the voters real faces and real stories of people damaged by taxes on "the rich."

wealthy Nevadan donates $138,320 annually.[12] This money goes to churches, higher education, hospitals, cancer institutes, and organizations that help the poor. Obama seems to think capping the charitable tax deduction would be no big deal.[13] Really? You mean if I donate $140,000 this year to charity, but I still owe 40 percent taxes on the money that I no longer have, I'll still make the same decision to donate? Monkeys must be flying again, and hell is certainly freezing over. One more certainty—Democrats are either completely ignorant, or their goal is the destruction of capitalism and churches at the same time.

But winning this argument isn't about facts or common sense. Just like all politics, it's about sales and marketing. It's about winning the public relations battle. Obama travels the nation stopping in the homes of middle class families and asking them how paying $2,000 in extra taxes would affect them. He does all this with cameras rolling, of course. *Brilliant.*

THE MYTH OF THE RETURN TO "CLINTON-ERA TAX RATES"

Obama claims he just wants to go back to Clinton-era tax rates.[14] What could be unfair about that? Well for starters, under Clinton there was no Obamacare. The new healthcare law raises taxes on the highest-income earners dramatically.[15] When you add income tax increases to Obamacare taxes, the highest earners will pay substantially more than under Clinton. Honestly returning to Clinton-era tax levels would mean scrapping the new Obamacare taxes. But this isn't an honest argument.

In any case, Obama is comparing apples to oranges. Economic growth is about more than taxes. It's about regulations, mandates, entitlements, and spending. So next time Obama suggests it's "fair" to go back to Clinton era tax rates, the GOP should say it's only "fair" if we can also go back to Clinton-era spending, regulations, and welfare reform. Let's agree to roll back all increases in spending, entitlements, government programs, and regulations enacted since Clinton. The overall economy under Clinton was good compared to today because the size of government, spending, rules, and regulations was so much smaller back then—and government-run healthcare was rejected under Clinton. That's the only return to the Clinton era that the GOP should agree to.

I'm sick of hearing Democrats call today's tax rates "historically low." That is another lie. There are many factors that determine your tax bill—including deductions and tax credits. Overall, we are all paying among the highest taxes ever. "Tax Freedom Day" in 2012 was April 17.[16] That means the average taxpayer had to give the government all the money he made for more than the first three and a half months of the year, just to pay his tax burden.

In 1917 "Tax Freedom Day" was January 24.[17] Facts don't lie, folks. If taxes are "historically low," then why does it take until April to pay our taxes, versus mid-January in 1917?

In any case, Obama is comparing apples to oranges when he compares tax rates today to those of yesteryear. Rates are lower today than in the past because many valuable tax deductions were eliminated. And we now face caps, phase-outs, and the dreaded Alternative Minimum Tax. Therefore quoting higher rates is a distortion of the truth. A tax rate of 70 percent from decades ago might actually yield a lower effective tax rate than today's rates once you include these factors.

Democrats defend high tax rates on the basis of the rates in the mid-twentieth century.[18] But that's another distortion. It is true that FDR raised the top rate in 1935 to 79 percent. But what we never hear is that it only applied to incomes over $5 million—the equivalent of $76,000,000 per year today. In 1935 only one man in the entire U.S.A. paid a penny at that rate—John D. Rockefeller.[19] The reality is that from 1935 through the 1970s the highest tax rates did pass 70 percent, 80 percent, and for a time even 90 percent, but those rates were aimed only at billionaire industrialists, not small business owners. Only a handful of taxpayers in America ever paid the top rates.[20] Today the highest tax rate (after the "fiscal cliff" deal) is 39.6 percent, but it hits incomes of $450,000 for married couples—in other words, it's aimed not just at billionaires, but at upper middle class small business owners.[21]

Obama says, "Taxes are lower on families than they've been probably in the last fifty years."[22] He leaves out the important fact that only in the last thirty years have we moved away from a cash economy. Tax rates at 70 percent or higher didn't matter prior to 1980 because most small businesses earned unreported cash. Today we have a computerized economy based on credit cards. Virtually every dollar that every business takes in is tracked and reported to the government. So the tax rates are immaterial—all of us are paying more in taxes than ever before.

Up until now, the American upper middle class small business owner like me has been able to live the life equivalent to that of a multi-millionaire in Europe. All because we keep more of our own money—we've had lower tax rates, and when the rates have been high we've been able to use deductions to offset high tax rates. What do we do with the money? We spend it or invest it. Both are great things for the U.S. economy. Then Obama came along.

Obama wants to take that money from us, to redistribute to his voters—who didn't do a thing to earn it. If I used to owe $15,000 to the IRS, but now I owe $25,000, that's money I don't have to save my business if the economy turns bad. That's money I don't have to save for retirement. That's money I don't have to pay for my kids to avoid failing public schools. That's money I don't have to invest in stocks or real estate. That's money I don't have to spend on the U.S. economy. How is this loss of money from millions of big spenders and investors good for the U.S. economy?

TAX AVOIDANCE BY OBAMA'S CRONIES AND HOLLYWOOD LEFTISTS

If taxing "the rich" is so great for the economy, why do Obama's super-rich pals keep avoiding high taxes however they can?

Why has Obama's buddy Warren Buffett been fighting a billion dollar tax bill for his company Berkshire Hathaway for many years? Why not just pay the taxes?[23]

Why did Denise Rich, a huge contributor to the Democratic Party and associated causes, renounce her American citizenship to save tens of millions in taxes?[24]

Why do ultra-liberal Hollywood movie and television producers choose to leave California, to make their movies in states with giant tax breaks (like Michigan or Louisiana)? In one state alone, Michigan, tax credits grew the movie industry from $2 million to $225 million overnight.[25]

Why did NBC Sports recently move their headquarters from high-tax Manhattan to Stanford, Connecticut—in return for $35 million in tax breaks?[26]

Why do the liberal, latte-drinking young whiz kids at Google rout their billions in revenues through a subsidiary headquarters in no-tax Bermuda to save $2 billion on taxes?[27]

Why did the governor of Oregon have to call a special session of his legislature this past December to give Nike a forty-year tax deal?[28]

Why did Eduardo Saverin, the co-founder of Facebook, renounce his U.S. citizenship to move to Singapore (with low income taxes and zero capital gains taxes)?[29]

THE POWER TO TAX IS THE POWER TO DESTROY

And if taxes are so good for the economy, why do politicians tax whatever they want to kill? Politicians constantly raise taxes on cigarettes, claiming the taxes will reduce their use.[30]

Obama raised taxes on tanning bed sessions—for exactly the same reason.[31] Politicians love to raise "sin" taxes on liquor and gambling.[32] Environmentalists frequently suggest raising gas taxes to force Americans to reduce their use of cars.[33] It seems to me that the same progressive and socialist politicians who claim raising taxes is a good thing are committing tax fraud. They know darn well that high taxes kill whatever they touch.

On the other hand, whenever politicians want to encourage something, they lower taxes. When Obama wanted Americans to trade in their old gas-guzzling cars, he offered a "cash for clunkers" tax credit.[34] When the government wanted to encourage home sales, they offered a tax credit for buying a home.[35] Liberal politicians and environmentalists desperately want to breathe life into the solar energy business, so they offer solar tax credits.[36] It's pretty clear that lowering taxes forces people to buy things, and raising taxes forces them to stop buying. The debate is over.

So please explain how raising taxes on "the rich" is good for the economy? The reality is Obama doesn't care. He is a Marxist. He just wants to punish "the rich" and take their money away. Then he wants to redistribute the loot to his voters. He believes the Marxist principle of, "From each according to his ability, to each according to his need." But he's not honest with the American people.

Look at the U.K., where the exact Obama tax-the-rich "solution" has already been tried…and proven a failure. The U.K. created a special "millionaires tax." Since it was enacted, two thirds of all the millionaires have disappeared. They've either left England, retired…or simply stopped working so hard. Result: tax revenues plunged and the U.K. economy was hurt. Now U.K. politicians are busy undoing the damage by bringing tax rates for "the rich" back down. In the end, they learned that high taxes don't increase revenues, they *depress* them.[37]

Just compare the GDP per capita of America versus European nations for the past few decades.[38] What accounts for America's magical success? The higher tax rates of Europe discourage hard work and financial risk-taking (entrepreneurship). First, because if government takes too much of your earnings, there is nothing left to spend or invest. Second, because with government taking more as you earn more, there is no incentive to work harder or longer. You might as well play soccer in the park with your kids, or go to the beach, or enjoy a three-hour afternoon siesta. It's just not worth it to work hard and keep so little of what you earn.

A recent commentary in the *Wall Street Journal* by a Nobel Prize winner in economics proves this point. It turns out things weren't always this way. When taxes were low in Europe in the 1950s, Europeans actually outworked Americans—working more hours per capita. Then tax rates rose dramatically in Europe. At that point, the number of hours they worked compared to Americans dropped dramatically. Today the average European adult works about 1,000 hours per year, versus about 1,400 a few decades ago (when taxes were lower), and versus American workers today who average just under 1,400 hours annually.[39]

Entrepreneurship, too, was stunted by high taxes and severe regulations in Western Europe. In America we have 30 million small business owners because lower taxes, less regulation, and smaller government all work together to encourage opportunity, mobility, ambition, financial risk-taking, and big dreams. The proof is in the economic facts that Obama doesn't want you to hear—our GDP, job creation, and economic success for the past quarter century have dwarfed Europe's in tandem with our lower tax rates.

With the "fiscal cliff" deal, Obama's tax fraud has paid off. He has succeeded in raising the top income tax rates back up to 39.6 percent. He has turned American tax policy in the direction that Europe's been going for the past fifty years. Great Obama Depression, here we come. We're one step closer to Obamageddon.

CHAPTER FOURTEEN

THE PERFECT TROJAN HORSE

DID YOU KNOW?

- Obamacare is the real game-changer—in long-term significance to America's future it dwarfs even Obama's near-$6 trillion in new debt
- Obamacare was sold as the solution to "the healthcare crisis." But before Obamacare, 70 percent of Americans rated their healthcare plan "excellent or good"
- Obamacare does not "bend the cost curve" downward; it is not even deficit-neutral; it adds $17 *trillion* in unfunded liabilities

Thanks to out-of-control taxes under Obama, American capitalism is on life support. *And Obamacare is designed to finish it off.* Obamacare is Obama's masterpiece. Obamacare is the keystone in the arch, the linchpin in his plan to destroy that great capitalist country known as the U.S.A.

Remember, the Cloward-Piven plan is to destroy capitalism by overwhelming the system. Obama's best scenario for accomplishing this is to add massive debt in response to a national crisis or emergency. Remember he aims to boil the frog slowly, until the frog is cooked without ever realizing what is happening. Obama learned well at Columbia University. He has a Ph.D. in slow-cooking frogs.

The key is Obamacare.

Obama learned deception from his radical mentors. (*Of course* Obama's not socializing the country. He's only making the system more *fair*.)

The nearly $6 trillion in new debt was supposed to save our economy. Obamacare was supposed to save our healthcare system. Do you see a pattern here? The things meant to tax us to death, enslave future generations to big government, and destroy American capitalism are always introduced during a time of crisis, when our defenses are down—to "save" us. As Obama sidekick Rahm Emanuel said, "You never want a serious crisis to go to waste. And what I mean by that, it's an opportunity to do things that you think you could not do before."[1]

What you need to understand is that the almost $6 trillion in new debt in Obama's first term was just a *starting point*—and a distraction from the main event. The main event, the real game-changer, was always Obamacare.

If we were thinking clearly we might have asked a few obvious questions:

- Before Obama was elected, polls proved that over 70 percent of Americans liked the present healthcare coverage they had—rating it "excellent or good."[2] So what exactly is Obamacare saving us from?
- Everyone who looks at the numbers agrees that government-run Medicare and Medicaid are going broke.[3] Unfunded entitlements are threatening to bankrupt the U.S. economy.[4] Even Obama must know that.[5] So how can we "save" the U.S. economy by adding 10 million new patients to Medicaid?[6] Even more to the point, how can we save our economy by putting the same government that runs Medicare and Medicaid…and has run up $100 trillion in unfunded liabilities…in charge of all our healthcare?
- If government can magically lower healthcare prices, how come some of the highest healthcare costs in America are

found in New York and New Jersey, the two states with the
highest level of government regulation?[7]

- If government has been wildly wrong on practically every
prediction they've ever made about the cost of every government program, why should this time be any different?[8]

Just as he learned from Alinsky, Cloward, and Piven, Obama manufactured a healthcare "crisis" and made us panic. So the American people sus-
pended our reason and common sense. That was the plan from day one.

Congresswoman Nancy Pelosi once said about Obamacare, "We have
to pass the bill so that you can find out what is in it." Well, the results are
in. Someone finally took her up on it, read the entire 2,700 pages, and did
the math. Obamacare isn't going to "save" anything. Senator Jeff Sessions
determined that the long-term debt Obamcare creates is off the charts—
rather than lowering the deficit, as Obama promised, it will add *$17 trillion*
to our debt.[10]

Yes, I said $17 trillion dollars—trillion with a "t." It's going to "bend
the cost curve" all right—but in the opposite direction from what the
president was promising.

I wish I could say I'm surprised. That's about the same
amount as the current entire
national debt. It's more than our
nation's GDP—all the goods and
services produced in America each
year. It's about the same amount
we already owe in unfunded liabilities for the entire Social Security
program.

Just so you know, Senator Sessions didn't use crazy math to
come up with this $17 trillion fig-
ure. All he did was read the entire
2,700 pages and apply standard

PUT FEDEX IN CHARGE

If government is so talented at running things, why does government
program after government program
fail so badly? Why do they all lose
money? Why did the U.S. Postal
Service lose $15.9 billion last year?[9]
Do we want the same people who
run the Post Office to run our
healthcare system? Why not put
FedEx in charge of healthcare
instead? They run circles around the
Postal Service—and make a profit!

federal government estimates and models to the law's spending obligations. In fact, since the $1.7 trillion added to the deficit is a government estimate, the true cost is undoubtedly several times greater.

When combined with the shortfalls for Medicare and Medicaid, this $17 trillion puts U.S. taxpayers on the hook for **$82 trillion** in long-term healthcare obligations.[11]

So you see, Obamacare is the heart of the plan to overwhelm the U.S. economy with debt. The current economy cannot survive $82 trillion in unfunded obligations. This new debt will force us to our knees, to beg government to save us. Taxes will have to be increased to unimaginable levels to feed the beast of big government. The Trojan horse that promised to save us is actually here to destroy us.

For those who hate capitalism, and hate America, the beauty is this Trojan horse will keep adding to the debt—destroying all that is great about this country—long after Obama is gone. No one ever agrees to give up a massive government program. After tens of millions experience "free" healthcare for their every sniffle, with no obligation to ever pay a dime in taxes, they will certainly never agree to give it up. It will live forever. This is the Obama plan.

If Obamacare isn't repealed, decades from now our children and grandchildren will be overwhelmed by huge debts, deficits, and unimaginable taxes—not to mention, terrible healthcare. (If you want a view into the future of healthcare in this country, just look at the horror story that is the National Health Service in Britain.)[12] Future generations may not even remember Obama's name, but he will have changed their lives and the economic system they live under.

In a bit of healthcare irony, Obamacare is like herpes—the gift that keeps on giving…long after the person who gave it to you is gone!

CHAPTER FIFTEEN

THE MASK IS OFF

DID YOU KNOW?

- Forty percent of Americans have less than $500 total in savings
- A quarter of the jobs in Obama's America pay below the federal poverty line
- *After* the election, the IRS revealed that the *cheapest* health insurance policy available through the Obamacare exchanges is estimated to have a price tag of $20,000 a year for a family of five

President Obama is making it a breeze to write this book! Every day brings a new outrage or travesty to add to the story. Let me quickly bring you up to date on how things have gotten even worse during the two months since his re-election. Through the election, Obama and his cronies—and his willing allies in the media—managed to keep a lid on some of the worst evidence that Obama's policies are heading America straight toward economic decline and disaster. But now the mask is off.

At this very moment (*before* it gets really bad, before a complete collapse), one quarter of the jobs in Obama's America pay below the federal poverty line. Obama is not only great at killing jobs—the jobs he *doesn't* kill still leave you in misery and poverty.[1]

But at least those people have jobs, a rare feat in the Obama economy. The Labor Department just reported that 8.5 million Americans left the labor force during Obama's first term. That leaves 89 million able-bodied adults NOT working in America (remember, this is before things get really bad).[2]

At this very moment over 40 percent of Americans have $500 or less in total savings.[4] But just wait until 2014 when all Americans will be required by law to buy health insurance. The IRS just disclosed their assumption that the cheapest health insurance plan available for a family of five by 2016 will be $20,000 per year. Wasn't the whole point of Obamacare to *reduce* the cost of health insurance? With 40 percent of Americans having $500 or less in savings and 89 million able-bodied adults *not* working, how can we expect them to pay $20,000 per year for health insurance? Heck, Obama classifies me as "rich" and I couldn't afford $20,000 per year for health insurance. If this were a movie plot, critics would say it's too ridiculous to believe.[5]

COMING SOON TO A CITY, TOWN, OR STATE NEAR YOU

One in three citizens of Illinois, Obama's home state, now lives at or near the poverty level.[3]

But wait—it gets even more ridiculous. Here is the latest "Government Gone Wild" story just out as I'm writing: as of January 2013 the government now classifies anyone with food allergies as "disabled."[6] Have you ever heard of anything so stupid? I've had severe food allergies my entire life. I'm gluten- and dairy-intolerant. But I'm certainly NOT disabled. I've lived a perfectly wonderful life without any help from the government. I can make my own decisions what to eat without government involved.

But this isn't about our health. This is another big government payoff to the Bar Association. Lawyers—like union members—are *huge* supporters of Obama. And declaring food allergies a disability opens the door to more lawsuits against business. Food manufacturers, distributors, super-markets, bodegas, and restaurants can all now expect to be sued because a "disabled" customer ate something that they manufactured, sold, or served them. This is completely typical of Obama's approach to the economy.

What's unclear is where the now "disabled" people with food allergies will buy their non-gluten, allergy-free food. Obama's FDA has proposed new labeling requirements that threaten to put supermarkets, convenience stores, delis, and bodegas out of business. It will cost over $1 billion in the first year alone. If a product on the shelves is mislabeled, grocers face crippling fines and *prison time*.[7]

Or read this one and weep. In January, a federal appeals court threw out EPA standards for biofuels and actually called those government standards "wishful thinking rather than accurate estimates." The American Petroleum Institute said, "The court recognized the absurdity of fining companies for failing to use a nonexistent biofuel." So how did the EPA respond? Only days later they came out with new standards—which almost *DOUBLED* the mandate.[8]

There is no longer any reason for anyone to wonder what has happened to the U.S. economy. Our income taxes were just raised to the same level as in Greece, at the same time Obama took away many of our legal exemptions and deductions.[9] Obama promises more to come. There are 60,000 new rules and regulations.[10] Obama created four times as many new regulations in his first three years as Bush in his first four years, at a cost of $46 billion to American business.[11] No small businessman can hope to keep up with them, let alone comply—so government has an excuse to raid, indict, and fine almost anyone in business, at any time. Obama's mandates and the EPA harassment of energy producers are going to make our utility bills skyrocket. The minute any business owner even thinks of hiring someone, the clock starts ticking for a future lawsuit. And the IRS is hiring thousands of new agents to harass us all. It's quite a depressing picture.

Here's the trillion-dollar question: Who would be willing to risk their life savings to start a business in this current environment? Now you know why the economy is so bad, there is no serious job growth, and the American Dream is becoming a distant memory. Obama has turned the entire U.S. economy into a "hostile work environment." Where's a good lawyer when you need one?

This is what a Great Depression II looks like. But no worry—our fear-less leader Obama is hard at work! We just found out in January that he closed down his Jobs Council. Eighty-nine million Americans no longer work. Why would we need a Jobs Council? No need for an ongoing dialogue about jobs, right? Silly me, I guess I'm just a worry wart! Again, if this were a movie, critics would say it's too ridiculous, far-fetched, and implausible to take seriously.[12]

So with the "Jobs Council" shut down, Obama and his socialist cabal must have some kind of plan, right? Of course they do. A liberal Washington, D.C., think tank has the solution—*we should all work less*. I'm not kidding. This is the best they've got. To reduce the effects of global warming, they suggest America adopt a "European work schedule" of fewer hours and more vacations. I wish I could say I'm making this stuff up. I wish I could say this is a skit from *Saturday Night Live*. But it's very real.[13]

But the U.S. economy actually looks good compared to Europe.

The French Labor Minister announced that France is "totally bankrupt."[14]

The U.K. is on the verge of its third recession in five years—a dreaded and unheard of "triple-dip recession." I think it's safe to use the words "Great Depression."[15]

And in Italy buses had to return to the bus depot because the government ran out of money to pay for gas.[16]

Is it any wonder the EU is failing? Their economic model sounds just like Obama's (and vice versa). Take Spain, the largest economic basket case in the EU. Spain has 26 percent unemployment, with over 50 percent youth unemployment, and staggering deficits and debt. Along comes Las Vegas Sands and its American billionaire Chairman Sheldon Adelson. They have agreed to build one of the largest resorts in world history, just outside Madrid.

It is called EuroVegas. It will take up 750 football fields, cost over $22 billion, and include twelve hotels, six casinos, a convention center, three golf courses, theaters, shopping malls, bars, and restaurants. It is estimated 260,000 jobs will be created. Doesn't that sound like a good thing?

Yet it took years to overcome the protests from leftist and environmental groups in Spain. The leftists complained that EuroVegas might actually promote gambling. We couldn't possibly allow that in a country with no jobs, could we?

They whined it might promote smoking, in a country with strict non-smoking laws. We couldn't possibly allow that in a country with no jobs, could we?

They complained that Las Vegas Sands might actually get tax breaks. We couldn't possibly allow that in a country with no job prospects and sinking tax revenues, could we?

And wait for the final zinger. Leftist groups claimed that EuroVegas will create low-level jobs. The left says young people need "higher skill jobs."[17]

Really? Last I checked, Spain needed *any* jobs *at all*. Its youth unemployment rate is over 50 percent.[18] Aren't young people better off waiting on tables, or cleaning rooms, or working at a hotel front desk, than unemployed, collecting welfare from the government?

This is the socialist attitude in a nutshell, folks. If it were up to the left, none of us would have a job. Not if the job actually involved real work. Not if anyone involved had to lower themselves to accept low wages—as opposed to no jobs and no wages. Not if anyone involved is smoking. Not if a barrel of oil is pumped out of the ground. Not if a tree is damaged. Not if a snake or mouse is harmed. None of it is worth the tradeoff for 260,000 jobs. This is why Spain and the entire EU are in economic ruin—and America soon will be. This is why no jobs can be created. The battle with the left is a battle for our very economic survival.

Whether America or the world economy can be saved is up for debate. Only time will tell. Although I'd argue that based on the progressive model of recommending fewer hours of work, shutting down factories, and taking more vacations—walking vacations, I assume, because plane trips add to global warming and gas for cars is too expensive—we're pretty much doomed.

CHAPTER SIXTEEN

WHY OBAMA'S DREAMS CAN NEVER WORK: BECAUSE GOVERNMENT FAILS AT *EVERYTHING* IT DOES!

DID YOU KNOW?

- The stock market goes up, on average, *seventeen times as fast* when Congress is not in session
- The War on Poverty has cost $20 trillion, almost three times as much as all the wars in American history combined
- When Medicare was introduced in 1965, the government estimated that in 1990 it would cost $12 billion; in reality, it cost $110 billion

While I'm sure by now you no longer have any doubt that Obama and his policies are dangerous and destructive to your well-being, it is critical to your survival to understand *why* government fails at everything it does.

The fact is, government is dangerous, incompetent, and corrupt. The bigger it is, the more dangerous, incompetent, and corrupt it becomes.

While Obama's goal is to turn America into a big government Nanny State, he doesn't realize his plans are doomed.

Why won't they work? Because government always fails, at everything it does. *Everywhere.* Pick a country. Any country. Not just socialist countries like Cuba, North Korea, Venezuela, the old Soviet Union, the old People's Republic of China, Angola—failures all. Those disasters are too easy to recite. Not merely "socialist-lite" countries like Greece, Spain, France, or Argentina; those disasters are also too obvious. Look at any country, even capitalist ones. Government everywhere screws up whatever it touches.

Governments are always verging on bankruptcy. Without the discipline of the marketplace, they survive by going heavily into debt, printing fake money, and raising taxes. They survive only by *stealing* from me, you, and future generations.

If you and I owned printing presses and had the right to print as much money as we wanted, and if we ever ran out, had the power to steal more from our customers (the way the government can always tax us more) I think we'd be in business for a long time. What do you think?

Government is quite simply a Ponzi scheme. First they take people's money and spend until it's gone. Then they spend more money that doesn't really exist (fake dollars created out of thin air by the Fed). And as in every Ponzi scheme, they take from the newest customers to pay the oldest (as in Social Security and Medicare). And they keep the Ponzi scheme running through pure fraud, gaming the numbers, stealing some more (raising taxes), and then using the money to hand out bribes to the masses to distract them from noticing how bad things really are—or at least from complaining about it. Of course, government's ultimate ace in the hole is that they own the prosecution and courts. No one can ever bring them to justice for their stealing and cheating. What a deal.

Government is the worst kind of thief and fraud, because it's also an addict—pathetically addicted to spending. Just like drug addicts, government blames the victim (taxpayers) for not giving them more of our money. No matter how much they spend, no matter how badly they screw up, it's always our fault for not paying higher taxes. In other words, we should be allowing them to steal more of our money to feed their addiction.

Other than the obvious fact that government is filled with thieves, frauds, and incompetents, why does government fail? Government is a failure because the people who work for government are not subject to marketplace competition and don't understand the most basic concept of business—treat your customers well. Especially your best customers. Business owners like me understand that

1. Your top 20 percent of customers produce 80 percent of your profits and success.
2. It's far less expensive to do whatever is necessary to keep your present customers than find new ones.
3. The customer is always right.
4. And if the customer is wrong, refer back to 3.

The world over, governments have no clue about these tenets of business. They just see taxpayers as targets of opportunity, to confiscate what is ours to feed their spending addiction. They see taxpayers as "suckers." And ironically, the government's top customers (that is, the highest earners) are treated the worst. The more we make, the more they demonize us, punish us, take more from us, and harass us with IRS audits. All government wants to do is spend more (to make themselves seem more important), regulate more (to control our lives), and hire more government employees (to make government bigger and their unions more powerful).

Politicians, bureaucrats, and central bank chiefs the world over keep repeating the mantra of big government: *If only you'll give us more time and money, this time we'll fix the problem.* But like clockwork, every time we give them more money, it gets worse. See the public schools, or the "War on Poverty." Then the addicts blame the victims some more. They say, *It failed because you should have given us more.*

As one of my heroes, Ronald Reagan, said, "Government is not the solution to our problems; government is the problem." It is this simple:

the economy will not improve until government stops interfering. The reality is that government is a walking disaster. Run away when you see it coming.

Don't take just my word for it. The Congressional Effect Fund, a mutual fund on Wall Street, has studied the effects of Congress on the economy for decades. Since 1964, whenever Congress is in session, the U.S. stock market is up about 1 percent on an annualized basis. During that same period, while Congress is on vacation, the stock market is up almost 17 percent.[1] *Coincidence?*

AN OLD JOKE

Q: How do you know when Congress is doing damage to our economy?

A: When they're in their seats and their lips are moving.

Want a longer view on the damage government does? That same Congressional Effect Fund reports that if you invested $1 in the stock market in 1897 only on the days that Congress was in session, you'd have $2 today. But if you invested that same $1 only on the days that Congress was on vacation, today you'd have more than $300.[2]

Yes, government is *that* bad.

Government is a failure everywhere. And the bigger government is, the more miserably it fails.

LET'S LOOK AT THE FACTS

Take the Veterans Administration. A federal appeals court has ruled the VA suffers from "unchecked incompetence." That incompetence is killing our brave veterans. I bet you didn't know eighteen veterans commit suicide per day. Or that 85,000 vets are on waiting lists for care. Even a severely depressed vet can wait eight weeks to see a psychiatrist. Still want government to run your healthcare?[3]

The U.S. Postal Service, by law, is not subject to competition. Yet it lost $15.9 billion last year.[4]

When Medicare was founded in the 1960s, government "experts" estimated its cost at $12 billion per year by 1990. Instead it cost $110 billion.[5]

We have spent just over $20 trillion (in inflation-adjusted dollars) since President Johnson launched the "War on Poverty" in 1964. Since all wars in American history combined have cost about $7 trillion, the War on Poverty has cost almost three times as much as all the wars in United States history COMBINED. With terrible results.[6]

When NASA started the Space Shuttle, their "experts" estimated its future cost at $10.7 million per trip. The actual cost has turned out to be $1.5 billion per launch.[7]

When the federal government took over Amtrak, they promised the turnaround would take two years and $1 billion. That was over forty years and $40 billion dollars ago. Today forty of Amtrak's forty-four lines lose money.[8] The losses never end. Each time a passenger sits down in an Amtrak train seat, U.S. taxpayers lose $32.[9]

Mistakes like these cost management their jobs in the private sector. But they're no problem for government employees. They just waste more of our tax money, raise our taxes, give themselves raises, and retire on $100,000 pensions.

The government-run school system is a shambles. The U.S. spends more per student than any country but Switzerland and yet still gets pitiful results. The Department of Education budget went from $40 billion in Bush's first year (2001) to over $130 billion in Obama's first year (2009)— including $98 billion in extra stimulus spending.[10] We tripled spending. Anyone see triple improvement? Only if you call the *worst* SAT scores in history "improvement."[11]

How about the Department of Energy? It was founded in 1977 to solve our energy crisis. It now has 115,000 employees and spends $24 billion per year. On what? Does anyone think we are more energy-independent than in 1977? We'd have been better off spending the entire budget on buying gas for the American people.[12]

Then there's the "War on Drugs." That war has cost $1 trillion over 40 glorious years. $33 billion was spent on "Just Say No" and other public relations campaigns. Attempts to control drug smuggling at the border have cost $49 billion. We spend over $120 billion annually to arrest and imprison 37 million non-violent drug offenders (10 million of them for marijuana possession).[13]

The results? Ten million more Americans use drugs today than forty years ago.[14] Drug overdoses among young Americans have skyrocketed to about 20,000 annually. More Americans are imprisoned for drug crimes than for property crimes.[15] Drug trafficking on the border is out of control. And the easiest place to find drugs? *Any prison.*[16]

Even the tax system proves the failure of government. Today, America has the highest corporate taxes in the industrialized world.[17] Yet while 30 percent of federal taxes were paid by corporations back in 1950, today—with those sky-high tax rates—corporations pay only 7 percent of federal taxes.[18]

Total individual taxes collected are about $1.2 trillion. Yet the cost of compliance is about $800 billion.[19] Taxpayers waste 7.6 billion hours complying with the most complicated tax code in the world.[20]

How about the Federal Reserve's track record? The Fed was created in 1913 with one main goal—protect the value of the U.S. dollar. Since the Fed's creation, our dollar has lost 96 percent of its value. With friends like that, who needs enemies?[21]

Worst of all is the cost of government employees themselves. The unfunded liability for the pensions of federal employees is now around $5.7 trillion dollars.[22] On the state and local level the unfunded liabilities for government employees is about $3 trillion.[23] One state alone, California, has unfunded liabilities of as much as $884 billion.[24] One California government employee earns $822,000. No wonder government is broke and desperately needs higher taxes.[25] There are a mind-boggling 22 million government employees.[26] Worst of all, the government employees on whom we're spending trillions of dollars have racked up four consecutive trillion-dollar deficits and a national debt of $16 trillion. With unfunded liabilities added in, the taxpayers owe an unimaginable $100 trillion.[27] That's well over 100 percent of GDP—not just U.S. GDP, but the GDP of the entire *world.*[28] What do 22 million employees do all day? Apparently their days are dedicated to thinking of new and creative ways to bankrupt us all.

If you're waiting for government to save you, get ready to wait for... ***eternity.***

The evidence is clear. Government is never going to save the healthcare system, or the economy, or us. It's just going to keep making things worse. Which is exactly how Obama wants it—because the worse the crisis, the bigger the opportunity for yet more rescue efforts, yet more socialism, and yet more government expansion.

Which, of course, will only make things worse. We'll go from Zombie Economy to Obama Great Depression to Obamageddon. Which is exactly where we're headed.

If that story was all this book had to offer, you'd be pretty darn depressed. But this isn't the end. It's only the beginning. I've painted the picture, so now you understand the Obama game plan. And you can observe that plan unfolding—slowly but surely—in front of your very eyes. Step one in solving any problem is to first understand what you are facing.

But that's just step one. Once you see the problem, you can start to see the opportunities. Just as in the original Great Depression, Obama's policies have triggered the beginning of the greatest wealth transfer in history. As I pointed out earlier, during that crisis more self-made millionaires were created than in any other period in U.S. history.[29] Those who were educated, prepared, empowered, understood what was happening, and had a game plan to capitalize on it . . . **that group didn't just survive, they THRIVED.**

I don't like what is happening to America under Obama. I'm leading the fight to stop it, and God willing we will. But in every tragedy lies great opportunity. Now I'm going to show you how to capitalize on that opportunity. Because what matters most isn't the world economy…or the U.S. economy…it's your own *personal economy*.

Never forget, Obama believes in incremental success—like boiling a frog slowly, until the frog is cooked before it ever realizes what is happening to it. Unfortunately, in Obama's world, you and I are that frog. This book is devoted to helping you recognize that the heat has been turned up to the point where you need to jump out of the boiling water.

Then, it is devoted to making you a Capitalist Evangelist…to helping you protect your assets…to giving you financial freedom…to making you mentally and physically strong like a Navy Seal…so you can prosper and protect your family from Obama and those trying to put them in the velvet handcuffs of governmental dependence.

To thrive you need to create your own Booming Personal Economy, not just in spite of what Obama is doing, but because of what he's doing. What he thinks is your loss will become your gain. I'm going to show you how to profit from this mess. Won't this be fun? It's like the "Inner Game" of Obama.

I can't wait. Let the fun and profits begin.

PART TWO

HOW TO SURVIVE, THRIVE, AND PROSPER DURING THE NEXT FOUR YEARS OF THE OBAMA DISASTER

B·y now we should be on the same page. If you had any doubt before, you now understand that America is headed for certain disaster under a president who is jealous of the rich; resents business owners; is economically ignorant; has zero experience at business or job creation; loves unions and lawyers; is addicted to spending, debt, and taxes; and wants (in the best scenario) to turn America into Europe. *This will not end well.* That could be why Obama and his socialist cabal suddenly seem so desperate to disarm the citizens.[1]

But you don't need to go down with the ship (of state)!

That's precisely why I wrote this book. You don't need to be unemployed, or living in misery. You can create your own Booming Personal Economy right in the midst of decline and collapse. As I've mentioned, more self-made millionaires emerged from the Great Depression (Great Depression I, that is) than from any other period in U.S. history. It's time to answer the question, "How do my family and I survive, thrive, and prosper during Obama's second term?"

I've criticized enough. Complaints and criticisms—no matter how completely justified—by themselves get you nowhere. Once you understand what's wrong, you've got to deal with the situation.

You have to do what you need to do, to make things right, at least for yourself and your own family. It's time for solutions.

The rest of this book is bursting with them. First I'll give you my own recipe for making lemonade out of socialist lemons.

Then in addition to my own advice, I'm including the advice of a few other, exceptional Americans. You see, I'm just one small businessman with my own share of common sense. But I've been blessed. I have a broad and diverse array of friends. The key to success in life is to know what you know, and know what you don't know. I readily defer to people smarter or more experienced than I am. So I've sought out some of the smartest minds in the country. I know when to shut up and listen. I interviewed a dozen friends who all have one thing in common—they're brilliant, self-made businesspeople—mega-successful millionaire CEOs, entrepreneurs, and financial geniuses. These superstars of business will give you their own personal strategies for surviving and thriving for the next four years.

We know Obama is boiling the frog slowly. So don't sit there and let yourself be cooked—hop out and take some action!

Strap on your seat belt. Eat your spinach. Take your vitamins. And put in your mouthpiece. By the time we're through, you'll be clicking your heels and whistling while you work. You're about to discover how the Obama Great Depression can be as lucrative and life-changing for you as the original Great Depression was for that record number of millionaires.

Here we go!

CHAPTER SEVENTEEN

LEARNING TO USE Y-PODS: YOUR PERSONAL OBAMA DEFENSE SHIELD

DID YOU KNOW?

- The Spanish government "invested" Spaniards' pension funds in government bonds—and the same thing is being threatened in the U.S.
- The Obama administration is silencing bond rating agencies, subjecting them to investigation and indictment if they dare tell the truth about our unsustainable government debt
- Ever more rounds of "stimulus" and "quantitative easing" are putting the United States in danger of hyperinflation

No amount of lies, exaggerations, misstatements, misrepresentations, or propaganda—of which President Obama and his cronies in the media are shoveling out record quantities daily—can change the fact that the U.S. economy under Obama is ugly and getting uglier every day.

But now it's time to stop whining and start winning. In these next chapters I'm going to focus on detailed solutions for creating your own Booming Personal Economy in the midst of Obama's Zombie Economy.

Millions of Americans have iPods, for fun and entertainment. But you need Y-PODS—Your own Personal Obama Defense Shield—for survival. Obama and his cronies are not looking out for you. Your survival depends on you—and it's serious business. It's time to break out the heavy artillery. It's time to learn how to use Y-PODS.

YOUR PERSONAL OBAMA DEFENSE SHIELD

Let's start with detailed advice on how to protect your assets and then move on to commonsense advice to improve your financial position, even if you are one of the millions of Americans with few or even no assets.

First up is what you can do to save yourself from the fallout of the biggest disaster Obama has created—the spiraling national debt caused by out-of-control government spending.

As you now know, the United States is in severe trouble. Historic trouble. "End of empire" kind of trouble. As I outlined earlier, we are indebted either past the point of no return, or damn close to it. We owe $100 trillion in debt and unfunded liabilities. And with annual trillion-dollar deficits, the debt gets larger every year.

Our national debt increases by $3 million per minute. The debt ceiling has been breached—again and again.

This can't go on forever, any more than you could go on eternally funding a lavish lifestyle with your credit cards. The difference is, when the entire United States runs out of money, credit, and options, the fallout is going to be bigger than any personal bankruptcy. The shock waves are going to be enormous. The entire world will go down with our ship.

So what will the U.S. government do about its debt, you ask? It may do what Spain has done. Spain stole their citizens' retirement accounts and "invested" the money in government bonds that no one else would go near. If Spanish bonds collapse (and at this point I'd say the odds favor that outcome), the pensions of Spain's citizens are gone forever.[1]

Do you really believe that can't happen in America under a socialist like Obama? The administration and Obama's allies in Congress may already be considering it.[2] Just imagine the temptation to get their hands on that money as the financial position of the federal government gets worse—as Obama's supporters riot in the streets because their checks are late or reduced. Do you really believe the U.S. government won't try to seize our 401(k)s and other retirement accounts? Well, you don't have to wonder, because it's already in the works.

You already know the so-called Social Security trust fund that we've all paid into for years is nothing but a box with potentially worthless IOUs, the government seizing the cash as it's paid into the system and spending it on whatever it wants. Now, Bloomberg is reporting the U.S. Consumer Financial Protection Bureau is weighing whether to take a role "helping" Americans manage the $19.4 trillion we have in our privately held retirement accounts. The bureau director has said that "we're interested in terms of whether and what authority we have." Authority to do what exactly? Help themselves to our $19.4 trillion?[3]

You don't think they'll do it? Remember, Obama has made it clear he wants us to be more like Europe.[4] Well let's take a look at Europe—up close and personal. Then you'll see why I'm giving you the advice that follows.

You already know Spain has taken its citizens' retirement money. In Italy they're searching citizens for cash and precious metals on the way out of the country (even just for a family vacation). You can leave Italy, but you can't take your money with you. You see, your money is *their* money.[5]

Spain and Portugal also have imposed financial controls—your money is no longer yours to do with it as you wish.[6] In Greece they've started outright confiscation of assets.[7] In France, the masses have decided to tax any money you make above $1 million at 75 percent.[8] How long before our Socialist in Chief Obama (the lover of all things European) emulates the EU's mode of doing business?

The answer is…not long. Obviously Obama has already been inspired by the way business is done in the EU. Audits of small business are sky-rocketing under Obama.[9]

A bill has already been introduced in the Senate that would stop us from leaving the country (for business or vacation) if we are accused of owing $50,000 or more to the IRS. *Accused.*[10]

And our government now demands we pay an "exit tax" for the right to leave the country with our own money.[11]

America is already so broke and desperate that some delusional Democrats have pushed the idea of minting a trillion dollar coin out of thin air, with the full faith of the U.S. Treasury behind it.[12]

A trillion dollar coin backed by "the full faith" of our government? Are you kidding me? We laughed when Zimbabwe printed a trillion dollar bill…is a coin any different? Stop kidding yourself. Zimbabwe recently reported having $217 left in the bank.[13] Not bad, considering the United States is negative $100 trillion. We could use that $217.

"AN UNSECURED LIABILITY OF A BANKRUPT GOVERNMENT"

The definition of the U.S. dollar, according to famous speculator and free market advocate Doug Casey.[14]

We are out of options with this president at the helm. We are indebted *squared.* Obama's re-election guarantees more insane levels of spending, more printing of money, and more taxing.

Don't believe me? Just listen to Obama's inauguration speech. He delivered it smack dab in the middle of my writing this book. It was the most frightening speech I've ever heard. On January 21, 2013, Obama took the presidency to new lows. He went on the warpath. He was vicious and vindictive. Never in the annals of presidential history has any president taken an inaugural speech to such levels of partisanship and acrimony.

Obama promised in that inauguration speech to pursue the most radical agenda in American political history. He promised to grow government even bigger. He made it clear that "we the people" is based entirely on government and what government can do for us. He promised to increase spending and protect entitlements. He made it crystal clear that cutting one dollar from the budget is not part of his agenda. He made it clear that debt and deficits are not a big deal to him.

He called for "collective action." That word "collective" should remind us all of the core belief of communism—collective ownership. Apparently he's not interested in growing the economy and can't be bothered to worry about small things like creating jobs or dealing with the debt—other than making it clear he will drive the country even deeper into debt.[15]

Obama has gone so far as to attempt to silence anyone telling the truth about the Ponzi scheme that our bankrupt and insolvent government is running. And with the active support of Obama's propagandists in the mainstream media, the U.S. government is now enforcing mafia-style loyalty and silence.

Two weeks after S&P dared to break their silence and downgrade America's debt for the first time in history, S&P was suddenly under SEC and Justice Department investigation. In February they were indicted by the Justice Department.[16]

Then a smaller ratings agency, Egan-Jones, dared to downgrade the U.S. credit rating three times in eighteen months. Sure enough, the SEC brought action against them within two weeks of their second downgrade. Rather than face disaster, Egan-Jones settled the case. Result? They are now banned from rating U.S. government debt for the next eighteen months.[17]

The mafia…I mean the government…has effectively intimidated and silenced the only entities capable of telling us how bankrupt our government actually is.

But surely there must be some good news somewhere? Isn't there any hope we can grow our way out of this economic crisis? Not likely. Perhaps the smartest economist—certainly one of the most quoted—in the world, Nouriel Roubini, predicts years of gloom ahead. Roubini recently said at a global economic forum, "History suggests that whenever [there is] a crisis with too much private debt first and public debt second, you have a painful process of deleveraging." As he pointed out, "That would imply many years, up to a decade of low economic growth…that's not going to change, unfortunately in the next few years."[18]

Folks, with Obama in charge for four more years, there is no quick fix. We're not reversing course, we are doubling down. So the die is cast. Obama will be forced to go to Vegas to bet the entire U.S. budget on red.

Just kidding … sort of.

Unfortunately my little joke is not far from the truth. Instead Obama will gamble it all on the Fed, which is just like betting on red—*red ink, that is*. As I was writing this book, the Fed announced an expanded QE (quantitative easing) stimulus. That means printing more fake money to the tune of $85 billion per month. Yes, I said per MONTH.[19]

So now the Fed has committed to printing even more money to try to save the U.S. economy. This fake money will be used to buy billions per month in U.S. government and mortgage debt that no one else will buy, to prop up the stock market, and save the biggest companies from going under. Why? To convince naïve fools—a.k.a. Obama voters—that the economy is in recovery. Obama is trying to keep the confidence game going for just a little while longer. It's not working. Walmart executives called the first two months of 2013 a "total disaster" and reported the worst sales results in seven years. The Ponzi scheme is falling apart.[20]

Bubbles always burst. The three biggest bubbles in world history have now grown to the size of the Hindenburg. They are sovereign debt, fiat currency (paper money), and big government spending. And they will end like the Hindenburg—in a ball of flames.

History has repeatedly proven when bubbles like these implode, the end result is hyperinflation—the Weimar Germany nightmare with wheelbarrows full of money needed to purchase anything of value. At best we are facing a lost decade (or two) of misery, malaise, and steady decline. At worst we are looking at a record-setting, one-for-the-books financial tragedy that could make the Great Depression of 1929 look like a walk in the park.

So where's the light at the end of the tunnel? There is one, and it's as bright as a spotlight. It is your personal economic recovery. Your salvation from Obama is coming up in the following pages—a plan to survive, thrive, and prosper.

It's time to learn how to use **Y-PODS: Your Personal Obama Defense Shield.**

CHAPTER EIGHTEEN

YOUR PRECIOUS METALS DEFENSE SYSTEM

DID YOU KNOW?

- The dollar has lost 80 percent of its purchasing power since 1971
- Russia and India have recently bought up hundreds of tons of gold
- If you had bought $1 million of gold in 1913, it would be worth *over $87 million* today

Gold and other precious metal asset classes must be the cornerstone of your plan for Obama's next four years. They are the foundation of your survival. They are your Golden Rule. Your "Precious Metals Defense System" is a vital subset of your Y-PODS, your defense against the Obama Great Depression. Precious metals can help you protect your assets, survive, thrive, and prosper on anything Obama throws your way.

Here are the tools in Obama's bag of tricks—this is what you're facing:

1. Open-ended money printing by the Fed which will continue to decimate the U.S. dollar, and with it your savings and assets.

2. Interest rates kept artificially low for many years to come (because any rise in rates would increase the interest on the national debt and destroy the entire U.S. economy).

3. Massive taxes, spending, debt, and regulations—all coming together in a perfect storm that will devastate business and the whole U.S. economy.

4. Income redistribution that will destroy your assets and drain your retirement plan, all with the purpose of achieving equality and "fairness"—that is, shared misery—and leaving you dependent on government.

5. Running the country by crisis. Following the model of Cloward and Piven, Obama understands the way to destroy capitalism is to manufacture and promote crisis, in order to panic the American people into taking action without thinking. *Have you noticed?*

During his first term, and now even more so after his re-election, Obama is fomenting crisis. First it was the fiscal cliff crisis, then a national gun crisis, then the debt-ceiling crisis, then the sequestration crisis. It is clear that this pattern of crisis, panic, and the Obama solution (always bigger government and wealth redistribution) will continue for the rest of Obama's second term.

You need a bag of survival tools to get through the crises to come. That's what this book is for. Meet the first survival tool—for everyone with assets to protect, gold and precious metals are the answer. Each new crisis is a reason to add to your gold and precious metals holdings. Not just to make money, but even more importantly to protect yourself from economic disaster. If at the end of this chapter you are asking yourself how much money you can make in precious metals, you will have missed my entire point.

As my good friend and go-to guy for precious metals, Michael Checkan, co-founder and CEO of Asset Strategies International (www.asi4gold.com) says,[1] gold is insurance first, and investment only second. You should buy enough gold to protect your assets before you think about the possibility of making money from appreciation.

In other words, you may make a fortune investing in gold, but that's not your number one priority. Gold, first and foremost, protects what you already have. Nothing is more important than protecting what's yours. Making more money is a wonderful thing—it's icing on the cake. But first make sure you keep what you have. That's the job of gold—wealth protection and preservation.

Take a look at the charts on the next few pages. I don't know how better to demonstrate the critical economic life-or-death importance of using precious metals as your defense shield than to have you study these charts and follow me through the examples below.

Your financial survival through four more years of Obamageddon hinges upon understanding that you must first and foremost (above all else) preserve your purchasing power. Gold is the *only* form of money *proven* to do this consistently for over five millennia. That is why gold has to be the cornerstone of your financial survival plan.

THE INCREDIBLE SHRINKING DOLLAR

Over time, dollars (like any fiat currency not backed up by real assets) buy less and less as they are weakened by the fiscal irresponsibility of the government that backs them. Over time, the price of gold increases mainly because we measure or price it with weakening dollars.

Let's look at a few flabbergasting examples dating back to 1913, the year the Federal Reserve was created.

Since the Fed was created in 1913, the dollar has lost over *96 percent* of its purchasing power. But what does that mean in practice? Here are some numbers to blow your mind!

If you had $1 million in 1913, and you held onto that same sum till this day, it would only buy today what $40,000 purchased back in 1913—there's that 96 percent loss. However, if you took that same $1 million in 1913 and purchased gold at the going price of $18.93 per ounce back then, you would have purchased 52,826 ounces of gold.

If you held that gold today, when gold is now worth approximately $1,660 per ounce (as of the day I wrote this chapter), you would have **$87,691,160 worth of gold,** the equivalent of over $3.5 million in 1913 dollars.

Now let's fast forward to another critical date in United States gold history—August 15, 1971, the day Nixon officially "closed the gold window," making U.S. dollars no longer convertible to gold and finally ending the gold standard.

Note: This is the day the wheels fell off of our fiat dollar. From this day forward, accountability and fiscal responsibility ended. Look at the following chart showing the price of gold in U.S. dollars from 1900 to the present. They say a picture is worth a thousand words. This particular picture is worth trillions of dollars in deficit spending!

Just since the day that Nixon "closed the gold window," the dollar has lost over 80 percent of its purchasing power. Again, the numbers are eye-opening. Facts don't lie. If you had $1 million in 1971, and you held that same sum to this day, it would only buy today what $200,000 purchased back in 1971—there's that 80 percent loss of value. However, if in 1971 you took that same $1 million and purchased gold (at the going price, back then, of $35.00 per ounce), you would have purchased 28,571 ounces of gold.

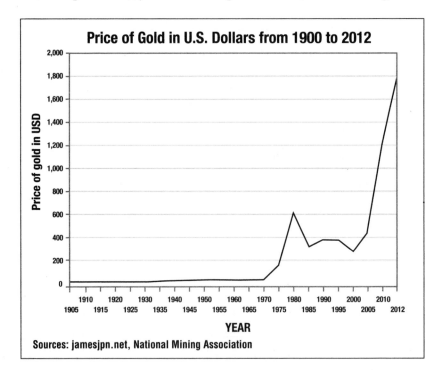

If you held that gold to this day (when gold sells for approximately $1,660 per ounce), you would have **$47,427,860 worth of gold** (the equivalent of just under $9.5 million in 1971 dollar terms).

Now, let's take a look at one last point in the past: the turn of this century, the year 2000, just before the current precious metals bull market began.

Since Y2K, the dollar has lost over 33.7 percent of its purchasing power. If you had $1 million in 2000, and you held that same sum to this day, today it would only buy what $663,000 purchased back in 2000—there's that 33.7 percent loss of value. However, if you took that same $1,000,000 in 2000 and purchased gold at the going price back then of $288.50 per ounce, you would have purchased 3,466 ounces of gold.

If you held that gold to this day (at approximately $1,660 per ounce), you would have **$5,753,560 worth of gold** (the equivalent of just under $2 million in year 2000 dollar terms).

One more remarkable fact. Warren Buffett is regarded as one of the greatest (and smartest) investors in the world. Yet since 2000, the price of gold has outperformed the price of Warren Buffett's publicly traded company Berkshire Hathaway stock by over 300 percent.[2]

Asset Strategies International is my trusted go-to company for all precious metals transactions. Its co-founder Michael Checkan has been in the gold and precious metals business for over thirty years. He has seen it all. Michael says,

> Over the years, I have encountered many people who have considered any investment in gold to be foolhardy. However, recently, I have been finding that more and more of them are beginning to change their minds. As their fears grow about the market and the future of the U.S. dollar, many are now seeing gold as a possible light at the end of the tunnel. . . .
>
> For the past three decades, ASI has been educating friends, family, clients, and anyone else who would listen, about gold. We viewed it as a long-term store of value that would protect their savings from inflation, the devaluation of the dollar, and a continuing increase in the money supply. Look at the results.

THE TWENTY-FIRST-CENTURY GOLD RUSH

Let's do precisely what Michael says—let's look at the remarkable results. Since the turn of the millennium, the price of gold has increased relative to *every currency in the world*. Specifically relative to the U.S. dollar, gold has increased in price from $288.50 per ounce in January of 2000 to $1,685.60 per ounce in January of 2013, or 484 percent.

But we are not really looking at a fundamental increase in the value of gold here. It is not gold that increases in value over time. Rather, it is paper currency that deflates in value, raising the price of gold.

INTRINSIC VALUE = ZERO

Two centuries ago, the famous French philosopher Voltaire said, "Paper money eventually returns to its intrinsic value of zero."

It's a simple matter of supply and demand. The supply of paper money is constantly increasing. Whenever the government needs more money to pay for entitlement promises, food stamps, free medical coverage, free public schools, free contraception, the interest on its massive debt—it simply resorts to printing more money. (Or, in modern times, creating it with a computer keyboard.) Quantitative Easing (QE) one through three is only the beginning of the currency devaluation. "QE Infinity" is likely. And the *more* of a currency there is, the *less* it is worth.

Is it any wonder that gold is such a promising investment? It cannot help but rise in value relative to every currency on the planet. Gold cannot be printed at will, so it is automatically more valuable. It will take more dollars, more Euros, more of every currency to buy the static supply of gold on the planet.

Just take a glance at the price of gold relative to these world currencies in the next two charts.

WHAT THE FED REALLY DOES

"We make money the old fashioned way. We print it."
—Art Rolnick, former chief economist of the Minneapolis Federal Reserve Bank

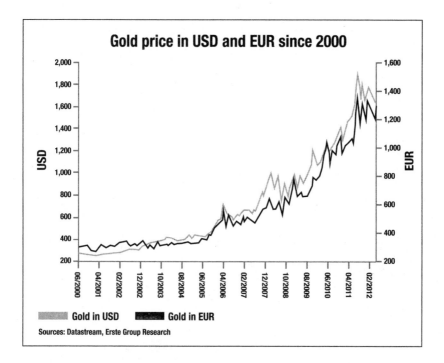

Gold price in USD and EUR since 2000

Gold in USD   Gold in EUR

Sources: Datastream, Erste Group Research

Over the last decade, this simple supply and demand configuration has not gone unnoticed by governments. India recently purchased over two hundred tons of gold from the International Monetary Fund. This is being seen as an attempt by the Indians to protect themselves against the falling value of the dollar.[3]

Russia has also been buying hundreds of tons of gold for its reserves.[4] Ironically, the one-time communist empire wants to protect itself against the continuing debasement and collapse of fiat currencies (paper money) in once great capitalist countries. Give them credit—the communists have learned a lesson from their own failures.

There have also been rumors that central banks in China, Dubai, and Japan are considering major commitments to gold and gold-mining companies. They all have the same concerns—a falling dollar turning into a falling knife, cutting the value of the U.S. debt they own.

For decades, we have seen a transfer of real wealth from the West to the East.

Annual gold performance since 2001 in various currencies (%)

	EUR	USD	GBP	AUD	CAD	YUAN	JPY	CHF	INR	MEAN
2001	8.10%	2.50%	5.40%	11.30%	8.80%	2.50%	17.40%	5.00%	5.80%	7.42%
2002	5.90%	24.70%	12.70%	13.50%	23.70%	24.80%	13.00%	3.90%	24.00%	16.24%
2003	-0.50%	19.60%	7.90%	-10.50%	-2.20%	19.50%	7.90%	7.00%	13.50%	6.91%
2004	-2.10%	5.20%	-2.00%	1.40%	-2.00%	5.20%	0.90%	-3.00%	0.90%	0.50%
2005	35.10%	18.20%	31.80%	25.60%	14.50%	15.20%	35.70%	36.20%	22.80%	26.12%
2006	10.20%	22.80%	7.80%	14.40%	22.80%	18.80%	24.00%	13.90%	20.50%	17.24%
2007	18.80%	31.40%	29.70%	18.10%	11.50%	22.90%	23.40%	22.10%	17.40%	21.70%
2008	11.00%	5.80%	43.70%	33.00%	31.10%	-1.00%	-14.00%	-0.30%	30.50%	15.53%
2009	20.50%	23.90%	12.10%	-3.60%	5.90%	24.00%	27.10%	20.30%	18.40%	16.51%
2010	39.20%	29.80%	36.30%	15.10%	24.30%	25.30%	13.90%	17.40%	25.30%	25.18%
2011	12.70%	10.20%	9.20%	8.80%	11.90%	3.30%	3.90%	10.20%	30.40%	11.18%
2012ytd	8.24%	3.15%	2.49%	1.89%	1.70%	3.53%	6.47%	5.93%	6.95%	4.48%
Mean	13.93%	16.44%	16.42%	10.75%	12.67%	13.67%	13.31%	11.55%	18.04%	14.09%
Median	10.60%	18.90%	10.65%	12.40%	11.70%	17.00%	13.45%	8.60%	19.45%	13.64%

Sources: James Turk, Goldmoney.com, Datastream, Erste Group Research

In 2007, China surpassed South Africa as the world's number one producer of gold. And there they have remained. With the final numbers in for 2012, China has produced more gold than any other nation on earth annually for the past six years. And in recent years, as a middle class has emerged in China, the government has opened up gold ownership to Chinese citizens (they were prohibited from owning gold in the past). As a result, China is on the verge of passing India as the world's number one gold consumer. Many believed this would happen in 2012, but surging consumption in India late in the year kept China in the number two spot.

The Chinese clearly have an affinity for real money. They are no longer happy seeing real negative returns on their U.S. dollar reserves. So they produce more gold than any other nation on earth. But interestingly, they do not export a single ounce of gold. China is a net importer of the yellow metal—and Chinese citizens are prohibited from taking gold out of China.[5]

What does all this mean? In the short term, gold produced by and imported by China is off the market. The Chinese thirst for gold will undoubtedly exhibit an upward pressure on the price of gold for years to come, as the rest of the world vies for a smaller supply of it to meet our needs.

In the longer run…I am reminded of an old saying— "He who has the gold makes the rules." Have you learned to speak Chinese yet?

As the dollar continues to weaken, we need to do what the Chinese, Russians, and Indians are doing. Buy gold.

Gold will increase in value as fiat currencies lose theirs. This is why countries and individuals alike are beginning to see the need for gold. When all else fails, gold does not.

A worldwide gold rush is underway. This one is fueled by need, not by greed. In this gold rush you don't need to load up your Conestoga wagon and head west. Just get your debit card ready and power up your laptop. It's easy to add the protection of gold to your portfolio. Just check out the "Digital Gold" section below for the latest in online gold buying and selling programs such as ASI Precious Metals Direct.

YOUR ASSET-INSURANCE POLICY

How well has gold done in the last thirteen years? Commodities, stocks, home prices, CD rates, and the U.S. 10-year note haven't even come close. It more than *tripled* the returns of the next-best asset class.

From January 2000 to January 2013, gold produced a thirteen-year return of 484 percent as measured in U.S. dollars. In that same thirteen-year period, investors earned 138 percent from bonds, 35 percent in real estate, and 25 percent in stocks.[6]

While investors were paying a pretty stiff penalty for holding these other, supposedly more traditional investments, gold did what it was supposed to do. It provided a strong and stable foundation as a store of wealth, as well as protection against the continued devaluation of the dollar.

Here's a record of gold's performance for the past thirteen years. You will see it made gains every single year. I defy you to find another popular asset class that can make that claim.

Gold Price Chart		
Year	Closing Price	% Increase
2000	$273.60	—
2001	$279.00	1.97%
2002	$348.20	24.80%
2003	$416.10	19.50%
2004	$438.40	5.36%
2005	$518.90	18.36%
2006	$638.00	22.95%
2007	$838.00	31.35%
2008	$889.00	6.09%
2009	$1,118.40	25.80%
2010	$1,413.00	26.34%
2011	$1,566.40	10.86%
2012	$1,675.20	6.95%

Now, keep in mind, past performance doesn't always predict future results. However, gold has consistently performed the same role—protecting assets from the ravages of inflation and fiat currency devaluation—for centuries. And we need that protection now! The dollar has already lost 96 percent of its value in the past century. And that was before we racked up obligations of about $100 trillion, including our huge national debt plus our even bigger unfunded liabilities.

Looking to the future, which is the more likely scenario? Will the U.S. government under Obama get spending and deficits under control and become a model of financial rectitude, restoring faith in the U.S. dollar? Or will they add more spending, more taxing, more debt, more dollar debasement? Our politicians live in a world reminiscent of the movie *Groundhog Day*—they make the same bad decisions day after day, year after year, while expecting different results. The protection against this madness is gold.

Author's Note: Like any other investment, gold and precious metals go up and down for a variety of reasons. My advice is to see any dips in gold and silver as buying opportunities. In this kind of economic environment, when gold goes down, it's a gift giving you the wonderful option to buy more at cheaper prices.

HOW TO BUY PRECIOUS METALS

The decision to buy gold and other precious metals has become an essential part of any protection and survival plan in this Obamageddon economy. There are a variety of ways to invest and to secure your position.

A POWERFUL COMPARISON

In January of 2000, three hypothetical young men, John, Sam, and Harold, each decided to invest $50,000 they received in an inheritance.

John had been told that the best place to put his funds was the stock market. So he decided to invest in five of the most widely held stocks. He purchased an equal dollar amount of AT&T, Coca-Cola, GE, Microsoft, and Merck shares. After thirteen years and more volatility than he ever dreamed he would encounter, his net gains came to 6.6 percent. His $50,000 was now $53,289.

Sam decided to diversify his portfolio by owning two classes of assets, both stocks and gold. Sam spent $35,000 on the same five stocks John purchased. But he also put 30 percent of his money, or $15,000, into gold bullion.

He purchased fifty-two ounces of gold in the form of Gold American Eagle bullion coins. In January 2000, gold was $288.50 per ounce. By January of 2013, bullion prices reached $1,685.60 per ounce. Since Sam had 52 ounces of gold, he saw the value of his bullion go from $15,000 to $72,600.

While his stocks gained 6.6 percent over that thirteen-year period, his gold went up 484 percent. Rather than a pathetic $3,289 gain, his account was up $74,902.30!

Our last investor, Harold, decided to make an even bigger bet on gold than Sam. He put 50 percent of his inheritance into the same five stocks John and Sam purchased. But he put the other 50 percent, or $25,000, into gold. After thirteen years, Harold's $25,000 investment in gold coins had increased 484 percent, to $121,600.

In other words, his diversified portfolio more than doubled in the thirteen-year span, from $50,000 to $172,644.50 . . . a gain of over 245 percent!

Precious metals used to be considered one "asset class." But because of the unique circumstances of our unsustainable debt, the incredibly reckless spending spree under Bush and Obama, and endless dollar printing by the Fed, combined with the economic crisis that is overwhelming the EU, our biggest trading partner, and Obama's re-election as president, I believe the definition of "asset classes" has to be modified.

Unique situations demand unique and creative solutions. Various precious metals options should now make up the foundation of your Obama Survival Plan. Each precious metal option should be considered an "asset class" of its own. This is your arsenal against Obama's massive nonstop debt creation and dollar devaluation.

There are many possible ways to invest in gold:

- physical gold (that is, bullion with a refined purity of at least 99.5 percent)
- certificates (warehouse receipts for physical bullion)
- gold mining stocks
- Exchange Traded Funds (ETFs)
- digital gold
- rare gold and silver coins
- futures
- options

PHYSICAL GOLD

Real gold bullion, in the form of bars, coins, and wafers, has been the only true currency for more than five thousand years. I'm talking about coins or bars that are sold based on their gold content, not for their rarity, age, or condition.

Many investors believe a one-ounce gold coin, such as the U.S. Gold Eagle, the South African Krugerrand, or the Canadian Maple Leaf, make the most sense to own. Other popular gold coins include the Austrian Philharmonic, the Australian Kangaroo, the Chinese Panda, and the American Buffalo. Each of these coins contains one troy ounce of gold, but because pure 99.99 percent gold is slightly soft, the Krugerrand and the Eagle are minted with an alloy, making them harder and more resistant to damage. These coins actually weigh more than one troy ounce, but the gold content is equal to that of the pure gold coins.

Bullion coins are all convenient and portable. Their weight, size, and purity are recognized worldwide, making them easy to purchase or sell virtually anywhere. There are other gold bullion products, including smaller fractional coins and gold bars ranging from 1/20th of a troy ounce to 400 troy ounces. Heavier bars can be purchased at lower premiums than one-ounce gold coins, however, they would most likely require you to assay them (prove their purity and weight) prior to selling them back. Bars bearing recognized hallmarks such as Johnson-Matthey, Credit Suisse, and PAMP Suisse are preferred.

For ease of storage and liquidity, you should probably start your gold collection with one-ounce coins. In times of need, it is easier to liquidate such a coin than a 400-ounce bar, or even a one-ounce bar.

When it comes to where to keep your gold, there are pros and cons to consider. Storing gold at home raises security issues. In the event our government begins confiscating gold again, as it did in 1933, having physical gold in the U.S. becomes problematic. Plus, gold is heavy, and transporting it can be difficult. Even so, in a financial crisis, I would much rather have a handful of gold coins than a suitcase full of paper currency.

CERTIFICATES

Purchasing physical gold through a credible certificate program is a way to own gold without the worry of storage or security. Certificates are warehouse receipts for physical gold stored in a third-party depository. Consider the Perth Mint Certificate Program (PMCP), which is offered by the Perth Mint in Western Australia. Our friends Michael and Rich Checkan at Asset Strategies International (www.asi4gold.com) are U.S. representatives for Perth Mint; in fact, they were instrumental in designing the original program.

Premiums for purchases through the PMCP are very low, just 2.25 percent over the spot price for unallocated gold, and 1.25 percent below the spot price when you sell. ("Unallocated" just means that your gold isn't in a separate cubbyhole with your name on it; you own it, but it's stored together with all the other gold bullion at the Mint.) The PMCP enables the investor to store gold, silver, and platinum offshore at the Perth Mint with a guarantee from the Australian government and no storage fees for unallocated metals. Your gold is insured by Lloyds of London at no additional charge to you. In the event of U.S. government confiscation, your physical gold is protected outside of the United States. You can even purchase Perth Mint Certificates for your IRA. Perth Mint Certificates can be a great way to own and store physical gold, knowing your holdings are insured, secure, and backed by a government with a Triple A rating.

GOLD MINING STOCKS

If you like volatility, have a speculative nature, and can handle dramatically fluctuating risks and rewards, then you might consider investing in the shares of mining companies. With mining stocks, you are betting as much on the management of a company as you are on the gold they discover or produce. The share price of a smaller mine can double, triple, or quadruple on news of a major discovery or the mine's purchase by a larger, better-capitalized mining company—even without the price of gold entering into the picture. An investment in a gold mining stock is *not* really an investment in gold itself. Rather, it is an equity, a stock security.

So while I urge caution toward gold mining stocks and generally suggest owning physical gold itself (see that track record above) over gold mining stocks, there is a unique opportunity developing today with regard to mining stocks. Gold mine stocks have plunged to ridiculous lows relative to the price of gold. Over the past decade or so, the ratio of the price of gold mining stocks to the price of gold itself has ranged from a high of 44 to a low of 14.[7] The higher the range, the better the opportunity to wager on mining stocks. As I write this chapter, the ratio is just below 40, near the high for the past decade. That means gold mining stocks are undervalued. Not just undervalued, but *very* undervalued.

But the news gets even better. Gold mining stocks are not just undervalued in relation to the price of gold. They are also undervalued in relation to the price of the S&P 500. This has resulted in not only great P/E (price to earnings) ratios, but very large dividend payouts. You don't get dividends when you buy gold bars or coins (or even the GLD ETF we'll be looking at in the moment). That makes gold mining stocks a historic bargain right now. You get to own gold and get paid a dividend in the bargain. "Quite a deal!" as my Yiddish grandfather used to say.

The price of gold rose nearly 7 percent in 2012, but the Philadelphia Gold & Silver Index (tracking the stocks of leading precious-metal mining companies), fell about 8 percent on concerns that mining costs and political risks are increasing. While gold has more than doubled over the past five years, the *Wall Street Journal* reported recently that the Philadelphia Gold & Silver Index has fallen to the lowest level on record (since tracking began in 1984). The *Journal*'s conclusion was that "the price of an ounce of gold today would buy more stock in gold-mining companies than at any point in a quarter century."[8]

The end result is that the largest gold mining stocks are cheap in comparison to both gold and the stock market. This is quite an unusual opportunity. If you believe gold will rise, then mining stocks, which are now historically undervalued compared to gold, have the potential to rise even further and faster than gold itself.

There's one more bit of good news about investing in mining stocks. A few years back, financial experts used to warn that successful investing in mining stocks required extensive homework and research into the individual mining companies. Today that has changed—and so has my advice. GDX, the Market Vectors Gold Miners ETF (Exchange Traded Fund), gives investors a diversified mix of worldwide gold mining stocks, including small-, mid-, and large-cap companies. (More about ETFs just below.) GDX has made investing in gold mining stocks as easy as Asset Strategies International has made buying and selling physical gold.

There is, however, one serious risk. It's the reason I will always tread carefully with mining stocks. It's the reason I'll always keep a much larger percentage of my assets in gold than in gold stocks. The risk is that gold mining stocks are still equities. If the stock market tanks because of bad economic news, all stocks—including even gold mining stocks—will be affected. With how I feel about this economy, I'd rather own real physical gold and silver than gold mining stocks, because of the risk of a serious stock market decline.

ETFS (EXCHANGE TRADED FUNDS)

Exchange traded funds are a relatively new financial option, but they have become a major driver of investment demand since their introduction over half a dozen years ago. The World Gold Council and State Street Global Advisors, the world's largest money manager, launched the first gold-backed ETF in 2004, under the symbol GLD.

Today, GLD holds close to $16 billion in gold in its various warehouses, and hundreds of millions of dollars' worth of its shares trade every day. Gold, silver, and platinum ETFs are available on most major exchanges worldwide. While they are an easy and convenient way of owning precious metals, as the owner of an ETF you simply cannot go to your broker and exchange your shares for equivalent ounces of gold. Plus, consider what would happen if trading were to stop, or if the government were to intervene, as it did in 1933. ETFs can be simple and convenient; but safety and security cannot be guaranteed (versus having gold bars or coins in your hand, or in your safe).

Still, because of the ease of investing in precious metals via ETFs, I have personally bought gold and silver over the past decade through GLD (SPDR Gold Shares ETF) and SLV (iShares Silver Trust ETF).

DIGITAL GOLD

Online gold purchases are the newest innovation in precious metal ownership. Purchasing gold through electronic platforms gives even the average investor access to the precious metals market twenty-four hours a day.

You can use a digital gold account as a precious metal investment, or utilize it to pay for goods and services, or both. This is how it works. Funds in a bullion-backed digital account are based on the market value of the price of gold. Your holdings are stored by weight (grams or ounces). This means it is easy to follow the price on the international bullion market.

Also, since you can use your digital account as a form of currency, you can have its value linked to a currency, such as the U.S. dollar, the Swiss franc, or the Euro. You can choose to pay for purchases in currency or in grams of gold.

The advantages include no set-up fees, no yearly membership fees, and backing by a reputable thirty-year leader in the field of precious metals.

Look for a trading platform like the one available through...you guessed it, our friends Michael and Rich Checkan of Asset Strategies International and their Precious Metals Direct program—www.asi4gold.com. You can trade gold here the same way you buy stocks at E*Trade. Just point and click your mouse on your desktop or laptop.

Here are the important features to bear in mind when you're selecting an electronic platform for digital gold holdings:

1. Ease of Use. It should be as easy to use from the comfort of your home as any online stock brokerage platform.
2. Safety. It should afford you equally high levels of security for your precious metals and for your personal information.
3. Storage Options. Cost-effective domestic *and* international storage options should be readily available.
4. Liquidity. The platform you choose should offer a ready two-way market for your precious metals. After all, what good is an investment you cannot sell when you need to?

SILVER AND OTHER PRECIOUS METALS

Of course, gold is not the only precious metal. But make no mistake, gold is the leader in the precious metals complex. The other precious metals—silver, platinum, and palladium—take their direction, up or down, from gold. Gold moves, and they follow in its wake.

Why? Simple. Gold is the very first thought of anyone considering precious metals. And rightly so. It is primarily a monetary metal and only secondarily an industrial metal. Silver, on the other hand, is primarily an industrial metal with a wide and growing array of applications and only secondarily a monetary metal. Platinum and palladium act like silver, but they're even more industrial...but gathering some steam as monetary metals in this bull market.

Many of the same considerations apply to all four precious metals. And once people start buying gold, they soon acquire enough of an allocation that diversification is prudent and wise. Though I can make a case for owning each individual precious metal on its own merits, for the purposes of Y-PODS (Your Personal Obama Defense Shield) diversification within the precious metals is enough of a reason to own them all. All four precious metals—gold, silver, platinum, and palladium—are real, intrinsically valuable assets that are rare and in demand. In other words, they're the type of things you should own when the supply of fiat currency (paper money backed only by the promises of worthless and reckless governments) is expanding out of control.

Just a few notes on silver in particular, which you'll naturally make the second precious metal to purchase once you've built a position in gold:

1. Silver is price-inelastic. There are very few pure silver mines in the world. Most silver is produced as a by-product of base metal mining. So if demand increases, you can't just go get more silver.

2. The silver market is much smaller than the gold market. So the same size investment in the silver market as in the gold market has a greater relative impact on the silver price than the gold price. As a result, we see the pendulum effect in silver prices. Silver starts to follow gold up in price and then it tends to outpace gold in appreciation. Then when gold reverses direction, silver will follow suit, tending to outpace gold to the downside as well. As a result we see wider price fluctuations (greater volatility) in the price of silver.

3. Silver is called "the Poor Man's Gold" for a reason. As gold climbs in price, folks who want to own precious metals will be a bit unnerved by the perceived "expensive" price of gold. The higher the price of gold goes, the more substitution buying of silver we see.

4. The best ways to buy silver is a mixture of SLV (the ETF) and the ownership of *physical* silver.

5. Pre-1965 "junk" silver U.S. coins are considered by many experts to be one of the best buys on account of several factors: A) cost-effectiveness B) the coins are easy to recognize C) old silver dimes and half dollars are one of the most divisible ways to own silver, and D) versatility—the coins are still U.S. legal tender.

You can consider precious metals as an investment. But that's not their most important role. Listen carefully to how I'm using the word "investment." An investment is when you plunk down your "risk money" with an eye toward making a profit.

But remember what Michael Checkan counseled? Gold and other precious metals are first and foremost about *asset protection—insurance against loss.* First you protect what's yours, then you take financial risks to create more. So separate from your investments, and in fact *before* you ever look to profit, I recommend protecting yourself and your assets with the wealth insurance of precious metals. Many experts suggest that 5 to 10 percent of your NET WORTH should be in gold—right off the top, as an insurance policy.

WHAT BUBBLE?

Gold has risen far and fast over the last thirteen years, and some so-called experts will tell you that we've come to the end of a bull market in precious metals. They'll even call the gold rise an "asset bubble."

They are wrong. The prerequisite for the end of a speculative bubble is broad participation by the general public. This happened in past stock bubbles, the huge real estate bubble of the last decade, and even the tulip bulb bubble in seventeenth-century Holland. But it has not happened in this decade-long gold rise.

Ask around. Speak to your friends, family, partners, and co-workers. Very few people own gold or silver, let alone gold mining stocks, or rare collectible coins. There is no "mania." The vast majority of Americans have never owned gold bars, or GLD, or SLV, or "junk silver" coins in their life.

Even more rare is the ownership of rare gold and silver coins. (Turn to the next chapter to learn about investing in rare coins.)

You'll be lucky to find one friend with assets in this category. But many of those same people in your circle of friends and associates own stocks, bonds, real estate, art, even baseball cards. What they don't own is gold or silver. This is not a bubble. Not even close.

The few friends you find that do own precious metals might have allocated 1 to 2 percent of their assets to precious metals. Or even less— maybe they've put away a few gold coins in their safety deposit box. That's their idea of an "investment" in precious metals. This is a pretty good indicator that there is no bubble in gold and silver.

Simply put, there is a long, long way for this bull market in gold to run. When you start hearing waitresses, taxi drivers, and your mailman bragging about their gold or silver investments, it will probably be time to get out of precious metals. But that's still a long way off. And based on the way the Fed is printing dollars by the trillion, and the size of our national debt, and how low interest rates are being artificially kept, this gold rally has only just begun.

ASSET ALLOCATION

Many investors believe precious metals fall under one blanket asset class. For all the reasons I've already explained in this book, and in this chapter, I believe all of that has changed with Obama's re-election.

Gold; silver and other precious metals; gold mining stocks; and rare gold and silver coins (more about them in the next chapter) are four different asset classes. In today's economic crisis they are all crucial elements of Y-PODS (Your Personal Obama Defense Shield). In years past investment advisors recommended 5 to 10 percent asset allocation in gold. In today's conditions, I believe that holding 30 to 40 percent of your assets in precious metals is warranted.

Within your PMDS (Precious Metals Defense System) I would recommend this allocation distribution:

First, set aside 10 percent off the top of all of your assets in gold for **Wealth Insurance.**

Then allocate 20 to 30 percent (or as much as you feel comfortable) of your total assets to the four asset classes of gold; silver and other precious metals; gold mining stocks; and rare gold and silver coins in the following distribution:

- 50 percent in gold
- 30 percent in silver
- 10 percent in gold mine stocks
- 5 percent in palladium and platinum
- 5 percent in rare gold and silver coins

As the dollar moves inevitably toward its true, intrinsic value (absolutely nothing) the rush to gold will continue and accelerate. As that happens, the price of the gold (or silver, or platinum) that you purchase will be less important than the fact that you own it. Many analysts believe the greatest transfer of wealth in history has already begun. It is

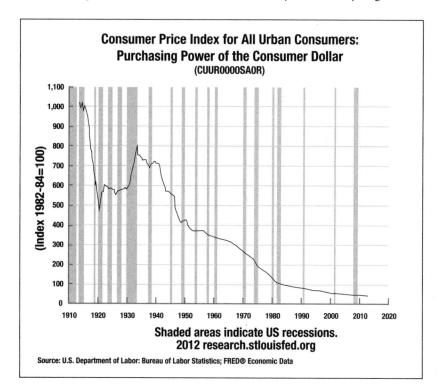

Consumer Price Index for All Urban Consumers: Purchasing Power of the Consumer Dollar
(CUUR0000SA0R)

Shaded areas indicate US recessions.
2012 research.stlouisfed.org

Source: U.S. Department of Labor: Bureau of Labor Statistics; FRED® Economic Data

the transfer of "money" from those whose assets are backed by debt to those whose wealth is backed by real resources, such as commodities.

Ninety-six percent of the U.S. dollar's purchasing power has evaporated since the Federal Reserve was created a century ago in 1913. Since the United States abandoned the gold standard in 1971, the U.S. dollar has lost more than 80 percent of its purchasing power. In just the past decade, the cost of the necessities that you have to buy every day has risen by more than 20 percent.[9] Those increases in the cost of food, clothing, medical insurance, and shelter mean our currency—the U.S. dollar—is losing purchasing power every day.

Yet consider this: as I point out in a later chapter, an ounce of gold today buys more oil than the long-term historical average. That's why precious metals play such a prominent role in this book—and why the PMDS (Precious Metals Defense System) is a crucial part of your Y-PODS. Precious metals are going to allow you to survive, thrive, and capitalize on the next four years of Obama.

Here are some resources for investing in precious metals:

- Purchase physical gold, silver, platinum or palladium through Asset Strategies International: www.asi4gold.com
- Trade precious metals through an online electronic platform (digital gold account) such as ASI Precious Metals Direct:www.asi4gold.com
- Purchase gold through a certificate program like the Perth Mint Certificate Program (PMCP) through Asset Strategies International: www.asi4gold.com
- Purchase rare coins (more on them in the next chapter!) through Rare Coin Portfolios: www.RareCoinPortfolios.com or www.RareGoldCoins.com

Or you can purchase shares in these Exchange Traded Funds:

- GLD (SPDR Gold ETF)

- IAU (iShares Gold Trust ETF)
- SGOL (Securities Swiss Gold Shares ETF)
- PHYS (Sprott Physical Gold Trust ETV)
- GDX (Market Vectors Gold Miners ETF)
- SLV (iShares Silver Trust)
- SIVR (Securities Physical Silver Shares ETF)
- PSLV (Sprott Physical Silver Trust)

And for riskier-minded investors:

- UGLD (VelocityShares 3x Long Gold ETN)
  *A 3x Leveraged Gold ETN
- USLV (3x Long Silver ETN)
  *A 3x Leveraged Silver ETN
- NUGT (Direxion Daily Gold Miners Bull 3x Shares ETF)
  *A 3x Leveraged Gold Miners ETF

CHAPTER NINETEEN

RARE COINS

DID YOU KNOW?

- The very rich—the 1 percent of the 1 percent, who have no financial troubles—are bidding up the prices of high-end collectibles such as art, cars, and rare coins
- In January 2013 a single rare coin sold for $10 million, for the first time
- A "Type 1" $20 Liberty dated 1850 brought $12,650 in October 2001 and then sold for $31,050 exactly ten years later

've put rare silver and gold coins in their own chapter because—though they should be an integral part of your Precious Metals Defense System, they have a unique niche market.

Notice that while 99.9 percent of the economic world struggles with rising debt and loses sleep over fiscal cliffs—you don't hear a peep out of the top 1 percent of the top 1 percent.

Why? Because they're not suffering. They sleep just fine knowing they will be rich no matter what. However, they are still investors.

Do you know what the richest of the rich are buying, and where they have created a bull market that runs contrary to everything you might think about the economy and the state of the world?

The really rich are buying exclusive high-end collectibles.

Business at the huge art show called Art Basel in Miami in December 2012 was booming.[1]

Antique car auctions in Arizona in January 2013 did the same—with vintage Ferraris worth $1–2 million a few years ago now fetching $8 million and up.[2]

And the biggest collectible opportunity of all right now might be in the most venerable of all collectibles—numismatics, popularly known as rare coins.

"Let me tell you why the right coins are poised for a big move in the years ahead," says Richard Spring of Rare Coin Portfolios (www.RareCoin-Portfolios.com).[3]

> There are thousands of paintings and hundreds of vintage automobiles (for example) that sell for more than a million dollars. Yet there are less than a hundred rare coins that sell for that amount or more. This applies throughout the market— where you can still find terrific coins with big upside for $10,000, while art or vintage cars in that range don't even make it to auction.
>
> In January 2013, we witnessed the sale of the first $10 mil- lion dollar coin (a 1794 Silver Dollar thought to be the first one ever minted by the United States Government) and I think it signals that some coins are going to catch up with the prices we're seeing for art and cars.[4]

Richard Spring says right now is a great time to be a coin buyer: "Stories like the sale of a $10M coin draw attention to the market. We're seeing growing interest in many areas of truly rare numismatics as a result."

"For the first time, we're seeing CEOs and Hedge Fund Managers tak-ing their personal money and putting it into coins," Richard told me. "There's a Texas billionaire who's invested over $300 million in the last few years. There's a Japanese asset manager who has placed more than $200 million in United States Proof Gold coins with his Asian clients. These sophisticated investors don't throw their money around without a purpose; they see a world full of fiat money and worthless paper and they're augmenting their gold and silver and precious metals holdings with historic tangible assets like rare coins."

The good news is that savvy investors don't need millions to invest: "There are still some coins in $10K price range with all the fundamentals for long term appreciation. Published auction records show lots of coins that were $10K ten years ago, now selling in the $60K range."

"A smart investor can acquire a fine coin portfolio for $50K–$100K and rest well at night knowing they've moved some of their liquid assets in a safe direction," Richard assures me.

"We have a growing number of investors who love American history and who fondly remember sifting through the change in Mom's purse or laying on Dad's night stand when they were kids, looking for that unique coin to add to their collection. Then they go off to school and their coin collection is forgotten. They raise a family and have other uses for their money. Then they wake up one day and they are Baby Boomers with money and nowhere to invest it. They become collectors again and it's those 50-somethings who are driving the coin market now and we think for many years to come."

Coins have significant advantages over most other historic tangible assets, says Spring.

First of all, numismatics is a huge hobby with millions of collectors who have driven the market for hundreds if not thousands of years (the first coin collectors were Romans).[5] In other words, coins are not a fad.

Second, coins are easily transportable and coin sales are a completely private transaction with no government reporting of any kind between buyer and seller.

Third, they are by far the most liquid of all artifacts, with ready buyers attending coin shows and bidding at auctions held somewhere in the country virtually every weekend—to say nothing of coins being one of the largest selling categories on eBay.[6]

There's lots more to the rare coin opportunity than I can share with you in this brief introduction.

To invest successfully, you need to find the right professional numismatist to deal with. Make sure they are members of the Professional Numismatists Guild (PNG), an organization that represents the finest numismatists and dealers.[7] Whatever you do, never buy coins blindly from someone selling over the phone. Don't buy "common" coins just because they are old, either.

Next, you need to have an area of interest on which to focus. You can't be all over the lot. If you love the earliest days of our Republic, you can actually own coins that might have passed through the hands of our Founding Fathers. If you're a Civil War buff, there are great coins from that Lincoln-Grant-Robert E. Lee era. If you're a "gold bug," what better way to add to your gold holdings than with historic gold coins from the days when gold fever drove miners to the hills of Georgia and North Carolina in the 1830s and then west to Sutter's Mill in 1849?

"The 1 percent of the 1 percent don't invest like you do," says Richard Spring. They're not worried about the economy on a day to day basis. They're not day-trading to pay the mortgage. They're not reading the *Wall Street Journal* for a tip. However, they do want to be remembered, and what better legacy than a historic collection of coins—telling the story of the American dream in the form of the coins that once were the driving engine of commerce!

In fact there is no collectibles market with more historic market and price information more readily available. A simple visit to PCGS.com will open the world of coins to you, and from there it's just a matter of building the right relationship with a professional who can guide you through the maze.

So, which coins are the right coins?

"The coins that have performed best in the past decade are major rarities," according to Richard Spring, "coins where there may be only five or ten known. They are coins with a good 'elevator speech.' Meaning you can explain them to your wife in less than a minute and she will say, 'Oh, I get it. It's OK that you just bought that.' They are great early coins, gold coins, coins with a strong collector base."

LOUIS ELIASBERG, RARE COIN INVESTOR

He was a Baltimore banker who set out to own the finest examples he could acquire—*of every single coin minted by the United States Government!* It took him thirty years. He invested around $300,000. After his death, his collection sold... *for more than thirty million dollars!* [8]

How would you have done if you had taken $100,000 ten years ago and bought rare coins? [9]

- A high grade $5 gold coin from 1805 sold for $18,975 at auction in 2002; the last auction of a coin of similar quality, in 2012, brought $63,250
- An 1883-O $10 "Gold Eagle" sold for $11,500 in 1999; it brought $20,700 a few years later; and then sold for $63,250 in 2011
- A "Type 1" $20 Liberty dated 1850 brought $12,650 in October 2001, and then sold for $31,050 exactly ten years later

These are not isolated examples. They reflect the overall strength of the market for true rarities, and that's what's attracting the billionaires.

Here's the good news: if you want to invest like "the 1 percent of the 1 percent," you don't have to be a billionaire. You can invest very intelligently and you don't have to be as rich as the richest investors. Some of the greatest coin collectors of all time didn't have the most money. They had the most passion. They got the best advice. And they held the coins they bought for a long time.

Here are some resources for investing in rare gold and silver coins:

- Richard Spring was the public relations strategist behind the launch of the Professional Coin Grading Service in 1987.

Since then he has advised more than fifty rare coin companies on their communications and marketing strategy. Richard Spring can be reached at www.RareCoinPortfolios.com or Richard@RareCoinPortfolios.com.

- Douglas Winter is a rare coin scholar and professional numismatist. He is the author of twelve books on rare coins and is widely acknowledged as the leading authority on early U.S. gold coins. Douglas Winter can be reached at www.RareGoldCoins.com or dwn@ont.com.

CHAPTER TWENTY

INVEST IN OIL, GAS, AND ENERGY

DID YOU KNOW?

- Oil has been the most efficient source of energy for the past 100 years, and it will remain so for the foreseeable future
- Historically, one ounce of gold has on average bought ten barrels of oil; if gold stays above $1,600 an ounce, oil would have to go up about $50 a barrel for us to return to that historical average
- The price of gas at the pump doubled in Obama's first term—when he needed to appear "moderate" to get elected; imagine how much it'll go up in his second term
- As incomes grow, there is a point of saturation at which the growth of energy consumption per capita slows and eventually stops. The EU countries and the U.S. have almost reached that point.[1] But as the rest of the world becomes more industrialized, they will need much more energy per capita

Granted, energy can come in many forms. But oil and natural gas have always been the least expensive form of BTUs on earth. The new so-called "green energy" sources such as solar, wind, and biofuels are considerably more expensive, and regardless of what President Obama says, it appears they will remain so for many years. (And so will nuclear energy.) The simple fact is that oil has been the most efficient source of energy for the last hundred years and it will remain so for any investment horizon less than twenty years.[2]

Worldwide oil production has been falling because of the rising costs of exploration, production, and delivery. In short, the low-hanging fruit has been picked, and I believe the price of future oil will continue to rise as the cheaper supplies are depleted.

The "peak oil" theory rests on the assumption that the worldwide supply of oil is finite and that what took 400 million years to produce as natural deposits can and will be consumed eventually as the worldwide population and the industrialization of world nations grows.

Granted, the technology of oil extraction has taken significant strides forward. But the normal tug-of-war between a diminishing supply, a growing worldwide demand, and the continued erosion of the purchasing power of the U.S. dollar means a future of ever higher oil and gas prices.

A PRESCIENT PREDICTION

In the 1950s, M. K. Hubbert used production data to show that growth in oil extraction had been slowing for decades and that it would eventually cease to grow in the mid 1970s. In 1974, the yearly increases in the yield of oil did in fact stop; since then, oil production has declined to approximately half the 1973–1974 peak.[3] To be specific, 10 million barrels per day (U.S. production) in 1974–76 now has fallen to 5 million barrels per day.[4]

One important factor to consider is the hundred-year historic average ratio of oil to gold: ten to one. That is, the average number of barrels of oil that could be purchased with one ounce of gold since the year 1912 has been approximately ten barrels. When oil was selling for $3–4 per barrel, gold was selling for $30–42 per ounce. When gold rose to $300 per ounce, oil was selling for $25–40 per barrel.[5] Today, oil is selling for about $100 per barrel. Gold prices of $1,600 to $1,700 would predict that oil prices should be at $160–170 already. The price of oil did, in fact, reach $140 in 2007–2008, but then it fell back below $100. The fall in the price of oil was undoubtedly due to the economic slowdown. The question is "How will this disparity from the normalized ratio of 10 resolve itself?" Are we to expect the price of gold to decline back to $1,000? Or is it more rational to expect oil to be selling for $150 to $200 per barrel soon?

The EIA (Energy Information Administration) is projecting the Brent crude oil spot price, which averaged $112 per barrel in 2012, will fall to an average of $109 per barrel in 2013 and $101 per barrel in 2014.[6] But I don't buy it. The EIA is, after all, an arm of the U.S. government, and therefore under pressure to issue projections that are favorable to the current powers that be. I believe it is much more likely that inflation and the continued decline in worldwide supplies will combine to move prices back into the $150–200 per barrel range.

Let me give you some really important advice when making any investment decision. Never forget that most sources of information are dependent, or at least invested, in a certain outcome or conclusion. Be aware of misinformation—the intentional dissemination of false information to support a certain view or to preserve (or change) the existing order. Always take into account the possible bias of your information source and the agenda of those behind it, and use your own common sense.

I have no doubt oil prices (and the value of oil-related stocks or ETFs) are headed higher…long term. But the price of oil and the value of equities dependent on it can and will fluctuate widely day to day, week to week, month to month, in the short term. Invest accordingly.

That was my disclaimer. Now let me tell you what I really think—based on common sense.

I'm a simple blue-collar S.O.B. (son of a butcher). Not a fancy-schmancy blue-blood economist or hedge fund manager. Here is the way I look at investing in oil, gas, and energy. Gas prices at the pump have doubled in only four years under Obama. That was in Obama's first term (when he needed to be "moderate" to get re-elected). Now, in his second term, we'll see and experience the REAL Obama—the radical "climate change"-obsessed, environmentalist Obama. The Obama that wants us all to live in equality (that is, shared misery). The Obama who wants to emulate Europe in all things—where gas is $8 per gallon (and higher) and where everyone drives tiny, ugly cars. My common sense tells me things will get much worse during Obama's second term.

As if on cue, the retail price of gas in the United States rose for thirty-four days in a row as I was finishing this book.[7] The price of a gallon of gas in February 2013 hit the all-time high for winter prices.[8]

Over the next four years Obama's EPA will try to deal the final fatal blow to the coal industry. Obama will limit oil drilling even more dramatically than in his first term. His EPA will never allow new refineries to be built. He has already rejected the Keystone Pipeline. He will continue to block the building of the Yucca Mountain nuclear waste repository in Nevada—thereby ensuring the nuclear industry cannot grow (because there is nowhere to store the waste). And of course, as he announced in his inauguration speech and State of the Union speech, he will double down on "green energy," a complete ineffective failure everywhere in the world it has been tried. It's madness, perpetrated by a man apparently intent on destroying our economy, the foundation of which is fossil fuel. The result of all of this is that you can bet on one thing: gas prices at the pump will rise much higher in the next four years.

So here's a simple bit of advice on how to survive, thrive, and prosper in the Obama era. Every time you fill up your tank you'll wince from the pain of seeing gas prices ever higher—*if* you don't own oil, gas, and energy stocks. Each time you fill up your gas tank, or pay your heating bill, you'll be sick to your stomach. But if you invest in oil, gas, and energy stocks, each time the price of energy rises, you'll profit. Each time you fill up your tank, you'll smile. Each time you hear the price of a barrel of oil went up, you'll dance a jig. For every $20 extra you spend at the gas station, you'll make $100 or $1,000 or $100,000 in your stock portfolio. That's a pretty good trade!

Like I keep saying—we are about to experience the greatest wealth transfer in world history (much like the last one, in 1929). Your job is to get on the right side to capitalize on this tragic mess that Obama is creating—and prosper despite the Obama Great Depression. I believe investments in gold, silver, mining stocks, rare gold and silver coins, and oil/energy puts you on the right side. These investments allow you to protect your current assets and empower you to earn a profit on the insanity that is Obama's socialist plan.

• • •

Author's note on natural gas: We all keep hearing about natural gas from fracking as the new energy source to replace oil. Fat chance. That may in fact happen twenty-five to fifty years from now, when supplies of oil have dwindled to nothing, or near nothing. In other words, it may happen out of need, but not out of choice. The reality is that natural gas is plentiful right here in America right now, yet the price of oil is still skyrocketing as I write this book. Why?

First, natural gas is obviously no threat to oil. It may be plentiful, but it's a massive money loser. Natural gas companies are losing money every single quarter, and that will not change any time soon. Companies are now turning away from natural gas and back to oil for profit.[9]

Second, natural gas has an efficiency problem. The number one use of oil is in our cars. To use natural gas in autos, natural gas must be compressed into liquefied natural gas (to approach the BTU capacity of gasoline). But the energy it takes to compress it makes it more expensive.

Third, natural gas also requires a specially adapted engine for your car and specially built refueling stations. Think of the logistical problems involved in replacing the already established nationwide infrastructure of gas stations. What seems cheap is actually a huge, high-cost undertaking that would require massive amounts of new investment.[10]

Fourth, natural gas has a volatility issue that makes it problematic as a replacement for gas in our cars. Liquefied natural gas is much more combustible than oil. Could a more explosive fuel make auto accidents much more deadly? When an auto accident causes a gas leak from your car, the gasoline flows out and evaporates unless flames are present. But liquefied natural gas can become a flamethrower. A natural gas explosion leveled an entire block in Kansas City while I was busy writing this book. Want that inside your car?[11]

Fifth, one of the main motivations behind the desperate search for an alternative to oil and gasoline is the idea of global warming. Natural gas burns cleaner than oil, producing 70 percent less carbon emissions. Yet the case for man-made global warming is (excuse the pun) evaporating. Even the ultimate global warming alarmist organization, the IPCC (Intergovernmental Panel on Climate Change) now admits it may very well be the sun that has the greatest impact upon climate change.[12]

Finally, the most important reason for the massive undertaking of converting to an alternative fuel such as natural gas is that oil is a finite natural resource—it is going to run out one day. That is the whole point of this chapter. If the world's supply of oil is limited, that makes it valuable. The price will therefore continue to rise. And in order to profit, you should own it.

Ironically, the best use of natural gas may be as an energy source to extract oil from the ground. It is used to power the equipment that produces the much more precious commodity—oil. However, natural gas is a cheaper energy source than coal and could replace coal in electricity production in the future. Natural gas makes sense for non-mobile uses, such as in the production of electricity, rather than in cars and trucks, where weight is a major design criterion. The storage devices for energy for non-mobile uses can be much heavier, safer, more protected; fixed supply lines can be built. Natural gas could also become "the next big thing" for export to Europe and Asia, where the cost of energy is far higher.

Here are some resources for investing in energy, gas, and oil companies:

- DIG (ProShares Ultra Oil & Gas ETF)
- XES (SPDR® S&P® Oil & Gas Equipment & Services ETF)
- CHIE (Global X China Energy ETF) is designed to track the performance of the energy sector in China
- RIG (Transocean Ltd) provides offshore contract drilling services for oil and gas wells worldwide
- FCX (Freeport-McMoRan Copper & Gold, Inc.) is a global natural resource company, combining mining of copper and gold with oil and gas exploration

CHAPTER TWENTY-ONE

INVEST IN FARMLAND AND AGRICULTURE

DID YOU KNOW?

- The average American consumes 250 pounds of meat a year; the average Chinese, just 100; and the average Indian, only 10—they have a lot of catching up to do
- Grain consumption has exceeded grain production in seven of the last eight years
- According to Monsanto, we'll need to produce more food, total, in the next fifty years than in the last *10,000* years

've told you about precious metals, gold and silver, oil and gas. Now let me tell you about another precious commodity: FARMLAND.

There are two primary reasons farmland is such a valuable commodity:

First, food demand worldwide will continue to increase. Emerging economies such as India, China, and Brazil are seeing a surge in their middle class. One of the first things people do as they move beyond a subsistence level is improve their diet, especially their intake of meat. We are looking at huge numbers of people whose current meat consumption is minuscule compared to Americans'. *Time* magazine estimates the average American consumes about 250 pounds of meat a year while the average

Chinese consumes about a hundred pounds and the average Indian less than ten pounds.[1] Given the demographics of the developing world, we can expect demand for meat to explode.

It is estimated that half of U.S. corn production is currently used for animal feed already[2]—foreshadowing a huge and rapid growth in the demand for grain as ever more meat is consumed in these emerging countries. But this is just the tip of the iceberg. Monsanto says grain consumption has already exceeded total production seven out of the last eight years; the company predicts that the world's farmers will need to produce more food in the next fifty years, total, than they have produced over the last 10,000 years.[3]

Note that I have not even mentioned the use of corn in ethanol production. Even though a commonsense analysis would suggest this is a poor use of a food crop, it appears that ethanol production is here to stay and undoubtedly increase.

Second, not only is demand for agricultural products increasing with no slowdown in sight—thus creating higher prices—but also technology is increasing yields. The fact is, during the past thirty years, genetically engineered seeds and improved farming techniques have dramatically increased yields per acre. There is no reason to believe this trend will slow.

This "double bonus" of higher prices for food crops and more yield per acre has boosted farm profits and made farm land significantly more valuable over the past few years. Meanwhile, Money Morning reports that the average price for farmland has been rising since 1980 and now exceeds $2,000 an acre. Prices for prime land in some parts of the country have gone as high as $6,000 an acre.[4] Given that both demand and technology appear to be accelerating and that the quantity of farmland is relatively fixed, it is only common sense that the price of farmland can be expected to continue to rise as well.

Here are a few other things to consider:

- Worldwide, water is becoming an ever more valuable, and limited, resource—ensuring that land that is productive without irrigation will remain a scarce, highly desirable commodity. As the saying goes, "They're not making any more of it."

- Timing is everything in life—and this would may be a unique time to invest. Farmland is typically sold only after the farmer retires or dies, and only if there isn't a son or daughter to take over the family business. The average farmer in the United States today is nearing sixty years of age and has a smaller family than prior generations.[5] USDA studies estimate that one-third of farmland owners have less than fifteen years to live.[6] The aging population of farmers may represent a window of opportunity for smart investors.

- Managing farmland is straightforward. Flat-fee, cash rents are prevalent, and every locality has farm management companies who, for a fee, will collect your rents and oversee your property—or, for the more adventurous owner, negotiate crop-sharing arrangements with local farmers. Also, unlike a rental home where roofs can leak and plumbing can back up, there is little ongoing maintenance or upkeep on farmland.

- Cash-on-cash returns on farmland are in the 4–5 percent per year range. This kind of return (plus the possibility of significant appreciation and historically low downside risk) makes farmland a solid investment—like owning a dividend-paying stock, except that the value of the land is not subject to the volatility of the stock market.

- Farmland is an opportunity to invest in a commodity very different from and historically less volatile than stocks, bonds, and energy-related commodities. However, for those of you who like the idea of farmland as an investment but do not have the capital base or the desire to own farmland itself, consider some of the limited partnerships or stock ETFs (Exchange Traded Funds) that invest in grain commodities, agriculture, and/or farmland.

- If you are a hunter or outdoorsman, owning farmland also offers non-monetary benefits. In the right location pheasant, quail, turkey, and even deer hunting can be done on your own property. Or you may want to keep horses or graze cattle, sheep, or goats on a portion of the property. There is something satisfying and "all-American" about owning a farm—even if it is just a weekend get-away that returns you a profit (both financial and mental).

Billionaire investment guru Jim Rogers pointed out recently that the best investment opportunities are where shortages are developing. How good is Rogers at predictions? He co-founded the Quantum Fund in the 1970s and in ten years posted returns of 4,200 percent before retiring at age thirty-seven. In 1999 he recommended gold at $252 and silver at $4.[7] Now Rogers says we are entering a period similar to the 1970s, when the world's economies were in crisis, inflation raged, and central banks printed far too much money. Result? Commodities boomed. Between the growing demand for food and the excess money printing, Rogers expects a similar boom in agriculture and commodities. Rogers told the *Financial Review* of Australia, "It's the farmers, the producers who are going to be in the captain's seat when the prices go through the roof."[8]

WORDS OF WISDOM

A friend of mine, an investor in farmland, is always telling me,

"Wayne, you can buy all the gold, silver, and precious metals you want. But you can't eat them. Nor can you eat stocks or traditional real estate. I hope the economy never gets so bad that all those other investments are worthless. But under Obama we are headed for some very bad times. So if the whole economy goes to hell, you're welcome to pull up your double wide on my farm and park it right next to mine. We'll all eat real well!"

Here are some resources for investing in agriculture:

- HAP (Market Vectors RVE Hard Assets Prod ETF)
- MOO (Market Vectors Global Agribusiness ETF)
- DBA (PowerShares DB Agriculture)

CHAPTER TWENTY-TWO

SHORT THE GOVERNMENT BOND PONZI SCHEME

DID YOU KNOW?

- Cook County, Illinois, owes *$108 billion*, mostly in unfunded pensions
- The population of Baltimore has dropped from 950,000 to 615,000 and the city has 16,000 vacant properties
- The Clark County, Nevada, public school teachers' health trust will run out of money to pay claims in *60–90 days*

I f you've read this far, you understand the magnitude of our debt and dysfunction. Our government is perpetrating the biggest Ponzi scheme in world history—the government debt bubble. One county alone (Cook County, Illinois, the location of Obama's home town, Chicago) owes a staggering, unimaginable $108 billion, most of it for unfunded government employee pensions.[1]

Chicago stands at the head of the class (of dunces). But many other cities are in almost as terrible shape.

The Pew Center on the States surveyed the biggest cities in all fifty states. They found that many U.S. cities look just like Baltimore, Detroit, and Chicago. The study found that U.S. cities need hundreds of billions to

JUST ANOTHER AMERICAN CITY ON THE VERGE OF BANKRUPTCY

As if on cue, just as I was finishing up this book, it was revealed that the city of Baltimore is on the road to financial ruin. How will they solve their massive debt and budget shortfalls? They already have the highest property taxes in Maryland and the highest income taxes allowed by state law. It's no wonder their population has dropped from 950,000 to 615,000. The city has 16,000 vacant properties. Twenty-two percent of the population lives in poverty. Who will pay for all of this?[2]

pay their retiree pension and healthcare promises. Guess what? That was in 2009, ancient news.[3] By now you can bet those numbers are far larger.

Now add in state pension shortfalls. And then of course the biggest Ponzi scheme of all is our federal government, with $16 trillion in debt, plus unfunded obligations of another $90 to $100 trillion. But at least the federal government can just print more money to pay its debts. Cities and states don't have that luxury. So what are they going to do?

My conclusion is that the jig is up—or very soon will be. As Bernie Madoff found out, the Ponzi scheme ends when the incoming monies slow. Suddenly there isn't enough new money to pay the old obligations, the fraud is out in the open, and collapse is imminent.

This is exactly what is now happening with unsustainable pension and healthcare obligations to government employees. The days of paying $100,000, $150,000, and even $200,000 annual pensions for life are quickly coming to an end…a tragic end. Local and state governments can't even afford the medical bills (see the story below about Las Vegas teachers), let alone the pensions. Why? Because, taxpayers are out of money.

Too many Americans are unemployed and unable to pay anything into the system. Too many Americans (and illegal immigrants) are on welfare, food stamps, disability, and a hundred other entitlement programs, taking too much out of the system. And, too many businesses are struggling or going out of business altogether—and there goes the golden goose that paid the taxes (that funded everything else). What this means in simple language is…the amount of money coming in to feed the Ponzi scheme has slowed to a trickle. Therefore the jig is up.

Here's a great example. In Clark County, Nevada, (home to Las Vegas) it was just reported that the public school teachers' health trust is going bankrupt. As in kaput, empty, out of money. And fast. The teachers' health trust is in such dire straits, it has only sixty to ninety days before it runs out of money. This was never disclosed until there were only days to go before disaster.[4]

The 17,000 teachers of the Clark County Education Association, the fifth-largest public school system in America, are up the proverbial creek without a paddle. The trust has an annual revenue stream of $148 million, yet that's not nearly enough to pay for the cost of claims.

What does this failure of the Las Vegas teachers' health fund tell you? This isn't an anomaly. This is happening all over America. The rest of the government employee unions just haven't yet disclosed how dire their situation is…*yet*. How do I know this? Because there isn't enough money to pay for the obscene health and retirement benefits in *any* school district. There are 22 million government employees in America—all of them have been promised unsustainable salaries, pensions, and benefits. This gigantic bubble is about to crash and burn. This is a ticking time bomb about to blow up in taxpayers' faces across the country.

On the federal level and across the globe, the Ponzi scheme has been aided by corrupt deals between countries and banks. Bernie Madoff could not have figured out a more brilliant scam. Countries and their central banks (including the Fed) bailed out the banks by buying bad loans and keeping interest rates artificially low—thereby fixing the game so banks couldn't lose.[5] Even a complete idiot (see bank CEOs) couldn't help but make billions by borrowing from the government at zero interest rates. Then to repay the favor, banks used the bailout money and the massive gains from government interest rate manipulation to buy government bonds.[6] It's just one big incestuous family of frauds and scammers.

The losers are always the taxpayers. We are on the hook for the debt and obligations created by this scam. Our children and grandchildren will be paying the interest on the debt a hundred years from now. Let me say it again—this is a Bernie Madoff-like Ponzi scheme. The only difference is that in this case no one will be prosecuted because all the prosecutors work for the government (and are looking forward to a government pension and free healthcare for life).

You probably didn't know that banks own much of the government debt. To complete the scam, government makes sure banks take almost no risk with their bond purchases, because no matter how broke the government is, they just raise taxes or run the printing presses to make sure the banks get paid every cent they are owed. This is what keeps the scam going.

How do you profit on this Ponzi scheme? Simple. First bet against U.S. Treasuries. Second, bet against Municipal Bond Funds. In other words, **sell short.** Basically you are betting on the potential defaults of hundreds of cities, towns, and counties (and eventually states, once Congress is forced to change the law to allow states to declare bankruptcy). It's only a matter of time before this whole gigantic Ponzi scheme implodes.

My good friend Thomas Noon (you'll be hearing directly from him later in the book) is a real estate consultant for one of the biggest New York hedge funds, with a knack for making good calls, early. In late 2004 he was already calling for a cessation of land inventory purchases at one of the country's largest homebuilders. When Thomas Noon talks—*I listen.*

Like me, Noon believes it's time to short government bonds—although he is very particular about which specific bonds to sell short. Noon warns that bonds that are collateralized by hard assets such as real estate should not be shorted at this time.

Noon says, "The bonds most prone to default are those issued by—and guaranteed by—the cities and states themselves (i.e., city development or redevelopment projects), where the sole source of repayment is the city or county or state revenues, again, especially those cities, counties, or states that have the highest ratio of debt to revenue base."

Moody's Investors Service rates all the states. Those in the worst shape (based on combined debt and unfunded pension liabilities) are Illinois, Connecticut, New Jersey, Hawaii, New Mexico, Mississippi, Kentucky, Rhode Island, Massachusetts, California, West Virginia, and Maryland.[7]

Meredith Whitney, an extremely sharp investment advisor, made this same prediction back in 2010.[8] She predicted 50 to 100 cities, towns, and counties would have significant municipal bond defaults. She wasn't wrong, she was just *early*. She simply misjudged the power of these municipalities to raise taxes to keep the Ponzi scheme alive. Desperate politicians can merely raise sales taxes, property taxes, and other fees to ridiculous levels (even if they destroy their own taxpayers in the process). Or, if they are really devious, they can float new bonds to pay off the principal and interest due on earlier bonds. This is the public version of the Ponzi scheme. If Bernie Madoff had had the power to tax, his scheme might have *never* ended.

The federal government has been engaged in this ritual for decades, increasing debt to the sky to pay the interest and principal of prior debts. Ponzi went to jail for his version of this plan, but any such scheme proposed by government is not only legal, but condoned by a populace that wants the scheme to go on forever (so long as their checks keep coming). Politicians around the world are willing to pass on a simmering disaster to the next generation, as long as they can retire from office without the final epic collapse on their watch. This fraud even has its own special phrase in politics; it is called "kicking the can down the road."

But government's ability to kick the can down the road by raising taxes ends if there is an economic collapse, or a nasty long-term decline, and taxpayers are finally out of money. It ends when so-called "bond vigilantes" wake up and realize the Ponzi scheme is coming to an end and start demanding much higher interest rates in return for the risk of buying bonds. That's when the whole fraud blows up.

It quickly becomes a vicious circle, and we're in it now. The worse the economy gets, the fewer bond buyers (a.k.a. suckers) remain. The higher the interest they demand, the more impossible it is for the government to pay the interest without starving other government spending. The people riot in the streets. Anarchy ensues. Just ask the Greeks.[9] The sad reality is…America is Greece. We're just a thousand times bigger and a little bit behind. But, don't doubt for a minute that our day of reckoning is coming.

On a federal level this descent toward disaster started even before Obama. He just put it on steroids. The Fed is now buying most of our

U.S. Treasury Bonds.[10] Even the Chinese have gotten worried about our "debt addiction."[11] Who would be foolish enough to bet on the U.S.A.—at least if they understood the Obama plan? Banks are still buying government bonds, but many financial experts believe they are under pressure from the government to continue playing this game of musical chairs—because the only way out of this debt crisis is to keep printing fake money to pay the bills, in other words, to inflate, inflate, inflate, so we can pay back the government debt with drastically cheaper dollars.[12] The result of this kind of plan is either an outright collapse of the financial system—or bond investors will be forced into accepting zero or negative returns.

Famous billionaire investor Jim Rogers said in a recent interview with Reuters that he believes the time is close for the U.S. bond bubble to pop.[13] He believes the collapse will come around 2014 and was only postponed until then by a presidential election year and trillions of dollars printed by the Fed to get Obama re-elected. Obama's ego is so inflated, and he has so little regard for America and its people, that he will keep the printing presses and mainstream media propaganda machine running—even if that means that the collapse will be that much bigger when it finally comes.

The thing to remember is that when you sell government bonds short you are not betting on a *complete* collapse of any individual muni bond fund or the entire bond market. You are simply betting on more people being concerned about a partial default and therefore selling, overwhelming the demand from new buyers. Thus the market price falls, perhaps to 50–70 cents on the dollar. This will be driven by new-money investors demanding higher interest rate yields.

A short position could rise in value 30–60 percent and the holder of the short position could buy back at a much lower price. That's a more realistic scenario than complete default—which is much less likely when the backer of the bond is a government agency that can simply raise taxes—or be forced by a court to pay back the borrowed money. The more likely "partial default" scenario could mean, for example, that government unilaterally cancels interest payments for a year so they can pay their pensions and employee healthcare costs. This abatement of interest payments would shock the bondholders, creating a rush to get out.

It's coming. The signs are everywhere. It can only be stopped with a sound money policy (a return to the gold standard would be the ideal) and sane government policy (lower taxes, drastic reduction in spending, balanced budgets). Yet Obama won't let it happen.

Unfortunately, it's probably out of your power to put the United States on the path to sound monetary and budgetary policy in the next four years. Your job is to understand what is happening and use that knowledge to protect yourself, your assets, and your family. Then become a realist and follow the advice in this book to protect your assets, in order to survive, thrive, and prosper amidst the self-destructive and suicidal Obama policies.

Learn about how to short municipal bonds:

John Carney explains the difficulties, risks, and rewards of shorting municipal bonds in a CNBC article you can find at this link: http://www.cnbc.com/id/41513958/How_to_Profit_From_a_Muni_Bond_Crisis[14]

Municipal bonds themselves are difficult or impossible to sell short, but you can short the insurers of these bonds (although many of them are now out of business due to the mortgage crisis) or you can directly short the Muni Bond ETFs (even those of individual states).

Here are some resources for shorting U.S. Treasuries:

- TBF (ProShares Short 20+ Year Treasury ETF)
- TBX (ProShares Short 7–10 Year Treasury ETF)
- DTYS (iPath US Treasury 10-year Bear ETN)
- TYO (Direxion Daily 10-Year Treasury Bear 3x Shares ETF)
- TBZ (ProShares UltraShort 3–7 Year Treasury ETF)

For the ultra brave financial risk-taker:

- TBT (ProShares UltraShort 20+ Year Treasury ETF)
- TMV (Direxion Daily 30-Year Treasury Bear 3x Shares ETF)

CHAPTER TWENTY-THREE

INVEST IN MEDICAL REAL ESTATE

DID YOU KNOW?
- Obamacare will add at least 30 million people to the health-care system
- Seventy-nine million baby boomers are beginning to retire
- Experts estimate that 60 million square feet of medical real estate will be developed across America

In the military they say, "Wait for the whites of their eyes…wait…wait …wait…shoot NOW!" This is my real estate philosophy. Be patient, buy gold and silver, and then more gold and silver…throw in some gold mining stocks and rare gold and silver coins. Then wait some more. Add in a little oil, gas, energy, and agriculture investment. Sell short government bonds. Exercise every option in your Y-PODS artillery. Then wait some more.

Once things get *really* bad over the next four years of Obama, after an economic collapse that makes 2008 look like child's play, only *then* will you find the greatest real estate bargains of all time. At that point a safety deposit box filled with gold will allow you to buy entire city blocks (just don't buy in Detroit). So, my real estate advice is to be patient and wait for the right moment. It's coming. Obama's re-election assured that.

In the meantime, if you have money for commercial real estate properties, there is one very specific kind of real estate I would be looking at right now: *Medical Real Estate.*

There are two reasons. First, Obamacare is here to stay. Like Social Security, Medicare, and Medicaid, this multi-trillion dollar government program is becoming entrenched. This boondoggle will inject its tentacles into every aspect of our lives. It's a disaster for the economy, but it doesn't have to be a disaster for your *personal* economy.

Just like my advice of investing in oil, gas, and energy so that every time the price of gas goes up at the pump, you'll be smiling because you're actually making money…here is a chance to profit from Obamacare. When the government is spending and wasting trillions, there is money to be made. *Lots of it.*

Thirty million people (or more) have just been added to the healthcare system.[1] It's all paid for by government, so you know no one cares how high the bill will go. The result will be a medical boom.

Medical real estate will make someone a fortune—it might as well be you. From medical office buildings…to long-term care facilities (nursing homes)…to rehab centers…to physical therapy centers…they are all about to expand and multiply like rabbits.

Second, we are an aging nation. Seventy-nine million baby boomers are headed into retirement.[2] They'll experience aches and pains, diabetes, arthritis, allergies, cancer, strokes, and heart disease. They'll need medical care, drugs, and rehab. And the tab is now covered by government, so the costs will skyrocket.

WHERE IT'S AT

Wayne Gretsky said, "I skate to where the puck is going to be." Medical real estate is where it's going to be.

This massive influx of new patients will create demand for more of everything from doctor's offices to long-term care facilities. Experts estimate 60 million square feet of medical real estate will be developed nationwide.[3]

This is a good time to get ahead of the curve. The smartest minds in business and finance are either buying or building medical real estate and/or investing in healthcare, biotech, and pharmaceutical ETFs.

Like it, or not, Obama has ensured the future of America is never-ending healthcare spending to keep poor people happy (and voting Democrat), illegal immigrants happy (and voting Democrat), the elderly happy (and voting Democrat), and millions of unionized healthcare workers happy and prosperous (and voting Democrat).

Here are some resources for investing in medical real estate:

- HCN (Health Care REIT, Inc.)
- VNQ (Vanguard REIT Index ETF)
- XHS (SPDR S&P Health Care Services ETF)
- PJP (PowerShares Dynamic Pharmaceuticals)
- XBI (SPDR S&P Biotech ETF)

CHAPTER TWENTY-FOUR

DIVERSIFY AND INVEST OUTSIDE THE U.S.A.

DID YOU KNOW?

- Your financial portfolio is already skewed toward American assets—just because you live and work here
- Australia, New Zealand, Canada, Singapore, Hong Kong, and Switzerland all came out of the 2008 crisis in better financial health than the United States
- The communist Chinese now enjoy some economic freedoms that we have lost in the United States

I t's a big world out there. The U.S.A. is in a precarious position. Our debt, our dollar, our economy are all hanging by a thread. We could face a long-term decline (like Japan), or a complete collapse. You are already overexposed to the U.S. economy—simply because you live and work here. Your home is here. You may own a vacation home or rental properties here. You may own a business here. Or you may be an employee of a U.S. company. So whatever happens to America affects your income, assets, and ability to retire comfortably. Do you really want to bet even *more* on America's future with Obama at the controls? Aren't your home, business, and career enough?

It's clear the U.S. economy and entire American way of life are in severe trouble. To be fair, it's not just Obama's policies damaging America's future. The structural problems and dysfunction started well before Obama. We are an aging nation with negative demographics. Too many Americans are aging and retiring. Too few are working to pay for the Social Security and Medicare the retirees need.

When people retire, they slow down their spending. That's bad for the economy. Manufacturers, distributors, and retailers all suffer. Then there's our aging infrastructure. Where will we get the trillions of dollars necessary to upgrade and replace our aging highways, roads, bridges, tunnels, airports, schools, water and sewer pipes, and electrical wiring? America has big problems.

The biggest problem of all is America's debt, a real national security threat. Because of the decisions being made by Obama now (and the voters' decision to re-elect him), we are headed for a debt implosion. Government does not know best. Government cannot create jobs. Government cannot solve a spending crisis with more spending, nor a debt crisis with more debt. Government cannot successfully print money we don't have, to pay debts we can't afford. The Fed can't be in the business of funding 100 percent of government deficit spending. Everyone can't work for government, or depend on government. Everyone can't be guaranteed free healthcare. It will end with hyperinflation and economic disaster. *It will not end well.*

Not every country is looking this bad. Some are younger and more dynamic, with bright futures. Some are still filled with ambitious, hungry citizens—*the way America used to be.*

Many countries came out of the 2008 financial crisis in much better shape than America: Australia, New Zealand, Canada, Singapore, Hong Kong, and Switzerland, to name a few.[1] It is not a coincidence that these countries top the Economic Freedom Index.[2] Economic freedom and capitalism lead to prosperity.

To protect your assets you need to invest in the futures of these countries by diversifying and balancing your portfolio. You also need to hold at least some portion of your savings, precious metals, and retirement funds outside of the U.S.A.

What are the countries I recommend? Invest in China, India, Brazil, and other Asian countries—Vietnam, Cambodia, Thailand, Indonesia, Laos, Singapore, Hong Kong. These countries are filled with people who remind me of what America used to look like. They are young, hungry, ambitious, relentless, and not interested in help from government. You don't survive in these countries on welfare, food stamps, disability, unemployment, housing allowances, or Medicaid. Their economies are not run based on affirmative action, "climate change," or social justice. They aren't politically correct. In Asia's emerging economies, you sink or swim. You work or starve. That's powerful motivation. It's like it used to be in America. These people want the brass ring. They have painted a target on America's back and they are coming to take what has always been ours—the highest standard of living in the world. You can make money by investing in their hunger, ambition, and relentlessness. Boatloads of money.

These countries have other advantages. Their population demographics skew younger than America's. So, their future is in front of them, not behind. The people of Brazil, China, India, Vietnam, Laos, Thailand, and Cambodia have years of earning power and consumer spending ahead of them.[3]

Most importantly, these countries aren't burdened by debt—either national debt or individual debt. So the citizens of those other countries can weather a world economic crash. American citizens are already too busy digging out from under mountains of debt.

Finally, I saved the best for last. These other countries have more freedom. Don't kid yourself. America doesn't enjoy economic freedom any more. Under Obama the taxes are too high, the rules, regulations, and mandates too cumbersome, to grow or encourage business start-ups or job creation. Yes, in many ways, even communist China enjoys more freedom than America under Obama. Not in civil rights, not in freedom of the press, not

NOT EVERYONE IS DROWNING IN DEBT

In China, surveys show, 90 percent or more of auto purchases are with cash. In America almost 90 percent are with loans (debt).[4]

in democracy, not in a woman's ability to procreate, but in freedom to start a business and in freedom to go as far as your God-given talents and individual work ethic and initiative will take you.[5]

It only makes sense to build your investment portfolio around their future. What will all these hungry, ambitious, foreign consumers buy? The same things we have bought in America for the past half century—homes, cars, clothes, jewelry, high-end electronics, fancy kitchen appliances, furniture, food, and medicine.

That means you'll want to invest in all those categories—in companies based in these countries that produce raw materials, natural resources, manufacturing, agriculture, technology, healthcare, biotech, and pharmaceuticals.

And, not just companies in those countries, but also the countries that *sell* to those countries, or manage their money—such as Australia, New Zealand, Singapore, Hong Kong, Canada (yes Canada is the main trading partner of the U.S., but their economy is based on hard assets like mining, minerals, oil, and agriculture, all desperately needed by these developing countries).[6] Add in the Netherlands, because they are a top exporter of agricultural products and energy.[7] And never leave out Switzerland, because of its banking, drugs, and chemical industries. The bottom line is you want to have investments in countries that sell stuff to China, India, Brazil, and the emerging economies of Asia.

The easiest way to accomplish this is to invest in ETFs (Exchange Traded Funds) of countries and sectors you like. Here's my recommended shopping list:

- International agriculture ETFs—because people in these growing and emerging economies will need to eat
- International energy ETFs—because they will need gas and energy
- International raw materials ETFs—because they will need to build homes, commercial buildings, and infrastructure
- International manufacturing ETFs—because these companies will get rich producing the products these people need to consume

- International technology ETFs—because all these ambitious people will want to buy the latest gadgets
- International pharmaceutical ETFs—because these people will get sick and need to buy drugs to treat their illnesses

One last bit of advice on diversifying your portfolio into foreign stocks. A very wise and wealthy man once told me the key to wealth is "to make money while you sleep." I asked him what he meant. The wise and wealthy man told me that he owned a bank and that banks earn interest all night long while he slept. He owned hotels and his hotel guests paid for the rooms all night long. And he owned oil wells and they pumped oil all night long. And he owned mines and they produced precious metals while he slept.

How do you accomplish this? Well you can certainly invest in banks, hotels, gold, silver, oil, and natural resources. But the other way is to invest in companies that pay big dividends. Dividends pay you interest while you sleep. With the right international companies, dividends pay out even when the U.S. economy is in crisis. So, it makes sense to invest in foreign companies that pay the richest dividends.

Other ways to bet on the success of these foreign countries is to buy international bond funds and hold foreign currencies like the Swiss franc, Australian dollar, or Canadian loonie. I'm sad to report that the future looks brighter for foreign bonds and currencies than U.S. bonds or the U.S. dollar.

Here are some resources for investing in international and Asian funds:

- iShares FTSE/Xinhua China 25 Index Fund (FXI)
- iShares MSCI Australia Index Fund (EWA)
- iShares Hong Kong Index Fund (EWH)
- iShares Singapore Index Fund (EWS)
- Direxion India Bull 2x ETF (INDL)
- EGS INDXX China Infrastructure ETF (CHXX)
- Global X China Consumer ETF (CHIQ)
- Global X China Energy ETF (CHIE)

- Global X China Financials ETF (CHIX)
- Global X China Materials ETF (CHIM)
- Global X China Technology ETF (CHIB)
- Guggenheim/AlphaShares China Real Estate ETF (TAO)
- AUSE–Australia Dividend Fund
- EWA–MSCI Australia Index Fund
- iShares MSCI Malaysia Index (EWM)
- iShares MSCI Singapore Index ETF (EWS)
- iShares MSCI Thailand Investable Market Index ETF (THD)
- Market Vectors Vietnam ETF (VNM)

CHAPTER TWENTY-FIVE

BECOME YOUR OWN BOSS

DID YOU KNOW?

- Owning your own business is a *legal* tax shelter
- Under Obama, it's still smart to start your own business—but just don't hire any full-time employees!
- Franchises and Multi-Level Marketing (MLM) businesses still offer great opportunities even in the Obama Zombie Economy

O kay, enough passive investing advice. How about investing in yourself? Obama has an agenda against small business owners. I think I've made that case convincingly. I've also told you why—because we are independent. We don't want or need government to help us. We don't want what he's selling. Obama resents that attitude. So he wants desperately to put us out of business.

No matter. If you're reading this book you already understand that for your own well-being you must defy Obama. If he doesn't want you to be a small business owner, your goal in life should be to become a small business owner. If Obama wants to stop you from doing it, it must be pretty darn good for you. It must be your shot at freedom.

I can tell you. . . it is.

With Obama in charge, owning a business will make you a marked man or women, because you no longer depend on government. But trust me, the freedom it gives you is worth the pain and intimidation. Anything worth doing is worth a little pain, is worth fighting for.

My father toiled as a low-paid butcher for twenty years until he saved enough to start his own butcher shop. It wasn't much, it was tiny, it didn't make much money, but it was his. He was the boss. He would never take orders again. To him, the air he was breathing in that little butcher store was the sweetest-smelling air on earth. On his deathbed my dad told me that becoming his own boss was the happiest day of his life (along with the birth of his two children). It was the defining moment of his life.

That's just what Obama is afraid of—people who don't want to take orders, who don't want to be told what to do, who think for themselves, who ask for nothing from government, who are skeptical and cynical about the intentions of government, and who don't trust politicians. It's no wonder almost all small business owners are conservatives.

If your ambition is sitting home, sleeping late, and watching eight hours of TV each day while waiting for your government check to arrive, you are a perfect Obama voter.

But what made America great, and can make it great again, is a nation of independent free-thinkers and courageous financial risk-takers. That's why I wrote this book, for people I call the "Financial First Responders." These are the people who live to own—own your own business, own your own home, own stocks, own real estate, own gold and precious metals…people who are stable, responsible, married with children, have a strong faith in God, and contribute to society. People willing to risk their own money to achieve success and mobility. Those are the people who made America great, and who still make America great today. They make the economy go and grow. God bless small business.

America needs more of you. The reason to own a small business is because it is still the best way to achieve financial freedom, and it's still one of the only legal tax shelters in this country. All your business-related bills are tax deductible. Use your auto for business—tax deductible. Use gas for that business car—tax deductible. Use your home as the office—tax deductible. Entertain clients—tax deductible. Your health insurance—tax deductible.[1] Major business expenses—tax deductible. Travel to Lake Tahoe or Hawaii or London on business—tax deductible. (At least for now.) Just keep meticulous records.

For more on the art of the legal tax deduction for business owners, professionals, and independent contractors, I advise everyone to read an article in the *Wall Street Journal* from April 5, 2011, entitled, "A Tax Man Takes Account of His Life: CPA Lives Better, Works Less Thanks to Art of Deduction."[2]

But there is a complication with owning a business. Obama and big government politicians (from both parties, but mostly Democrats) have made it much more difficult. They've damaged the American Dream with big taxes, too many rules and regulations, too many unions, too many lawyers and lawsuits. In California and many other states, they've made it almost impossible to do business any more, and completely impossible to have employees.

So if at all possible, you want to stay away from hiring anyone except part-time employees, temps, and independent contractors. The costs for full-time employees—payroll taxes, workers' comp, health insurance, minimum wage laws, big office space, rules and regulations that force you to hire human resources managers, and the legal fees to defend against possible future lawsuits—are just not worth it. I hear it every day from my smartest and wealthiest friends. They no longer want the hassle, headaches, and expense of employees. How sad.

If you're a politically correct liberal, union member, or government employee, I can hear you blaming and complaining right now: "That Wayne Root. He's a typical greedy capitalist conservative who doesn't want to pay employees." Well, you've got it backward. I've been a job creator my whole life. I love people and would like to hire and give them a salary that allows them to live the American Dream—but unfortunately those days are over. It's simply unaffordable. Obama, the progressives, liberals, socialists, unions, labor lawyers, and politicians have made it so expensive that no one can afford employees any more. Blame them, not the small businessperson trying to make a go of it. Obama and his socialist cabal have turned the job market into a "hostile work environment." They are the reason companies aren't hiring.

There's a price to be paid when you demonize and punish business owners. It always sounds so good in theory. But as my dad pointed out forty years ago, "Son I'd love to hate rich people, but no poor person has ever given me a job." My father understood if you treat rich people with disdain, eventually there are no jobs. And the middle class pays the price. Congratulations Mr. Obama—you've succeeded.

Because of this, there is now an asterisk in this Obama economy. You need to build your own business and be your own boss. *But, only if you can do it *without* employees. Here are four ways to accomplish that:

Option #1) What still works is "One-Man-Army" businesses: lawyers, doctors, dentists, accountants, financial planners, stockbrokers, insurance agents, real estate agents, mortgage brokers, hairdressers. Build a business where you are the only employee (or at least have just a handful of support staff, preferably part time). Or build a business where all those working for you are commissioned, performance-based, independent contractors with no weekly payroll, health insurance, or other benefits. Or, become one of those independent contractors yourself. For all intents and purposes, you are your own boss.

In my case I have multiple One-Man-Army careers. I'm a television host and producer, author, and spokesman for multiple companies. They all pay me as an independent contractor. I'm my own boss and I'm paid based on performance.

Option #2) Build a web-based business. A website is national, or global, yet it can be run in cyberspace from your bedroom with no overhead, no office space, no payroll, and no employees. It's just you, or you plus a network of independent contractors (such as your webmaster, and a fulfillment house if you are selling products).

In my case, I've built a prototype web business. Consumers from all over the country buy from me while I sleep, with a point and click, no employees needed. This is the future of entrepreneurship.

Option #3) Invest in and build a franchised business. Franchises range all the way from simple work-at-home, small-investment businesses to multi-million-dollar chains of fast food restaurants. I won't begin to try to tell you what type, or what specific franchise might be best for you. What I will tell you is that there are some very good ones and some very bad ones, so do your due diligence. The advantage of a good franchise is that you have a business model to follow that has already proven to be successful, along with a detailed game plan. Plus you have a support team to get you through all the red tape of starting and operating your business. If you have no experience in the type of business you would like to start, I strongly advise a franchise. For years a close friend of mine kept a sign on his wall: "EVERYTHING IS EASY WHEN YOU KNOW WHAT TO DO!" The only way you can know how to do something is either by "paying your dues" and learning it through the school of hard knocks, or buying a franchise that has already got the plan down to a science.

Option #4) Here's a recommendation that has been successful for millions of people across the globe and that virtually anyone can do. Start a home-based direct selling or MLM (Multi-Level Marketing) business.

The advantages of MLM are numerous. Here are twelve of them:

First, you don't have to be rich to start an MLM business. The cost of entry is low. There are few, if any, barriers to entry. It's an equal opportunity business—no one cares if you're male or female, white or black, what religion you believe in, or whether you're from Yale or jail. As long as you are enthusiastic, and relentless, you are in like Flynn.

Second, you don't need a fancy college diploma. If you believe in yourself and can show and share your product or message with passion and enthusiasm, you'll be a star and can make a fortune. It's all about your willingness to learn.

LUCRATIVE OPPORTUNITY DESPISED BY LIBERALS— WHAT ELSE IS NEW?

Multi-Level Marketing has gotten a bad rap. Liberals hate it. They think it's low class, beneath them. Or they think it's a rip-off because many people who try it fail. Well, I personally know a dozen MLM members who make $500,000 to $2,000,000 per year. If I personally know a dozen people with that kind of income, can you imagine how many MLM business opportunities are out there for someone to achieve financial freedom? What are you waiting for? Stop complaining about Obama and do something!

Third is flexibility—you can build your MLM career part-time in coordination with a full-time career that gives you a base salary with a safe paycheck. I know many people who started out as teachers, policemen, firemen, secretaries, plumbers, and in their spare time on weekends, mornings, evenings, and summers they added $25,000, $50,000, or even $100,000 to their income. Once your MLM income surpasses that of your full-time job, you may want to quit and make MLM your main career (as so many have already done).

Another way to do it is to have one spouse with the safe, steady job with a regular paycheck (plus health insurance), while the other spouse builds an MLM business full-time. What a great way to have your cake and eat it too. You get to have both safety and performance-based commissions (which is always where the big money is).

Performance-based commissions are so important simply because you can't get rich with a "safe salary." A salary limits your income. The salary is a ceiling. Ignore Obama's obsession with "safety nets." Taking risks in the business world is the only way to achieve financial freedom. So you need another career based on performance, where you are guaranteed nothing, but where the sky is the limit. MLM allows you to do that while keeping your day job.

Fourth, the beauty of MLM is you own your own business. You get all the advantages of being a business owner. But you can base it at home around spouse and family. Once you get used to working at home and seeing your kids all day, you can never go back to an office.

Fifth, you can build a legacy for your children. They can take it over after you retire or die, or sell it. You can't do that with a traditional career or job. But MLM generates residual income. You make money while you sleep, and your revenue stream keeps going after you retire or die.

Sixth, you can do it alongside your family. Everyone, even the kids, can participate. My wife grew up as part of an MLM family. Her dad was a hospital CEO with over 600 employees. Her mom sold MLM products. The MLM parties, conferences, and training sessions are some of her fondest memories of childhood. She learned to host events and sell products from a young age. It made her into the outgoing dynamic women that I fell in love with and married.

Seventh, just as my wife experienced growing up, you can use your MLM business to travel the world (tax deductible), recruiting and training new members to join your downline (all of whom are independent contractors). My wife and her family traveled on business to Hawaii, Europe, Australia, South Korea, Finland, and Japan. They built downlines (the MLM term for the people who work your business under you) all over the world. Some might say, "The family that sells together, stays together."

Eighth, MLM is mobile—you can do it from anywhere in the world. You can run it from your vacation villa in the south of France, a beach in Maui, a mountaintop in Park City, Utah, or move to Singapore. It's the perfect high tech business. It can be run without employees, with a laptop, email blasts to your database, text, cell, website, online sales, and Internet back office.

Ninth, when you are your own boss, you finally get paid what you're worth. When you're an employee, you work hard and the lion's share of the benefits and rewards go to your boss (the owner). When you own your own business, you build assets for *yourself*.

Tenth, since your MLM is based at home with no commute, you are doing what liberals preach—reducing your carbon footprint. You are using no gas, no wear and tear on your car, no damage to the environment.

Eleventh, owning a small business creates financial independence because of the many legal tax advantages it provides. As I've already pointed out, businesses are the last great legal tax shelter allowed by government—with legal deductions for your expenses, investments into the business, legal fees, accounting services, office supplies, business-related expenses at your home, business use of your car, business travel, and business entertainment.

Last, the greatest tax advantage of all is that when you invest your time and money in a business, build equity, and eventually sell out, the money you make is taxed at the lower capital gains rate (rather than as income). The most recent data from the IRS about the richest Americans shows that the key to their wealth is building a business, owning a business, and selling it (or stock shares from the business) at the lower capital gains tax rate.[3] Also according to extensive research and government data, most members of the capitalist "wealth" class own their own business, own a home, are married with children, and have a college degree. It's a pretty simple formula.[4]

In the next chapter, I'll even show you a way to build a multi-milliondollar pension that only works for a family-owned One-Man-Army business. You're in luck.

This is how you beat Obama at his own game. You own a business, you remain independent, you never rely on government, you build it all around God and family, but you do it all *without* employees.

This will drive Obama crazy. More small business owners, more people with an independent streak, more people who don't trust or rely on government, more people earning financial freedom and legally reducing their tax burden, and yet no new employees for Obama's economy. I'm smiling from ear to ear as I write this.

I may do a few back-flips too.

CHAPTER TWENTY-SIX

A BIG BUSINESS PENSION OPPORTUNITY FOR SMALL BUSINESS

DID YOU KNOW?

- Defined-benefits plans for government employees are helping drive America into bankruptcy
- But that very kind of plan could be a great and completely legal tax shelter for certain kinds of small businesses
- Unlike contributions to an SEP IRA, there's no cap on what you can contribute to a defined-benefit plan

So here's how you take a "One Man Army" small business—or you plus a few family members—and create a big business pension plan to salt away millions of dollars for your retirement. Do I have your attention?

We keep hearing about pensions going away—look at the airline industry, automobile industry, and so forth.[1] And I constantly hear small business owners complain that they have no pension at all (that includes yours truly). But according to David Bray of Bray Financial (www.brayfinancial.com), this can be remedied.[2]

For small business owners, or one-person professional Subchapter S corporations (lawyers, doctors, dentists), or independent contractors (stockbrokers, real estate brokers, and mortgage brokers who work for performance-based commissions), this could be one of the great unknown opportunities in the tax world!

I believe "defined pension plans" for government employees are a disaster for the U.S. economy. But that's only because they are using our taxpayer money to fund their pensions. Many government employees retire on $100,000 per year of our money. That heinous practice has to end—and quickly.

But when it comes to small business owners, a "defined-benefit pension plan" may be the ideal way to salt away enough money to fund a wonderful, prosperous retirement.

My accountant has told me many times over the years that I know more about taxes and legal deductions than anyone he has ever met in his life who isn't a CPA. And yet I had never heard of a small business using a defined-benefit pension plan. Enter David Bray of Bray Financial.

David Bray's brilliant idea allows profitable family-owned small businesses to take advantage of the kind of old-school pension plan traditionally used by large corporations with thousands or even hundreds of thousands of employees.

The tax breaks may be substantial. In fact, according to Bray, if these plans are funded with insurance contracts, 100 percent of the plan contributions may be tax-deductible. While an SEP IRA (Simplified Employee Pension Plan), permits a business owner to save thousands of dollars for retirement annually, the amounts are limited by government rules. That leaves a huge chunk of your net income to be taxed at above 40 percent (39.6 percent plus state income taxes, plus Obamacare taxes).

But with Bray's recommended defined-benefits pension plan, there is literally no cap on how much you can contribute and save. Business owners have the potential to accumulate millions of dollars for the future through such a vehicle. In other words, if you've been so successful that you can go without a salary, Bray says you can structure a plan to put your entire annual salary (or most of it), however large, into your pension plan. Or in a less extreme example, you can set aside two-thirds or half your salary. So this isn't for everyone, but it sure is for smart business owners!

For the record, the IRS does limit the yearly retirement income that a participant in a defined benefit plan may receive (that is, take out). In 2012, the pension benefit resulting from such a plan may not exceed A) $200,000 annually, or B) 100 percent of the participant's average compensation across his or her three highest-paid consecutive years of service.

Bray says if you are earning well into six figures and you are forty-five or older, you may have entered the "sweet spot" when it comes to defined-benefit plans. You will presumably be in your peak earning years, allowing you to accelerate retirement savings. A defined benefit plan offers the possibility to sock all or most of that money away.

What are the downsides? Cost and complexity. Actuaries have to be involved (and paid) when you have one of these plans; you need an actuary to perform regular and annual calculations and valuations to see that the plan is being properly funded. In addition, the pension benefits need to be insured through the federal government's Pension Benefit Guaranty Corporation (PBGC); and in exchange for that service, the business must pay the PBGC annual premiums.

An actuary must determine the annual employer contribution amount needed to fund the plan (typically adjusted yearly in light of investment performance) and the actuarial formula used to make contributions per worker. You could get stuck funding the plan year in and year out, even in a bad year. Setup costs may be cheaper than you think, however.

Certain financial services firms (such as Bray Financial) have made a niche of helping small businesses implement these pension programs. Instead of a fifty-page plan agreement, Bray can help design a document a tenth that long, or less.

Getting a defined benefit plan up and running for under $5,000 is not unheard of these days. You may also have the option to annually "duck out" of the pension plan in case your business hits hard times.

A long-established family business with a payroll made up of a few family members may find one of these plans highly attractive. The plan contributions can be large, and the benefits can go directly to family members and/or their spouse.

What businesses are good candidates? Those "One Man Armies." Accounting, consulting, legal, and medical practices are often good fits for these plans. And seeing how many baby boomers have elected to continue working as consultants, you may see interest rising in them during the coming decade.

With Obama raising taxes toward the sky, this could be one of the few ways left to legally protect your income from taxes. (This one tip alone could help you create a multimillion-dollar retirement fund. Not bad for the price of a book!)

For more information on setting up your retirement account, contact David Bray at Bray Financial (www.brayfinancial.com, david.bray@ brayfinancial.com).

CHAPTER TWENTY-SEVEN

GUNS FOR PROTECTION AND PROFIT

DID YOU KNOW?

- There were more than 65 million background checks for weapon purchases in Obama's first term
- The NRA gained a *quarter million* new members in the weeks after the Sandy Hook massacre
- The U.K., with much stricter gun control than the U.S., has *three and a half times* as much violent crime
- Smith & Wesson stock was up on average 16 percent per year for the past decade and Sturm, Ruger & Co. 21 percent—compared to 7.1 percent for the S&P 500
- $10,000 invested in the S&P 500 in 2002 would be worth $19,193 today; the same amount invested in the VICE fund (guns, gambling, alcohol, etc.) would be worth $25,295

Over 250,000 new members joined the NRA in the few weeks after the Sandy Hook elementary school tragedy.[1]

Why? Well probably for the same reasons I joined for the first time in the days after Sandy Hook. As an Ivy Leaguer and former member of the mainstream media, I'm certainly not your typical NRA member.

I'm not a big gun guy. I'm not a collector. I'm not a hunter. Being around guns is not second nature to me. But I know one thing—I want them legal. I want the right to own them. I want the right to protect myself and my family. I want to protect the Second Amendment. I don't want government telling me what to do. And if any of those rights are going to be threatened, then it's time for me to stand with the NRA.

Here are some commonsense reasons why guns should always be legal in America:

First, I believe it's clear that our politicians have come to the wrong conclusions. Why should we rush to ban guns, when almost all our worst mass murders and most of our violent crimes occur in places with the strictest gun controls? Why rush to create more "Gun Free Zones" when the Sandy Hook tragedy occurred in a "Gun Free Zone?" It makes absolutely no sense.

The most violent crime and murders in America occur in places with the strictest gun controls—places like Chicago, Cleveland, Detroit, and Washington, D.C.[2] By the way, the state of Connecticut has among the strictest gun control laws.[3] Did those gun controls stop the Sandy Hook tragedy?

Strict gun control only disarms honest, law-abiding citizens, leaving them helpless and defenseless. Criminals have no problem acquiring guns. Therefore gun laws are not only useless, they are dangerous.

Don't just look at America. Look across the Atlantic Ocean for the best example. Our friend and ally England has made obtaining a handgun or even a shotgun almost impossible. Guns were banned in 1998.[4] The result? The U.K. violent crime rate is three and a half times as high as in America. The FBI reports 386 violent crimes per 100,000 people in the U.S.A. The U.K. Home Office reports 1,361 violent crimes per 100,000 in England.[5] Gun controls may be a failure in lots of places, but the U.K. experience proves that gun bans are an unmitigated disaster.

> **GROUCHO MARX SAID IT BEST:**
>
> "Politics is the art of looking for trouble, finding it everywhere, diagnosing it incorrectly and applying all the wrong remedies."

But this is nothing new. Leftist, big government, Nanny State politicians always come to the wrong conclusion about most issues.

As I pointed out earlier, Rahm Emanuel says "You never want a serious crisis to go to waste."

Our leftist big government politicians are turning a terrible tragedy into a gun crisis, because it will give them the opportunity to demonize and ban guns. It doesn't matter to them that the Newtown tragedy wasn't a gun problem, it was a mental illness problem.

Thank goodness the American public has more common sense than the politicians and media propagandists. A recent Rasmussen poll shows that while 27 percent think stricter gun control laws are the solution, 48 percent believe the answer is more action to treat mental health issues.[6]

It is obvious that a majority of Americans have not overreacted to this tragedy. Most reasonable people agree that while guns in the wrong hands may kill, more often guns save lives and prevent violence.

Here are a few proven facts that are too often missing from the gun debate (thanks to Gun Owners of America and ZeroHedge.com for these statistics):

- Based on a 2000 study, Americans use guns to *defend* themselves from crime and violence 989,883 times annually. Banning guns would leave about 1 million Americans defenseless from criminals who have no problem acquiring guns illegally.[7]
- A nationwide survey reported that over a five-year period, 3.5 percent of households had a member who used a gun to protect themselves, their family, or their property. This also adds up to about the same 1 million incidents annually.[8]
- Each year about 200,000 women use a gun to defend themselves from a sexual crime or abuse.[9]
- The Carter Justice Department found that of more than 32,000 attempted rapes, 32 percent were actually committed. But when a woman was armed with a gun or knife, 97 percent of the attempted rapes were thwarted.[10]

- Newer studies all point toward a figure of 2.5 million—
  that's the new expert guesstimate of how many times Americans defend themselves from violent criminals each year.[11]

The facts are in and show clearly that guns save lives. The hypocrisy about gun control is mind-numbing. The politicians and Hollywood celebrities screaming the loudest about disarming citizens all have armed security protecting them. Big-mouth leftist filmmaker Michael Moore has armed bodyguards.[12] New York City Mayor Michael Bloomberg has armed security.[13] President Obama obviously has an army of armed security. But more to the point, Obama sends his girls to the exclusive Sidwell Friends School with armed Secret Service agents to guard them. Don't get me wrong, I agree with him. I just want the same right to protect my children.

And then there's Washington, D.C., itself—the place where all the elite anti-gun snobs who govern the peasants they want so badly to disarm work. If it's so great to be in a "Gun Free Zone," why aren't they making all federal buildings in Washington, D.C., "Gun Free Zones?" If it's so safe to disarm, let our leaders show us the way. If it's good for the goose, it's good for the gander.

For me it's always been more a personal and emotional argument than a factual one. I'm a proud Jewish American. Over six million of my fellow Jews were enslaved, starved, tortured, and then slaughtered by Adolf Hitler. It could never have happened without Hitler first banning gun ownership for Jews.[14]

That act on November 11, 1938, (one day after the infamous Kristallnacht) was the beginning of the end for German Jews. Hitler only started his murderous genocide after first ensuring his victims were disarmed, defenseless, and helpless.

The reality is that throughout history, the first thing all tyrants do is disarm the citizens.[15] Then the citizenry is much easier to control and even kill.

In the end we must remember our Second Amendment was written not to protect us from criminals and random crime; it was put in place to protect the citizens from government.

Isn't the very fact that the politicians and elites who trample our rights and violate the Constitution on a daily basis want citizens to be disarmed positive proof of the necessity for the citizens to be armed?

That's why I joined the NRA in the days after Sandy Hook. Now more than ever, we need to stand behind the NRA. Now more than ever, we need to protect the Second Amendment.

So let's address how we protect our right to bear arms—and how to profit from investing in them. Because both are very good ideas in our current circumstances.

As to how to protect the citizens' right to bear arms, I have a creative idea that settles the issue. It's based on states' rights. The Second Amendment reads:

> A well-regulated militia being necessary to the security of a free state, the right of the people to keep and bear arms shall not be infringed.

I propose Texas lead the way and play the hero (so what else is new?). Since the only possible valid constitutional argument by liberals, progressives, and socialists to limit gun rights is that the right to bear arms refers specifically to militia members, I propose the governor of Texas propose a bill in the next session of the Texas legislature that says,

> We declare that every citizen of Texas who owns or desires to own one or more firearms is hereby made a member of the Texas State Militia. It is the duty of that citizen to obtain, safely secure, properly maintain, and become proficient in the use of the firearms of his or her choice in the event the militia is called to active duty to defend the State of Texas and/or the United States of America.

Within days of that bill passing, I predict that the same law will be proposed in at least twenty other states across America. Soon the issue will be settled. If citizens want their gun rights protected, safe and secure, they'll move to the states that protect them.

Let Obama and his progressive liberal cohorts chew on that for awhile.

Do you know how to use a gun? Does your daughter? Owning firearms is important, but every member of your family also needs to know how to use them safely and effectively. And you need to make sure you have plenty of ammunition—stock up while you can! (Details in Chapter 31, "Invest in Survival.")

As for investing and profiting from guns—I have a way for you to do that, too. The only trouble is, you're a little late to the game. I recommended guns and bullets in my book from four years ago, *The Conscience of a Libertarian*. The subtitle said it all: *Empowering the Citizen Revolution with God, Guns, Gold & Tax Cuts*. The past four years have seen the greatest gun and bullet-buying binge in history. There were over *65 million* background checks for weapons purchases in Obama's first term.[16]

Firearms manufacturers' stocks are already at stratospheric heights. Smith & Wesson soared by 5.7 percent on the day Obama proposed stricter gun control laws in January 2013. It's hard to find stocks that go up 5.7 percent in a *year*, let alone a *day*. Smith & Wesson went up 8.3 percent that same week.

On February 27, gunmaker Sturm Ruger & Co. reported that 2012 earnings were up 77.7 and sales up 49.7 percent. Sturm Ruger stock is up 789 percent since the day Obama took office. As one gun dealer said, "Obama is the greatest gun salesman of all-time."[17]

But firearm makers are no Johnny-come-latelies. For the past decade the S&P 500 Stock Index is up 7.1 percent annually. Smith & Wesson gained an average of 16 percent annually and Sturm, Ruger & Co. gained 21 percent annually for that same decade.

So is it too late to profit? Obama will undoubtedly inspire more gun and ammo sales, but even I don't think the pace of firearm sales can be sustained at the levels of the last four years. So many guns and so much ammo have now been bought that common sense says it has to slow down, at least a little. I'm betting firearms makers' stocks will continue to go up under Obama, just not at the same rate as during Obama's first term, unless, of course, it appears that draconian gun control legislation will actually be passed by Congress—regardless of its constitutionality.

Here's one possibility to profit on the upside, without the huge downside if firearms makers underperform: **VICEX, the Vice Fund.**

This contrarian stock fund concentrates on investments in often under-valued industries that some might classify as "sin" or "vice." Stocks like these scare away Obama, socialists, Greenpeace nuts and flakes, and the politically correct crowd. The main investments of the VICE Fund are alcohol, tobacco, gambling (casinos/gaming industry), firearm makers, and military (defense/weapons) stocks.

Over the years VICE has far out-performed the S&P 500 Index. Since its inception in 2002, it has produced an annual return of 10.41 percent, versus 7.09 percent for the S&P. If you had put $10,000 into the S&P back then, today it would be worth $19,193—versus $25,295 for the VICE Fund. So much for politically correct "socially responsible" investing.

The fact is, in times of crisis and stress, many people invariably turn to vice (although hopefully not you). Since that is the nature of many people and since the next four years of Obama are almost certain to bring crisis, financial decline, collapse, unrest, rioting, and the threat or reality of war (because of Obama's perceived weakness by our enemies), Obam-aggedon will most certainly lead Americans to drink more, smoke more, gamble more, buy guns and bullets for personal protection, and demand stronger national defense. That could all lead to success for investors in the Vice Fund.

CHAPTER TWENTY-EIGHT

ESCAPE FROM HIGH-TAX STATES

DID YOU KNOW?

- Between 2000 and 2010, over half a million people left California for Texas, which has no state income tax or estate tax
- Since Connecticut adopted a state income tax in 1992 there have been on net *no* new jobs created in the state
- According to *Science* magazine, the happiest people in America live in low-tax states

I t is time to address your ultimate survival option—MOVING. Some of my wealthy friends are leaving the country. Many others are exploring that option, and I'll address it at the end of this chapter. But my personal choice is to stay and fight to save America. I'm betting most of you will make the same choice.

If you're going to stay, if you love America as I do, and will not give up on her, then it is imperative to consider moving to a low- or no-tax, low-regulation, friendly-to-business state. Millions of Americans are doing exactly that. Join them. The money you save can make the difference for you, your family, and your business's survival.

Ironically, the tax rebellion was started by people you'd never expect—sports stars, actors, actresses, and high-profile billionaires, many showing their true hypocrisy. Whether it's moving out of California or moving out of America, they've put a spotlight on the issue.

One thing is clear, Mr. Obama—if even celebrities who fawn at your feet won't pay your taxes, you have a big problem. You may own the media, so you were able to control the Benghazi disaster. But you have no control over the tax rebellion that's started and is growing bigger by the day. Let's look at just a few recent examples.

Phil Mickelson is one of the most famous athletes in the world. Last year he made almost $50 million. Yet in January he announced publicly how angry he is with California's taxes and stated that he plans to make "drastic changes." Leaving California is at the top of his list.[1]

Tiger Woods is even more famous and worth perhaps $1 billion. Yet he came out in support of Mickelson. Tiger admitted he left California in 1996 for the exact same reason—high taxes.[2]

In the same week, famed boxing promoter Bob Arum announced that superstar boxer Manny Pacquiao's next fight would almost certainly not be in held in America. The man who makes tens of millions per fight refuses to pay Obama's higher U.S. income taxes. He is considering Mexico City, Asia, or Dubai for his next fight. Can you imagine? One-hundred-million-dollar men are choosing Mexico City over America because of Obama's taxes.[3]

Tina Turner went public only days later. She renounced her U.S. citizenship to become a citizen of Switzerland—which just happens to have lower taxes than Obama's America (including capital gains taxes of zero).[4]

This all happened in a span of a few days. The dam is breaking. Remember, these are just the rich celebrities courageous enough to go public. This is merely the tip of the iceberg. The rich are fleeing in droves. The Obama tax-and-spend Ponzi scheme is imploding.

California taxes have been high for a while. What changed? The technology revolution has made it possible to do business from places where taxes are lower (or nonexistent) and where government treats highly productive people better. Obama had better learn this lesson fast, because this tax rebellion is spreading to millions of Americans with far smaller incomes and assets than Tiger Woods, Phil Mickelson, or Manny Pacquaio. How do I know? Friends are telling me about their decisions daily.

Why is it so easy to move nowadays? Technology!

I'm a New Yorker. I love New York, can't get it out of my blood. Technology allows me to watch Yankee games and the New York local news on DirecTV. I can read the *New York Post* every morning on my iPad. I can speak to and see my New York friends and relatives on Skype—for free. I can jet to New York for $500 on JetBlue and get my "New York fix" whenever I want. I can eat out in my adopted hometown, Las Vegas, at any number of New York restaurants, delis, and pizza joints. I can even get bagels in Las Vegas made with water flown in from New York.

So I chose to live in Las Vegas with sunshine 330 days a year and no traffic jams. Best of all, I've used the hundreds of thousands of tax dollars I've saved by living in no-tax Nevada to make life even more wonderful for me and my family. The real question is, "Why does anyone live in New York anymore?"

Technology allows many businesspeople to run their business from anywhere in America…or anywhere in the world. We're not tied to one place anymore. We're not prisoners. This has to give Mr. Obama and his socialist cabal nightmares. It's a primary reason progressives are so intent on keeping people poor and dependent—so they don't have the resources to escape. But, for those that do, the jail-break is on.

Smart people have figured out that when a government takes our money and gives us almost nothing in return, it's time to find a different government. I'm happy to pay for police, firefighters, courts, national security, national parks, and infrastructure, but that could all easily be paid for with a 10 percent flat tax.

The money I saved by moving away from New York and California (where I lived for a decade) allowed me to buy a mansion on a world-class golf course, inside a gated country club, overlooking five lakes, seven waterfalls, and the entire twinkling Vegas Strip, *for free.*

That's right, the money I saved in state income taxes, state capital gains taxes, lower payroll taxes, lower workers' comp, lower insurance rates, lower sales taxes, and lower property taxes, paid my Las Vegas mortgage. I got the mansion on the golf course for *free.* Imagine how many other

New Yorkers or Californians could move here, or to another low-tax state, and get a free home too (with enough left over for private school tuition and a family vacation to Maui each year).

I lived in New York for twenty-seven years, then California for a decade. What did I get for all those taxes I paid? *Nothing.* What did I miss when I moved to tax-free Las Vegas? *Nothing.* There isn't one single thing that I'm missing.

But I did gain something fantastic—a much higher quality of life. The money I saved paid for home-school tutors for my oldest daughter. She was accepted to Harvard University. She's now attending Oxford in the U.K. Would she have been able to attend the two best universities in the world if I had been forced to send her to public schools (because of higher taxes that left me without the resources to pay for her education)?

Lower taxes changed my life...and the lives of my family. They can change yours too. Trust me, folks, you're not missing anything when you leave a high-tax state. The money you get to keep in a no-tax state is yours to enjoy. And you don't need to feel guilty about it—you earned it; it's *your* money in the first place.

The signs are everywhere that a tax rebellion has begun. The latest U.S. Census shows the states with the lowest taxes enjoyed the fastest population growth. Here are the top fifteen fastest-growing states (in order) in America for the past decade:

1. Nevada
2. Arizona
3. Utah
4. Idaho
5. Texas
6. North Carolina
7. Georgia
8. Florida
9. Colorado
10. South Carolina
11. Wyoming

12. Washington
13. Alaska
14. New Mexico
15. Virginia

Notice anything interesting? All fifteen states are low-tax, no-tax, business-friendly, and/or Republican red states.[5] Six are states with no income tax: Nevada, Texas, Florida, Wyoming, Washington, and Alaska. Keep in mind there are only nine no-tax states in all of America—and six are on this list.[6]

Also keep in mind *Science* magazine reported the unhappiest people in America live in high tax states. The happiest people live in low tax states. Coincidence?[7]

Maybe these citizens are happier because the economy grows so much faster in no-tax states. The *Wall Street Journal* reported on a study from the Kansas Policy Institute that shows that states without an income tax had significantly better private sector GDP growth (59 percent versus 42 percent) over the last ten years. They increased the number of jobs by 4.9 percent while jobs in the rest of the states declined by 2.6 percent. No wonder states without an income tax gained population (+5.5 percent) from domestic migration, while all other states as a whole lost 1.3 percent of their population between 2000 and 2009. Think how much better the entire U.S. economy would be with lower taxes.[8]

Not surprisingly, the states losing the most population are all high-tax states: California, New York, New Jersey, Connecticut, Michigan, Maryland, and of course Obama's Illinois.

Examples abound of Americans with high incomes and assets escaping from high-tax states. California has lost over 1.2 million net residents in the past decade. Between 2000 and 2010, 551,914 people left California just for one state—Texas, taking $14.3 billion in income. Texas has no state income tax or estate tax.[9]

Maryland has much higher taxes than its next-door neighbor, Virginia. Between 2007 and 2010 over 40,000 residents escaped from Maryland to become Virginia residents. They took $2.17 billion with them.[10]

The Tax Foundation reports that 612,520 people renounced their citizenship in New York State and moved to Florida in the past decade, taking with them $19.7 billion in adjusted growth income.[11]

In Connecticut a third of the millionaires have vanished from the tax rolls since taxes were raised.[12]

High taxes don't just chase away residents, they kill jobs. Since 2001, according to the California Manufacturers and Technology Association, the state has lost 440,000 high-wage jobs.[13]

HIGH TAXES WORK *THAT* FAST

Illinois passed a 67 percent tax increase in 2011, and in only a few months they had lost 89,000 jobs.[15]

The Yankee Institute notes the astounding fact that since 1992, the year Connecticut added a state income tax, businesses in Connecticut have hired a grand total of *zero* net new workers.[14]

The exodus from high-tax states is a sign of what's to come in Obama's second term. The pattern could easily change from Americans leaving high-tax states to leaving the country. The states that Americans are running from are all governed just the way Obama wants to govern the entire country. Will the same Americans running away from California, New York, and Illinois soon be running away from America?

Ask Eduardo Saverin, the co-founder of Facebook, who recently renounced his citizenship and left for Singapore (where the capital gains taxes are zero).[16]

Ask big-time Democratic contributor Denise Rich, who recently renounced her citizenship to leave for Austria (where she'll get major tax breaks).[17]

The trickle is turning into a torrent. Record numbers of wealthy Americans are giving up their citizenship—*eight times more* than before Obama became president.[18]

Of course we already know that only one year after the U.K. imposed a "millionaires tax" two-thirds of the millionaires in England had disappeared off the tax rolls.[19]

We already know that millionaires are escaping France at a record pace because of high tax rates imposed by the new Obama-clone socialist president of France. Even leftist actors like Gerard Depardieu are abandoning the country they love.[20]

The famous actor isn't alone. Requests by citizens to leave France are up 500 percent.[21]

Then came the coup de grace. Former French President Nicolas Sarkozy announced he is leaving France because of taxes. High taxes are even chasing former presidents out of their own countries![22]

That's why I moved to Nevada. And I'm certainly not alone. During the past decade over 1.2 million residents escaped California.[23] When I add it up, chasing me away may have cost California about $2 million in taxes (from me personally, my business, and the employees I took with me). Multiply that times thousands of other high-income, high-net worth business owners among the 1.2 million citizens who have escaped California…and you see why California is broke, insolvent, dysfunctional, and desperate.

Californians' vote last November to stupidly raise taxes even higher will only accelerate the exodus and move California ever closer to bankruptcy. And let me give a big warning to all you Californians…you want to be gone *before* that happens. Desperate times call for desperate measures, and there is nothing more dangerous than desperate politicians with the authority to tax and confiscate your property.

You know what they say about pigs—*they get slaughtered*. The "PIIGS" in Europe (Portugal, Italy, Ireland, Greece, and Spain) have already chased away their richest citizens and business owners.[24] They have nothing left, their tax base is destroyed. High tax states are the PIIGS of America and like the European PIIGS, they are all going down.

If we let big government progressives have their way, California and Europe's tragic story will be America's also. But it doesn't have to be yours.

If you (like me) have chosen to stay and fight Obama and his attempts to end the American Dream, punish success, and destroy capitalism, then move to a state where you can keep more of your own money. At the very least your move will help offset the effect of Obama's federal tax increases on your family budget. Use any extra money you save to start a business, invest in precious metals, educate your children away from the failing public school system, and support conservative candidates and causes.

That's how you beat Obama at his own game. That's how we will fight, survive, thrive, and prosper. **Do the math. If you save $50,000 per year by moving to a no-tax state, that's $500,000 per decade. Invested wisely in gold or oil or international stocks, that could easily rise to $1 million. Over four decades of working, that's an extra $4 million for your retirement (and to leave your family).**

RETIREES: THINK GLOBAL

I've made the point about the necessity, of moving to a low-tax state, and have also made it clear I'm not yet ready to consider leaving America, but I realize that some of you are looking at that option. So I want to include some thoughts about such a move, especially for those of you at or near retirement.

First, let me say, I'm devastated that anyone would have to make that decision. When I ask my wealthy friends how to survive Obama's America, many answer the same way: "Leave the country, or at least move your money out of it. It's a big, beautiful world and there are any number of countries that want and welcome your money with open arms."

But the *very* wealthiest people I know respond slightly differently. They add, "You mean you don't already have money and assets in other countries? We've been diversifying geographically for years." Just ask the ultra-wealthy hypocrites (who claim to support higher taxes) like the Kennedys, various Democrat U.S. Senators including John Kerry and Diane Feinstein, George Soros, or Obama's new pick for Treasury Secretary Jack Lew where they've been moving and investing their money all these years.[25] Of course we know plenty of rich Republicans also park their money outside of the U.S.A.—ask Mitt Romney.[26] But at least Mitt is honest—he is a capitalist.

Let me make it clear that while getting at least some of your assets out of the way of this Obama economic train wreck is undoubtedly a good idea, I am not about to try to cover the hows, wheres, and whats of protecting large assets for yourself, your family, and your heirs in any great detail. That's for lawyers and estate experts. If you're wealthy, I'm betting you already know the answers.

Ironically, those who need some educating about offshore options are hardworking middle class Americans nearing or at retirement age. The fact is Obama's economic and fiscal policies are destroying your retirement income, limiting your options, and damaging your plans to enjoy a comfortable retirement here in the United States. Under Obama your retirement options are quickly being narrowed down to:

Leaving the U.S. for a more affordable and friendly environment, or...joining the parade of American citizens now being forced to live in poverty and on food stamps.

"Never!" you say. Think again. Most retirees depend on fixed incomes primarily from interest and dividends; wealthier retirees live on capital gains from the sale of their homes, stocks, or business. Obama just dramatically raised taxes on interest, dividends, and captial gains. Plus Obamacare taxes will take an additional 3.8 percent from the sale of your home, stocks, or business. Obama's new taxes are aimed directly at seniors.

But the true time bomb Obama has set to destroy middle income retirees is a two-headed monster. It is a monster that could only be foisted upon unsuspecting citizens by someone who is either totally ignorant of how money and the economy function, or by someone whose purpose is to destroy the American economy and the American dream. Take your pick.

The first head of Obama's two-headed monster is the Federal Reserve's fiscal policy of printing money to pay the ever-increasing national debt, thereby supporting Obama and his socialist cronies' insatiable appetite for spending. The result of reckless money printing is always the same—economic disaster. Retirees who are living on fixed incomes will see the purchasing power of their income plummet and their standard of living destroyed. If you still doubt this, you don't even need to look at other countries. All you need do is look at what happened in America during the administration of President Jimmy Carter. With inflation, your dollars suddenly become quarters.

You're going to survive and thrive in the coming inflationary environment with your Precious Metals Defense System (PMDS) and the other commodities in Your Personal Obama Defense Shield (Y-PODS).

But the second head of Obama's two-headed monster is the inevitable collapse of Social Security. I assume anyone reading this is not so naïve as to believe those trillions of dollars we've all been paying into Social Security for our retirement years have actually been set aside into a "lockbox" (as we were promised). The so-called "lockbox" actually holds nothing but a bunch of IOUs. All it takes is an Obama, or a future Obama-like administration, with the cooperation of administration lackeys in Congress, to decide America has other priorities and all those IOUs become worthless. Social Security payments are then drastically cut or stopped altogether.

Today, in Obama's America, "fairness" means income redistribution—the rich should pay more. How long do you think it will be until "fairness" means the retired don't need all that Social Security income? They don't have kids to pay for, no longer need two cars, don't need to take vacations, or live in such a big home. It could never happen, right? Think again…this is Obama's America we're talking about. An America where no matter how hard you worked and saved, "you didn't build it." Therefore, you must share it with the collective.

What do you do if you are one of the 20 million Americans already retired, or soon to be one of the 10,000 Americans retiring daily?

One option is to consider moving to a foreign country where your dollars will go a lot further. Every month thousands of middle class Americans are moving to low-cost foreign countries. I'll have a list of these countries at the end of this chapter.

Several of these countries not only welcome American expats, they have financial incentive programs including discounts on everything from restaurants to airfare that actively encourage you to relocate there. Anyone with a little adventure in their soul should spend some time on the Internet researching opportunities.

So many Americans have chosen this route that if you don't know someone who has moved offshore, I'm willing to bet your neighbor does. Ask around. People I know who have chosen to move to one of these low-cost foreign countries as a retirement option tell me about wonderful experiences (in addition to the obvious one of making your retirement dollar stretch further). Later in this book you will read and be able to learn from the experiences of one of my friends who chose this route.

I've done some investigating on behalf of my readers and have also found the best places to move if money is no object (if you have serious assets and a high income). These are countries that have a high cost of living or expensive entry requirements, but offer tax savings and fewer business regulations (more economic freedom). I'll have a list of these possible choices at the end of this chapter also.

There are also specific countries with the best corporate business environment (lower taxes and less red tape, mandates, and so forth) also listed at the end of this chapter.

Escaping high U.S. taxes is not the only reason to look at other countries. As discussed elsewhere in this book, investment opportunities outside the U.S. abound. But another reason to look offshore is because Mexico, Costa Rica, Panama, and Colombia have long been destinations for low-cost dental work and surgery. Europeans, Canadians, and those from other countries with national healthcare (like we are soon to have with Obamacare) have long traveled to low-cost countries for medical care. As my friend who moved to Panama writes later in this book, he regularly met people, especially Brits and Canadians, who came there for hip and knee replacements. As he says, their stories were always much the same. "Being over sixty-five, I'd been on the list for a knee replacement for over a year with no way of knowing when or even if the government would ever let me have it done. I could have had it done in the U.S. [this is before Obamacare] for $35,000. In Panama the cost is $12,000 and it is done in a Johns Hopkins-affiliated hospital by a U.S.-trained doctor."

Thailand, for a fraction of the cost in the U.S., has a thriving business in skilled-care nursing homes. I understand similar opportunities are becoming increasingly available in other low-cost countries. If your spouse needs this kind of care you are easily looking at $100,000 a year or more in the United States. If you limit your options to America, the normal course would be to quickly spend yourself destitute, then let the government pay for your spouse's nursing home care while you live in poverty. Wouldn't it be much better to move to a place where the nursing care is good and affordable for both spouses?

While we're discussing ways to survive and thrive in Obama's economy, here is another action you should consider. If moving offshore to stretch your retirement dollars, or to just "survive" Obama's depression, isn't possible (because of family and friends, or a desire to stay in America forever), another possibility is to downsize, not just your living space, but also your community.

The difference between the cost of living in a large city or a suburban area and truly rural America can be huge. America is filled with small towns and communities—and by "small" I do mean small—population 10,000 and under. These communities tend to be extremely safe and inexpensive. Churches abound, libraries, garden clubs, parks, and senior centers—most probably within walking distance of your home—are filled with friendly people. While grocery and gas prices are the same as elsewhere, home purchase or rental prices can be a fraction of city and suburb prices. Your employment opportunities may be limited, but for anyone with initiative, drive, and personal responsibility there are always opportunities, especially when your "monthly nut" is dramatically reduced—particularly given the technology that now allows anyone to work from their own homes.

Possible choices for saving money by retiring in low-cost foreign countries:

Panama, Mexico, Belize, Costa Rica, Dominican Republic, Nicaragua, Chile, Uruguay.

Possible choices for saving on taxes in foreign tax havens—these are expensive places to live, but ideal for retirees with large assets:

Singapore, Hong Kong, Switzerland, Australia, New Zealand, Cayman Islands, the Bahamas, Bermuda, Monaco, St. Kitts and Nevis, and (believe it or not) a name that keeps popping up in my conversations with tax experts: Canada.

Countries with specific business-friendly and corporate tax advantages:

The Cayman Islands, the Bahamas, Belize, Singapore, Switzerland, Liechtenstein, the Netherlands, Ireland, Belgium, U.A.E. (the United Arab

Emirates), Oman, Belize, Vanuatu, the Seychelles, the Maldives, and once again surprisingly Canada keeps popping up in my conversations with tax experts.

Best corporate tax havens within the United States:
Delaware and Nevada.

CHAPTER TWENTY-NINE

INVEST IN YOUR CHILDREN

DID YOU KNOW?

- In 2011, critical reading scores on the SAT reached their lowest level *ever*
- Twenty-five percent of American teenagers are unaware that Hitler led Germany during World War II; the same number think Columbus discovered America around 1750
- Homeschooling has increased by 74 percent since 1999
- Homeschoolers score 72 points above the national average on the SAT

Much of this book is focused on economic solutions to save you, your income, and your assets from the overreaching grasp of Obama. Education is also an economic issue, perhaps the most important economic issue of our time—but it's not *only* an economic issue.

Plain and simple—our children are the future of America. They are the workforce, the entrepreneurs, the CEOs of the future. And, as with virtually every political, economic, or social issue in this country, less government and more freedom is the solution.

The freedom to live the American Dream starts with a quality education. The pursuit of happiness that our Constitution guarantees is dependent upon a quality education. And a quality education is dependent upon parents choosing the best education for their children—and having the power to make that choice.

All the terrible economic statistics quoted throughout this book are child's play (excuse the pun) compared to the results of our failing government-run education system. The dramatic and accelerating decline of our public school system is the shame of this once great country. Generations of children mis-educated in our dumbed-down public schools certainly played a major role in the re-election of Obama. Millions of voters had no clue about the definition of socialism. They knew nothing about economics. No one has ever taught them how government fails at everything it does. No one has ever exposed them to the heroes of the U.S. economy—small business owners. The younger generation didn't vote for a leader, they voted for "the American Idol."

"EVERY CHILD LEFT BEHIND"

That's the only accurate description for our government-run public school system in Obama's America.

This dumbing down of America has condemned millions of young people to a future with no hope, no advancement, no good jobs, perhaps no jobs at all. The American Dream of each generation doing better than the past has been relegated to the dustbin of history. It is a national disgrace.

Pause for a second, take a deep breath, and reflect on the quagmire called "the public school system." In 2011 SAT scores in critical reading reached their lowest levels EVER.[1] "Ever" as in the history of America! Combined math and reading SAT scores were the lowest since 1995.[2] This, despite our country spending the most money on education *ever*. Since 1970 education spending is up 375 percent, while reading scores have declined by 25 percent and our children's math and science scores are in the bottom third for developed nations.[3] Education is the only institution I know where the worse they do, the more money they demand…and get!

Studies find that fewer than 50 percent of students know when the Civil War was fought, 25 percent are unaware that Adolph Hitler was Germany's leader in World War II, and only 23 percent of students can identify George

Washington as our first president. These are the students taught by "state-certified" teachers.[4]

Our public schools are failing miserably compared to the school systems of other industrialized countries. Children are dropping out of high school in record numbers. A study by the Education Trust shows that one in four U.S. children drop out of high school. Among minorities the dropout rate is more than one out of three. The system has deteriorated so far that young people today are less likely to receive a diploma than their parents.[5]

But wait, it gets worse. In the fifty largest U.S. cities, the dropout rate is almost 50 percent, with minority dropout rates as much as 25 percent higher than white students. Approximately 1.2 million students drop out each year, one every twenty-six seconds. Where do these statistics come from? Direct from the Department of Education.[6]

How important is the dropout rate? Researchers report that those who have not graduated from high school are eight times more likely to wind up in prison.[7] This is no small problem—there are 6.2 million high school dropouts.[8] How shocking and sad. These are the results of the public school system of the richest nation in the world.

The worse the statistics get, the more money teachers' unions demand as a reward for their failure...and the more the unions demand teachers' pay *not* be based on performance, merit, or accountability.[9] Well now we know why. If pay were based on performance, record numbers of public school teachers—and administrators—would be fired.

But worst of all, the more the teachers' unions fail, the more they demand no other options be allowed—that their monopoly be strengthened. And they have the full support of progressives and liberal politicians in holding America's children hostage to their incompetence. If a dumbed-down, ill-educated, unemployable, dependent electorate is their dream, then they are achieving that goal with flying colors!

Remember Barry Goldwater's words back in 1959:

> Education is one of the great problems of our day... [lobbyists] tend to see the problem in quantitative terms—not enough

schools, not enough teachers, not enough equipment. I think
it has to do with quality: How good are the schools we have?
Their solution is to spend more money. Mine is to raise standards. Their resource is the federal government. Mine is the
local school board, the private school, the individual citizen—
as far away from the federal government as one can possibly go.
And I suspect that if we knew which of these two views on
education will eventually prevail, we would know also whether
Western civilization is due to survive, or will pass away.

Well, we now see the results of half a century of higher spending
on education, more involvement by the federal government, and more
meddling by the teachers' unions. The results are devastatingly clear.
Goldwater was right—the survival of Western civilization is in doubt.
The only way to solve our educational crisis is by reducing the role of
the federal government.

When President Bush took office in 2001, Education Department
spending was just under $40 billion. By the first year of Obama's presidency
it was almost $140 billion, including an extra $98 billion from Obama's
stimulus program.[10] Add up the numbers. Does anyone think public education is three times better today than it was twelve years ago?

It's no surprise that President Obama and Education Secretary Arne
Duncan are in panic mode. They are handing out waivers to opt out of
"No Child Left Behind" like candy—at least thirty-four of fifty states have
been granted waivers so far.[11]

What is the Obama administration's amazing solution? Dumb down
the standards. Have you ever heard of such a dumb (excuse the pun) solution? Only in Obama's America.

Despite all this gloom and doom, there are rays of hope. In localities
where competition has been allowed in the form of charter schools and
voucher programs, a number have flourished and are achieving enviable
results. Another continuing success story is that of homeschooling. The
Department of Education reports a 74 percent increase in homeschooling
since 1999.[12]

There is a good reason for this dramatic increase in parents choosing homeschooling. I am the proud father of one of those remarkable educational success stories. I've mentioned my "Homeschool to Harvard" story, but now I want to fill in the details.

HOMESCHOOL TO HARVARD

My daughter, Dakota Root, was homeschooled here in Las Vegas. Dakota scored perfect SAT scores of 800 in reading and writing. She was a National Merit Scholar and Presidential Scholar nominee. She was accepted by many of this nation's finest universities including Harvard, Stanford, Duke, Columbia, Penn, Brown, Chicago, Virginia, and Cal-Berkeley. She actually had the confidence to turn down an early admissions offer from Yale before she had gotten any of her other acceptances. *My kid turned down Yale!*

At Harvard, she has earned straight As and the John Harvard award for being in the top 5 percent of her class. Today she attends Oxford University in England. Harvard and Oxford are rated as the best colleges in the world.[13] Dakota is a scholar and an athlete. Fencing for the elite Harvard team, she earned Second Team All-Ivy League honors. I am proud to say Dakota is among the best and brightest ever produced by the great state of Nevada. She represents what all of us hope and pray for our children.

What makes Dakota's story so remarkable is that she was educated in the same city (Las Vegas) that produces some of the worst public education results in America. So how did it happen? What was in the water at the Root household? Can others learn from Dakota's story? Can others replicate her remarkable Homeschool to Harvard story? YES they can!

It doesn't take a village…or a government…or a teachers' union to raise a child—it takes a mother and father who give a damn.

The key is the same as achieving success in all other areas of life: taking action, taking charge, taking personal responsibility, and being RELENTLESS. It requires taking back the power from government. Dakota Root's story is a testament to the power of the individual and understanding that when it comes to educating our children, government is too big to succeed.

My advice as the homeschool dad of a Harvard and Oxford superstar scholar and athlete: Take control. Take charge. Take action. Be proactive. Become the CEO of your child's future. "If it is to be, it is up to me." Only through self-reliance, personal responsibility, and rugged individualism can a parent change their child's direction and super-charge their future.

Here's what it comes down to. You can't trust the government to educate your children—any more than you can trust them to guarantee your retirement, provide your medical care, or deliver the mail without losing $15.9 billion per year.[14] "Free" public education may have been a great deal in the past—just as Social Security was a bargain for the first recipients, who paid into the system for only a few years (and were paid much more than they ever contributed). But it's only the early investors in Ponzi schemes who make out like bandits. By this point, Americans entrusting their kids to most public school systems are just being cheated.

Education is not "free" if it ruins your child's prospects in life. The worst SAT scores in history and the low rankings of our students compared to other countries prove that we aren't getting any bargain. "Free" in this case is very expensive.

With Great Depression II waiting around the corner, family is going to be more economically important than it has been since the original Great Depression. When the government's promises to take care of us all from cradle to grave are finally proven to be completely empty, where will we turn in emergencies? To family. In those dire circumstances, the families that will survive, thrive, and prosper are going to be the families where each person in that family is an independent, highly productive, creative, and resilient individual, capable of lending a hand to brothers and sisters, parents and grandparents in a serious crisis.

Do you want to let the public schools educate your children to be dependent clients of the welfare state? Or do you want them to get a real education that will make them independent achievers? If you want them to grow up to be people you can be proud of, you're going to have to take their education into your own hands.

What did we teach Dakota that isn't being taught in the public schools of Nevada? Since the day she was born, her mom and dad taught her a work ethic. She learned that to succeed she would have to outwork, outshine, outsmart, and out-hustle every other student. She was taught talk is cheap, there are no short cuts. The foundation of success is to get up early, do the work, make the sacrifices, live with discipline, and fight passionately and relentlessly for your dreams.

We taught her to relish competition and embrace winning. We taught her to build her life around detailed and specific goals, to set the bar high and aim for the stars. We taught her that dreams became goals with a plan and that she must be willing to risk courageously to turn her dreams into reality. We taught her to embrace and learn from failure, but to always get right back into the battle. And we taught her to never settle for anything less than her definition of success.

From birth we set the bar at Dakota's acceptance at either Stanford or Harvard. For eighteen years we talked about it, planned it, dreamed it, and worked for it. We took her on campus tours of Stanford and Harvard so she could see her goals clearly. The result? The first classroom of Dakota Root's life was inside the hallowed halls of Harvard.

And it happened right here in Las Vegas—without government, teachers' unions, or education bureaucrats involved. *I hate to think what might have become of our incredible daughter if she had been subjected to the national disgrace known as public education.*

What were the sacrifices? Many. While other kids spent their school days being indoctrinated to believe competition and winning are unimportant, Dakota was learning to relish competition and value winning. While other kids were becoming experts at partying, Dakota was learning about sacrifice and discipline. While other kids were busy getting their driver's licenses at age sixteen, Dakota was studying for SAT exams, taking piano lessons, Spanish and French lessons, swimming lessons, tennis lessons, and fencing lessons and being tutored for academic excellence. While other kids shopped, dated, and gossiped, Dakota was debating with her dad about politics and current events at the dinner table (while devouring books on science, math, history, literature, politics, and business). While others were out experimenting with alcohol and drugs, Dakota was practicing the sport she loves with dedication, intensity, and passion—fencing.

While other kids came home to empty houses, Dakota's mom, dad, or both were home every day to share meals, a bedtime kiss, and prayer with our four homeschooled kids. Dakota got to travel with her dad to major business and political events across the country. She watched, studied, and absorbed her dad conducting business like a Zen master.

Then when the moment of opportunity called, she took advantage. I asked her to give my nomination speech for president of the United States on C-SPAN at the age of sixteen. Dakota delivered the first speech of her life like a pro in front of 1,000 delegates and media, and a national TV audience at the Libertarian Convention in 2008. Google "Dakota Root." The speech is the first thing that pops up. Watch a sixteen-year-old deliver a speech on national television like a professional politician.

After eighteen years of hard work, dedication, discipline and sacrifice, Dakota achieved "overnight success" with her acceptance at Harvard. And even better than her Harvard degree is her understanding that that's how "overnight success" usually happens—it's the reward for many years (sometimes decades) of hard work.

Is Dakota's story unusual? Actually, no. A recent study shows that homeschooled kids score almost twice as high on exams as public school students. Other studies show that homeschooled kids score 72 points higher than the national average on SAT exams.[15]

Homeschoolers are more likely to attend college, are more likely to graduate, and have higher college GPAs (Grade Point Averages) than other students.[16]

The old wives' tale spread by the teachers' unions (who are afraid of competition) is that homeschoolers are not "socialized." Well, the facts are in. Homeschoolers are almost twice as involved in their local community or church as public school students, and almost three times as involved in politics.[17]

Homeschooled children also have far fewer behavioral problems.[18]

But why are homeschool success stories like Dakota's not covered by the mainstream media? Why are these remarkable statistics that prove the success of homeschooling blacked out by the media? The media doesn't just ignore positive stories about homeschooling, they appear to go out of their way to feature *negative* stories. The only news stories I've seen in recent years about homeschooling portray it as a form of inferior education practiced by "ignorant" backwoods people or supposed "religious extremists."

To the contrary, I'm here to educate readers that homeschooling is becoming mainstream—and in cases such as mine, preferred by parents who could afford to pay for elite private schools. My family is the symbol of the change in the image and acceptance of homeschooling.

So why does the media bend over backward to try to smear homeschooling? Is it possible that the success of homeschooling threatens the liberal establishment? Is it possible that teachers' unions believe that if more citizens are exposed to the success of homeschooling, parents might be emboldened to take their children out of failing public schools? Are they afraid that the success of homeschooling might lead to lower funding for failing public education, weaker teachers' unions, and even a national push for school choice?

Our Root family brand of homeschooling melded parental education with tutoring by hand-picked retired teachers and college professors, combined with a personally chosen curriculum. You may be able to get great results with a slightly different combination of resources. There are myriad homeschooling resources out there, from curricula you can subscribe to, to online classes for kids, to homeschooling support programs (which will even allow your child to play high school football). The crucial factor isn't what program you pick, or whom you hire to teach your children, or how much of the actual tuition you and your spouse take on yourselves. There are infinite variations in how you arrange your children's education. The crucial factor is that you realize it's your responsibility, as their parent, to take charge of their education. "If it is to be, it is up to me" applies to your children's education just as much as to achieving financial success.

By the way, I respect and applaud teachers. I think most work hard, sacrifice, and care for their students. Dakota owes her homeschool success to several retired teachers who are like members of our family. Those same retired teachers are now teaching a new generation of my children—ages five, eight, and thirteen.

Unfortunately teachers' unions and education bureaucrats are a far different story. Education in this country has deteriorated for decades under their leadership. Homeschooling worked for our family because we took the best of education—dedicated parents and professional educators—and eliminated the worst—unions and government bureaucrats.

Dakota Root doesn't just prove the success of homeschooling. She proves the success of the individual over dependence upon government. She proves the success of alternative education, parental freedom, and school choice. Her tremendous success as a scholar and athlete proves it doesn't take a state-licensed teacher to educate a child. It takes two caring, motivated parents with the willingness and courage to seize control and take responsibility for their children's future.

And the homeschooling success story continues. Fast-forward to 2011. We had our son Hudson, then in sixth grade, take the same nationwide exam as Dakota took all those years ago. Same results. Hudson, a sixth grader, scored P.H.S. (Post High School) in every category. Our seven-year-old Remington took the same nationwide standardized exam for first graders in 2011. He scored at sixth-through-ninth-grade level in every category.

So now you have a remarkable pattern. One child achieving those results is fantastic, two is remarkable, but all three performing the same way (a decade apart) is proof positive that we are on to something special. So special it can be a "model" for every parent in America.

My final advice: You are the CEO of your child's future. Don't wait for opportunity to knock. Don't wait for the approval or permission of others. Don't wait for the cavalry. Don't leave it to fate, or luck, or Big Brother. Don't depend on Obama. In the end, no one cares or loves your child like you do. It is up to you to seize opportunity and take control of your child's future. Dakota's story proves the American Dream is alive, if only we'd stop depending on government to save us.

CHAPTER THIRTY

BACK TO BASICS: COMMONSENSE ADVICE REGARDLESS OF YOUR FINANCES

DID YOU KNOW?

- Whatever your net worth, you should be preparing for the Obama Great Depression by cutting expenses and acquiring new streams of income
- In some places, it is actually cheaper to rent than to own your own home
- You could save hundreds of dollars by cutting back on restaurants and on going out to movies—Netflix costs just $7.99 a month

You've learned about the Precious Metals Defense System and other Y-PODS that can help you protect your assets and investments in the Obama Great Depression. But in this Zombie Economy, not everybody *has* assets. This chapter is devoted to commonsense advice that applies to you regardless of your net worth or asset status. This is the aspect of Y-PODS that applies equally to *everyone* who wants to survive and thrive during the next four years of Obama. These are the steps you should be taking right now:

1) Cut spending and downsize. This advice applies to your personal life as much as to any business you may own or be associated with. To protect yourself and your family, it is imperative to minimize debt. If that means downsizing—then do it. Certainly don't buy that new car or bigger TV. Now is not the time for the new kitchen you've been planning on— remodeling can wait, especially if you have to go into debt (credit card or otherwise) to pay for it. Save the money!

If you have a spare bedroom, rent it out to a college kid or a once-a- month visiting businessman. If you have a second home, rent it out. If you can't rent it for enough to cover the mortgage, taxes, and upkeep, sell it. Unburden yourself from as much debt as possible, because Mr. Obama is coming for your money. He doesn't care about you or your commitments.

The banks we, the taxpayers, bailed out, don't care about you or me. They feel no responsibility to us. So it's time to walk away. If necessary, short sell your home and become a renter. A house with a $3,000 mortgage, plus $500 property tax, plus $200 insurance, plus $200 repairs, quickly adds up to $4,000 per month—whereas the same house might rent for half that amount. There are some areas of the country where it is actually cheaper to rent than to own a house.[1]

Don't ignore the small things. Cut back on restaurants and going out to movies. Netflix costs just $7.99 a month. Start looking at your cable, Internet, and phone bills. You might be surprised how much can be saved with a little shopping around. Rather than an expensive family vacation at a resort, visit relatives or friends…or go camping.

2) Multiply yourself to create additional sources of income. Get a second

HOW TO REALLY SAVE MONEY

Don't worry about keeping up with the Joneses. Think of yourself as *being* the Joneses, a smart family prepared to weather Obama's economic storm—and let your neighbors try to keep up with you!

job, a third job—or, better yet, start your own business. This author has a dozen careers and still took on another to write this book. I can sleep when I'm dead. Until then, I owe it to my family to work sixteen hours a day (minimum) to survive and thrive. That is how you create financial freedom and independence.

These are things Obama hates. He wants you desperate, hopeless, and dependent on him. But those of us willing to work sixteen-hour days, seven days a week, don't need Obama or the government. Therefore we aren't beholden to him.

Let me give you an example. I hear people who work for government complain they don't make enough money. First, that's a lie. They might make $60,000 or $70,000 (which isn't a fortune), but that doesn't count their benefits, healthcare, or pension. In reality their $60K salary is $120,000 with benefits added in.[2] The rest of us have no lifetime pension. Please stop whining. More importantly, government employees enjoy fantastic work schedules. Some of them work only until 3 p.m. Others work three days on, four days off. They are off on weekends. They are off on every holiday. Some are off the entire summer. Most retire after twenty to twenty-five years.

If this is you, rather than complain, see it as a gift from heaven. You have a guaranteed job for life, plus pension and healthcare, with an easy schedule most of us would die for. That's your base, your foundation. You are the luckiest person on earth. Now build a second career and income source.

The same advice applies to all of you with a steady, secure job in the private sector (if there is such a thing any longer), and even more so to those of you who are unemployed, underemployed, or at risk of losing the job you have. You may not have the job security for life enjoyed by public sector employees. They have the perfect foundation to start a business or sell real estate, stocks, cars, insurance, or mortgages on the side, in their spare time. But private sector employees should certainly have an equal or greater motivation.

If you don't know where to start, I suggest you look into buying a franchise, or starting a "One Man Army" online business, or joining an MLM (multi level marketing) company, as I discussed in detail in a previous chapter.

By the way, the people I've met in MLM would all love to have a $75,000 government job, with tenure, free healthcare, and a pension as a base…to go with their $100,000+ MLM income. The people I know who work in sales, MLM, or own their own business all have one thing in common—they have no job guaranteed for life, no pension, no free healthcare. Yet they don't complain, they just work. Hard. Long. Weekends. Mornings. Nights. That's how you build financial freedom and a legacy for your children. Instead of complaining, you work. Instead of watching TV or playing golf, you work.

Yet those who have the safe weekly check and guaranteed government job for life seem to always be complaining that they aren't paid enough. No one is guaranteed a prosperous life. You have to work for it. Instead of watching TV three hours a night, and playing around on weekends…WORK. Take a second job, or build a third career, or both. Wait tables on the weekend. Instead of retiring with a $60,000 pension, go get a new job, or build a career that doubles your income to $120,000 in "retirement." Do that and you'll soon have nothing to complain about.

3) Be proactive. If you are insecure in your current job, or unsure about the future survival of the company for whom you are working, don't wait to be fired, or for it to close. Then it's too late.

As you know, over the years I've owned several businesses. I have always told my employees to know their value and have encouraged them to leave for greener pastures if available. It is so easy to settle into a routine and "go with the flow." This is absolutely NOT the time to do either. As you are now aware, Obama is destroying the economy. If you have even a hint that your job may be one of those being destroyed…take action now. It's always a thousand times easier to get a new job while already employed. Once you're unemployed and desperately looking for a job, you've lost a ton of value. Sad, but true.

4) Talk to your teenaged children. One of the many areas where public schools fail our children is teaching them about money. They don't. And, they certainly aren't telling them about the disaster Obama is making of their future. It is your duty to educate them. Anyone who has read this far is well aware, we are facing an economic crisis unlike any ever faced before. Now is not the time to be reluctant to discuss personal finances with your teenaged children, especially if your job or family finances are in a precarious position.

Teenagers are old enough not only to understand, but also to help and contribute. Obvious ways are to get a part-time job to save for college, or even help pay current household expenses. A frank and honest discussion about your situation and concerns can help them understand why you are resisting getting them the newest iPhone, latest video game, latest fad article of clothing, and so forth. My experience has always been if you are honest with your kids, they will be honest with you.

5) Talk to your grown children. I have a good friend who is an investment advisor. She tells me she is approached weekly by at least one of her long-term clients…often more than one…whom she has carefully planned, guided, and invested into a comfortable retirement. The issue is always the same:

> My married (or divorced) son/daughter has just lost their job. One of our grandkids is in college, the other two will be soon. They have no savings and are facing foreclosure. They have asked if we can help. Oh, and you know how you told us not to countersign any loans…well, we only did it once…to help them out when they bought the house. What do we do now?

You don't think it can happen to you? It is happening all across America, and Obama's plan for the economy will continue to make it worse. I'm not going to try to advise you what to do if you are caught in this tragic situation. Only you can make that decision. Just be prepared for it, it may be sooner than you think.

This is all part of Obama's plan. He doesn't like rich people (except his lefty millionaire campaign donors and Hollywood pals). He doesn't want you to have independence or financial freedom. He wants everyone dependent on government. In Obama's perfect world, no one should have rich parents who can help in a crisis. That's "unfair." He wants to bleed us with taxes so no one has the extra money left to help their kids in an emergency. Then the kids will have to turn to the government. Obama wants government to be your only Sugar Daddy.

My advice to everyone reading this who has any concerns they may end up with relatives or close friends coming to them to ask for money, is to have an honest and straightforward discussion with them *now*. Forewarned at least provides the opportunity to plan and explore options. For exactly the same reason, if you are one of those who think you may need to turn to family or friends for help, I strongly suggest the "open and frank" discussion as early as possible.

I tell you this because this sad story of grown children across America asking mom and dad for financial help is like a blinking neon billboard to convince you to:

Work harder with a second or third job or career…and cut back on spending and build a savings nest egg. You are going to need it.

6) Be prepared for a serious crisis. Understand that crisis is on the way—whether it be rioting and unrest (when the government can no longer afford to keep the checks coming), terrorist attacks (provoked by the Obama administration's weakness), economic collapse, or other disruptions in the supply chain for food, water, and fuel. Be prepared. Make room in your garage or basement for an ample supply of food and water. In a prolonged period of crisis, food and water are more precious than gold. For more detailed advice on this topic from a world-class professional, please read the next chapter.

Last, if you don't own a firearm already, now is the time to acquire one, along with a large quantity of ammunition. Your access to the firearms you need may soon be severely limited—it could become very difficult to buy a gun or find ammo in Obama's America.

Many of you reading this book will scoff at this last recommendation. Let me share a story. Back in 1992, I lived in Los Angeles, surrounded by Hollywood liberals. Does that year ring a bell? Think **L.A. riots.** I remember looking out from a nearby mountain hiking trail and seeing the entire city burning, fires in all directions. Sirens were wailing from every corner of the city. News reports warned of heavily armed gangs headed for wealthy neighborhoods. The police were out-manned and out-gunned. They refused to go into violent neighborhoods. Store and homeowners were on their own. It was every man for himself.

Politically correct Hollywood liberals panicked, especially our friends with children. Guess who it was that they called? *Yours truly.* Our friends knew I was armed. They knew because they had argued with me for years that individuals had no right to own a gun.

In the middle of crisis and violence, with the smell of smoke in their nostrils, suddenly my liberal friends exhibited a change of heart. All of them, and I mean all, called to ask if they could come to our home with their families to stay. They knew the police could not protect them so they turned to Wayne Root for protection. For several days we had a full house, while I kept watch, armed and ready to defend my home, family, and friends. But I wasn't alone. Entire neighborhoods in the Hollywood Hills were patrolled by armed homeowners, who set up checkpoints and road-blocks with guns and walkie-talkies. Only residents with proof of ID were let in. The police were nowhere to be found.

With Obama in charge there is no doubt that day will come again. And, when it does it will be one thousand times worse. Are you ready? You'd better be, because this time I can't house you all!

You may not believe it will ever come to this... BUT, in case it does, in the next chapter I turn to a friend who has been in the special forces—to give you his advice on how to survive when survival means literally saving the lives of you and your family. Read on.

CHAPTER THIRTY-ONE

INVEST IN SURVIVAL— FOR YOURSELF AND YOUR FAMILY

DID YOU KNOW?

- The first thing to understand about a situation of national emergency and civil unrest is that *you cannot count on the government to come to your rescue*
- You need to plan ahead whether your family will hunker down in your domicile or depart for a safe location
- If you plan to leave, you should have supplies prepared so that you can escape within *ninety minutes* of the disaster, when your neighbors are still waiting for the government rescue

Let's face it. In the worst-case scenario, surviving, thriving, and prospering in Obama's next four years of disaster could at some point boil down to actual, physical *survival*. If there is a complete collapse— either of the U.S. economic system or of the global financial system or as a result of terrorism—we will all have much bigger worries than preserving our assets for retirement. We'll be concerned about our physical survival amidst unrest and anarchy.

Will it ever get that bad? Who knows? But I believe in being prepared—especially when the lives of my family are involved. I'm no expert on survival. So I turned to one of my close friends, a former elite U.S. Special Forces operative who served in intelligence, in counterterrorism, and as a member of the Joint Special Operations Command (JSOC). He is also an expert in biometrics and nonlethal defense technology. He is a man we can reliably turn to for professional advice on how to prepare for disaster. Here is his exclusive and valuable advice, in his own words:

SURVIVAL AS DEFINED BY A SPECIAL FORCES EXPERT

In this book, Wayne defines surviving and thriving much differently from someone like me. For the next few pages let's focus on defining survival at its most basic level—staying alive.

It is paramount to be prepared and have options when a national emergency or Act of God occurs. We have no control over events unfolding globally or nationally just as we have no control over catastrophic events. However, I can tell you, without a doubt, if you don't have a contingency plan that will allow you to execute a step-by-step process when the unthinkable occurs, you and your family are doomed to disaster.

Please listen to my advice now. You'll believe me later after a catastrophic event **THE GOVERNMENT WILL NOT COME TO YOUR RESCUE.**

Let me say it another way. Any significant event will result in the immediate stoppage of food, fuel, and essential services to which you are so accustomed. You, and you alone, will be responsible for yourself and your family. There will be no FEMA, no fuel, no food, no garbage collection, and very likely, no electricity or water.

What's your plan? Are you prepared to hunker down in your domicile and wait it out? How long can you last? Do you have water supplies and food supplies? What are you waiting for? Simply put, you are waiting for gloom and doom. I'm sorry to be so blunt but that's exactly what you're doing. Time is of the essence. Within the first ninety minutes after an emergency, while the masses are waiting for help to arrive, you must be proactive and put your plan into action. Your contingency plan is now your roadmap to survival.

What's included in your roadmap? Do you have an exit strategy to get out of the affected area? Are you prepared to hunker down and protect your fortress? The first and most important requirement is food and water—followed by shelter, heat, power, and self-defense. If you do not have at least a thirty-to-ninety-day supply of basic, easy-to-fix meals for yourself and your family, now is the time to start to put that in place. At the end of these pages I will provide a few websites where you can obtain key elements for your contingency plan, and rest assured I am in no way connected to any of these sites. I'm prepared and I hope you are. But, you have to take responsibility to "pack your own parachute."

If your plan includes departing your location, be sure you have a safe location already identified. Then, you must be prepared to leave in ninety minutes or less. Whatever you are taking with you must be easily accessible and ready to load in thirty minutes or less. Your family members must be aware of the plan and have a rally location or return immediately to aid in the loading and move out order. Don't worry about your existing domicile. Once gone there is nothing you can do to stop looters and those in dire need from gaining access. Do not inform anyone where you're going, or even let them know you are going.

Trust me when I say the operational security of your plan is essential to your survival. When the situation melts down, and it will, your neighbors, friends, and associates are going to get desperate, and by desperate I mean they are going to want what you have. It will be dog eats dog, and the untrained and ill-prepared will be the first collateral victims.

As part of your plan, know who your threats are and identify the potential they have to derail your plans. The Billy Bad Ass down the street who has constantly raved about his assault rifles and his knowledge will be the first to act in an unconventional manner. That is why speed is of the essence. You must be gone before he has a chance to act in a violent way. Do you have a plan if your exit is blocked by him or a group of these types? Hesitation will get you killed! Have multiple exit plans from your neighborhood. However, in a worst-case situation you must do what you are not trained to do to survive. Yes, you understand what I'm saying, and as hor-rific as that sounds it's your will to survive and to protect your family that will make you act. Remember avoidance and deception are key to your uninterrupted departure.

What else does it take to put together a cohesive and doable plan? It must prepare for contingencies and be simple. Do not over-plan. The most important part is to practice and rehearse.

U.S. Special Operation forces are so effective in combat for three reasons:

1. Highly intelligent operators
2. Best equipment in the world
3. Training, training, and more training

Training is everything in life. Just as you practice a sport or study for a test, you must practice your plan to be ready to put it into action. You will learn during these exercises what works and doesn't work. You will improvise the plan so that it becomes seamless. It has to be second nature.

Given your unique situation I cannot tell you what kind of plan you should have. But, sources of information are abundant on the Internet for you to create an executable and successful roadmap.

When developing a plan, understand your surroundings and also your end-game location. If your plan is to ride things out at home, then prepare for that. Are you going to secure the entire home or just a couple of rooms? Who will be in your neighborhood network of trusted parties? Where will your water come from? Your swimming pool? How will you filter it? How will you dispose of your waste? Are you prepared to share with those who were not prepared? Do you have auxiliary power gen-eration? Fuel generator? Solar power? And the last and probably the most important question to ask yourself is once you have the logistics and plan for your family in place, how are you going to defend and protect your fortress?

Know that, however much you might want to, you are not going to be able to reason or negotiate with those in dire straits. You must be prepared to provide security by force. And, by force I mean you need firepower. Make no mistake, your neighbors will also have weapons, and when all else fails they will resort to their weapons to obtain food and life essentials. Many families today have guns. However, I can assure you they are not well trained, and they don't possess sufficient quantities of munitions to sustain a fight. Don't be one of them. If you are prepared, they will move on to some other soft target to get what they need. So in your plan you must have a defense component that includes training, a sufficient quantity of weapons, and an over-supply of munitions.

It is not my intent to put the fear of God in you. It is my intent to open your eyes to the possibility of a major disruption of essential needs. I see people living their lives every day and how they react when their cellular service goes down. Imagine what happens when you can't procure food and fuel! Imagine no electricity, and no communications. Actually, you don't even need to imagine it. Look at what happened when events as minor as an electrical outage happened in several major U.S. cities…the gangs and looters came out en masse. Remember the L.A. riots? The police were afraid to protect us.

For events other than natural catastrophes, there are always warning signs. It is your job to be aware and heed them. Most people are sheep, living their lives one day at a time, paycheck to paycheck, expecting everything will remain the same. They don't realize they are just waiting to be slaughtered.

I am not one of those types…don't you be either. I've traveled the world, lived life, and endured hardship. I've defended my country with my life and love America with all my heart. I know I must be prepared to defend what is mine and what is near and dear to me! That is my family, loved ones, and my team members. We have a bond that transcends itself for the greater good of survival. It is a code of brothers that causes us to be prepared and to act. It is our hope that disaster never comes, but we would be naïve to think it won't. We will be prepared and we will practice. It is infinitely better to be prepared and never have to implement than to not be prepared at all!

I'm not telling you to be an extremist. I'm telling you to be vigilant, alert, and prepared! Nothing more, nothing less.

While it is your decision, know that your life and the lives of your family depend on it. Do you really want to put your lives in the hands of others? If you believe like me, take responsibility for your decisions, and intend to be ready for the day we all hope will never come, continue reading. If not, skip the rest and continue on with the rest of book. There you will receive incredible insight into what the brightest minds are doing to survive a financial meltdown to our markets, currency, and financial way of life. For those of you still with me, I will guide you through establishing the minimum requirements for survival of life.

Okay, you're still here, the brave, practical ones who have the ability to envision a modern civil meltdown. Let me walk you through what you will need. Establishing your minimum requirements is dependent upon your needs and experience; I would suggest that you evaluate your needs based on your location and/or evacuation location.

As I stated earlier, your human priorities are as follows:

1. Food and water
2. Shelter
3. Heat
4. Power
5. Self-defense

SELF DEFENSE

I choose to start with what I feel most comfortable with and that is, at a minimum, having one weapon for each individual capable of providing support. I recommend a handgun and would also suggest one shotgun for every two individuals. Shotguns are perfect for home and close-quarter protection, and you don't have to be a marksman to take down or ward off an aggressor. In the event you're looking for standoff protection, acquire a rifle or assault weapon.

Here are your weapons requirements in a snapshot:

1. .40 Caliber Hand Gun (Glock Model 22, 27 or equivalent)
2. Shotguns (Mossberg Model 500 Series)

3. Assault Weapons (XCR-L Series)
4. Ammunition (as much as each person can carry)

To make life easier you should also have some type of backpack system. Your choices are based on individual needs and comfort. **The choices are MOLLE or ALICE:**

MOLLE = Modular Lightweight Load-carrying Equipment

ALICE = All-purpose Lightweight Individual Carrying Equipment

My recommendation is MOLLE Large as it is the most modern and allows you to add and subtract pouches as needed; it offers the ability to add Commercial Off The Shelf (COTS) sleep systems. The only drawback is the plastic frame. However, for value it is the perfect bug-out bag that facilitates "grab and go" scenarios, saving precious time. Each member in your team should be fitted and equipped. You should have the contents of the bag fully defined and packed. It should at a minimum include:

1. Food (enough for three days)
2. Water and water purification systems
3. Medical kit
4. Extra set of clothes, socks, etc.
5. Knife and entrenching tool
6. Chem (snap and shake) flashlights
7. Fire starter
8. Sleep system
9. Flares
10. Ammunition

Special Note: Have a supply of cash, silver, and gold and an emergency hand crank AM/FM radio.

I could spend pages addressing each of these elements, but you can identify sources via the Internet for the right setup for yourself and your team. Keep in mind that loads vary by person and you have to manage that carefully. Remember, you are only as strong as your weakest link.

Now, you are asking "if I'm basing my survival from my existing domicile why would I need the bug-out bag?" Quite simply, it is vital for many reasons. I keep mine in the trunk of my car and if I have to abandon my vehicle during a time of crisis, I have the essentials to get home. What happens if your home gets overrun? Even if your plan is to stay put, plan an exit strategy to a predetermined safe haven…just in case.

FOOD AND WATER

Have sufficient supplies of both food and water. "Sufficient" depends upon your location. If you lose power, utilize food on hand that will spoil first. Save the recommended freeze-dried foods for later.

Fill your bathtubs and other containers with water. Do this first. You never know how long city water sources will be available. If you have access to a stream, river, lake, or swimming pool, make sure you have adequate filtration equipment.

Ration your food, and be disciplined from day one. Above all, do not panic and NEVER communicate about your food supplies to anyone. Operational security is paramount to your survival. The last thing you want is to make your location a target.

SHELTER, HEAT, AND POWER

Wherever you are, step one is to limit access. Board up all first floor windows and reinforce doorways. There are simple ways to do this without a major renovation. Place lookouts on the second floor to ensure these areas are not breached.

Have a supply of firewood if you have a fireplace, or space saver heaters in the event that you don't. Acquire a gas-powered generator to be used only to power essentials, and locate it on a secure balcony with an adequate supply of fuel.

This is all about prior planning, dress rehearsals, and trial and error from these practice rounds.

When I was asked to contribute to this *Ultimate Obama Survival Guide* I was at first hesitant, as I didn't want to be perceived as a nut job, but after talking to Wayne and really understanding where we are as a nation, I felt compelled to offer a brief overview of my definition of "survival." Pray to God you never need it.

My intent here is simply to open your eyes, give you a brief overview, and let you determine how much or how little you will be prepared.

Let me end by pointing out America is at a crossroads. Our government has become a spending addict. When elected, President Obama turned on the spending faucet like no president before him. What have we gotten for it? Absolutely nothing! Ayn Rand's *Atlas Shrugged* is a work of fiction quickly becoming reality.

Who is John Galt? Wayne, is it you? I hope so.

People, it is time to start preparing, or get in line with the rest of the sheep.

Survival resources:

Weapons:
- http://us.glock.com/
- http://www.mossberg.com/
- http://xcr.robarm.com/

Food:
- http://www.preparewise.com/
- http://www.wisefoodsupply.com/

Survival:
- http://www.tacticalintelligence.net/blog/top-10-most-influential-survival-and-preparedness-blogs.htm

CHAPTER THIRTY-TWO

ACT LOCALLY

DID YOU KNOW?

- The groundwork for Obama's election and re-election was laid by leftists working for years at the local level
- While we were busy watching the president and Congress, local radicals were changing our laws and dumbing down our children
- With commonsense reforms that required state employees to pay a little more for their own benefits, Wisconsin went from a $3.6 billion budget deficit to a surplus in one year

All the Y-PODS we've talked about so far focused on *you*—saving your family, your business, your personal economy. But Your Personal Obama Defense Shield also has to include making a difference—to your neighbors, to your fellow citizens, to your country. Given Obama's re-election, we may not be able to stop Obamageddon from descending on the United States. But we can do our best to save America one town, one school district, one judge at a time. This is personal, too—because without the right laws, the right education system, the right business environment, the right court system, all else is lost. We are all in this together. During the Revolutionary War our Founding Fathers figured it out. In Benjamin Franklin's famous words, "We must all hang together, or assuredly we shall

all hang separately." The left figured that out a long time ago. They have had a big head start. *But it's not too late.*

You've probably heard the ancient Chinese saying: "A journey of a thousand miles begins with one step." Assuming you, like me, have chosen to stay in America and fight, here is the way to take that first baby step. Here is how we beat Obama and win our country back for our children and grandchildren. That's as personal as it gets. It all starts by committing to a plan to take back America one precinct at a time.

Let's beat former Obama Chief of Staff Rahm Emanuel with his own words. Rahm said, "You never want a serious crisis to go to waste." The left has used crisis to change our country from the ground up. They understood it all starts locally. Well, two can play at that game.

Now is the time to get back to basics and work harder than ever politically. Don't wait for the next presidential or even Congressional election. TODAY (this moment) is the right time to focus at the local level. Start with your city council, mayor, judges, and school board. And, don't forget zoning boards and water boards. Most of us pay little attention to these local elections and local positions of authority. That strategy needs to change. Often these local officials affect our lives far more than a president, senator, or congressman.

These offices and positions are not glamorous. They don't make media headlines. No one gets famous as a school board member or water commissioner. But this is how the Marxists, socialists, progressives, and liberals (or whatever they are calling themselves nowadays) have taken over America—from the ground up. They understood if you take control of the schools, courts and laws, zoning, and local decisions on taxing and spending—you control the agenda. The groundwork for a socialist takeover has been laid for several generations. While we were busy watching the president and Congress, the local radicals were changing our laws and dumbing down our children.

Let's point out the crisis. Let's not let it go to waste. Is there a crisis bigger than our failing public schools? How about our debt-ridden, bankrupt local and state governments? And what about the pension crisis of our local government employees? Not to mention activist leftist judges changing and violating our Constitution?

Over the next few years not letting the financial and debt crisis of local government "go to waste" is going to be a powerful tool to elect officeholders who understand economics and who will implement fiscally responsible policies. Recent history proves how successful this can be. Conditions became so bad that states such as Michigan, Ohio, New Jersey, and Wisconsin—long bastions of liberal spending and powerful unions—actually elected fiscally conservative governors and legislators.[1]

Wisconsin proved the solution is E-A-S-Y. Simply limit the spending on government employees, make them contribute more to their own pensions and healthcare, and overnight your state goes from insolvent to healthy. Wisconsin went from a $3.6 billion deficit to a surplus in one year. There is no magic here. It's all about cutting government spending, laying off government employees (in many cases through attrition—meaning no one that wants a job will lose a job), and asking government employees to contribute just a little more.[2]

Now is the time! With the crises that Obama has created, we can beat him at his own game. We can use these crises to turn this Obama disaster into an opportunity to take control of government and schools starting at the grass-roots level. But you must commit to taking positive action. Walk your neighborhood, precinct, or district. Man a phone bank. Donate money. Write letters to the editor. Run for office yourself. Commit to devoting two to four hours a week to making a difference, and recruit two other friends to do the same. If every conservative and libertarian in America committed to this plan, we'd take back our country within four years. Let's start today.

• • •

Author's Note: That concludes your introduction to my Ultimate Obama Survival Plan's Y-PODS: Your Personal Obama Defense Shield. Now we're going to be taking it up to the next level. Coming up next is a once-in-a-lifetime opportunity to earn your MBA degree. Consider this next section a crash course in economics, business, and finance taught by a group of American business superstars. I'm proud to call them my friends.

PART THREE

BUSINESS SUPERSTARS OFFER THEIR ADVICE

The key to success is to know what you know, and what you don't. Always seek out the best and brightest, who know more than you. Then shut up and listen.

So for this book I've sought out, among my friends, the smartest, sharpest, wealthiest minds in the country. I thank God that this small businessman was blessed to become a vice presidential nominee and then a Fox News regular guest and national media personality. These opportunities have allowed me to meet a group of business superstars a guy like me normally would never have access to.

I've interviewed eighteen friends—millionaire superstars of business. They all have one thing in common; they are brilliant, self-made businesspeople. Forget IQ. These unique people have something very rare: EIQ—Economic Intelligence Quotient.

I asked them all a simple question: **"How do you intend to survive, thrive, and prosper in the next four years of Obama, and what can the rest of us do?"**

Then I sat back, shut up, and listened. In the following pages, you'll have the benefit of the advice they gave me. It's like having a team of business geniuses whispering in your ear.

Keep in mind I'm not a billionaire or the CEO of a multinational company. Nor do I have an MBA from Harvard. When I came up with the idea of asking my wealthiest friends for advice, I didn't realize it would be the most enlightening, empowering, and educational experience of my life. Forget grad school. This one month of interviews with these business superstars was better than getting an MBA and Ph.D. in economics, finance, and business.

I'm clicking my heels as I walk. I'm smiling from ear to ear. I've never had so much fun learning about business in my life. These aren't boring college professors (who, by the way, know nothing about business other than what they've read in books). These are people who risked their own money (and are still risking it today) to build billion-dollar companies, or manage billion-dollar hedge funds. Their advice is *priceless*.

But it won't be just me benefiting. You're about to gain access to the exact same advice. You're about to get your Ph.D. in real life business and economics. Congratulations. And remember you didn't pay $100,000 for two years at Harvard or Stanford Business School. Your only cost was the price of this book. Pretty cool!

Here's one more revelation that I want to share about this experience. About 90 percent of the advice from these business superstars came in after I finished writing my personal advice on how to survive, thrive, and prosper in the Obama era. Without an MBA, without being a billionaire…relying solely on a lifetime of small business experience, combined with common sense, I had arrived at a lot of the very same conclusions as my superstar millionaires had to offer. Their advice reinforced everything I had written. Quite frankly, that gave me great confidence about facing the next four crucial years. It should give you great confidence, as well.

In the following chapters you'll discover what these business superstars believe are your best solutions to survive, thrive, and prosper in the face of Obamageddon. Read, absorb like a sponge, learn, then take action. This advice has the power to change your life.

CHAPTER THIRTY-THREE

DR. MARC FABER

D r. Marc Faber is a leading investment advisor and fund manager. Faber was a managing director at Drexel Burnham Lambert Ltd. Hong Kong from the beginning of 1978 until 1990. In 1990 he founded Marc Faber Limited, based in Hong Kong. Known for his contrarian investment philosophies, Faber is also an advisor to a number of investment funds that focus on emerging and frontier markets. Faber also invests and acts as a fund manager to private wealthy clients.

Dr. Faber is often quoted in national and international financial media and is a frequent guest on CNBC and Bloomberg TV programs. He is a regular speaker on the investment circuit and writes often for leading financial publications, including *Forbes* and the *Wall Street Journal*. He serves on the board of directors of numerous companies.

Dr. Faber is perhaps best known as the publisher of the widely read monthly investment newsletter the *Gloom Boom & Doom Report*, which highlights unusual investment opportunities. He is also the author of the bestselling *Tomorrow's Gold: Asia's Age of Discovery* and was the subject of a 1998 book entitled *Riding the Millennial Storm: Marc Faber's Path to Profit in the Financial Markets*.[1]

Dr. Faber is famous for advising clients to get out of the stock market one week before the October 1987 crash. He predicted the rise of oil, precious metals, other commodities, and emerging markets, especially China. He also correctly predicted the slide of the U.S. dollar (since 2002) and the

5/06 and 2/07 mini-corrections. He has gained a reputation as a contrarian investor.

Faber was born in Switzerland, studied economics at the University of Zurich, and obtained his Ph.D. magna cum laude at the age of twenty-four. He resides in Thailand.

DR. MARC FABER'S ADVICE

"Government is the great fiction, through which everybody endeavors to live at the expense of everybody else."

—Frederic Bastiat, French economist (1801–1850)[2]

The great part about being a pessimist like me is to wake up every morning and be pleasantly surprised that whereas it may be spinning, my head has not yet fallen off or been hit by a drone sent by some evil government. So, every day, over coffee, before taking my daily bath, I think about the huge problem we have in the most advanced economies of the West.

There are far too many people who vote for the living they get in one form or another from a government handout. In fact, if the U.S. government were to use GAAP accounting standards (under which the fiscal deficit would be annually over $5 trillion), it would by now have become obvious to everyone that the Obama socialist system is fast running out of "other people's money."[3]

Now, I cannot blame Mr. Obama alone for this mess. Mr. Greenspan and Mr. Bernanke's expansionary monetary policies created a colossal inflation in all asset prices from which the wealthiest ¼ of 1 percent of the population (including myself) benefited the most.

By keeping interest rates artificially low (negative in real terms) it also enabled the federal government to finance growing fiscal deficits at—for now—no cost. But to be fair to the academics at the Federal Reserve (who wouldn't know how to run a simple laundry or grocery shop in a million years) we have to assume some responsibility because, as Harold Laski observed already in 1930, "A State divided into a small number of rich and a large number of poor will always develop a government manipulated by the rich to protect the amenities represented by their property."[4]

Therefore, we now have a situation which my favorite American historian, Will Durant, described in *The Lessons of History* as follows: "In progressive societies the concentration of wealth may reach a point where the strength of number in the many poor rivals the strength of ability in the few rich; then the unstable equilibrium generates a critical situation, *which history has diversely met by legislation redistributing wealth or by revolution distributing poverty* [emphasis added]."[5]

In other words, we hard-working people, whose asset values admittedly benefited from the Fed's "money printing," are doomed one way or the other because our wealth will be decimated either sooner by taxation or later by revolution. (While some call me a pessimist, I call myself a realist.)

The good news is that in turbulent times there are great opportunities for the "thoughtful" and "prudent" investor and businessman. In my humble opinion, the opportunities are not necessarily to make money, but to make sure you lose far less wealth than the majority of other investors. I know, some people will laugh at me. But I have met so many families that lost everything (Russia in 1918, Eastern Europe 1947, China 1949, Egypt 1955, Vietnam 1975), whereas families that had diversified their wealth into a variety of asset classes (real estate, stocks, currencies, commodities, precious metals, businesses, etc.) **in different sovereign jurisdictions** might have lost "only" 80 percent of their wealth.

Believe me, if in the future your assets are still worth 20 percent of what they are worth now (most likely in real terms), and provided you are still alive (a big if—I might add), you will be very affluent because most other people will have lost 100 percent of their assets.

How would I *try* to protect my assets?

I am not an American but if I were, I would support **Wayne Allyn Root** as a presidential candidate.

I would accept the fact that our Western Society is in *relative decline* compared to the emerging economies of Asia, Latin America, the former Soviet Union, and Africa. I would also understand that if the U.S. hopes to maintain, for a while longer, its superpower status ("forever" has never happened in history), the best chance is by shrinking its foreign "adventures."

As Hemingway observed, we also need to accept that "The first panacea for a mismanaged nation is inflation of the currency; the second is war. Both bring a temporary prosperity; both bring permanent ruin."[6]

Therefore, I would own some assets outside the U.S. and make sure the custody of these assets is also outside the U.S.

I would ensure that I could live without Internet, mobile phone, job, credit card, paper money, electricity, and be food self-sufficient if my "optimistic" scenario should come to pass. Therefore, I would own a house in the countryside and make sure I would have the ability to get to it in case of an emergency.

Most importantly I would always keep in mind the wise words of Milton Friedman who opined, "If you put the federal government in charge of the Sahara Desert, in 5 years there'd be a shortage of sand."[7]

CHAPTER THIRTY-FOUR

JOE SUGARMAN

Joseph Sugarman is an American business icon. A lifelong innovator in sales, direct marketing, and advertising, Sugarman has sold over $1 *billion* worth of products in his career. The founder and chairman of BluBlocker Sunglasses, Sugarman has sold over 20 million pairs of sunglasses across the globe. The company just celebrated its twenty-eighth anniversary.

The *New York Times* called him a "Mail Order Maverick." Using direct marketing, Sugarman implemented trend-setting concepts in how marketing should be conducted. Sugarman is credited with introducing the very first pocket calculator in 1971. In 1973 he was the first to use toll-free (800) phone numbers to take credit card orders—a new innovation that was responsible for dramatically expanding the entire mail order industry. In 1986 he was among the first to use half-hour TV infomercials to market his products. His products were also sold on QVC home shopping network. His company, JS&A Group Inc., grew to become the leading marketer of space-age products including the pocket calculator, the digital watch, telephones, recording devices, and home computers.

For the past six years, Sugarman has focused his entrepreneurial skills on Stem Cell Products, LLC, a company he founded to sell anti-aging products, including skin care, hair growth, and immune building solutions. (No embryonic stem cells are used by Stem Cell Products, LLC— only adult stem cells.)

JOE SUGARMAN'S ADVICE

This is my Financial Protection Plan. I don't know just how bad things are going to get. I do know, however, that now is the time to prepare for the worst. Here are my recommended steps on how to survive and prosper in the era of Obama:

1) **Precious metals.** If you don't already own gold, you should. Silver and gold are the best insurance against hyperinflation. There is no better way to weather the fiscal crisis we are in. Gold has been considered real money for thousands of years.

2) **Real Estate.** Buy real estate that has the potential to grow in value. Ocean-front property is one example. Real estate is a storehouse of value. As inflation increases, so does the value of your property.

3) **Collect Art.** Another storehouse of value is art by famous artists.

4) **Get a Gun.** It appears that Obama is making those who have worked hard and saved objects of greed and envy. Protect yourself.

5) **Stock up.** Now is the time to stock up on food and water. You can buy food that will last twenty-five years. Be prepared for the worst.

6) **Invest in You.** In other words, own your own business. One of the freedoms we have as Americans is the "freedom to fail." And to make that freedom work there are all types of procedures in place either to assist a company to completely fail, or to give them another chance. There's Chapter 11, Chapter 13, and Chapter 7 bankruptcy—each one not requiring government takeovers, or bailouts. So keep trying to succeed in your own business, knowing that you won't be disgraced if for any reason you don't achieve success. And let's keep government out of the process.

7) **Move to a tax-free state.** I was based in Chicago running a nice business that was starting to expand rapidly. Realizing the high Illinois taxes I was facing, I packed my bags and transferred my entire staff to Nevada—where there is no corporate tax or personal income tax, and where I was welcomed with open arms. The following year, I was able to give my staff large bonuses and invest in a new computer system—all from the savings in taxes I no longer had to pay. I've been based there ever since. I'll never leave—as long as they keep state income taxes at zero.

It is amazing to me that the high tax states don't realize that part of the reason for their financial difficulties is their high taxes. And now with all the recent publicity from famous sports stars moving to avoid paying high taxes, it is no wonder there is a lot of awareness of the subtle effect high state taxes can have on an individual's (and a company's) financial stability and viability.

As well as actions to take as individuals, here are some suggestions as to what tactics we as citizens might take, or encourage our elected officials to take:

1) **Scandals.** There is enough scandal in the Obama administration to last several lifetimes. An effective way to stop Obama is to tie him up in investigations, inquiries, and exposés. This requires an aggressive Congress and aggressive GOP leadership. Some of the scandals that should be investigated include Benghazi and Fast and Furious.

2) **Regulations.** Another tactic would be for small business owners to stand up and voice major complaints about the torrent of Obama regulations stifling the economy. As difficult as it is to break through the adoring Obama-loving media, it is critical the public hears about this. Major employee dismissals due to regulation, higher taxes, and the implementation of Obamacare will be the biggest news story of Obama's second term. These job losses may be so bad that they can actually attract the attention of the media, despite their bias.

Finally, let me leave you with this piece of positive advice:

Now that you have the basis for surviving, there is something important to understand. In any economy there is opportunity. The best definition of luck I know is "Luck is where opportunity meets preparation." Many millionaires were created during the last major depression. My point is there are always opportunities and in this book my great friend, Wayne Allyn Root, has identified many for you. Now, it's up to you to grab one of those opportunities, or identify your own, and then "go for it." I know Wayne will inspire and energize you to take action.

CHAPTER THIRTY-FIVE

MAX JAMES

Max James is a graduate of the U.S. Air Force Academy. After a distinguished career in the Air Force including over two hundred combat flight missions in Vietnam, Max earned his MBA from the Stanford Graduate School of Business. Following a successful career in real estate and the hospitality industry (including owning eighteen hotels), Max founded and currently owns American Kiosk Management, LLC, and North American Kiosk, LLC, which operate in over eight hundred locations in the United States and Canada with more than 1,200 employees and revenues exceeding $150 million annually. Because of his success, Max James was the first inductee into the $25 billion Specialty Retail Hall of Fame.

Max's latest endeavor, and the one of which he is most proud, is founding and serving as the Chairman of the Camp Soaring Eagle Foundation (www.campsoaringeagle.com), a medically-assisted camping program for children with life-threatening illnesses.

Max has received numerous honors for his business and philanthropic endeavors including being selected for the Air Force Academy's most prestigious honor, the Distinguished Graduate Award. He currently serves on the CEO Advisory Board of the St. Jude's Children's Hospital and on the Founders' Board of Directors of the United States Air Force Academy Endowment Foundation and supports the Muhammad Ali Parkinson's

Research Center, the Boys and Girls Clubs, and other worthy charitable organizations.

While Max's resume is impressive, it tells only part of the story of this remarkable man. His two hundred Vietnam combat missions were as a Jolly Green rescue pilot, and Max lived the creed: "That Others May Live." Shot down twice himself, he rescued ten fallen comrades. For his heroism, Max received three Distinguished Flying Crosses and eight Air Medals. Max James is a true American hero, and I am proud to call him my friend.

MAX JAMES'S ADVICE

First let me say, Obama's goal of "wealth redistribution" seems to me to be quite different from "helping our fellow man." There are many trite expressions to support the better concept, perhaps the most notable one: "A helping hand, not a handout."

It now appears the next major "planning inputs" from "The Hill" for conservative Americans will be how to respond to even more taxes, increased medical costs for our employees, and fewer charitable deductions.

Here are some of the steps I'm taking to survive Obama:

1. Government actions and monetary policy make inflation inevitable. In addition to planning for inflation with the securities and precious metals I'm investing in, I'm also focusing on increasing my business retained earnings, as well as my personal savings, to handle increased pricing of goods and services in both my corporate and personal life. Now is the time to begin to adjust (reduce) consumption to prepare for inflation.

2. Healthcare costs will go up for my company or, alternatively, healthcare coverage for employees will be reduced or eliminated. Some of the doctors that I currently see will no longer be in business for themselves, many by choice, not necessity.

3. I'm preparing for some of my employees to defer the date
    that they are planning on retiring because of inflation and
    increased health care costs. I'm also aware that increased
    taxes on dividends and capital gains will result in less cash
    flow, necessitating deferring retirement for many.
4. It's a good time to refinance your mortgage at low fixed
    rates, rather than variable.
5. Look to re-balance your securities portfolio, increasing
    selected international equity investments. Reduce exposure
    to bonds—as local governments move deeper and deeper
    toward insolvency. Some will not make it.
6. Search for niche real estate markets: housing stocks, indi-
    vidual rental opportunities, commercial building invest-
    ments, etc.

Let me finish with a personal note everyone should consider. Several
years ago I fled California, moving my businesses and life to Tennessee and then Nevada. It simply didn't make sense to continue to fight
California's unfriendly business environment and certainly didn't make
sense to continue paying an additional 10 percent (now much higher)
in income taxes (plus much higher property taxes too), payroll taxes,
corporate taxes, plus lawyer fees (for such a litigious place) just for the
weather.

I've been able to use the dollars I saved for what I, not the government,
believe is important in life. For me, that is philanthropy. I was able to found
a charitable organization, Camp Soaring Eagle, in Sedona, Arizona, that
helps kids with cancer and other serious life-threatening illness. Here is
the camp's mission statement:

To give kids with serious illnesses and their families a chance
to discover the healing power of laughter and the sheer joy of
play that sickness has too long denied them by providing camping experiences filled with excitement, challenge and fun in a
medically safe setting—at no charge to the children or families.

Camp Soaring Eagle is the greatest thing I've ever done. We've been able to give sick children joy. That's priceless—for them and myself. I highly recommend such an undertaking to anyone with the resources to do so. If you know a child who could benefit, or have the ability to help us with a donation, go to the website www.campsoaringeagle.org. Your help is greatly appreciated.

So, my final advice is that any time is a good time to leave your high-tax state and move to a low-tax state so you can use more of your hard-earned money as you choose, not as government dictates. I know that thousands of sick children who have received joy from Camp Soaring Eagle would agree.

CHAPTER THIRTY-SIX

DR. PETER H. DIAMANDIS

Peter is my best friend from childhood. We played together as little boys from the age of five to about ten. It's nice to have a childhood best pal who played "Star Trek" with you in your basement every weekend grow up to be the real-life "King of Private Space Travel"... and perhaps one of the top ten smartest guys in the universe! He runs some of the top space and innovation companies around, as you can see from his bio below, and on his boards and among his investors he counts folks like Larry Page, CEO of Google; Elon Musk, CEO of SpaceX and founder of PayPal; and producer James Cameron; as well as business titans like H. Ross Perot Jr. and Eric Schmidt.

Below are Peter's thoughts on surviving and thriving for the next four years under Obama. He is the most apolitical of my friends. He has no political agenda or axe to grind. He just sees opportunity where others cannot. I asked him to share his vision with my readers. He was kind enough to do so, but only if I made it clear that his opinions, views, and predictions are *not* about politics. I said "YES" (loudly)—because when you get a chance to listen to the views of a genius, you put politics aside.

I'm so one-in-a-billion lucky to have grown up with a boy genius as my best friend and neighbor. As you're about to see, I hit the lottery. Here are Peter's thoughts on surviving and thriving for the next four years.

Dr. Peter Diamandis is the chairman and CEO of the X PRIZE Foundation, which leads the world in designing and launching large-incentive prizes to drive radical breakthroughs for the benefit of humanity. Best known for the $10 million Ansari X PRIZE for private spaceflight and the $10 million Progressive Automotive X PRIZE for hundred-mile-per-gallon-equivalent cars, the Foundation is now launching prizes in Exploration, Life Sciences, Energy, and Education.

As co-founder and chairman of the Singularity University, a Silicon Valley based institution partnered with NASA, Google, Autodesk, and Nokia, Dr. Diamandis counsels the world's top enterprises on how to utilize exponential technologies and incentivized innovation to dramatically accelerate their business objectives.

Dr. Diamandis attended MIT, where he received his degrees in molecular genetics and aerospace engineering, as well as Harvard Medical School where he received his M.D.

Peter Diamandis's personal motto is: "The best way to predict the future is to create it yourself!"

DR. PETER DIAMANDIS'S ADVICE

When Wayne asked me to write about how to survive in the next four years under Obama, my first inclination was to decline because I prefer to stay apolitical. However, in thinking about it further I do have a "future-looking message" that is important for everyone to consider for their survival, or as Wayne likes to put it, their thriving over the next four, ten, twenty, or even thirty years—regardless of their political views.

1) This next decade is going to see an explosion of key, exponentially growing technologies that will create the next Googles of the world, the next multi-hundred-billion-dollar companies. Currently the U.S. is still the most likely birthplace for these companies. We're still the hotbed of capitalism and entrepreneurship because you're still allowed to take risks, fail, and start over again. Overregulation, however, may end up pushing such innovations to arise in other economies. For me there are a number of key "exponential technologies" that you need to keep educated on. These are so important that I started an entire institution named Singularity University (www.singularityU.org) to teach these areas to executives. The

University, based in Silicon Valley, is partnered with NASA, Google, Autodesk, Genetech, and others to study the most rapidly changing technologies in society today. Areas to focus on:

A. Synthetic Biology. The ability to design/create life forms that will be able to produce foods, fuels, and vaccines. Some of the leading thinkers in this arena include Dr. J. Craig Venter and Dr. George Church. Over time, these technologies will disrupt multi-trillion-dollar arenas. Think about using designer life forms as small machines to build the molecules you need. During the next few decades we're going from "evolution by natural selection" (Darwinism) to "evolution by intelligent direction."

B. 3D Printing/Digital Manufacturing. Imagine the ability to build anything you want, anywhere, any time…in your home, your office, your closet. Think of the future "printers" that don't just print an image in two dimensions, but an object of your choosing, fully functional, in three dimensions. Practical applications of these technologies are being demonstrated now. They will democratize the world's manufacturing base.

C. Artificial Intelligence (AI). Google is basically an AI company. Many more will materialize. AI will drive robotics as well. Think of computers that can really truly understand you—your spoken word, your written word, and your very intentions. Then imagine that these computers have access to all the knowledge in the world. They will do your bidding, help you recall what you've forgotten, help you answer any question you might have. This isn't something decades from now, this is capability coming on line this decade that will transform healthcare and education in a massive fashion.

2) Think Globally. Technology created in the U.S. can rapidly be used everywhere. National borders are porous. Ideas flow between nations, and

those nations that put up regulatory blocks will simply find that their top scientists and ideas move to other nations that are supportive.

3) Healthcare and education will be massively disrupted by technology in this next decade. Like banking, the healthcare and educational systems here in the U.S. are a mess, way too expensive and providing small results per dollar. Technology will fundamentally change both these industries. In looking where to invest, I would bet on start-ups, not large players, who have too much of self-interest to protect. They will eventually crumble under the weight of innovative competition.

4) Joblessness will continue to increase because of innovation as Artificial Intelligence, distributed manufacturing, and robotics increasingly come on line over the next three to ten years. How the current or next administration tries to battle this, I do not know. I remain hopeful that we humans are continuing to "integrate" with technology, allowing us to do more and more complex work, but the low-end labor—stocking shelves at Walmart or manning a toll booth—is rapidly on the way out, much in the same way America transitioned from being an agrarian society 150 years ago with two-thirds of our citizens tending to farms, to the point where less than 2 percent of us grow the food we now eat.

5) In the long run, the basics required to support us—food, energy, education, healthcare—will become "demonetized." By that I mean technology will ultimately make these critical elements of life close to free—much the same way it has done for knowledge (Google), Banking (Paypal), telephones (Skype), Digital Cameras (think iPhones, etc.). This is the thesis of my new book, *Abundance: The Future Is Better Than You Think*, available on Amazon for those interested in more detail. A new economy will be emerging over the next twenty years…and there is much turbulence ahead as it does.

Let me leave you with a couple of passages from *Abundance*:

> In areas like chronic disease, where governments spend billions
> of dollars, the offer of a massive incentive prize seems like a
> no-brainer. AIDS costs the U.S. government over $20 billion a
> year, that's over $100 billion during a five-year period. Imagine,
> for example, a $1 billion purse offered for the first team to

demonstrate a cure or vaccine. Sure, the marketplace is vast and the corporation that creates this cure will reap huge rewards, but what if the government's $1 billion was paid directly to the scientists who made the discovery? How many more brilliant minds might be turned onto this problem? How many graduate students might start day-dreaming about solutions?

Now apply this thinking to Alzheimer's, Parkinson's, or your cancer of choice. Whatever you like. The advantage here is an army of brilliant people around the world thinking about your problem and working on their own nickel to solve it. Properly executed, this mechanism offers the potential for fixed-cost science, fixed-cost engineering and fixed-cost solutions. I've always believed (to paraphrase Alan Kay) that the best way to predict the future is to create it yourself. In my five decades of experience, there is no better way to do just that than with incentive prizes.

Here are some prizes the government should be offering:

GRADUATION COMPETITION

School system against school system for increasing graduation rates (or other metric).

1,000 HOUSEHOLDS X PRIZE—$50 MILLION

Grand Challenge: The majority of energy today is used to heat and cool buildings, yet most people do not take the time to insulate their homes, seal their windows, or even know if their homes need further insulation. Similarly, tremendous steps can be taken to reduce electricity consumption at the household level. There are countless improvements that could be made if consumers were sufficiently aware and incentivized.

Draft Guidelines: In this competition, any group of 1,000 households can register to compete as a team. The winner will be that team of 1,000 households which reduces their energy consumption (oil, gas, electricity) by the greatest percentage over a two-year period, as compared to the average energy consumed over a historical two-year period. Each household in the winning team will receive $50,000. The competition will obtain the partnership of the utilities.

TRANSFORMING PARENTLESS YOUTH X CHALLENGE— $1 MILLION

Grand Challenge: The most vulnerable members of our society are children without parents. In the U.S., an astonishing 80 percent of prison inmates have spent time in the foster care system. In California, 50 percent of the foster children become homeless when they turn eighteen. Currently, there is little political will concerning their plight.

Draft Guidelines: The purse will be awarded to those parties, such as individual foster children programs or entire states, that cut key rates for former foster children, such as incarceration and unemployment, in half.

CHAPTER THIRTY-SEVEN

KIP HERRIAGE

K ip Herriage is CEO and co-founder of Wealth Masters International, a direct-selling financial education company with members in over one hundred countries. He is publisher and editor of the acclaimed *Vertical Research Advisory* (*VRA*) investment newsletter. Herriage's timely economic forecasts and uncanny predictions over the years have earned him the nickname "the Nostradamus of Investing." He is the author of *Crashproof Prosperity: Becoming Wealthy in the Age of Risk.* Prior to forming Wealth Masters, Kip spent fifteen years as vice president, financial advisor, and money manager for two of the most respected investment firms on Wall Street.

KIP HERRIAGE'S ADVICE

What's the scarcest commodity on the planet today? Could it be water, food, energy, raw materials, or precious metals? All of those things are getting tougher to come by, but the most urgent shortage facing all of us at this very moment is a shortage of the TRUTH! Your financial survival in the months and years to come may depend on hearing and responding to the truth.

From my fifteen years on Wall Street, to the birth of the *VRA* (my investment newsletter) in 2003, I have been committed to searching for and reporting on the truth. While some say "the truth" is entirely subjective, history provides us with a clear roadmap for discerning fact from fiction. The *VRA* research that I publish is backed by hard data, combining my twenty-three years in the financial industry with the research of "true experts" I have come to know well.

While my focus has been on the financial markets, it has become impossible to separate our financial future from the realities of the brand of global governance being practiced today by our elected (and unelected) officials. The financial risks that our leaders are forcing upon us now are completely unprecedented, both in size and in scope.

GLOBAL COUNTERFEITING PONZI SCHEME

For the first time in history, the entire planet is engaged in something that I can only call a "Global Counterfeiting Ponzi Scheme." The fact that it is a coordinated event between the U.S., Europe (via the EU), Japan, and China (among many others), should be enough to scare the hell out of everyone paying attention. In the past, countries have placed a tremendous amount of value on their sovereignty, a.k.a. doing the right thing for their citizenry. Their view now appears to be that because we live in a global economy, our solutions must also be global in scope. Certainly, there are times when this mindset makes more sense than others (military conflict, nuclear agreements, disease epidemics, etc.), but the globalized financial collusion we are seeing today between central banks and their commercial bank partners in crime is unprecedented. I fully expect this collusion to become a major issue…almost certainly a black swan event…an economic catastrophe brought on by our banking and political cartels, and one that few see coming.

For the last five years the world has been in various stages of financial panic, and their solitary solution has been…drum roll please…**Print More Money!** How has this fiat currency counterfeiting solution worked so far? After all, central banks around the planet have flooded the world with more than $10 trillion in freshly printed funny money in just the past few years, so the end result should have been astonishing. As you will see, reality is far different.

Esteemed economist and researcher Laurence Kotlikoff of Boston University is the foremost expert on the subject of sovereign debt. His latest figures show the U.S. now has a grand total of $222 trillion in debt, which means we can forget about that "official" $17 trillion figure.

Incredibly, this equates to $2.8 million in debt for a family of four in the U.S., which places us on par with that financial bankruptcy called Greece.

Make no mistake, this is debt that cannot...and will not...ever be repaid. And we have not even covered the equally obscene financial destruction happening throughout the rest of the world, namely every country in Europe (outside of Germany), along with Japan's mega-disaster in waiting.

With unprecedented currency and debt creation globally, the resulting benefits should be equally sensational, yes?

Let's take a quick look at the macro scorecard. Global unemployment rates are still 60–400 percent higher than their pre-collapse 2007 levels. Stock markets are anywhere from 10 to 60 percent below their 2007 highs. Inflation, that draconian hidden tax that robs us of our wealth even while we sleep, is seeing a dramatic increase with energy prices rising 40–60 percent and food prices increasing at an alarming level.

Currency inflation means price inflation to you and me, and this unprecedented wealth transfer process is exactly how the middle class has been destroyed. Yet incredibly, few are actually aware of this most deadly financial killer.

Since the creation of the Fed in 1913, more than 96 percent of the U.S. dollar's value has been destroyed. Based on my research, along with that of every true financial expert that I have come to know and trust over these past twenty-three years, the question has now become not if but WHEN the next global financial crisis will become reality. For those caught unprepared, the bursting of history's two largest bubbles (fiat currency and sovereign debt), will be devastating. Conversely, those that take action in advance of the coming global hyperinflationary depression will become the new wealthy. Make no mistake about it; we are at the early stages of what will become a massive, and multi-generational, wealth creation opportunity.

In my book *Crashproof Prosperity: Becoming Wealthy in the Age of Risk*, I outlined why 2013 to 2014 were the most likely years for this historic collapse, and the current actions of our leaders only help to further cement my predictions. The following represents these major forecasts going forward.

THE BEGINNING OF RUNAWAY INFLATION

Price increases as drastic as the ones I have laid out above should be one of the biggest stories of the year. Instead, we are lied to—more on that in a moment. However, the magnitude of these price increases is, and will continue to be, one of the biggest negative surprises going forward. Unfortunately, they will come with devastating consequences.

You may not believe what you are about to read, and I would not fault you for your skepticism. Unfortunately, this is all too real. Incredibly, the U.S. government obscures the level of inflation with their incredibly unreliable Consumer Price Index (CPI), and something it calls "core" inflation. In what should be known as one of the biggest cover-ups around, the government actually strips out *food and energy* prices from these core inflation numbers.

In 2013, look for a dramatic increase in the level of inflation, and know that as I write, in February of 2013, the real number already stands at close to 10 percent. Remember the late 1970s to early 1980s? Inflation rose by more than 15 percent and interest rates stood as high as 21 percent. How the government handles our current debt and spending problem will determine how quickly we approach these levels. With Obama receiving a second term, I see little reason to be optimistic. I will simply quote the president from his appearance on Jay Leno's *Tonight Show*, where he told Jay, "Well, the math stuff I was fine with up until about seventh grade."[1] Talk about famous last words…historians will wonder why we didn't take him seriously.

Regardless of the decisions our leaders make today, given our $222 trillion in total debt, plus the ongoing hunger for deficit spending, there remains just one thing the government and our central banks can do...continue to print massive amounts of fiat currency...which will ultimately turn inflation into hyperinflation. Actions must have consequences, and 2013 (2014 at the latest) is the year this subject will no longer be denied or ignored. The seeds for major inflation have been sown. Now is your time to prepare for this eventuality.

THE KEYNESIANS HAVE WON—GLOBAL MONEY PRINTING GOES INTO HYPERDRIVE

The battle is officially over...not the war mind you, but the global battle between Keynesian economics and Austrian economics most certainly is...and in the not too distant future we will have skyrocketing interest rates and rampant inflation as the end result.

For those new to this discussion, here's a quick snapshot of these two dominant schools of economics.

John Maynard Keynes is the father of Keynesian economics, and Barack Obama is a Keynesian through and through. Believers in pure demand-side economics, at all costs, and that the government is the answer to the problem rather than the problem itself, Keynesians now have the majority of political power globally. Now that his re-election campaign is over we get to see the real Obama: tax-and-spend policies, income redistribution, deficit spending, and lots and lots of money printing and debt issuance.

This is the exact opposite of Austrian economics (fathered by economist Ludwig von Mises), which is based on the belief in a free market system. Austrian economics is the belief that governments should not pick winners and losers, but instead should get out of the way and let entrepreneurs battle it out. The end result? A "laissez-faire" economy that flourishes...which then produces increased tax revenues to the government...for a win-win all around.

For the next several years we will continue to have to deal with a Keynesian economy, Big Brother increasing government regulation, taxes, fees, and fines in order to bring more money into Washington...so they can redistribute it. Or maybe they will spend it directly on things like roads and bridges…or solar and wind power companies. They'll even pay people to dig a hole and fill it back in. A Keynesian sees any government expenditure as a good investment.

So how has that worked for the president? Well, here are his numbers, comparing 2008 to 2012.

The government spent so much money that the federal debt increased by $5.4 trillion. That's over a trillion-dollar deficit each of the president's four years in office…unprecedented until Obama. And what did all that federal spending get us after about four years? An unemployment rate 2.1 points or 34 percent higher than when he took office. According to the government's official inflation figures, inflation fell, but it did nothing for GDP.

Now, take a look at our true inflation costs, from just the past twelve to eighteen months. Food prices have increased at an alarming level. Meat prices have increased some 35 percent, bacon prices are up 40 percent, cereal prices 50 percent, corn prices 80 percent, and incredibly, coffee prices are up 145 percent. The hard reality is that the effects of currency inflation are just beginning to make their way through the economy. And in many parts of the globe, rising food costs have a much more dramatic effect on the population than in Western civilization.

We see the same negatives in energy, where prices have soared 108 percent under our Keynesian president, while the median income plummeted 7.3 percent…the worst decline in real incomes since the Great Depression…and the continued destruction of the middle class. No nation becomes or remains an economic superpower using Keynesian economics. Yet here we are.

In just the past few months we have seen announcements from one country after another, each enforcing their commitment to embracing the Keynesian model. In Japan, the new prime minister just announced an unlimited amount of purchases in government debt, with an official inflation target of 2 percent per year. The collapse of Japan's economy will likely be a black swan event in 2013. Europe continues to provide bailout money for one country after another. Greece's issues have now spread to Portugal and Spain, where even the "official" unemployment rates surpass 25 percent. And the issues are not isolated in Europe…the unemployment rate for the entire EU now stands at a record 11.9 percent...where Keynesian economics rules the roost.

In China, we see the same Keynesian approach in what they officially call "state-sponsored capitalism." However, their massive stimulus programs over the past few years have translated into levels of inflation that are resulting in riots. China's response is to close the Internet and to imprison those that dare attempt to report on the truth. Here we see Keynesianism at its most ugly. Massive cronyism in a communist country, with the poor left to survive on their own. Can we be far behind?

So if Keynesian economics is a failed economic model, why has the entire world embarked on this approach? The answer is simple really...our Roman Empire-like leaders desire re-election...and giving the masses what they want is the easiest path to staying in power. The masses want easy money and all the wealth redistribution that comes with it. So...that's what they will get.

The planet is on a Weimer Republic money-printing binge—a Global Counterfeiting Ponzi Scheme. In the Keynesians' eyes, this is an economic war, and they intend to win, regardless of the amount of currency debasement and debt issuance that it takes. Make no mistake, they have made the decision to embark on this course and nothing will change their minds. The end result...similar to the one that brought us 20 percent interest rates in the early 1980s...will hit us with a much harder blow this time. That's the effect that spending all of your income to simply service your debt will have. This is when global currency inflation turns into global hyperinflation.

Prepare Today with These Strategies:

- Buy Precious Metals/Short the U.S. Dollar (the first massive bubble). With the combination of unlimited money printing and the coming global currency war, the U.S. dollar will continue its multi-decade collapse. Gold and silver will be huge winners, with increases of several hundred percent.
- Short Government Debt (the second massive bubble). Once interest rates begin to skyrocket, the exodus from government bonds will be breathtaking. Imagine the situation in Greece, except in your own backyard.

- Diversify AWAY from Your Bank. Think your money is safe in your bank? With banks holding less than 1 percent of their depositors' funds, imagine what will happen when the next great run on banks begins. The black swan event for this criminal cabal of bankers will come from the $1.2 quadrillion derivatives market, which will make the 2008 banking crisis look like a walk in the park.
- Avoid the stock market. Keep an eye on the two-hundred-day moving average. Once we cross beneath this and stay beneath it for more than two weeks, sell stocks and short the stock market.
- Food storage. The most devastating effect of hyperinflation is the increase in food prices, followed by food shortages. Government-mandated price controls will come first, followed by empty grocery store shelves. Stock up by purchasing long-term food storage.
- Become an entrepreneur. With unemployment headed past 15 percent, do not depend on someone else to pay you a salary and fund your life.
- Finally, prepare for the next world war. History teaches us that countries go to war in times of economic collapse. World War II ended our first Great Depression, and the situation in the Middle East today will be grounds for WWIII.

By making these moves, you, your family, and your business will not only survive the coming calamity, but will be positioned to prosper greatly as well. The long-term goal is to take profits from the recommendations spelled out above and to then use those funds to purchase cheap real estate, undervalued stocks and failing businesses. This simple axiom is how the wealthy become wealthy: buy low and sell high. In order to do this, you must first have the courage to act with the informed minority…*the smart money.*

CHAPTER THIRTY-EIGHT

THOMAS F. NOON

Thomas F. Noon is a real estate consultant to one of the biggest hedge funds on Wall Street. He earned a Bachelor of Science in Civil Engineering from the University of Illinois and his MBA at Stanford University. Following stints as division president of Shea Homes and DR Horton (two of America's largest homebuilders), Mr. Noon was Chief Operating Officer for DR Horton. He then founded Raintree Investments in 2008 where he currently serves as president and CEO.

THOMAS F. NOON'S ADVICE

Obama won re-election—now what to do to protect your assets?

Consider this chapter as a warning about a meteor falling from space. This meteor is a metaphor for a national economic and social cataclysm.

After an engineering undergraduate and Stanford graduate business school education and forty years of massive amounts of reading and investing in stocks, private equity, mutual funds, oil/gas exploration, and real estate, the following is my attempt to give the reader the benefit of the good things I've learned, and the useless things I've learned never to do again. Anything the reader takes as actionable advice, however, you do at your own risk.

The following is a plan for protection against what can be called the Obama economic disaster. Why infer this is all on Obama? The answer is simple: he is president during this period of a rampant upward spiraling of the U.S. national debt, and he championed programs such as "Cash for Clunkers." "Cash for Clunkers" accomplished with $1,000 what could be accomplished with $5–10 by any government with sanity and common sense. It's just one example of the rampant recklessness that has characterized this period of government idealism and ideology.

"Cash for Clunkers" was a multi-billion-dollar program sold to the American public as economic stimulus to create jobs and improve the environment by encouraging consumers to retire older vehicles and purchase more fuel-efficient new vehicles. The effects of this program on new vehicle sales and the environment were meager at best, a total waste of money. Only an ideology totally ignorant of basic economics, or with no concern about economic or monetary stability, would endorse such a waste of tax dollars and increase in the national debt.

Using Canada as the control group, the program increased new vehicle sales by only about $360,000 during July and August of 2009. Those sales were stolen from subsequent quarters, implying nearly none of the spending went to consumers who would not have purchased a new vehicle anyway. Studies suggest there was no net gain in new car sales for 2009 and only a temporary reduction in CO2 emissions, which would have occurred anyway because of normal obsolescence. As if this were not enough, the cars bought under the program were primarily built overseas, making the jobs "created" not only temporary and stolen from subsequent periods but also not American jobs. And what did it cost the American taxpayers? THREE BILLION DOLLARS!

Is this a government that instills confidence it can handle the much more complicated issues affecting our savings, our assets, or our jobs? Of course not.

So in the midst of this economic and monetary chaos, what is a household to do if it is concerned about possible future loss of incomes and/or devaluation of its resources and savings?

There isn't one single strategy to protect your household from monetary and economic weakness. The base strategy that I recommend is to diversify, do your homework, and be frugal. Your individual plan will vary, depending on the amount of assets you are trying to protect and the income you are expecting to earn. But make no mistake, you need to plan and act to take advantage of the coming shifts in the world and national economies.

The following is a menu of actions you should consider:

- Buy gold, silver, mining stocks, residential real estate, and the ETFs that hold portfolios of the above assets.
- During this time of depressed real estate, consider deploying 15–20 percent of your pool of funds into rental property. A growing portion of the population is broke and has poor credit, so many people will have to rent long term.
- Buy agriculture stocks, producing farmland with strong water sources and no environmental restrictions—because food shortages will result from disruptions in supply due to civil unrest, unstable governments, and disruptions in distribution channels.
- Buy oil and other energy stocks because the population continues to rise while new discoveries of oil topped out in the late 1970s and have been declining ever since. Own water sources and natural resources, and consider where you will live if social unrest begins. More details on these strategies follow.

But first, some warnings and thoughts; there are risks in all these strategies:

- Agricultural stocks and lands are subject to possible government intervention, environmental restrictions, and/or confiscation, so pick your country well.
- Rental homes can be impacted by governmental rent controls.

Another personal strategy is to lower future taxes by relocating to a state with low taxes, low debt, and lower risks of increased taxes, such as Texas. Avoid the states listed in the *Forbes* article "Do You Live In A Death Spiral State?"[1] These states include California, Illinois, New Mexico, Mississippi, and New York.

These "death spiral" states are in deep debt and are defined as having a positive ratio of "takers" to "makers," meaning they have more people who take from the state's GDP than they have people remaining to create and build that GDP. California is particularly bad in this regard with a ratio of 1:39.

You may want to consider the ultimate relocation plan. Singapore and Switzerland have very low income taxes and low to zero long term capital gains or estate taxes. Unfortunately, the United States is among the very few countries that tax their citizens no matter where they live in the world, so you would need to renounce your citizenship in America and become a citizen of another country in order to stop your U.S. tax liability.

Any relocation like this must take into account that the United States will still impose federal taxes on all income earned anywhere, until you renounce citizenship.

DEVELOPING A SURVIVAL PLAN—DEFINING THE PROBLEM

There is an old expression: "Pessimists complain about the weather, optimists expect it to improve, realists adjust the sails." The following are some basic characteristics of the problem of the Obama economy and options for addressing it. Wayne Root calls it Obamageddon.

Very simply, Obamageddon is characterized by diminishing revenues from those sources capable of paying taxes and ever-increasing, voracious demands on that government revenue by constituents in need of financial support.

Rather than getting caught up in what the world should be, I'd rather be pragmatic and deal with what is. The pessimist complains about the current state of political madness; the optimist expects it to get better soon; the realist, which is what I'm advising you to be, just keeps adjusting the sails as conditions warrant and moves ahead. Never be static.

So, what is an investor to do?

1. Invest wisely by following basic rules of investing,

2. Adjust your investing sails to the reality of a taxation system that is intent on dissuading you from investing and making a profit, and

3. Avoid or defer taxes legally.

SOME BASIC RULES TO INVEST BY

*Note: If you don't know what I'm talking about when I write about "puts," "calls," "limit orders," etc., do your homework before becoming an investor on your own. However, my advice to not go to a "full service" broker remains. If you are unwilling to put in the time to be educated about stock investing, either don't do it or at least do the research necessary to invest in a mutual fund that makes sense to you.

1) I learned from experience to never go to a "full service" broker. Open an account at TD Ameritrade, Schwab, or E-Trade. This way, the transaction costs will be a minimal part of the sales or purchase price. TD Ameritrade will likely offer you ten to twenty-five free trades either to open a new account or to add $100,000 or more to an existing account. And don't be afraid to ask for $8.95 instead of $9.95 per trade after the free trades are used up.

Don't go to a "full service" broker because they are in the business of transactions. They will sell you anything that means you will make as many trades as possible and will recommend mutual funds that generate them the biggest commissions. I never take the advice of stock brokers. They spend all of their time selling and very little time becoming informed about what they are selling.

2) When buying stocks or ETFs or mutual funds, always enter a "limit order" and never enter a "market order." Market orders can get bad executions due to temporary market conditions when your order hits the market. NO MARKET ORDERS.

3) USE PUTS TO BUY ANY STOCKS OR ETFS AND TO ENHANCE RETURNS. Sell puts to buy any stock or ETF at a discount to the current market price. For example, if you enter a $42 limit price when the stock is

selling for $44, the stock may never dip to $42 and so no progress will be made. So rather than put in a limit order of $42 when a stock is at $44 and hope for a dip, sell a put with a strike price of $43 for $1–2 per share. If the stock doesn't dip to $43 at the date of option expiration, you keep the $1–2 per share and move on the next buying move. If the stock dips below the $43, the put option will get exercised and you will buy it for the price of $43, but your net-price-in will be $41–42, lower than your desired buy price of $42. The guide you should use is the NET price at which you would be happy to buy and use that price as the target for the net price if the put option gets exercised. Remember: selling puts is a BULLISH move. It means you've concluded the general market is going to be flat to up during the term of the put and that the drop/rise ratio for the target stock is small.

4) SELL COVERED CALLS TO SELL EQUITIES AND/OR AS INSURANCE TO REDUCE VOLATILITY OF YOUR ACCOUNT. Sell covered calls to sell any stock at or above the current market price . . . or as insurance against a drop. For example, if you enter a $47 limit sell price when the stock is selling for $44, the stock may never rise to $47 and no progress has been made. So rather than put in a limit order of $47 to sell when a stock is at $44 and hope for a rise, sell a "covered call" on the stock that you hold with a strike price of $45 for $2 per share with an expiration of 30-60-90 days. If the stock doesn't rise to $45 at the date of option expiration, you keep the $2 per share and move on to the next selling move. If the stock rises above $45, the call option will get exercised and you will sell it for the price of $45, but your net sales price will be $47 total. The guide you should use is the NET price at which you would be happy to sell the stock and use that price as the target for the total net price if the call option gets exercised.

5) Never buy on "tips," whether heard from friends, flyers on a rack at your discount broker's office, or a "gotta move now" call from your broker, or read in a financial magazine. Nothing replaces the grunt work of research, research, research. You need to invest more than your money—you need to invest your time. You need to know as much as you can about the company and/or industry in which it operates. Take good notes and keep them for years.

6) One of the key problems in financial markets is that everyone tends to become a specialist, expert or otherwise. Their entire careers (and the way they are paid) are dominated by a single asset class or financial product. They will not tell you to invest in an asset class that does not pay them; they will only sell you what they have to sell. Warren Buffett once said, "Don't ever go to a barber to ask if you need a haircut—unless you want one." Nobody should be surprised to learn that a professional municipal bond specialist sees no sign of a bond bubble—that is, a strong probability of a steep correction in prices—in the one asset class that feeds him. So when seeking advice, remember to keep in mind the source of the response. Biases are everywhere.

7) You cannot become a jack of all stocks. Specialize. Decide what industries or products you know the most about—investing in an industry in which you have years of experience cannot hurt—and focus on that for years. Don't be impetuous or jump from one area of investing to another. That's like jumping from lily pad to lily pad—eventually you will end up in the swamp and lose a leg to an alligator.

8) Don't get greedy. Don't get emotional. Remember, a net gain of 2-3-4 percent per quarter will give you a very respectable 8–16 percent annual return. It will put you in the top 10–15 percent of all mutual fund results in the country. Stock investing is not like buying lottery tickets where you lose and lose until you become a millionaire (which never happens—you just lose). Stock investing is a slow and steady process of making small gains with the idea of making 8–16 percent per year and minimizing risk of loss. Selling to stop a loss is a viable, sane option. But selling out of fear is not wise. You will sell out of fear if you violate rule #7.

9) Don't be overly affected by tax considerations. It seems like every time I sell or don't sell to save on taxes or to avoid paying them, I do the wrong thing. If it's time to sell, SELL. If it's time to hold, then HOLD. Pay the taxes and move on. But do consider living where the tax effects are minimal.

10) Be biased by the overall direction of the market. Remember that a rising tide lifts all boats. If the market has a general trend toward rising, it will mean an upward bias on all stocks. If the general sentiment is nervousness or

negativity, even the best stocks will drop. So study overall economic trends and read, read, read.

MY ECONOMIC OUTLOOK

The government needs to raise taxes and limit spending during strong economies, not during a recession. During a recession or post-recession, they need to focus on growing GDP, although that seldom seems to be what's done.

If they agree to another debt limit increase and add another trillion in debt, it will be good for gold, silver, and GDX and lead to higher prices on lots of other things too (like oil). And, all this would be okay until the recession dangers pass and unemployment falls—except this administration cannot follow the path they need to, which is to build GDP. Building GDP means cutting taxes and regulations, drilling for domestic oil and natural gas, and increasing tax deductions for capital investment in business. Does any of this sound like something Obama believes in?

So here's a sample investment portfolio given current conditions and politics.

SUGGESTED PORTFOLIO (AS OF 1ST QUARTER 2013)

GLD: Gold bullion ETF.

GDX: Large Cap Gold Miners.

DIG: Energy Oil & Gas Ultra ETF

SLV: Silver Bullion ETF

IYR: iShares Real Estate ETF

Oil Refiners—Select

Banks—Select

Why GDX? Gold producers are currently in disfavor. Stock prices are down. Stock prices have fallen 22 percent over the last twelve months. But they appear to be a buy at these prices.

Why GLD or SLV? Money printing must continue for the foreseeable future to avoid a bigger problem with unemployment and the imbalance in trade. In addition, the devaluation of the dollar provides an erosive effect on the U.S. debt of $16 trillion. If the dollar falls in value by 50 percent, the U.S. can pay off that debt with cheaper dollars. The danger is that the interest on that debt may rise as a result of this money printing, which could cause a dangerous spike in that debt because the government would be forced to print even more money to pay the interest.

Why IYR Real Estate? Real estate is recovering now from multi-decade lows relative to incomes. That is, housing is now so affordable in major metropolitan communities that this factor overpowers the higher unemployment in those cities. As unemployment falls and interest rates remain low (a promise of Ben Bernanke until unemployment falls), housing prices should be strong, and builders should be making money.

Banks and Oil Refiners. As general asset classes, I believe both present reasonable security and upside. Do your homework and choose those specific stocks which you believe give you the best of both.

ROTH IRA vs. Standard IRA. Should you convert your IRA to a ROTH IRA?

This depends on your opinion of what the future holds. If you had converted to a ROTH IRA prior to 2013 and lived in California, you'd be very happy right now because you would have paid a maximum of 9.3 percent to California and 35 percent to the feds. As of January 2013 those two are 13.3 percent and 39.6 percent.

So if you fear higher tax rates for your income tax bracket, you'd be better to convert today at the lower tax rates. Is a ROTH better than a traditional IRA? If you assume the tax rates stay the same from the day of contribution to the day of withdrawal and that the yearly gain percent is flat, there is no difference between a standard IRA and a ROTH IRA. The cumulative amount after withdrawal and taxes are paid at the end is the same.

Two advantages of a ROTH:

1) The biggest advantage of converting to a ROTH is protection from higher future tax rates when you withdraw the money. This could happen either from higher rates or if your income increases, pushing you into a higher tax bracket. After conversion, your account basis and any future

gains are tax-free forever. If either the yearly gains or your income has a chance of spiking up at any time in the future, it would be good to shield all of that gain from any higher tax rates.

2) The advantage of the conversion law I liked best was that I could pay the taxes with money outside the IRA. In that respect, it's like a one-time additional contribution of 42–44 percent, if you live in California.

(A word of caution: this decision is based on the assumption that the government doesn't amend the ROTH law and tax ROTH IRAs at some level as the funds are taken out in the future. The government has shown over and over again the ability to renege on any promise.)

So those are my thoughts as to why and how to put together your own survival plan. My most important advice is "Make a Plan." This is not a time to drift along. And, when making that plan, be neither an optimist, nor a pessimist. Be the realist who is continually "adjusting the sails."

CHAPTER THIRTY-NINE

PHIL GORDON

B.est known as a professional poker player and the host of Bravo's *Celebrity Poker Showdown*, Phil Gordon has led a "No Limits" life filled with adventure, challenges, entrepreneurship, and philanthropy. A National Merit and Presidential Scholar who entered college at fifteen, Phil began his professional life as a computer scientist after earning his degree from Georgia Tech.

He was the first employee and principal architect for Netsys Technologies, which was acquired by Cisco in 1997 for $95 Million. Following the sale of Netsys, Phil took off on a four year, 50+ country solo backpacking journey around the world that included stops at the top of Kilimanjaro and the outback of Australia, an elephant safari in Thailand, and the "greatest road trip in U.S. sports history," a 138-event, 40,000-mile, year-long trip in an RV dubbed the "Ultimate Sports Adventure."

In December 2011 after nearly ten years as a professional player, Phil retired from poker and returned to the world of technology, founding Jawfish Games and serving as CEO and chairman of the board. Phil is an active angel investor and accomplished public speaker, having delivered keynote addresses on business and entrepreneurship for many of the Fortune 500, including Google, ATT, iTron, Yahoo, IBM, Citrix, and Cisco.

Phil supports and regularly volunteers time to charities around the world. His hobbies include bridge (he's a two-time national champion), golf, tennis, beach volleyball, woodworking, piano, backgammon, fishing, and photography. He's raising two young sons (his greatest challenge to date), Xander (four) and Zachary (two). Phil, his wife Barb, and the boys live in Newport, Washington, on a ranch, along with their menagerie of four donkeys, two llamas, one horse, two dogs, six cats, three goats, and a host of bears, moose, elk, deer, beavers, ospreys, and fish.

PHIL GORDON'S ADVICE

Government and the global economy are blowing hurricane-like forces against most business and entrepreneurs. My advice is "Go where there's a tail wind."

Here are some tail-wind areas that I believe will experience explosive, world-wide growth in the next four years, despite Obama (or any future political leader, government bureaucrat, or policy):

- **Mobile.** More than one million mobile devices are being activated world-wide every single day. These devices have great connectivity and capabilities that will only grow during the next few years. Anything and everything is moving to mobile. Already 40 percent of website visits are via mobile handsets. Apps are just the tip of the iceberg.
- **Health and Wellness.** I have no doubt the healthcare system is facing collapse. People will have little choice but to start taking more responsibility for their own health and wellness. Invest in fitness and organic food production, locally produced items. Sell short anything with high-fructose corn syrup and the like. Intelligent people have been moving this way for years. It is a trend that will escalate.
- **Homeschooling and Internet-Enabled Education.** Government has failed at education. Every smart parent knows it. Few may be able to homeschool as Wayne has done, but everyone has access to the Internet. There are some amazing resources already online and more on the way: KhanAcademy, General Assembly, Skillshare, and Treehouse are a few. Others are also tackling this issue and will

be big, big winners. There isn't a caring, smart parent who believes their children are going to get a good education without supplements. The Internet is a perfect delivery system.

- **Self-Defense, Alarm Companies.** Big growth is coming here. How much civil unrest will it take before more people become concerned that they need to look out for their own self-defense? When we're running trillion-dollar annual deficits, there is no doubt that civil unrest is coming. Just look at Greece. Martial arts, gun training, home alarm systems, bulletproofing, and dog obedience training will all be big winners in the next four years.

- **Idaho, Montana, Wyoming, Nevada, the Dakotas.** States with limited government and where there aren't many people will be big winners over the next few decades. California is already dead. Most states in the Northeast and upper Midwest are not far behind. Yes, they might have great weather (California), or be your long-time ancestral home, the place you were born, but that doesn't matter much if you're homeless.

On a personal note regarding places to live, we moved to Las Vegas primarily for my previous profession as a professional poker player. However, when we decided to move from Las Vegas, we purposefully excluded all states with state income taxes. (It's interesting to note how many governors are currently promoting getting rid of income taxes in their states.)

For an entrepreneur and job creator like me, finding a state that had a talented pool of technologists along with a corporate and personal tax-friendly and business-friendly environment made the most sense for us. Washington state was an easy choice.

I hope this helps. If you don't agree with my specific suggestions, identify your own. Just be sure to "Go where the wind is at your back."

CHAPTER FORTY

DAVE BEGO

Dave Bego is president and CEO of Executive Management Services, Inc. (EMS), an industry leader in the field of environmental workplace maintenance. EMS employs approximately five thousand workers in thirty-eight states across the country.

Honored as a finalist for the Indiana Entrepreneur of the Year Award, Bego has guided EMS to a prestigious listing as one of the nation's top Building Service Contractors.

Dave Bego is the author of *The Devil at My Doorstep* and *The Devil at Our Doorstep*, detailing his firsthand experience waging war with Andy Stern and the powerful SEIU (Service Employees International Union). Unlike so many business owners who fold or "compromise" under the power and relentless pressure of this powerful union, Dave Bego had the courage to stand up for what he believes, protecting his employees against the loss of their freedom to vote in secret ballot elections. Dave Bego is a patriot and American business leader who strongly believes in entrepreneurship, free enterprise, and capitalism.

DAVE BEGO'S ADVICE

As a business owner and CEO, as well as a concerned American citizen, the results of the disappointing presidential election in 2012 have forced me to evaluate options for the future of my business, family, and employees, and ultimately for retirement plans for me and my wife.

Barack Obama was elected the 44th president of the United States of America. The president's anti-business, pro-union, social justice, and pro-socialism agenda, combined with his utter disregard for the American Constitution, has placed business leaders in a position of reexamining and reevaluating their business strategies and future plans.

When faced with the possibility of an imminent collapse of the American economy, or even a long slow decline for decades to come, all entrepreneurs should be rethinking their business models and developing a list of personal priorities should they need to make quick decisions. Thus I embarked on developing a list of priorities for business owners, to assist as they evaluate the most prudent means for surviving a potential government takeover. The following points are areas that any concerned business owner should consider and reevaluate:

- Increase liquidity by moving the largest percentage of investments to precious metals such as gold, and into cash
- Consider moving the business to a low-tax or taxation-friendly state
- Invest in land in tax-friendly states, or in countries that embrace free markets and that are not under U.S. jurisdiction
- If your company is positioned to do so, consider purchasing companies outside the U.S. that provide a future exit strategy and preserve wealth. Should the need arise, be prepared to sell companies and relocate family and all assets out of the U.S.
- Obtain current passports for all family members for quick and easy exit from the U.S. in case of emergency (collapse of economy or loss of our civil rights).
- Immediately reduce costs to prepare for increased taxes and costs from Obamacare. Sadly, many industries will find that the implementation of Obamacare may require job reductions and movement from full-time employees to part-time employees. As this occurs, we will see the proof

that Obama policies are killing jobs and destroying the middle-class.

- Meet frequently with tax advisors to assess both short- and long-term impact and implications of Obamacare, payroll tax increases, expiration of Bush-era tax cuts, and other corporate "penalties" imposed by the administration.
- Expand current businesses through acquisition and aggressive sales growth to counter expected increases in taxes and healthcare costs.
- Move liquid investments offshore.
- Become involved in politics and aware of how changes made in Washington, D.C., can impact you and your business.
- Fight to take America back and restore American exceptionalism! Expose this administration's radical agenda. Don't compromise with those looking to wreck our country and bankrupt business owners.

These scenarios are truly scary and the decisions at hand will be difficult. We must stand tall and fight back to make our voices heard. America is at a tipping point, but together we can restore our nation to its greatness. I pray that God helps us return to our Christian values and that we find our way back to freedom.

CHAPTER FORTY-ONE

J. T. FOXX

J. T. Foxx is a serial entrepreneur, real estate investor, national radio host, and one of the top speakers and business coaches in the world. He has traveled across three continents to spread his wealth-building message. He is also founder of Mega Partnering, where elite entrepreneurs gather to network, learn, and rub shoulders with the power elites from across the globe (www.JTFoxx.com). Speakers and teachers at J. T.'s events have included Gene Simmons of KISS, former presidential candidate and New York mayor Rudy Giuliani, former Disney CEO Michael Eisner, Eric Trump, the co-founder of Apple Steve Wozniak, and of course, Wayne Allyn Root.

J. T. FOXX'S ADVICE

The United States of America was built on the backbone of small business. What President Obama does not seem to understand is that entrepreneurs are motivated by taking risks. It's taking on risk that leads to opportunity, but being an entrepreneur isn't easy in today's most challenging business environment. How can any business owner expect to succeed under such negativity?

Yet we do! Entrepreneurs thrive. That's the amazing strength of small business owners with a dream. However, on top of that we are under constant threat from getting sued, because it is far easier for people to make money on lawsuits, rather than work for the money. Sometimes it seems that government and the legal system is setting us up to fail.

CHANGE ENTREPRENEURS SIMPLY DON'T BELIEVE IN

Change entrepreneurs don't believe in takes the form of higher taxes, which punish us for taking risk. What do you think entrepreneurs do when taxes rise? They work less, of course. After all, why work twice as hard for less pay? That, in turn, reduces tax revenues and brings the country to a screeching halt. That's what happens in an upside-down world where we reward some people for doing absolutely nothing and paying no taxes, yet punish people who expect and want nothing from their government.

Of course people who pay no taxes are going to want "the rich" to pay more, because they have no skin in the game. In order for this country to thrive, it needs to be run like a business. If I ran my businesses, or anyone in this book ran theirs, like the government, we would be either out of business or in prison.

MY ADVICE...JUST BEING HONEST

I am going to take a very contrarian approach to my fellow entrepreneurs in this book…DO NOTHING DIFFERENT. You can't focus on what the government is doing. Instead, focus on creating your own economy. If you don't like the current policies, taxes, regulations, and mandates, vote Republican in the next election, and spend money backing candidates and policies you like.

We need to get on the same boat and sail together toward prosperity in unison rather than trying to sink each other's ship.

My best advice is that the current administration's policies that embrace spending and debt will certainly cause a tidal wave of inflation in the future. When inflation rages, real estate goes up. Buy with both hands.

Second, there is a big world out there—much of it unaffected by President Obama and his advisors. That means you should consider buying real estate in stable countries with good infrastructures, young demographics, reliable banking systems, and lower national debt. Two nations come to mind instantly—Canada and Switzerland.

Third, to nullify the impact of new taxes, smart entrepreneurs should relocate to low-tax or preferably no-tax states like Nevada, Texas, and Florida. That is precisely what I have done both personally and with my businesses.

Enough complaining. I have work to do, so I can pay for the person who prefers unemployment rather than working. I love this country and it's still the best country in the world (for the moment). But we just have to start acting like it, and take action to keep it that way, rather than just saying it to ourselves so we can fool ourselves into believing it's true. As Ronald Reagan said,

> Freedom is never more than one generation away from extinction. We didn't pass it to our children in the bloodstream. The only way they can inherit the freedom we have now is if we fight for it, protect it, defend it, and then hand it to them with the well-taught lessons of how they in their lifetime must do the same. And if you and I don't do this, then you and I may well spend our sunset years telling our children, and our children's children, what it was once like in America, where men were free.[1]

CHAPTER FORTY-TWO

MARK SKOUSEN

D r. Mark Skousen was recently named one of the top twenty most influential economists today.[1] He has had an unusual career, working for the CIA; as a professor at Columbia Business School; and as president of a non-profit organization, the Foundation for Economic Education. Skousen has written over twenty-five books including *The Making of Modern Economics* and *Investing in One Lesson*. His latest book is *The Maxims of Wall Street*, the first collection of all the Wall Street sayings. By profession, he is a Ph.D. financial economist who has written a successful investment newsletter since 1980. He has been a columnist for *Forbes* magazine, written for the *Wall Street Journal*, and appeared regularly on CNBC's *Kudlow Report*.

He is also the producer of FreedomFest, the world's largest gathering of free minds, in Las Vegas every July (www.freedomfest.com). As a direct descendant of Ben Franklin, Skousen completed Franklin's *Autobiography* covering the last thirty-three years of his life (*The Compleated Autobiography by Benjamin Franklin*, published by Regnery in 2006). The business school at Grantham University has been named after him. He is married to his first wife, Jo Ann; together they have five children and four grandchildren. They have lived in Washington, D.C.; Nassau; the Bahamas; London, England; Orlando, Florida; and now New York. He has visited and lectured in seventy-four countries. He is the editor of *Forecasts & Strategies*.

MARK SKOUSEN'S ADVICE

"The uniform, constant, and uninterrupted effort of every man to better his condition, the principle from which the public and nation, as well as private opulence is originally derived, is frequently powerful enough to maintain the natural progress of things toward improvement, in spite both of the extravagance of government, and of the greatest errors of administration."[2]

—Adam Smith (1776)

Whether Barack Obama is a European-style social democrat or a hardcore socialist, there is no doubt that he and his supporters are taking the country down a dangerous path— bigger government, unsustainable debt, more regulation, and higher taxes. As a result, I expect a sluggish economy at best, and another financial crisis at worst.

As the author of *The Wealth of Nations*, a declaration of economic independence in 1776, Adam Smith contended, "Little else is requisite to carry a state to the highest degree of opulence from the lowest barbarism, but peace, easy taxes, and a tolerable administration of justice … "[3] Unfortunately, we are seeing less of all three. In today's world, more and more of everything is either prohibited or mandated.

According to the Economic Freedom Index, the United States has been in steady decline in terms of economic freedom since 2001. Size of government, property rights, sound money, and regulation have all moved in the wrong direction.[4] We can blame both Republican and Democrat leaders for this loss of freedom.

Our theme this year at FreedomFest is "Are We Rome?"[5] Many historians have warned that the West is going the way of the Roman Empire. Rome was the #1 superpower 2,000 years ago, and then collapsed. When the British historian Edward Gibbon began publishing *The Decline and Fall of the Roman Empire* in 1776, the British were worried that Britain, the #1 superpower at that time, would lose its dominance in the world…and it did within a century.

Now many experts fear that the United States and the West in general are on a road to decline and financial collapse. In 1947, Pulitzer-prize winner

H. J. Haskill wrote a book called *New Deal in Old Rome*, making apt comparisons between Rome and the welfare state. Harold Bloom, the famed literary critic at Yale, recently warned, "Twenty-first-century America is in a state of decline. It is scary to reread the final volume of Gibbon these days because the fate of the Roman Empire seems an outline that the imperial presidency of George W. Bush retraced and that continues even now. We have approached bankruptcy, fought wars we cannot pay for, and defrauded our urban and rural poor.... We have no Emerson or Whitman among us."[6]

Yet all is not lost. There is plenty of opportunity still in America, and around the world, and I remain optimistic. As Adam Smith once said, upon hearing of the British loss of Saratoga in the American Revolution, "There is much ruin in a nation." In today's parlance, you can still turn lemons into lemonade.

Technology is still advancing. New inventions are taking place. Bargains are to be found in the stock market, real estate, collectibles, and commodities.

There are a couple of good sayings on Wall Street that apply here:

"We cannot direct the wind, but we can adjust the sail."

—Anonymous

"Muddy waters make for good fishing."

—Daniel Drew

"Businessmen can profit handsomely by taking advantage of the pessimistic auguries of self-appointed prophets of doom."

—J. Paul Getty

Yet being a millionaire on a sinking ship is not victory. We need to do our part to reverse the tide. Here are some universal principles of personal finance that every reader of this book should follow:

1) Get your house in order. Live within your means, pay off your debts as quickly as possible, and have plenty of cash on hand. As Poor Richard says, "There are three old friends—an old wife, an old dog, and ready money."

2) Having plenty of cash on hand (or retained earnings if you are a business) allows you to pick up bargains when they become available. Many a speculator has made his fortune buying stocks or real estate at the depths of a depression.

3) Avoid credit card debt and high interest rates. Don't fall into the consumer debt syndrome, wasting your money on high-priced retail consumer goods and services. Buy used cars, used houses, used goods.

4) Save, save, save! Don't buy into the myth that consumer spending drives the economy. The real keys to economic growth and a higher standard of living are on the supply side: saving, investing, education, training, improving tools and equipment, productivity, entrepreneurship, and technology. This is known as Say's Law—supply creates demand.

5) Invest your savings productively. Use your savings wisely by investing in what you know best, whether it be in a successful business, or other people's successful businesses (via the stock market).

6) Don't let taxes ruin your life. Keep your taxes to a minimum, but don't get involved in suspect tax avoidance and estate planning schemes, or moving to your favorite tax haven just to avoid taxes. There's more to life than taxes.

7) Adopt Ben Franklin's three virtues: industry, thrift, and prudence.

No president, no matter how powerful or wrong-headed, is going to keep us independent Americans from succeeding. Good luck!

CHAPTER FORTY-THREE

BILL (ANONYMOUS)

Bill (not his real name) is a self-made Wall Street superstar and mathematics whiz. He arrived in Las Vegas over thirty years ago with $3,000 to his name and now has well over $100 million. He wishes to remain anonymous.

BILL'S ADVICE

I have the following points for your readers to consider:

1) For Investors. Over the next four years consider that the United States will go through something similar to what Japan has experienced over the last twenty years. If you do not know what Japan has endured, then I strongly suggest you do some research before deciding where to invest. Japan has endured almost two decades of decline and contraction.

So my advice is

    A. Diversify for either inflation or deflation. Most likely we will experience stagflation. But be prepared to move quickly when "know-it-all" political elite break the system and cause something very bad to happen. And they will.

    B. Capitalize on misguided policies by government. If you stay knowledgeable and alert, you can make a fortune off their mistakes and ignorance. That's exactly what I've done my entire life.

2) For Business Owners.

  A. If you have over fifty employees, your goal should be to cut the hours of as many employees as possible to under thirty hours per week to avoid the expense and penalties of Obamacare. (Having under fifty full-time employees, you'll avoid any penalties.)

  B. Use technology and any other means possible to minimize the number of employees.

3) For Everyone. Starve the "Beast" (Government).

  A. Use the best tax planning possible.

  B. Vote for fiscally conservative legislators for all public service positions—national, state, and local. We need politicians who are citizen politicians, not lifelong politicians. We need people in office with private sector business experience, people who believe in less spending, reduced debt, and smaller government.

  C. Move to states with low or no state income tax. I've followed this philosophy for thirty years by living and basing my business in Nevada—a state with no personal income taxes or business income taxes. If you're smart, you'll do the same. Certainly get the heck out of California!

4) Read this remarkable book, listen to Wayne Root's opinions, and take action based on Wayne Root's advice. And of course, listen to the advice of Wayne's very smart friends who contributed to this book.

CHAPTER FORTY-FOUR

LARRY
(NOT HIS REAL NAME)

L arry is a dear friend and mentor. He is retired after a mega-successful career in the garment industry. He was the exclusive distributor for several famous clothing brands.

ADVICE FROM LARRY

About four years ago, recognizing Barack Obama was going to do everything possible to diminish the value of the dollar, I made some important financial decisions. The first was to watch Obama closely and follow the money, therefore making sure my investments coincided with his actions.

The second was to keep somewhere around 20 percent of my net worth in cash. Then I bought a lot of gold at $895 an ounce. Of course if I could do it again I would have bought much more. But who knew? To prove I'm human, at the same time I sold my Apple stock at around $100 a share. If I was smart, that actually was an amazing place to keep money. Look back at March 2009. That month you would have been a genius buying either gold or stocks. Throw a dart at the Dow and win. Hindsight is 20/20!

During that time Obama was making decisions that were amazing. Every single move he made, I would have done the exact opposite. It became obvious to me Obama has a crew of businesses (run by his friends and contributors) that he will not let fail. They were not exactly the ones anyone financially savvy would have chosen. If you watched him closely it was clear he was making sure GE wouldn't fail, given his closeness to GE CEO Jeffrey Immelt. At the time GE was around $12 a share.

Others Obama will not allow to fail are any businesses associated with NBC or the *New York Times*. Even though people are not reading newspapers as before, Obama needs a willing voice, especially after losing *Newsweek*. So he finds ways to get money to his friends' companies through bailouts, stimulus, or, his favorite, so-called green "investments." He has his buddy list.

I see no change in strategy during his second term. Obama's love for solar didn't really become public until after several companies failed and Fox News exposed the incredible amount of government waste. Smart businessmen are still amazed he invested in these failing companies. Unfortunately, I don't see all these failures changing his priorities going forward.

Let me say this up front. I'm writing this in first quarter 2013. By the time you read this, things may have changed. But it is clear to me that for the last four years Obama, ON PURPOSE, has not only been allowing the country to fail, but has been taking actions and implanting policies to ensure that it does. I'll tell you why a little later.

Right now I believe it's imperative you take the following actions:

1) Have NO DEBT. Make sure all your bills are paid—no mortgage, obviously. Under Obama it will not be a benefit. He doesn't want "the People" to have power, and in this case power is ownership of ANYTHING. A person who owns his or her own house without a mortgage has power; that person doesn't need "Obama money." That kind of person is Obama's worst nightmare. Obama's dream is a society dependent on government.

2) Obama is all about POWER. His goal is to have you NEED government. Obama has a plan to make us all dependent on government and he is following it to the letter. If the economy fails, more people become dependent. He will be orchestrating this all, while finding ways to blame the Republicans.

3) Your only protection is to have a major portion of your portfolio in cash (no matter its real value) and no outstanding bills, no debt! Then sit back and see how bad Obama's economy gets. With money/assets in hand you have power. Real estate deals will come your way, but not yet. Not unless it's so incredible you can't lose. It is important to Obama not to allow the real estate bottom to happen. One of Romney's major points was to find the bottom so we could grow from there. The news media used it as a tool against him. But Romney was right. Obama will fight to keep us away from the bottom in order to maintain the economy in an uncertain crisis state.

4) This is not the time to spend excess money on anything other than something that has VALUE. That might be art, at the right price. Specifically, salable art of famous artists: Picasso, Warhol, Chagall, etc. Make sure it's authentic, documented art; there are tons of phonies out there. Alongside art come precious metals. I'm an avid believer in a combination of gold and silver. As the dollar shrinks gold will grow. Silver, poor man's gold, will grow as well. Every portfolio must have gold and silver. Be sure to buy it as close to the strike price as possible. Art, gold, and silver should be approximately 10 to 20 percent of your net worth, your primary real estate in the 50 to 60 percent range, with the balance in LIQUID CASH. I know it's not easy. But when the crisis comes you don't want to try paying bills with a fancy car you have to sell. This is a buyer's market.

5) Be aware that Obama is doing everything in his power to destroy the value of the dollar, working with Bernanke dumping billions into the market to keep interest rates artificially down and the stock market up. We are living in a fake economy. The stock market is a huge fraud propped up by all this fake money printing. As I said earlier, IF you feel you must be in the stock market my advice is to follow the friendships of Obama. As of now Apple, Google, and Facebook. Be careful, it's all artificial. Personally, I SOLD ALL my stocks months ago. That doesn't mean I am right. But ask yourself about all the spending Obama is racking up. He has clearly made the decision to ignore debt. One day it simply has to explode.

Even though gold is high, many experts believe $5,000/oz. is not unreasonable. In my opinion, the only downside is if Obama somehow allows our economy to flourish, and that isn't going to happen. It goes against Cloward and Piven and everything he believes. Obama's goal is to destroy America and then reboot it. Each day Obama says the right thing and then does the exact opposite; the exact opposite of what he said, and what should be done. Why? Cloward and Piven. Their plan is to destroy the economy and the wealthy with the goal of making everyone the same economically...except them, and their ruling elite friends, of course. That is Obama's plan and goal. Protect yourself!

CHAPTER FORTY-FIVE

DAVE
(NOT HIS ACTUAL NAME)

Dave is a well-known hedge fund manager who prefers to remain anonymous.

DAVE'S ADVICE

I stated to my dear friend, Wayne Allyn Root, that I would like to remain anonymous (for business reasons), but still provide his readers with the benefit of my twenty-five years in the hedge fund and investment environment.

Following are ten investment ideas that most clearly define the existing U.S. economic conditions relative to the world.

But first, here is the most important advice. If you have to remain a citizen of this country, it is a no-brainer to move to a state with NO STATE INCOME TAX such as Florida, Texas, Nevada, Wyoming, or Tennessee. Kansas, Nebraska, and Louisiana are in the process of removing their state income tax burdens on their residents as well and could be alternative choices in the future.

My top ten investment ideas for the next four years during President Obama's second term are as follows:

1) Gold should be at the top of all investment portfolios for any citizen of the United States. It is the oldest living currency and holds its value. Unlike the U.S. dollar which is being depreciated this year by another $1 trillion increase by the Federal Reserve Bank led by its Chairman Ben Bernanke, the supply of gold has been relatively flat over the last fifteen years. I expect gold to approach $3,000–5,000 an ounce by the end of Obama's second term because of hyperinflation concerns.

2) Silver, referred to as "the poor man's gold," is in a similar position. Like gold, silver is a precious metal and will hold its value as the world follows our central bank's lead in printing more paper currency. The ECB, Bank of England, Swiss National Bank, and Bank of Japan have all announced and implemented quantitative easing policies in their own currencies. Silver will benefit along with gold as a true alternative to paper holdings.

3) Platinum is in short supply because of the South African labor problems as well as an increase in demand from auto manufacturers for catalytic converters. Companies like Platinum Metals Group (PTM-Toronto) which is developing a new mine in the platinum belt region in South Africa will be regarded in high esteem as platinum prices increase.

4) My fourth investment idea is to start selling ten- and thirty-year U.S. Treasury bonds in the second half of 2013. Although they have already sold off some in January, I expect a bigger sell-off begins in the second half when our deficit approaches $17 trillion, then $18 trillion and beyond. Realizing this president will never cut social spending programs like Medicare, Food Stamps, and Social Security, foreign owners of our bonds will demand higher interest rates for their risk on these longer-term treasury bonds.

5) Sell U.S. dollars and dollar-denominated assets. Given my first four investment ideas, as well as the next five, the reason is self-explanatory.

6) Buy Canadian dollars! The Canadian government got their budget in order starting in 1995 as they brought their debt-to-GDP ratio down from a high of 78 percent to a more manageable mid-30 percent range. As well, the Canadian banks did not need a bailout in the 2008 financial col-

lapse in the U.S. They are very strong and well-diversified versus their U.S. counterparts.

7) As I write, Canadian gold mining stocks are almost priced back to their 2008 valuation lows. With gold at $1,675, the senior mining stocks are pricing in the $1,300 range, while the junior producers are valued at $1,200. Clearly, there is a disconnect between company valuations and current gold prices, but even more so on future prices that I expect to see at $3,000–5,000 per ounce.

8) Buy Brazilian assets, and I mean all of them including stocks, bonds, commodities, and real estate. Brazil is the "best of the best" of the emerging markets with an abundance of natural resources. Their banks and government budgets are stable and healthy.

9) Buy Australian companies and buy all of them if you believe in the China growth story resuming.

10) Finally, buy Sprott Resources (SCP-Toronto). Sprott is based in Toronto and all their assets are in Canada. Presently, the stock is yielding 10 percent paid monthly versus quarterly (higher time value of money) and valued at a discount to its net present value. Sprott currently manages the largest farm in North America and plans to expand it over 1 million acres. It also holds oil and gas interests in Canadian shale deposits.

CHAPTER FORTY-SIX

JOHN
(ANONYMOUS)

John (not his real name) is a hard-driving lifelong entrepreneur. He is street-smart, never having attended a day of college. He has built a hundred-million-dollar fortune twice (in two different industries). He was once profiled on the cover of one of the world's most famous publications for his outsized success.

JOHN'S ADVICE

Think globally, not locally. There are now stronger countries and economies in the world.

Find a bank where you can have your money in a foreign currency. Since I believe the U.S. dollar is going to continue to decline, your net worth will decline as well, unless you hedge by having your personal and business funds in a stronger currency. Right now, I recommend the Canadian dollar since Canada has a much stronger economy, government, and banking system.

U.S. real estate could well be a strong investment. While I don't fully know whether the market has hit bottom yet, I do believe it is at or near it. If you are in a position to invest in rental properties, now is a good time to do it.

Underwater homeowners should consider a short selling or a more drastic approach, strategic default. I know it's tough to leave one's home in either manner, but it could be a good financial move.

If you're a mid- to high-net worth person, it's advisable to acquire a second passport. You never know, it may come in handy down the road. Who knows what America will look like in ten, twenty, or thirty years.

Where you live is important. Some are choosing to leave America. But if you choose to stay, or need to stay (because of business or family), you should relocate to states with lower or preferably no state income taxes. Those most desirable states with no taxes and business-friendly attitudes are Nevada, Texas, Florida, Wyoming, and South Dakota. There are others, but these are the best of the best. With the high taxes imposed by Obama, you need to find a way to shield your income from the claws of government. I could have built my businesses anywhere in the U.S.A., but I chose Nevada. The tax money that I've saved has been instrumental in my success.

CHAPTER FORTY-SEVEN

BIG MO
(NOT HIS REAL NAME)

ig Mo is the retired CEO of a public company. His wealth is enormous. He is one of the brightest men I've ever met. He now lives in Nevada, a no-tax state.

BIG MO'S ADVICE

My primary advice is to be happy and save money. Now is not only a time to live within your means, but more importantly, **below your means.** Going without is better than worrying about how to pay for things that often are just that, "things"—things you can do without.

It's the same advice our government should be following—when times are tough and business is bad, CUT, CUT, CUT, and CUT SOME MORE. Slow down your spending. That's how you save yourself. Unfortunately government does the opposite, spending more, while expecting us to pay for it all with higher taxes. This is the definition of insanity.

Here are a few other words of advice:

- Refinance your home and lock in low rates now. Rates are the lowest in history, meaning this is the opportunity of a lifetime—and it is temporary. Do it now, before the moment is lost forever. This one act can lower your cost of living for the rest of your life.

But don't refinance to a thirty-year loan, or as some are pushing, a forty-year loan. A fifteen-year mortgage will make a dramatic positive difference in your financial picture.

On every $100,000 of mortgage at 3 percent the fifteen-year payment is $690.58, versus a payment of 421.60 on a thirty-year mortgage. The difference is $268.98 less in monthly payments on the thirty-year. That sounds good, right? Wrong. That ignores the fact that the interest on every $100,000 of mortgage for fifteen years is $24,304.40 versus $51,776.00 for thirty years. The difference is $27,472 in *additional* interest for the same loan amount.

I know they tell you to take out the thirty-year mortgage and pay it back quicker, but that takes discipline, which 99 percent of people don't have.

- If you don't own a home, now is a great time to do so, even if it's smaller than you would like. Rents are headed much higher and will soon exceed what you'll be paying for a fixed mortgage. It's not the size of the home that's important, it's the security you will have locking in a fixed rent for the rest of your life.
- Invest at least 35 percent of your net worth in precious metals.
- Invest the 65 percent balance of your capital in a diversified basket of biotech, healthcare, technology, and consumer staples.
- For the security of your family, buy term life insurance that doesn't expire as long as you pay the premiums. It's much cheaper than whole life and doesn't expire like five- or ten-year terms. Lock in the premium for life.

- Move to a no-tax state like Nevada, Texas, or Florida. I spent most of my career in New York paying high taxes. I got nothing for it. That tax money should have been invested in stocks, bonds, real estate, gold and silver, and collectible coins instead. It adds up—FAST. If I had figured out this idea of moving to a no-tax state thirty years sooner, I'd have an extra few million dollars. But better late than never.

- Now I have enough money to live anywhere I want in America. Yet I choose Nevada—because of zero income tax, zero business tax, zero capital gains tax, zero inheritance tax, and low property taxes. Add it up—it's enough to dramatically change your quality of life. When I took a company public a few years back, I relocated the entire company to a no-tax state. It was one of the best decisions of my life.

- I've owned my own businesses all my life. Be your own boss. It's the only way to achieve independence and financial freedom.

- And be a contrarian. Never follow others off a cliff like a sheep. Think for yourself. Usually following others is a recipe for disaster. If everyone is running for the exits, you should do the opposite. One of the best examples of this philosophy was right after 9/11. New Yorkers panicked and offered their homes for fire sale prices. I bought up several prime properties for a fraction of what they were selling for only months before. Soon New York real estate skyrocketed and I made a fortune. The people that sold to me made a big mistake—they panicked, overreacted, and followed "group think."

CHAPTER FORTY-EIGHT

GREG
(NOT HIS ACTUAL NAME)

reg is an eight-figure real estate investor in Florida. He owns investment properties and homes across the U.S.A.

GREG'S ADVICE

Here are some thoughts relating to surviving Obama for the next four years.

As an eight-figure investor in income-producing properties, whereby I reap returns on my investments, I actually look forward to inflation during the Obama administration.

It's actually pretty simple…Obama has huge bills to pay. He is setting records for spending, entitlements, and debt. To accomplish this, he has to print lots of money. That creates inflation in the near future. And perhaps massive hyperinflation in the more distant future.

The Fed policy of maintaining low interest rates will be forced to come to an end soon. This will allow higher-cap rates on all my future real estate ventures. A higher percentage of invested return = more cash for me!

In essence, since my main business is commercial real estate investments, I will keep doing "business as usual" until such time that I need to make a change. But I don't see that happening any time in the near future.

Obama's re-election means spending and debt will only grow bigger, and therefore inflation is coming. Guaranteed.

Obama's terrible, dangerous, and reckless policies are bad for America. They are deadly for the economy. But I'd be ignorant not to take advantage of his errors, mistakes, or pure stupidity. The inflation coming from his bad moves will add up to prosperity for real estate investors.

My future is real estate, real estate, and more real estate. Three cheers for Obama—inflate, inflate, inflate!

Two other key points. I could choose to live anywhere. I make my homes in Florida and Nevada—both zero-income tax states. That is no coincidence. Tiger Woods made the same choice back in 1996 when he left California for Florida. Now it appears Phil Mickelson is making the same move. Three quarters of professional golfers make their homes in Florida, Texas, or Nevada. Why? They make millions of dollars per year, just as I do. They are worth eight figures (or higher) just as I am. Yet they choose to protect their money from the greedy clutches of government. If the smartest and richest people in the world understand this concept, shouldn't you? You'd be a fool to give your valuable and hard-earned money to state governments who give you nothing back in return, then waste it on inefficiency, greed, incompetence, and corruption.

Last point. Work for yourself. I've never worked for anyone else. You cannot become rich paying high taxes or working as an employee for others. *Period.* Solve those two and buy real estate—and you've figured out how to succeed at life!

CHAPTER FORTY-NINE

DR. JOHNNY (ANONYMOUS)

J ohnny (not his real name) is a well-known doctor (M.D.) from a hard-scrabble background. He was one of seven children born to parents with seventh grade educations. His parents made it clear that paying for an education beyond high school would be his responsibility. Knowing that, he worked forty-eight-hour weeks during his last two years of high school, saving all he could. Those savings were supplemented by a $100 gift from his parents upon graduating from high school. To get through college he worked as many as five jobs and had a college degree before a car.

Accepted to both law and medical school, he chose medicine with plans to become a brain surgeon. He was accepted for residency at Harvard Medical, but turned it down in favor of a military scholarship. Graduating in three instead of four years, Dr. Johnny served in the Air Force as a staff surgeon. Here is his advice on Obamacare and the future of healthcare in America.

DR. JOHNNY'S ADVICE

There is grave concern among practicing physicians about the future state of America's healthcare delivery system under the Affordable Care Act passed into law during Obama's first presidential term. We have all

heard the words of Congresswoman Nancy Pelosi encouraging quick pas-
sage of the bill so Congress could then find out what's in it.[1]

There was a promise of transparency and bipartisan input, but this did
not occur. What resulted was a "cram-down" of the single largest healthcare law ever passed, voted on without our elected officials even reading
it! Although the bill is over 2,700 pages with some 500 provisions, there is
already an additional 13,000 pages of regulations surrounding the bill to
make it the largest government attempt to take over every facet of health
care in America!

Patient privacy will be a thing of the past as government databases
contain everything in our medical histories. Currently, physicians face
felony charges under HIPAA laws for breaching patient privacy, but our
federal government will have no similar restrictions under Obamacare.
The days of patient-doctor confidentiality will be gone forever.

Throughout our careers, we physicians have seen continuous meddling
by politicians at the national, state, and municipal levels as they add layer
upon layer of regulations with very little input by the very professionals
that are trained to provide the complicated "business of healthcare." Most
physicians realize the healthcare bill was more about control by the government than about improving the healthcare of its citizens.

All physicians wish for healthcare for everyone, and every physician I
know has given lots of care to patients who were uninsured or unable to
pay. An example is the requirement to be on emergency room call for
uninsured patients, to keep hospital privileges. Sadly, the system is already
so overloaded that pushing another 30 million people into it will only
ensure poorer and poorer care until the system collapses. And collapse it
will.

Regardless of the endless denials, rationing of care for the "less likely
to survive" to make care available for the "more likely to survive" is a large
part of the Obamacare legislation. A panel of appointees will be providing
the checklist criteria to the healthcare providers for what treatment options
are allowed and to whom. This is no different from insurance companies
determining what their policy-paying members can or cannot receive in
pre-approved care.

Physicians knew that healthcare reform was not the intent of this bill—simply because they noticed the glaringly obvious issues not addressed:

- Tort reform to decrease defensive medical practice with exorbitant additional costs
- Illegal alien care ahead of American charity care
- Medicare and Medicaid reform
- Diminished compensation to physicians who are going bankrupt at alarming rates because of their inability or unwillingness to increase patient loads to the numbers required to fund their practices

An attempt to see more and more patients only further frustrates the patients waiting for hours for a few precious minutes with the doctor. Patients resent the lack of attention as the doctor is noticeably distracted as he hurriedly reviews the charts and hastily refills prescriptions, while patients are desperately trying to express concerns about frightening symptoms.

This new system will make the whole situation far worse! Out of necessity, care of patients will be shifted to nurses and physician assistants, without a physician's input. But then, perhaps that's the intent…unless, of course, you are a politician or government bureaucrat, in which case you will get to see an actual doctor.

Care for the elderly will be at the patients' homes rather than a hospital or office facility since an aggressive approach for these patients will not be cost-effective and therefore it will be disallowed. At best this care will be provided by nurses and physician assistants, but more likely by personnel with even less training.

The only group with a superior option will be Congress and the other Washington elites, as is the case already. They will be receiving none of the Obamacare mandates forced on us!

The federal government has no appetite for making tough decisions regarding the survival of the growing Medicare and Medicaid population.

Life expectancy has dramatically increased since the beginning of Medicare—to over eighty years at present and increasing with advancing medical technologies.

Medicaid is even worse. Recipients pay nothing for their care, abuse is rampant, malpractice claims are among the highest, and compensation for Medicaid patients' care is the lowest. Through Obamacare, the federal government's solution will be to offer less care through rationing, based on treatment protocols dictated by the appointed panels, and offer less compensation to the care providers.

There are already doctor shortages in many areas of the country, and they're rapidly getting worse. American medical schools are having trouble filling the seats in their classes, and foreign medical graduates with poor English-language skills are arriving every day to fill the void. It is apparent that a career as a physician is not what it used to be in our country. Not only does it require a long, expensive education, but the fear of malpractice suits (which force physicians to practice "defensive medicine") only complicates the career. As compensation diminishes, the need to work longer and harder and see more patients robs the physician of the enjoyment and personal satisfaction of the profession. There is little personal time left to enjoy your family and a reasonable lifestyle with the increasing work load.

When I was a young man looking for a promising career, acceptance into medical school was a "dream come true." I never imagined that in one generation the most honored and cherished profession (albeit at the end of a long, hard road of training) could be transformed by meddling politicians into such a difficult existence. This rewarding and honorable profession has been regulated by those knowing nothing about what they are regulating, and we will continue to see further deterioration under Obamacare.

There are simple and straightforward solutions that could significantly decrease the cost and improve the quality of healthcare in our country:

1. Seal the borders to eliminate more illegal immigrant health care. We can't afford the healthcare costs of American citizens, how can we pay for more?

2. Tort reform with elimination of contingency fees for settlements. Attorneys could still accept cases and bill hourly rates against the awards granted (after the doctors have their day in court). Doctors do not get a contingency fee and a percentage for saving a billionaire's life, only his fee for service. Why should attorneys have such a lucrative arrangement, with patients negotiating settlements against a physician who has never been proven at fault?

3. Pain-and-suffering caps will drive the cost of care down. It can be a fair cap, say $500,000, not the tens of millions of dollars often awarded in a single case. This would curb trivial lawsuits and stop defensive medical practice, while still keeping doctors liable for gross negligence.

4. Medicaid recipients should be required to pay something, even if it's just a small co-pay. If the patient has no cost at all, it encourages over-utilization and waste.

5. Medicare is provided to those sixty-five years and older under the current arrangement. But now that life expectancy is so much longer, we should go back to the original intent of offering care the last two years of life. If life expectancy moves upward, then the age at which coverage begins automatically should move upward.

6. Offer preventative programs, not just symptom-based treatment. Symptom-based treatment is a great system for hospitals, pharmaceutical companies, and insurance companies, but greatly increases cost. It is shameful that 80 cents of every dollar spent on healthcare for an American is spent the last two months of their lives.

7. Physicians in this country are considering new options for themselves and their families. Many are retiring, moving to other countries, and/or going into non-medical businesses. If you're smart enough to be a brain surgeon and will work 120 hours per week, you probably have a skill set to make a living doing something else. We must get the

government, lawyers, and pharmaceutical giants with K Street clout out of the business of healthcare and give it back to the doctors who give their lives to care for the sick.

8. Consider a concierge or "direct pay physician." Meaning if you have the money, go outside the system and hire the best physicians money can buy. One way to afford that is to set up an HSA (Health Savings Account).

9. Consider "medical tourism"—pay out of pocket for your surgeries in other countries where the costs are much cheaper.

10. The simple, quick, easy way to make healthcare affordable and therefore encourage the uninsured to purchase health insurance isn't to put the wasteful inefficient federal government in charge. Simply make health insurance policies 100 percent tax deductible for individuals (just as they are for employers now).

CHAPTER FIFTY

DAN
(NOT HIS REAL NAME)

Dan is a Midwest farm-boy turned Stanford MBA. He spent his career building and turning around businesses, many of them public companies. Today he has retired to Texas. I asked Dan to write about his experiences moving out of the United States. His story is fascinating.

DAN'S ADVICE

When my long-time friend Wayne asked if I would share with his readers my experiences of retiring and moving offshore, I told him I would be glad to do so. Hopefully my experience will be helpful.

Although I enjoyed a nice career managing a number of start-up and turnaround businesses, I am not one of Wayne's friends retiring with tens or hundreds of millions of dollars. My retirement nest egg is much, much more modest, so a retirement plan where my wife and I get good "bang for the buck" is paramount. I'm sure many of you reading this book are in the same situation (retiring with assets in the million dollar plus or minus range), or soon will be. Fortunately, we were able to save enough to not be solely dependent upon Social Security. With Obama's never-ending tax obsession you may not be so fortunate. It's clear his goal is for everyone to be dependent on government checks, living a retirement of "shared misery."

When my wife and I retired, we decided to re-locate to Panama. The decision was based as much on "adventure and opportunity" as a desire to stretch our retirement budget.

Why did we choose Panama? Over the years I've learned two important lessons. First, "Dreams become goals only when you have a plan." And second, "Everything is easy when you know what to do." For some time my dream upon retiring had been to head off on that adventure from which I didn't need to return. To do that, I knew we needed a plan, and for a plan, we needed an expert—someone who knew "what to do."

As retirement approached, I began investigating living offshore. Starting with the Internet, I requested information and attended a seminar sponsored by International Living (www.internationalliving.com). International Living is a very successful private company making its money from seminars, books, newsletters, and real estate. I subscribed to their newsletter and attended one of their seminars. I have never bought any real estate they promoted; however, I have found the places in the world they are promoting are the precise places that those of us with a little adventure in our souls and a desire to stretch our retirement dollars should consider. Their choices are "on the money."

We chose Panama primarily because it was easy. It's close, a two-hour flight from Houston. The language is Spanish, but most Panamanians speak at least some English, and many were educated in the States. (The current president of Panama attended Texas A&M.) During America's years managing the Panama Canal, we built them a good infrastructure. The currency is the American dollar. And, here's the clincher, even for noncitizens, it's easier to do business (including buying and owning real estate) in Panama than in California.

There were other positives about Panama. Healthcare is excellent and reasonably priced; our local hospital was affiliated with Johns Hopkins, and our doctor attended medical school in the United States. We regularly met Europeans and Canadians who came to Panama to save money on medical procedures, especially hip and knee replacements. Best of all, you

can drink the water everywhere. I get "Montezuma's Revenge" just thinking about Mexico.

The other reason for choosing Panama is that they have a sane government that welcomes and encourages retirees to live there. The same certainly cannot be said of the U.S., especially a number of high-tax states like
California and New York. Panama understands that even though they may
not pay much in taxes, retirees support the local economy by buying real
estate, cars, food, and clothing and use few government-provided services.
Shouldn't California and New York want people like that? We are dream
residents. Yet high-tax states in America chase us away.

Consequently, Panama has passed laws to encourage moving and living
there. The U.S. would be smart to do the same. Allowing people to spend
their retirement money in the States could do nothing but help the economy.
As *jubilados* (retirees) in Panama, we enjoyed numerous discounts of 25
percent and more in restaurants and even on airfares. Another benefit was
separate express lines at banks, movies, and government buildings.

Other savings were even more advantageous. To encourage construction,
Panamanian law exempts new and renovated homes and buildings from
property taxes for twenty years. The result is lower rents; and, if you buy as
we did, no property tax means thousands of dollars in annual savings.

The cost of living is also much lower. First-run movies are $2, and a
maid can be hired for $10 a day. We paid ours $20 a day and were ostracized
by the locals for "ruining the economy."

We purchased and renovated a condominium for our home. The purchase process is similar to that in the States. Real estate prices are similar
to those here, although renovation can be done for much less, primarily
because labor is less than half the cost. We worked with a wonderful
Panamanian contractor who spoke passable English. My wife wanted to
adopt him. When asked how he was going to accomplish a difficult renovation task, he would respond, "Tenemos gente para eso." Translation: "We
have people for that." That saying became our Panamanian mantra and is
one of the truly wonderful memories from living there.

We met wonderful people, both expats and native Panamanians. To
this day our maid calls on New Year's Day, just to stay in touch.

Since the U.S. is one of the few countries that demand its citizens pay taxes regardless of where they live, or from where they earn their income (equivalent to having to pay New York taxes if you were born there, even after you moved elsewhere), several U.S. expats we met in Panama had given up their U.S. citizenship. Most, however, including us, had not taken such a drastic step, although almost all had established residency in a U.S. state without an income tax before their move (so at least they did not have to continue paying state income taxes).

Note that giving up U.S. citizenship is not an easy task. As I understand it, current U.S. law requires a draconian tax payment on all your assets. However, for those with large stock portfolios, such a move could be beneficial over the long run since Panama does not tax income made outside their country.

Although we were living well (especially for the cost) and had made some great friends, after three years my wife decided Panama was too small of a country and we returned to the States.

We were not, however, ready to give up on the idea of retiring offshore. We decided to explore what living in Europe would be like by living in different places a month at a time. We were able to do this on a reasonable budget by a combination of monthly rentals and home exchanges. There are several rental and exchange websites. Two we relied on were www.homeforexchange.com and www.vrbo.com.

Through these sites we arranged month-long stays in England: the Cotswolds for a month, with a second month in a flat in London; three months in Italy: one month in Tuscany, a second on the Adriatic in *The Marche*, and a third in Puglia, the heal; a month in Denmark; and a month in Majorca, Spain. Except for airfare, the home exchanges were done at no additional cost—we even exchanged cars. And we were able to rent some magnificent homes by going in the off-season and negotiating. The owner's asking rental price and calendar availability are listed on the website. I would find four or five great looking homes in the area we wanted to visit that were not booked during the off season. They might be asking $2,000–5,000 a week. Seeing they had no bookings, I'd email the owner, explain that our budget was limited, and offer $1,500 or $2,000 for the MONTH, pointing out it was better having us, even at this price, than having it sit empty. We got great rates, negotiating this way.

We had a wonderful time. Living in one place for a month was a great adventure. We'd shop in the local markets and explore the area at a leisurely pace, while meeting an interesting mix of locals and expats—the Brits are everywhere! It is amazing how many people are out and about in the world.

A few other cost-saving tips:

1. Rent cars from Peugeot and Renault. The way it was explained to me is that France has a very high new-car tax, so these companies rent new cars outside France for up to three months at very reasonable rates, making up the difference by then selling them as used cars in France without the tax.

2. Negotiate. We wanted to spend Christmas in Venice. Again, December is the offseason and a few weeks earlier there had been floods with warnings to avoid Venice. I went on Priceline.com and looked up five-star Venetian hotels. The average price was $640 U.S. dollars per night. I offered $105. My offer was accepted. We stayed for three nights in an amazing hotel. The highlight was Christmas morning mass at St. Mark's Basilica, celebrated by the Cardinal. After mass the bars opened stands on the street and handed out glasses of sparkling wine mixed with Aperol, a drink called "A Venetian." It was one of those truly magical moments.

As we boarded the plane in London after our last home exchange, I told my wife, "I've done this enough." She replied, "Me too. Let's go to the Texas hill country, build a home, and nest." *And, that is exactly what we've done.*

Those of you who don't live in Texas have probably noticed when meeting a Texan living elsewhere, they are only there temporarily; they are always "going back to Texas." To that, my wife (a Texas girl herself) says, "Yes, and every Texan wants to retire to the Hill Country." The Hill Country is the area of rolling hills, rivers, and beautiful lakes between Austin and San Antonio. It's now our home.

As you've already read in Wayne's "Cowboy Capitalism" chapter, Texas is the best damn country in America. It has everything. The state income taxes are zero, the capital gains taxes are zero, regulations are low, guns are welcome, and lawyers are kicked to the state line. It's the best we've got in America. If things get bad enough in the next four years under Obama, millions of Americans will escape to Texas.

Eventually Texas might be forced to secede—that is no longer a joke. And, if things get really bad, and even Texas can't save us, then it may be time to consider Switzerland, Singapore, Australia, Canada, or New Zealand (for the wealthy), or Panama, Belize, Mexico, Costa Rica, or Indonesia (for those of modest means). With the economic disaster happening in Europe, you might want to keep your eye on Greece, Spain, Ireland, or even France—soon the cost of housing there will be REALLY cheap. But for now, Texas will do.

So there's my story. I turned my dream into a plan with the help of those who "knew what to do." And although my "dream" didn't turn out to be what I thought I wanted, at least I won't live my life thinking "If only I would have, could have, should have," which, of course, is always followed by an "Aw s***!"

Hopefully, my experience will give you the confidence to head off on your own adventure and not hesitate to try moving offshore to survive regardless of what Obama and the liberals are doing to this great country. There's a big world out there. We love America, but it's not the only place in the world to live a nice life. And if it continues to decline, more and more Americans will look for greener pastures.

Why not? You only live once. And, as our story shows, you can always come back home…to Texas.

CHAPTER FIFTY-ONE

IN CONCLUSION: THE WINNING MINDSET AND PSYCHOLOGY YOU'LL NEED TO SUCCEED

You've heard my strategies for surviving Obamageddon, and you've been able to profit from the insights of the millionaires I'm lucky enough to call friends.

You now know *what* actions to take. It is time you learn *how* to take them. Quite frankly, it is not as easy or straightforward as it may seem. Why? Because most people are afraid of change. The key to taking action and implementing all these ideas is having a winning mindset. Let me explain.

A winning mindset consists of three parts: **conservative values, a competitive and enthusiastic spirit, and a relentless attitude.**

By now, I'm sure you agree with me about the need for smaller government, lower spending, lower taxes, and more power to the individual. But, if you have any doubt, let me tell you why long-term studies show these CONSERVATIVE VALUES are not just good for your bank account, they're also good for your spirit.

Amazingly, these studies prove that simply believing in the power of the individual versus the power of government makes all the difference in being successful and satisfied in life. What a bonus—a political and economic philosophy that not only leads to wealth and financial freedom, but also leads to a happier and more fulfilling life in the bargain.

In October 2008, newspapers across the country trumpeted the news that Republicans were much happier than Democrats. How much happier? Try 68 percent happier. Yes, the study found that conservative Republicans were 68 percent more likely to be happy than liberal Democrats.[1]

This wasn't the first study to reach this conclusion. In the journal *Psychological Science*, two NYU professors, Jaime Napier and John Yost, reported on multiple studies showing conservatives not only to be happier, but to possess a more positive outlook, more optimism, and more moral clarity.[2] You might argue that Republicans are wealthier, and money buys happiness. You'd be wrong. The four-decade study showed that poor Republicans are happier than poor Democrats, middle class Republicans are happier than middle class Democrats, and rich Republicans are happier than rich Democrats.[3] This result was first shown by the Pew Social & Demographic Trends Project. The dramatic partisan "happiness gap" that Pew found in favor of Republicans has held steady for decades, through good times and bad. No matter what you do to us, Republicans and conservatives are cheerful people.

Happiness obviously has nothing to do with political party identification. It is however about a belief system—a subconscious mindset that helps to create high levels of optimism and satisfaction.

What this is really about is *a belief in the individual.*

It's a belief in the principle that *you*, not government, are in control of your own destiny. How do I know that? Because the Pew study found that a key factor for happiness is whether you believe success is determined by outside forces, or by "personal initiative." Even the biased liberal *Washington Post* got it right, "The hypothesis: Those who think they can control their destinies are happier."[4] That life-changing core belief in personal initiative is what Republicans, fiscal conservatives, and free market libertarians share the world over.

If you believe government can make your life better and are waiting for handouts, entitlements, bailouts, and stimulus checks to save you, you are destined to be disappointed, unhappy, and depressed.

By the way, it isn't just that government leaves you disappointed, it's also about the reality that what government does provide cannot create happiness. Government won't make you rich, or successful, or bring you the perfect mate. All government can do is deliver a small check that leaves you in "shared misery" with no sense of accomplishment, and no hope for a better tomorrow.

Individuals who feel in control of their destiny always have hope for tomorrow. When times get difficult they become *more* committed, tenacious, and determined to succeed. Individuals with this kind of positive mindset don't wait for opportunity. *They create opportunity.*

If it is to be, it is up to me.

To conservative values we must add the second element of a winning mindset—A COMPETITIVE AND ENTHUSIASTIC SPIRIT.

If we're going to get out of this mess it will come from entrepreneurship and capitalism, not from a nation hooked on handouts and entitlements. It won't come from denigrating, discouraging, and punishing successful citizens for their success. It won't come from redistributing their money to people who don't have enthusiasm or a competitive spirit. It won't come from running the country in the name of "social justice." It won't come from unemployment, food stamps, and disability payments. It will come from enthusiastic, competitive, courageous entrepreneurs willing to risk their own money to start up businesses and create jobs.

In this Obama economy, you better find a way to muster the most enthusiasm of your life. That is your best chance to survive and thrive. That's how you turn the Obama nightmare into the American Dream. With a smile, a whistle while you work, a spark in your eyes, and an excitement level never before seen or felt. It's not "low class." It's not beneath you. It's not ignorant. It's your best chance to survive Obamageddon.

Conservatives need only look at presidential politics to see the difference enthusiasm makes. Barry Goldwater is the father of conservatism in America. Yet he lost the 1964 presidential election by a landslide. Ronald Reagan took Goldwater's exact philosophy, but spread it with tremendous enthusi-asm. With the exact same political philosophy and agenda, Reagan won the presidency in *two landslides*. Enthusiasm was the difference.

The second example is sports. This past Super Bowl Sunday, John and Jim Harbaugh were the two coaches left standing out of thirty-two NFL teams. They also happened to be brothers, born just fifteen months apart, who slept in the same room, in adjoining beds for their entire childhood. They played each other for the greatest prize in sports, in front of the big-gest audience in American television history. Amazing.[5]

Their favorite saying since childhood:

"Attack each day with an enthusiasm unknown to mankind!"[6]

Now, let's add the third and final leg, the overwhelming POWER OF A RELENTLESS ATTITUDE. Even in this Obamageddon economy, there is hope. It isn't found in your IQ or your education. What separates the winners from the losers is your mindset. And the most important piece of that mindset, the piece that allows people the world over to succeed against difficult, even impossible odds is to be RELENTLESS.

I'm not any smarter than the next guy or gal—I can barely answer a question on *Jeopardy*. I'm certainly no math whiz—without a calculator, I'm lost. I'm no high tech genius—I need my eight- and thirteen-year-old sons to help me navigate anything difficult on the Internet. Saying that I can't dance or sing would be an understatement. The list of things I can't do is long. But what matters isn't the list of what you can't do well. What matters is finding what you do well, and focusing on it like a laser-guided missile, to become the best you can possibly be.

Challenges, obstacles, and insurmountable odds—just figure out a way around them, or run right through them. Never let rejection or failure stop or even slow you. You'll hear "NO" early and often. But, "NO" is only the start of a long negotiation. Successful, relentless people eat "NO" for breakfast.

That's the one common ingredient in virtually every success story. And in this economic crisis, now more than ever we all need the power of RELENTLESS.

W.A.R. isn't just my initials. Actually, it stands for *"Wayne is always RELENTLESS."*

It certainly takes the power of RELENTLESS to go from a Las Vegas oddsmaker, small businessman, and homeschooling dad to presidential candidate, vice presidential nominee, and national media personality—whose political opinions are featured on the Fox News Channel, in *Time* magazine, and on hundreds of conservative talk radio shows from coast to coast. My business opinions and predictions have been featured by CNBC, *Forbes, Fortune, Equities*, the *Wall Street Journal*, and *Investor's Business Daily*. How does something like that happen? Only with the power of RELENTLESS.

I want to leave you with one personal story that literally defines RELENTLESS. It's the story of the last hours of the life of my mother, Stella Root. As you'll see, relentless is in my genes.

My mother and father died of cancer twenty-eight days apart in 1992, the toughest year of my life. I spoke at my father's funeral in New York and returned to my home in California only to get a call a few days later from my sister telling me that our mom had gone into a tailspin after the funeral. Only days later, she was gone. But it was the remarkable last hours of Stella Root's life that I will remember and cherish forever.

The call came from my mother's doctor: "Wayne, I'm sorry to tell you, but your mom is gone. She no longer shows brain activity so we're disconnecting life support. Please don't rush home. She's gone. Be careful, take care of yourself, breathe deeply, and don't rush home. Doctor's orders. Got it?"

Then, he handed the phone to my sister who whispered "Wayne…ignore the doctor. Rush home. You and I both know mom won't die until you get here. *Rush home.*"

I raced to the airport and caught the red eye that night out of Los Angeles to New York. By the time I walked into my mother's hospital room, it had been twelve hours since I got that terrible call; twelve hours since life support had been disconnected; twelve hours since that doctor said, "Don't rush home, your mom is gone." Yet when I ran through the door to her room, I heard the most beautiful sound I'd ever heard: **beep…beep… beep…beep.**

It was her heart monitor. Despite being disconnected from life support, her heart was still beating. My sister had sat by her bedside all night saying,

"Mom, hang on, Wayne is on the way. Don't die, Wayne is on the way." Medical science may have determined her brain was dead, but that beeping heart monitor told another story. She'd lived through the night on sheer willpower. Some might call it a miracle. I simply call it RELENTLESS.

I hugged my mom, grabbed her hand, kissed her cheek. I couldn't stop crying. I told her, "Mom, I love you. Thank you for waiting for me. I know how hard that was. But you made it. I'll remember forever what you did for me. I love you…but now it's time to go. Your body deserves a rest. Heaven is waiting. It's time to *let go*. You have Lori's and my permission."

Ten seconds later…beep…..beep (fainter)……….beeeeeep……….flat-line.

And she was gone.

Medical science may have considered her brain dead, but somehow, some way, my mother had understood. How did she will herself to live all the way until the next morning? How did she know that her only son, Wayne, was on the way?

My mother may not have had any brainpower left, but she had will-power. She had *heart*. And that's the most important thing in the world— no matter what your goals. All success, all progress, all the miracles in this world are based on heart, on spirit, on will, on being enthusiastic…and on the power of being *RELENTLESS*.

Stella Root defined relentless.

We're all going to need to muster the power of RELENTLESS to defeat Obama and his socialist game plan. We're going to need it to overcome the brainwashing of the education system. We're going to need it to overcome the biased, Obama-adoring, leftist media and the banana republic they've created. We're going to need it to overcome $100 trillion in debt and unfunded liabilities. We're going to need it to overcome the damage Obama has done to our economy…and our children's future.

You are now armed with detailed information and advice from me, and my business superstar friends. You now know how to not only survive, but to thrive, capitalize, and prosper during the next four years of Obam-ageddon. If you apply the advice with a RELENTLESS attitude—nothing can stop you.

Now, put on your armor. Lock down your helmet. Turn on **Y-PODS: Your Personal Obama Defense Shield.**

It's time for battle. Go create your own Booming Personal Economy. Go protect your family. Go take back this country. Your mission is to survive, thrive, and prosper despite Obama. Godspeed for a safe and prosperous journey.

And most importantly, God Bless America.

Wayne Allyn Root
Las Vegas, Nevada
February, 2013

ACKNOWLEDGMENTS

Let me start with God. God is my foundation, my motivation, and my source of inspiration. I pray to God to start every day. I prayed to God for the creativity and wisdom to write this book. I now pray that this book will empower, educate, enrich, and elevate the lives of every reader. I hope (and pray) that this book encourages Americans to fight for smaller government, reduced spending, lower taxes, more economic and personal freedom, and more respect for the Constitution. I pray that the taxpayers, capitalists, and patriots are able to take back this country from those looking to destroy it.

Now I want thank a few friends and family who were instrumental in my ability to write this book.

First, I want to thank my publisher. Regnery Publishing is the finest publisher I have had the honor of working with. Special thanks to Marji Ross, the president of Regnery. It has been an honor to work with one of the most influential conservative dynamos in the country. Elizabeth Kantor was my editor. And what an editor! I could not have written this book without her brilliant direction and research. She is the ultimate pro. Alberto Rojas headed up our public relations campaign. I am forever grateful for all of your faith, professionalism, work ethic, and teamwork.

Doug Miller is my best friend and mentor of the past thirty years. Doug is a Nebraska farm boy turned Stanford MBA who specialized in turning around companies. We desperately need people like Doug to turn around the U.S. economy. Unfortunately we have the Obamas of the world instead. What a tragedy.

All those many years ago (1983), Doug was the first adult to ever believe in me and my talents. He saw tremendous potential and then helped turn that potential into real achievements over the next three decades. I can never repay my debt of gratitude. Everyone needs a friend and mentor like Doug Miller. Doug reviewed and edited every word I wrote in this book. His talents and creative ideas can be found throughout.

Doug has written his own book of fatherly advice to his two sons, Alexander and Zachary (my godsons). It is full of an incredible amount of basic, commonsense parenting advice that I would recommend to everyone. It's available as an ebook at Amazon: *Never Give Up on Love: Life, Love, and Fatherly Advice.*

Then there are Michael and Richard Checkan and their executive team at Asset Strategies International (ASI). Michael and Rich shared their time, talents, and extensive knowledge about gold and precious metals with me. Their generous spirit, hard work, unmatched knowledge, and brilliant insights about gold and precious metals helped to make this book far better. If only America had adults like Michael and Rich running the economy, I guarantee you capitalism would be safe for centuries to come. Special thanks to ASI team members Elena Keller, Thomas VanBuskirk, and Steve Emerick, as well as Adriane Berg and Stuart Bochner of Generation Bold, for their contributions.

As important as the Checkans and ASI were to my precious metals education, Richard Spring was that important to my rare coin education. What a wonderful learning experience. Richard, you are a master at your craft! If anyone in America knows more about rare gold and silver coins, I haven't met him.

Special thanks goes to Thomas Noon, a consultant to one of the largest hedge funds on Wall Street. Thomas is a new friend whose brilliant mind added quite a few interesting ideas to this book. Thomas is a true American patriot. In the middle of managing hundreds of millions of dollars, he found the time to advise and educate me about gold, energy, ROTH IRAs, and equities. What can I say, except thank you from the bottom of my heart.

Thanks to each of the business superstars who contributed their advice to this book. What would America be without economic geniuses like Kip Herriage, Marc Faber, Joe Sugarman, Phil Gordon, Dr. Peter Diamandis, Max James, Dave Bego, J. T. Foxx, and Dr. Mark Skousen? And to my superstar friends who wanted to remain anonymous in the book, thank you for your contributions. You are all my heroes. You are what made America great, and your brilliance and extraordinary talents continue to give me hope for the future.

"Team Root" is fueled by the world's greatest publicist Sandy Frazier; my personal attorney and great friend of over twenty years Lee Sacks; and my accountant of over twenty years Allyn Moskowitz. My television partner is Michael Yudin. My book agent is Nancy Ellis. My television agent is Richard Lawrence. My radio agent is Paul Anderson. And then there's Kraig Kitchin, one of the most important players in American radio, who has given his time and effort to support my career every step of the way— just out of friendship. Whenever I formulate a plan, or have a question, these professionals are there to answer it, or make it happen. Your friendship, advice, and counsel have made all the hard work and struggles worthwhile.

Thanks to the economic gurus and financial mavens whose knowledge of finance and capitalism I rely on: Kip Herriage, Dr. Mark Skousen, John Mauldin, Marc Faber, Jim Rogers, and Peter Schiff. Thank you for your financial insights on a daily basis.

And a special thank you to Mark Skousen for inviting me to be a part of the "greatest financial event on earth"—FreedomFest. It's four amazing days every July in Las Vegas that everyone should experience.

Thanks to a few personal friends who gave me great inspiration for this book: Lee Lipton, whose friendship, counsel, and daily rants about politics inspire and motivate me! Lee's ideas can be found in so much of what I write.

Other friends who I owe a debt of gratitude to include Robert Sanchez, Dane Andreeff, Roger Harrison, Hollis "Harvard" Barnhart, George Abraham, Monte Weiner, Jim Feist, Dr. Joseph Williams, Matthew Schiff, Bob Bright, Carter Clews, and Larry Ward. Your friendship and counsel have been invaluable to my success and happiness.

A few media stars stand out for how helpful you have been to my career—Bill Cunningham (the GREAT American), Rita Cosby, Eric "Mancow" Muller, Bob "Sully" Sullivan, Andy Dean, Captain Matt Bruce, and Alan Stock, to name a few.

Thanks to Fox News and FoxNews.com for giving my career a boost. Special thanks to Bill Shine, Lynne Martin (of FoxNews.com), *Fox & Friends*, Bill O'Reilly, Sean Hannity, Glenn Beck, Neil Cavuto, Governor Mike Huckabee, Greta Van Susteren, and Judge Andrew Napolitano. Appearances on your shows were instrumental in building my media career.

Thanks to websites including FoxNews.com, PersonalLiberty.com, TheBlaze.com, Newsmax.com, Forbes.com, Breitbart.com, Washington-Times.com, and DailyCaller.com, which have so often spread my opinions and "Root Rants" to millions.

Thanks to my political heroes who inspired me from a young age—Barry Goldwater, Ronald Reagan, Ron Paul, and Jack Kemp. Today Jim DeMint of the Heritage Foundation, and Tea Party Senators Rand Paul and Marco Rubio carry on this great tradition. Thank you for your heroism and inspiration.

I saved the best for last—my family. Thank you forever to my wife Debra for giving me the four most perfect children in the world. Thank you to my children Dakota (twenty-one), Hudson (thirteen), Remington (eight), and Contessa (five). Hudson gets special kudos for directing, producing and editing all of my videos since the age of nine. This kid will be a superstar of TV and movies someday. You all make my life worth living, make all the work seem effortless, and all the struggles seem like a walk in the park. You are the lights of my life. Everything I do, I do for you.

AUTHOR'S NOTE

Do you have your own "Obama survival story?" Have you found a unique way to survive, thrive, and prosper in spite of Obama, or because of Obama? If so, please share your story with me. It could be part of my next book! I'm looking for interesting and unique personal stories of Obama survival.

W.A.R.
Wayne Allyn Root

Send your personal stories or unique advice to
Wayne@ROOTforAmerica.com

Or mail them to me at
Wayne Allyn Root
c/o ROOT for America
2505 Anthem Village Drive, Ste. 318
Henderson, NV 89052

WE HOPE YOU ENJOYED WAYNE'S BOOK.

TO CONTACT WAYNE, EMAIL

Wayne@ROOTforAmerica.com

IF YOU WANT TO FIND OUT MORE ABOUT WHAT WAYNE IS UP TO, PLEASE GO TO

www.ROOTforAmerica.com

or

www.WayneRoot.com

TO JOIN WAYNE'S FACEBOOK FAN PAGE:

https://www.facebook.com/WayneAllynRoot

TO FOLLOW WAYNE ON TWITTER PAGE
AND READ HIS DAILY TWEETS:

http://twitter.com/WayneRoot/

TO BOOK WAYNE FOR SPEECHES, SEMINARS,
KEYNOTE ADDRESSES FOR BUSINESS, CORPORATE,
OR POLITICAL CONFERENCES OR CONVENTIONS, GO TO

www.ROOTofSuccess.com

Or contact

The ROOT of Success

2505 Anthem Village Drive, Ste 318

Henderson, NV 89052

TOLL FREE: (888) 444-ROOT

FAX: (702) 407-5188

NOTES

PART ONE

1. H. L. Mencken, *In Defense of Women* (1918).

CHAPTER ONE

1. "Obama Says Jobs Numbers Show That Economy Is Improving But Too Many Looking For Work," Huffington Post, February 3, 2012, http://www.huffingtonpost.com/2012/02/03/obama-jobs-economy-arlington-va_n_1252603.html.
2. Michelle Jamrisko, "Consumer Spending in U.S. Climbs Even as Taxes Hurt Incomes," Bloomberg, March 1, 2013, http://www.bloomberg.com/news/2013-03-01/consumer-spending-in-u-s-climbs-even-as-taxes-hurt-incomes.html.
3. Moe Lane, "The grim labor force participation rate graph," RedState, January 21, 2013, http://www.redstate.com/2013/01/21/labor-force-participation-rate/; Erika Johnsen, "BLS: Americans 'not in labor force' increased by 8 million+ during Obama's first term," Hot Air, January 21, 2013, http://hotair.com/archives/2013/01/21/bls-americans-not-in-labor-force-increased-by-8-million-during-obamas-first-term/; "Male labor participation rate in the US hits the lowest level on record," Sober Look (blog), Credit Writedowns, September 9, 2012, http://www.creditwritedowns.com/2012/09/male-labor-participation-rate-in-the-us-hits-the-lowest-level-on-record.html.
4. Jim Geraghty, "Obama's Debt-Reduction Promises Continue to Expire," The Campaign Spot (blog), National Review Online, January 31, 2012,

http://www.nationalreview.com/campaign-spot/289729/obamas-debt-reduction-promises-continue-expire.

5.   Amy Payne, "Morning Bell: $16,000,000,000,000," The Foundry (blog), The Heritage Foundation, September 5, 2012, http://blog.heritage.org/2012/09/05/morning-bell-16000000000000.

6.   Ibid.

7.   Donovan Slack, "Obama: I'm not a socialist," Politico, December 14, 2012, http://www.politico.com/politico44/2012/12/obama-im-not-a-socialist-151997.html.

8.   "Jobs & The Economy: Putting America Back To Work," White House website, http://www.whitehouse.gov/economy.

9.   "Eurozone unemployment hits new high EU unemployment 26 million," Information Daily, January 10, 2013, http://www.theinformationdaily.com/2013/01/10/eurozone-unemployment-rate-hits-new-high.

10. Terry Miller, "In the Index of Economic Freedom, Liberalization Slips," Wall Street Journal, January 14, 2013, http://online.wsj.com/article/SB100014241278873233745045782180626653964032.html.

11. Jeff Mason, "Obama: Markets Will Have 'Adverse Reaction' to Fiscal Cliff Fail," Huffington Post, December 30, 2012, http://www.huffingtonpost.com/2012/12/30/obama-markets_n_2384315.html.

12. Jeanne Sahadi, "CBO: Fiscal cliff deal adds $4 trillion to deficits," CNN, January 18, 2013, http://money.cnn.com/2013/01/01/news/economy/fiscal-cliff-deal-cbo/index.html.

13. Terence P. Jeffrey, "73% of New Jobs Created in Last 5 Months Are in Government," CNS News, December 7, 2012, http://cnsnews.com/news/article/73-new-jobs-created-last-5-months-are-government.

14. "Obama on Economy: 'We're Moving in the Right Direction,'" 24Wired.TV, http://24wired.tv/26537/obama-on-economy-were-moving-in-the-right-direction/.

15. Daniel Halper, "Food Stamp Growth 75X Greater than Job Creation," Weekly Standard (blog), November 2, 2012, http://www.weeklystandard.com/blogs/food-stamp-growth-75x-greater-job-creation_660073.html; Marica Heroux Pounds, "Long-term unemployment benefits part of 'fiscal cliff' deal," Sun Sentinel, January 2, 2013, http://articles.sun-sentinel.com/2013-01-02/business/sfl-longterm-unemployment-benefits-fiscal-cliff_1_long-term-unemployment-benefits-weeks-of-state-benefits-part-of-fiscal-cliff.

16. Jennifer Epstein, "Obama talks up housing recovery," Politico, October 20, 2012, http://www.politico.com/news/stories/1012/82654.html; Jason Oliva, "Obama Administration: The Housing Recovery Continues," Reverse Mortgage Daily, January 14, 2013, http://reversemortgagedaily.com/2013/01/14/obama-adminstration-the-housing-recovery-continues/.

17. Hubble Smith, "Las Vegas sees $120 million in commercial loans go into default," Las Vegas Review-Journal, January 5, 2013, http://www.lvrj.com/business/las-vegas-sees-120-million-in-commercial-loans-go-into-default-185700681.html.

18. Chris Moody, "Apple has more cash than the federal government," The Ticket (blog), Yahoo! News, July 29, 2011, http://news.yahoo.com/blogs/ticket/apple-more-money-federal-government-163023405.html.

19. Tyler Durden, "Here Are The 29 Public Companies With More Cash Than The US Treasury," Zero Hedge (blog), July 15, 2011, http://www.zerohedge.com/article/here-are-29-public-companies-more-cash-us-treasury.

20. "Transcript of Obama on '60 Minutes,'" Fox News, September 24, 2012, http://www.foxnews.com/politics/2012/09/24/transcript-obama-on-60-minutes/.

21. Ira Stoll, "Yes, Actually, Obamacare Is the Biggest Tax Increase in History," Reason.com, July 9, 2012, http://reason.com/archives/2012/07/09/yes-actually-obamacare-is-the-biggest-ta.

22. Nuno Fontes, "United States Inflation Rate At 1.7% In December of 2012," Trading Economics, January 16, 2013, http://www.tradingeconomics.com/united-states/inflation-cpi; "Gas Prices Doubled, Obama Locks Up National Reserve," Investor's Business Daily, October 16, 2012, http://news.investors.com/ibd-editorials/101612-629552-obama-bans-drilling-in-national-petroleum-reserve.htm?p=full; Kimberly Amadeo, "Why Are Food Prices Rising?," About.com, February 5, 2013, http://useconomy.about.com/od/inflationfaq/f/Why-Are-Food-Prices-So-High.htm; "Food prices are at their highest for six months. Get all the data since 1990," Datablog, Guardian, http://www.guardian.co.uk/news/datablog/2012/oct/04/global-food-price-index-rise-data.

23. Tyler Durden, "Six Month + Delinquent Mortgages Amount To More Than Half Of Bank of America's Market Cap," Zero Hedge, December 19, 2012, http://www.zerohedge.com/news/2012-12-19/six-month-delinquent-mortgages-amount-more-half-bank-americas-market-cap.

24. Tyler Durden, "Guest Post: The Social Security System Is Already Broke," Zero Hedge, January 12, 2013, http://www.zerohedge.com/news/2013-01-12/guest-post-social-security-system-already-broke.

25. Christina Bellantoni, "Obama: Rich can afford tax hike," Washington Times, March 19, 2009, http://www.washingtontimes.com/news/2009/mar/19/obama-assures-town-hall-rich-can-afford-tax-hike/.

26. Veronique de Rugy, "Cronyism Lives On," The Corner (blog), National Review Online, January 3, 2013, http://www.nationalreview.com/corner/336865/cronyism-lives-veronique-de-rugy#.

27. "Remarks by the President at a Campaign Event in Roanoke, Virginia," July 13, 2012, White House website, http://www.whitehouse.gov/the-press-office/2012/07/13/remarks-president-campaign-event-roanoke-virginia.

28. "How Much?," Defeat the Debt, http://www.defeatthedebt.com/understanding-the-national-debt/how-much-do-we-owe/.

29. "Issues," White House website, http://www.whitehouse.gov/issues.

30. S. Fred Singer, "Obama's EPA Plans for 2013," American Thinker, October 25, 2012, http://www.americanthinker.com/2012/10/obamas_epa_plans_for_2013.html.

31. Mary Clare Jalonick, "FDA: Rules make food safer," Washington Times, January 4, 2013, http://www.washingtontimes.com/news/2013/jan/4/fda-proposes-sweeping-new-food-safety-rules/.

32. Investor's Business Daily, "Health Premiums Up $3,065; Obama Vowed $2,500 Cut," Yahoo! News, September 24, 2012, http://finance.yahoo.com/news/health-premiums-3-065-obama-224300715.html.

33. Hope Yen, "Postal Service Loss of $15.9 Billion Sets Record," Huffington Post, November 15, 2012, http://www.huffingtonpost.com/2012/11/15/postal-service-loss-_n_2137033.html.

34. "Great Depression Millionaires," HubPages, November 1, 2009, http://greatdepression.hubpages.com/hub/Great-Depression-Millionaires.

CHAPTER TWO

1. Wayne Allyn Root, *The Conscience of a Libertarian* (Hoboken: John Wiley & Sons, Inc., 2009); Wayne Allyn Root, "Obama's agenda: Overwhelm the system," *Las Vegas Review-Journal*, June 6, 2010, http://www.lvrj.com/opinion/obama-s-agenda—overwhelm-the-system-95716764.html; Wayne Allyn Root, "Let the Obama Disaster Begin:," *ROOT for AMERICA!* (blog), November 18, 2008, http://root4america.com/webroot/oldblog/index.

php?entry=entry081118-081333; Wayne Allyn Root, "The Truth About The Obama Agenda," *ROOT for AMERICA!* (blog), January 27, 2009, http://root4america.com/webroot/oldblog/index.php?entry=entry090127-191952. Wayne Allyn Root, "Welcome to Obamaville! Obama Bankrupts America with $9.7 Trillion on Bailouts and Stimulus, as CBO Confirms the Best Choice is to do Nothing.," *ROOT for AMERICA!* (blog), February 6, 2009, http://root4america.com/webroot/oldblog/index.php?m=02&y=09&entry=entry090206-111704. Wayne Allyn Root, "OBAMA HAS DECLARED WAR ON SMALL BUSINESS: The Real Story of Why Obama Hates Self-Made Entrepreneurs From Obama's College Classmate and The Only Small Businessman to Run for President in Modern History," *ROOT for AMERICA!* (blog), March 3, 2009, http://root4america.com/webroot/oldblog/index.php?m=03&y=09&entry=entry090303-103128. Wayne Allyn Root, "Barack Obama: The great jobs killer," *Las Vegas Review-Journal*, July 4, 2010, http://www.lvrj.com/opinion/barack-obama—the-great-jobs-killer-97758294.html.

2. Jim Geraghty, "Obama's Debt-Reduction Promises Continue to Expire," *The Campaign Spot* (blog), National Review Online, January 31, 2012, http://www.nationalreview.com/campaign-spot/289729/obamas-debt-reduction-promises-continue-expire.

3. Amy Payne, "Morning Bell: $16,000,000,000,000," *The Foundry* (blog), The Heritage Foundation, September 5, 2012, http://blog.heritage.org/2012/09/05/morning-bell-16000000000000.

4. "CLOWARD-PIVEN STRATEGY (CPS)," DiscoverTheNetworks, http://www.discoverthenetworks.org/groupProfile.asp?grpid=7522.

5. John Sexton, "'DOC FIX' MAY END: REAL SPENDING OFFSET BY FAKE CUTS," Breitbart, December 19, 2012, http://www.breitbart.com/Big-Government/2012/12/19/Doc-Fix-May-End-Costs-Offset-by-Obama-s-Gimmick-Cuts.

6. "Obama's 'Fiscal Cliff' Proposal: $1.6 Trillion in Tax Increases," CNBC, November 29, 2012, http://www.cnbc.com/id/50016612/Obamarsquos_lsquoFiscal_Cliffrsquo_Proposal_16_Trillion_in_Tax_Increases.

7. Tami Luhby, "Fiscal cliff deal raises taxes on 77% of Americans," CNN, January 3, 2013, http://money.cnn.com/2013/01/03/news/economy/fiscal-cliff-taxes/.

8. Barnini Chakraborty, "Fiscal deal emboldens Obama to seek more tax increases," Fox News, January 2, 2013, http://www.foxnews.com/

politics/2013/01/02/fiscal-deal-emboldens-obama-to-ask-for-more-tax-increases/.

9. Jeanne Sahadi, "CBO: Fiscal cliff deal adds $4 trillion to deficits," CNN, January 18, 2013, http://money.cnn.com/2013/01/01/news/economy/fiscal-cliff-deal-cbo/index.html.

10. Veronique de Rugy, "Cronyism Lives On," *The Corner* (blog), National Review Online, January 3, 2013, http://www.nationalreview.com/corner/336865/cronyism-lives-veronique-de-rugy#.

11. John D. McKinnon, "Deductions Limits Will Affect Many," *Wall Street Journal*, January 3, 2013, http://online.wsj.com/article/SB10001424127887323689604578217850195921128.html.

12. "Alaska senators join lawmakers who want Obama to rescind pay raise for Congress," Fox News, January 1, 2013, http://www.foxnews.com/politics/2012/12/31/obama-gives-congress-pay-raise/.

13. Veronique de Rugy, "How Much of Federal Spending is Borrowed for Every Dollar," Mercatus Center, July 11, 2011, http://mercatus.org/publication/how-much-federal-spending-borrowed-every-dollar.

14. "Collected Quotations," jim.com, http://jim.com/liberquo.htm.

15. Jim Hoft, "Obama Locks Up 1.6 Million Acres From Oil Development," Gateway Pundit, November 10, 2012, http://www.thegatewaypundit.com/2012/11/obama-locks-up-1-6-million-acres-from-oil-development/.

16. William Bigelow, "BOOK: OBAMACARE DESIGNED TO CREATE 21 MILLION UNION JOBS," Breitbart, August 20, 2012, http://www.breitbart.com/Big-Government/2012/08/20/Book-Obamacare-designed-to-create-21-million-union-jobs.

17. Grace-Marie Turner, "As 2013 Begins, Get Ready For An ObamaCare Tax Onslaught," *Forbes*, January 2, 2013, http://www.forbes.com/sites/gracemarieturner/2013/01/02/as-2013-begins-get-ready-for-an-obamacare-tax-onslaught/.

18. "IRS seeks 4,000 agents, $303 million for Obamacare," *Washington Examiner*, March 28, 2012, http://washingtonexaminer.com/irs-seeks-4000-agents-303-million-for-obamacare/article/416051.

19. Ed Morrissey, "ObamaCare bends the cost curve … upward," Hot Air, September 9, 2010, http://hotair.com/archives/2010/09/09/obamacare-bends-the-cost-curve-upward/.

20. Patrick Louis Knudsen, "Obamacare Loses Again in Deficit Reduction Debate," *The Foundry* (blog), The Heritage Foundation, August 22, 2012,

http://blog.heritage.org/2012/08/22/obamacare-loses-again-in-deficit-reduction-debate/.

21. Matt Cover, "Obama Budget Doubles National Debt to $26.3 Trillion in 10 Years," CNS News, February 14, 2011, http://cnsnews.com/news/article/obama-budget-doubles-national-debt-263-trillion-10-years.

22. Alister Bull, "Obama casts Republicans as party of the rich," Reuters, July 17, 2010, http://www.reuters.com/article/2010/07/17/us-obama-republicans-idUSTRE66G0LD20100717.

23. Peter Eavis, "Mortgage Interest Deduction, Once a Sacred Cow, Is Under Scrutiny," *New York Times*, November 26, 2012, http://dealbook.nytimes.com/2012/11/26/mortgage-interest-deduction-once-a-sacred-cow-is-seen-as-vulnerable/.

24. Tony Martignetti, "Will Obama's Proposal to Cap Charitable Deductions Affect Giving?," Financial Planning Association, http://www.fpanet.org/journal/BetweentheIssues/LastMonth/Articles/ObamaProposalto CapCharitableDeductions/; Richard A. Epstein, "The End of Charity?," Hoover Institution, January 29, 2013, http://www.hoover.org/publications/defining-ideas/article/139186.

25. Byron Tau, "Trumka: Card check will happen in second Obama term," Politico, November 5, 2012, http://www.politico.com/politico44/2012/11/trumka-card-check-will-happen-in-second-obama-term-148483.html.

CHAPTER THREE

1. Peter Ferrara, "President Obama: The Biggest Government Spender In World History," *Forbes*, June 14, 2012, http://www.forbes.com/sites/peterferrara/2012/06/14/president-obama-the-biggest-government-spender-in-world-history.

2. Tyler Durden, "'Fiscal Cliff' Distracts As 'Fiscal Abyss' In Japan, UK and U.S. Cometh," *Zero Hedge*, December 28, 2012, http://www.zerohedge.com/news/2012-12-28/'fiscal-cliff'-distracts-'fiscal-abyss'-japan-uk-and-us-cometh.

3. Amy Payne, "Morning Bell: $16,000,000,000,000," *The Foundry* (blog), The Heritage Foundation, September 5, 2012, http://blog.heritage.org/2012/09/05/morning-bell-16000000000000.

4. "U.S. debt exceeds annual economic output," CBC News, January 9, 2012, http://www.cbc.ca/news/business/story/2012/01/09/us-gdp-debt.html.

5. Martin Crutsinger, "U.S. deficit tops $1 trillion for fourth year," *Komo News*, October 13, 2012, http://www.komonews.com/news/business/US-deficit-tops-1-trillion-for-fourth-year-174041751.html; Terence P. Jeffrey, "Obama's Now Borrowed More Than All Presidents from Washington to W," CNS News, November 30, 2012, http://cnsnews.com/news/article/obama-s-now-borrowed-more-all-presidents-washington-w.

6. Stephen Dinan, "U.S. marks 3rd-largest, single-day debt increase," *Washington Times*, July 7, 2010, http://www.washingtontimes.com/news/2010/jul/7/us-marks-3rd-largest-single-day-debt-boost/?page=all.

7. Andrew Malcolm, "New national debt data: It's growing about $3 million a minute, even during his vacation," *Los Angeles Times*, August 23, 2011, http://latimesblogs.latimes.com/washington/2011/08/obama-national-debt.html.

8. Tracy Withers, "U.S. to Get Downgraded Amid Fiscal 'Theater,' Pimco Says," Bloomberg, October 17, 2012, http://www.bloomberg.com/news/2012-10-17/u-s-to-get-downgraded-amid-fiscal-theater-pimco-says.html.

9. Charles Riley, "Family net worth plummets nearly 40%," CNN, June 12, 2012, http://money.cnn.com/2012/06/11/news/economy/fed-family-net-worth/index.htm.

10. Michael, "Things Are Getting Worse: Median Household Income Has Fallen 4 Years In A Row," *The Economic Collapse* (blog), September 12, 2012, http://theeconomiccollapseblog.com/archives/things-are-getting-worse-median-household-income-has-fallen-4-years-in-a-row.

11. Jeff Cox, "US Housing Crisis Is Now Worse Than Great Depression," CNBC, June 14, 2011, http://www.cnbc.com/id/43395857/US_Housing_Crisis_Is_Now_Worse_Than_Great_Depression.

12. Fred Lucas, "BLS: Obama Unemployment Rate Above 8% Longer Than Any Other President Since 1948," CNS News, September 18, 2012, http://cnsnews.com/news/article/bls-obama-unemployment-rate-above-8-longer-any-other-president-1948; "Number of Months With Unemployment Above 8 percent," *Twitter*, https://twitter.com/kesgardner/status/247924140126896128/photo/1.

13. John Williams, "Alternate Unemployment Charts," Shadow Government Statistics, http://www.shadowstats.com/alternate_data/unemployment-charts.

14. Michael, "Unemployment Is Not Going Down: The Employment Rate Has
     Been Under 59 Percent For 39 Months In A Row," *The Economic Collapse*
     (blog), December 9, 2012, http://theeconomiccollapseblog.com/archives/
     unemployment-is-not-going-down-the-employment-rate-has-been-under-
     59-percent-for-39-months-in-a-row.

15. Ibid.

16. Catherine Rampell, "A Look Behind the U.S. Decline in Global Competi-
     tiveness," *Economix* (blog), *New York Times*, September 6, 2012, http://
     economix.blogs.nytimes.com/2012/09/06/a-look-behind-the-
     u-s-decline-in-global-competitiveness/.

17. Michael, "There Are 100 Million Working Age Americans That Do Not
     Have Jobs ***UPDATED***," *The Economic Collapse* (blog), May 3, 2012,
     http://theeconomiccollapseblog.com/archives/there-are-100-million-
     working-age-americans-that-do-not-have-jobs.

18. "Time Not on Side of the Jobless," *Wall Street Journal*, March 26, 2012,
     http://online.wsj.com/article/SB10001424052702303812904577299982932
     070176.html.

19. Kenneth Bozarth, "All unemployed people in the United States would
     constitute the 68ᵗʰ largest country in the world!!," *Greater Phoenix Tea Party
     Patriots* (blog), September 5, 2011, http://phoenixteaparty.ning.com/
     profiles/blogs/all-unemployed-people-in-the-united-states-would-consti-
     tute-the?xg_source=activity.

20. Ibid.

21. Lila Shapiro, "U.S. Economy Trades High-Paying Jobs For Low-Paying
     Positions, Report Finds," *Huffington Post*, February 24, 2011, http://www.
     huffingtonpost.com/2011/02/23/us-economy-trades-high-pa_n_827360.
     html.

22. Sherle R. Schwenninger and Samuel Sherraden, "The American Middle
     Class Under Stress," New America Foundation, April 2011, http://growth.
     newamerica.net/sites/newamerica.net/files/policydocs/26-04-11%20
     Middle%20Class%20Under%20Stress.pdf.

23. Michael, "53 Percent Of All Young College Graduates In America Are Either
     Unemployed Or Underemployed," *The Economic Collapse* (blog), April 22,
     2012, http://theeconomiccollapseblog.com/archives/53-percent-of-all-
     young-college-graduates-in-america-are-either-unemployed-or-underem-
     ployed.

24.   Matt Cover, "Unemployment Rises for Women, African-Americans in December," CNS News, January 4, 2013, http://cnsnews.com/news/article/ unemployment-rises-women-african-americans-december.

25.   Mamta Badkar, "Mary Meeker's Definitive Guide To The American Public Debt Crisis," *Business Insider*, February 25, 2011, http://www. businessinsider.com/mary-meeker-usa-inc-february-24-2011-2.

26.   Christopher Goins, "Medicare Faces Unfunded Liability of $38.6T, or $328,404 for Each U.S. Household," CNS News, April 23, 2012, http:// cnsnews.com/news/article/medicare-faces-unfunded-liability-386t-or-328404-each-us-household.

27.   Michael, "More Than 100 Million American Are On Welfare," The American Dream, August 8, 2012, http://endoftheamericandream.com/archives/ more-than-100-million-americans-are-on-welfare.

28.   See Wayne Allyn Root, "Welcome to Obamageddon," *Washington Times*, March 16, 2011, http://www.washingtontimes.com/news/2011/mar/16/ welcome-to-obamageddon/?page=all; "The Distribution of Household Income and Federal Taxes, 2008 and 2009," Congressional Budget Office, July 2012; http://www.cbo.gov/sites/default/files/cbofiles/ attachments/43373-AverageTaxRates_screen.pdf.

29.   "'Dismal' prospects: 1 in 2 Americans are now poor or low income," NBC News, http://usnews.nbcnews.com/_news/2011/12/15/9461848-dismal-prospects-1-in-2-americans-are-now-poor-or-low-income.

30.   Frank Marshall Davis, "Rave This; if Obama has buried you for the past four years," SodaHead, October 2, 2012, http://www.sodahead.com/united-states/rave-this-if-obama-has-buried-you-for-the-past-four-years/ question-3216431/.

31.   "One Million U.S. Students Homeless, New Data Show," National Law Center On Homelessness & Poverty, June 2012, http://www.nlchp.org/ view_release.cfm?PRID=148.

32.   Mark Leland, "School lunch waste costing taxpayers," FOX 11 Online, September, 25, 2012, http://www.fox11online.com/dpp/news/local/on_ assignment/school-lunch-waste-costing-taxpayers.

33.   Rohit Chopra, "Too Big to Fail: Student debt hits a trillion," *Blog*, Consumer Financial Protection Bureau, March 21, 2012, http://www.consumer finance.gov/blog/too-big-to-fail-student-debt-hits-a-trillion/.

34.   Shushannah Walshe and Steven Portnoy, "Fact Check: Paul Ryan's Jimmy Carter Comments," *The Note* (blog), ABC News, September 3, 2012, http://

abcnews.go.com/blogs/politics/2012/09/fact-check-paul-ryans-jimmy-carter-comments/.

35. Harry Bradford, "Nearly Half Of Americans Have Less Than $500 In Savings: Survey," *Huffington Post*, October 22, 2012, http://www.huffington post.com/2012/10/22/americans-savings-500_n_2003285.html.

36. "30-YEAR LOW – Let's Stimulate the Startups!," *Forbes*, April 9, 2012, http://www.forbes.com/sites/thesba/2012/04/09/30-year-low-lets-stimulate-the-startups/?goback=%2Egde_138439_member_106417128; Lucia Mutikani and Lisa Von Ahn, "U.S. business startups rate at record low," Reuters, May 2, 2012, http://www.reuters.com/article/2012/05/02/us-usa-economy-businesses-idUSBRE84113G20120502.

37. Catherine Rampell, "A Look Behind the U.S. Decline in Global Competitiveness," *Economix*, (blog) *New York Times*, September 6, 2012, http://economix.blogs.nytimes.com/2012/09/06/a-look-behind-the-u-s-decline-in-global-competitiveness/.

38. Howard Portnoy, "83% of doctors say they might quit over Obamacare, according to new poll," Examiner.com, July 11, 2012, http://www.examiner.com/article/83-of-doctors-say-they-might-quit-over-obamacare-according-to-new-poll.

39. Simon Black, "When Priced in Gold, the US economy is at Depression-Era levels," Sovereign Man, December 31, 2012, http://www.sovereignman.com/highlight/when-priced-in-gold-the-us-economy-is-at-depression-era-levels-10286.

CHAPTER FOUR

1. John Williams, "The US Has $100 Trillion in Debts & Obligations," *King World News*, (blog), December 30, 2011, http://kingworldnews.com/king worldnews/KWN_DailyWeb/Entries/2011/12/30_John_Williams__The_US_Has_$100_Trillion_in_Debts_%26_Obligations.html.

2. NoLibZone, "Cook taxpayers owe $108 billion, country Treasurer Pappas says: Greg Hinz [Chicago, Ill County]," FreeRepublic, June 21, 2011, http://www.freerepublic.com/focus/f-news/2737919/posts.

3. Dennis Cauchon, "Federal workers starting at much higher pay than in past," USA TODAY, December 27, 2011, http://www.usatoday.com/news/washington/story/2011-12-26/federal-starting-salaries/52236360/1.

4. David Wallechinsky, "Thousands of Federal Retirees Receive $100,000 a Year Pensions … Including Newt Gingrich," *AllGov*, January 22, 2012,

http://www.allgov.com/Top_Stories/ViewNews/Thousands_of_Federal_
Retirees_Receive_100000_Dollars_a_Year_Pensions__Including_Newt_
Gingrich_120122.

5.   "Study: $3.9 trillion in unfunded pension liabilities," FOX News, June 16,
     2012, http://video.foxnews.com/v/1692134075001/study-39-trillion-in-
     unfunded-pension-liabilities/.

6.   "Illinois Gov't Pensions Over $100,000 Up 27% Since Last Year," Taxpayers
     United of America, May 30, 2012, http://www.taxpayersunitedofamerica.
     org/latest/illinois-govt-pensions-over-100000-up-27-since-last-year.

7.   Tyler Durden, "Guest Post [by Jim Quinn]: The Social Security System Is
     Already Broke," *Zero Hedge*, January 12, 2013, http://www.zerohedge.com/
     news/2013-01-12/guest-post-social-security-system-already-broke.

8.   Mark Leland, "School lunch waste costing taxpayers," FOX 11 Online,
     September 25, 2012, http://www.fox11online.com/dpp/news/local/on_
     assignment/school-lunch-waste-costing-taxpayers; "National School
     Lunch Program," Food and Nutrition Service, June 21, 2012, http://www.
     fns.usda.gov/cnd/lunch/.

9.   Tami Luhby, "Government wants more people on food stamps," CNN, June
     25, 2012, http://money.cnn.com/2012/06/25/news/economy/food-stamps-
     ads/index.htm.

10. Daniel Halper, "Food Stamp Growth 75X Greater than Job Creation,"
     Weekly Standard (blog), November 2, 2012, http://www.weeklystandard.
     com/blogs/food-stamp-growth-75x-greater-job-creation_660073.html.

11. "USDA partnering with Mexico to boost food stamp participation," Daily
     Caller, July 19, 2012, http://dailycaller.com/2012/07/19/usda-partnering-
     with-mexico-to-boost-food-stamp-participation/.

12. "House GOP questions legal grounds for changes to welfare work require-
     ments," FOX News, July 23, 2012, http://www.foxnews.com/
     politics/2012/07/23/house-gop-questions-legal-grounds-for-changes-to-
     welfare-work-requirements/.

13. "86 Teens Pregnant at One Memphis High School," FOX News, January 14,
     2011, http://www.foxnews.com/health/2011/01/14/teens-pregnant-men-
     phis-high-school/.

14. Steven A. Camarota, "Immigrants in the United States, 2010: A Profile of
     America's Foreign-Born Population," Center for Immigration Studies,
     August 2012, http://cis.org/2012-profile-of-americas-foreign-born-
     population.

15. Steven A. Camarota, "Welfare Use by Immigrant Households with Children," Center for Immigration Studies, April 2011, http://cis.org/immigrant-welfare-use-2011.

16. Robrt Longley, "Illegal Immigration Costs californioa Over Ten Billion Annually," About.com, December 2004, http://usgovinfo.about.com/od/immigrationnaturalizatio/a/caillegals.htm.

17. "Adolescent and School Health," Centers for Disease Control and Prevention, January 28, 2013, http://www.cdc.gov/healthyyouth/obesity/facts.htm.

18. "The United States of Diabetes: Challenges and opportunities in the decade ahead," UnitedHealth Group, November 2010, http://www.unitedhealthgroup.com/hrm/unh_workingpaper5.pdf.

19. "The Cost of Diabetes," American Diabetes Association, http://www.diabetes.org/advocate/resources/cost-of-diabetes.html.

20. Terence P. Jeffrey, "8,753,935: Workers on Disability Set Another Record in July; Exceed Population of 39 States," CNS News, July 23, 2012, http://cnsnews.com/news/article/8753935-workers-disability-set-another-record-july-exceed-population-39-states.

21. John Merline, "5.4 Million Join Disability Rolls Under Obama," *Investor's Business Daily*, April 20, 2012, http://news.investors.com/business/042012-608418-ssdi-disability-rolls-skyrocket-under-obama.htm?p=full.

22. "Fiscal Fix Should Include Disability Reform," Bloomberg, January 7, 2013, http://www.bloomberg.com/news/2013-01-07/fiscal-fix-should-include-disability-reform.html.

23. See Wayne Allyn Root, "Why we are on the brink of the greatest Depression of all time," FOX News, August 23, 2012, http://www.foxnews.com/opinion/2012/08/23/why-are-on-brink-greatest-depression-all-time/; Alex Kowalski, "Number of US workers claimging Social Security Disability Insurance climbs 22% in 5 years," *Bangor Daily News*, May 6, 2012; http://bangordailynews.com/2012/05/06/business/number-of-us-workers-claiming-social-security-disability-insurance-climbs-22-in-5-years/.

24. Marilynn Marchione, "U.S. vets' disability filings reach historic rate," USA TODAY, May 28, 2012, http://www.usatoday.com/news/health/story/2012-05-28/veteran-disability/55250092/1.

25. "U.S. Students Still Lag Behind Foreign Peers, Schools Make Little Progress In Improving Achievement," *Huffington Post*, July 23, 2012, http://www.

huffingtonpost.com/2012/07/23/us-students-still-lag-beh_n_1695516.
html.

26. "US Tax Freedom Day Clock 2011 Released," *actionamerica.blogspot.com* (blog), March 31, 2011, http://actionamerica.blogspot.com/2011/03/us-tax-freedom-day-clock-2011-released.html.

27. "US Tax Freedom Day Clock 2011 Released," *ActionAmerica.blogspot.com*, March 31, 2011, http://actionamerica.blogspot.com/2011/03/us-tax-freedom-day-clock-2011-released.html.

28. "General Electric Pursues Pot of Government Stimulus Gold," *Wall Street Journal*, November 17, 2009, http://online.wsj.com/article/SB125832961253649563.html.

29. Donald Lambro, "Renewable energy dollars for Obama's cronies," *Washington Times*, August 2, 2012, http://www.washingtontimes.com/news/2012/aug/2/renewable-energy-dollars-for-obamas-cronies/?page=all.

30. Liz Peek, "Obama's Auto Bailout Was Really a Hefty Union Payoff," *Fiscal Times*, October 17, 2012, http://www.thefiscaltimes.com/Columns/2012/10/17/Obamas-Auto-Bailout-Was-Really-a-Hefty-Union-Payoff.aspx#page1.

31. Mark Modica, "GM's Government Fleet Sale and Truck Inventory Rise," National Legal and Policy Center, July 5, 2012, http://nlpc.org/stories/2012/07/05/gm's-government-sales-and-truck-inventory-rise.

32. Julie Crawshaw and Forrest Jones, "Fed Buying 61 Percent of US Debt," Moneynews.com, March 28, 2012, http://www.moneynews.com/Headline/fed-debt-Treasury/2012/03/28/id/434106.

CHAPTER FIVE

1. Meg Sullivan, "FDR's policies prolonged Depression by 7 years, UCLA economists calculate," *UCLA Newsroom*, August 10, 2004, http://newsroom.ucla.edu/portal/ucla/FDR-s-Policies-Prolonged-Depression-5409.aspx.

2. Veronique de Rugy, "1920s Income Tax Cuts Sparked Economic Growth and Raised Federal Revenues," Cato Institute, March 4, 2003, http://www.cato.org/publications/commentary/1920s-income-tax-cuts-sparked-economic-growth-raised-federal-revenues; Bucky Fox, "Calvin Coolidge Cut It Big Time As President," *Investor's Business Daily*, July 24, 2012, http://news.investors.com/management-leaders-in-success/072412-619282-calvin-coolidge-cut-taxes-and-spending-effectively.htm?p=full.

3.   Alonzo L. Hamby, "Presidential Pleasure Principles," *New York Times*, October 20, 2011, http://www.nytimes.com/roomfordebate/2011/07/20/presidents-and-their-debts-fdr-to-bush/presidential-pleasure-principles.

4.   David Weinberger, "Hoover, FDR and Clinton Tax Increases: A Brief Historical Lesson," *The Foundry* (blog), The Heritage Foundation, October 20, 2010, http://blog.heritage.org/2010/10/20/hoover-fdr-and-clinton-tax-increases-a-brief-historical-lesson/.

5.   Burton Folsom, Jr. and Anita Folsom, "Obama, FDR, and the Strategy of Massive Spending," *The Corner* (blog), National Review Online, July 27, 2011, http://www.nationalreview.com/corner/272901/obama-fdr-and-strategy-massive-spending-burton-folsom-jr.

6.   argusfest, "'I've abandoned free market principles to save the free market system' – George W. Bush," YouTube video, January 14, 2013, http://www.youtube.com/watch?v=Tmi8cJG0BJo.

7.   Weinberger, "Hoover, FDR and Clinton Tax Increases: A Brief Historical Lesson," *The Foundry* (blog), The Heritage Foundation, October 20, 2010, http://blog.heritage.org/2010/10/20/hoover-fdr-and-clinton-tax-increases-a-brief-historical-lesson/.

8.   William Beach, "'We're Spending More Than Ever and It Doesn't Work'," *The Foundry* (blog), The Heritage Foundation, January 14, 2009, http://blog.heritage.org/2009/01/14/were-spending-more-than-ever-and-it-doesnt-work/.

CHAPTER SIX

1.   Daniel Fisher, "Detroit Tops The 2012 List Of America's Most Dangerous Cities," *Forbes*, October 18, http://www.forbes.com/sites/danielfisher/2012/10/18/detroit-tops-the-2012-list-of-americas-most-dangerous-cities/

2.   Terence P. Jeffrey, "Obama's America Will Become Detroit," CNS News, December 12, 2012, http://cnsnews.com/blog/terence-p-jeffrey/obamas-america-will-become-detroit

3.   And so have a number of other cities, some of which are not far behind Detroit in decay and collapse—think Washington, D.C., Chicago, . . .

4.   Daniel Howes, "State laying groundwork for managed bankruptcy for Detroit," *Detroit News*, December 7, 2012, http://www.detroitnews.com/article/20121207/OPINION03/212070365.

5.   Timothy P. Carney, "Obama DID 'Let Detroit Go Bankrupt'," *Washington Examiner*, September 6, 2012, http://washingtonexaminer.com/obama-did-let-detroit-go-bankrupt/article/2507182#.UQfapfJBA-4.

6.   Liz Peek, "Obama's Auto Bailout Was Realy a Hefty Union Payoff," *Fiscal Times*, October 17, 2012, http://www.thefiscaltimes.com/Columns/2012/10/17/Obamas-Auto-Bailout-Was-Really-a-Hefty-Union-Payoff.aspx#page1.

7.   "Romney: Obama Claus bought election with gifts for voters," MSN, November 15, 2012, http://now.msn.com/obama-gifts-to-blame-for-election-loss-mitt-romney-says.

8.   "Detroit councilwoman to Obama: We voted for you, now bail us out," myFOXdetroit, December 5, 2012, http://www.myfoxdetroit.com/story/20264712/detroit-councilwoman-to-obama-we-supported-you-now-support-us.

9.   "Moody's Downgrades Detroit Bond Ratings," Huffington Post, March 12, 2012, http://www.huffingtonpost.com/2012/03/21/moodys-downgrades-detroit-bond-ratings_n_1369341.html.

10.   John Williams, "The US Has $100 Trillion in Debts & Obligations," *King World News* (blog), December 30, 2011, http://kingworldnews.com/kingworldnews/KWN_DailyWeb/Entries/2011/12/30_John_Williams__The_US_Has_$100_Trillion_in_Debts_%26_Obligations.html.

11.   Jeffrey Hadden, "Detroit in denial," *Detroit News*, December 5, 2012, http://www.detroitnews.com/article/20121205/MIVIEW/212040447.

12.   Dennis Cauchon, "Federal retirement plans almost as costly as Social Security," USA TODAY, September 29, 2011, http://usatoday30.usatoday.com/news/washington/story/2011-10-11/federal-retirement-pension-benefits/50592474/1.

13.   Michael, "The Death Of Detroit," *The Debt* (blog), October 21, 2010, http://thedebtweowe.com/the-death-of-detroit.

14.   "Mowtown's Mental Breakdown," *Wall Street Journal*, December 3, 2012, http://online.wsj.com/article/SB10001424127887323852904578129262547384972.html.

15.   Jeffrey, "Obama's America Will Become Detroit."

16.   Ibid.

17.   Daniel Fisher, "Detroit Tops The 2012 List Of America's Most Dangerous Cities," *Forbes*, October 18, 2012, http://www.forbes.com/sites/danielfisher/2012/10/18/detroit-tops-the-2012-list-of-americas-most-dangerous-cities.

18. United Press International, Inc., "Detroit Murder Rate Tops In The Nation,?" Personal Liberty Digest, January 4, 2013, http://personalliberty.com/2013/01/04/detroit-murder-rate-tops-in-the-nation/.

19. Steve Curtis, "Gun Control Facts: Detroit Crime Rate is the Result Of Gun Control," PolicyMic, http://www.policymic.com/articles/22835/gun-control-facts-detroit-crime-rate-is-the-result-of-gun-control.

20. Chris McGreal, "Detroit homes sell for $1 amid mortgage and car industry crisis," Guardian, March 2, 2010, http://www.guardian.co.uk/business/2010/mar/02/detroit-homes-mortgage-foreclosures-80.

21. Ashley Woods, "Wayne County Foreclosed Property Auction: Jerry Paffendorf And Alex Alsup Talk No Property Left Behind," Huffington Post, November 27, 2012, http://www.huffingtonpost.com/2012/11/27/wayne-county-foreclosed-property-auction-2012-jerry-paffendorf_n_2193845.html.

22. Jeffrey, "Obama's America Will Become Detroit," CNS News, December 12, 2012, http://cnsnews.com/blog/terence-p-jeffrey/obamas-america-will-become-detroit.

23. Ashley Woods, "Detroit Gun Violence: Murder Rate, Violent Crimes Threaten youth And City's Future," Huffington Post, December 17, 2012, http://www.huffingtonpost.com/2012/12/17/detroit-gun-violence-murder_n_2316323.html.

24. Michael, "The Mayor Of Detroit's Radical Plan To Bulldoze One Quarter Of The City," The Economic Collapse (blog), March 9, 2010, http://theeconomiccollapseblog.com/archives/the-mayor-of-detroits-radical-plan-to-bulldoze-one-quarter-of-the-city.

25. "Report: Nearly Half Of Detroiters Can't Read," CBS Detroit, May 4, 2011, http://www.nccp.org/media/releases/release_136.html.

26. Ibid.

27. "Mowtown's Mental Breakdown," Wall Street Journal, December 3, 2012, http://online.wsj.com/article/SB10001424127887323852904578129262547384972.html.

28. Ibid.

29. "Section 218 Training," Social Security Administration, http://www.ssa.gov/section218training/.

30. John Hall, "Tax Exile? Gerard Depardieu to leave France for Belgium," The Independent, December 10, 2012, http://www.independent.co.uk/news/world/europe/tax-exile-gerard-depardieu-to-leave-france-for-belgium-8399142.html.

31. "Detroit is in financial emergency, state-appointed review finds," Fox News, February 20, 2012, http://www.foxnews.com/politics/2013/02/20/detroit-is-in-financial-emergency-state-appointed-review-finds/.

32. "Left in The Dark: Copper Thieves Rob Detroit Freeways of Light," CBS Detroit, February 15, 2012, http://detroit.cbslocal.com/2013/02/15/left-in-the-dark-copper-thieves-rob-detroit-freeways-of-light/.

33. Scott Garner, "Northeast Leads U.S. In Outbound Migration, United Van Lines Study Finds," blog, Moving.com, January 4, 2012, http://www.moving.com/blogs/2012/01/04/northeast-leads-u-s-in-outbound-migration-united-van-lines-study-finds/.

CHAPTER SEVEN

1. Elizabeth Harrington, "Escape From New York? High-Taxing Empire State Loses 3.4 Million Residents in 10 Years," CNS News, May 28, 2012, http://cnsnews.com/news/article/escape-new-york-high-taxing-empire-state-loses-34-million-residents-10-years.

2. Michael B. Sauter, Samuel Weigley, Alexander E. M. Hess, and Brian Zajac, "States with the highest and lowest taxes," USA TODAY, October 28, 2012, http://www.usatoday.com/story/money/personalfinance/2012/10/28/state-taxes-states-highest-lowest/1654071/.

3. Ashley Ebeling, "California Voters Sock It To The Rich (And The Fate Of Other State Tax Ballot Measures)," Forbes, November 8, 2012, http://www.forbes.com/sites/ashleaebeling/2012/11/08/california-voters-sock-it-to-the-rich-and-the-fate-of-other-state-tax-ballot-measures/.

4. Tony Lee, "HUNDRED OF THOUSANDS FLEE DEMOCRAT-RUN CALIFORNIA," Breitbart, September 29, 2012, http://www.breitbart.com/Big-Government/2012/09/29/Report-225-000-Californians-A-Year-Escaping-State-s-High-Taxes-Burdensome-Regulations-Economic-And-Public-Sector-Instability.

5. Meena Krishnamsetty, "2010 Census Results: Top 10 States With Largest Percentage Increase in Population," Insider Monkey, December 22, 2010, http://www.insidermonkey.com/blog/2010-census-results-top-10-states-with-largest-percentage-increase-in-population-1494/.

6. "Texas Dominates List of Fastest-Growing Large Cities since 2010 Census, Census Bureau Reports," U.S Census Bureau website, June 28, 2012, http://www.census.gov/newsroom/releases/archives/population/cb12-117.html; Morgan Brennan, "America's Fastest Growing Cities," Forbes, January 23,

2013, http://www.forbes.com/sites/morganbrennan/2013/01/23/americas-fastest-growing-cities/.

7. Patrick Gleason and Jason Russell, "Perry's 'loser pays' is an economic winner," *Washington Times*, September 1, 2011, http://www.washingtontimes.com/news/2011/sep/1/perrys-loser-pays-is-an-economic-winner/.

8. Adam Feit, "Tort Reform, One State at a Time: Recent Developments in Class Actions and Complex Litigation in New York, Illinois, Texas, and Florida," *Loyola of Los Angeles Law Review*, March 1, 2008, http://digital commons.lmu.edu/cgi/viewcontent.cgi?article=2626&context=llr&sei-redir=1&referer=http%3A%2F%2Fwww.google.com%2Furl%3Fsa%3Dt%26rct%3Dj%26q%3Dtexas%2520is%2520most%2520difficult%2520state%2520to%2520file%2520class%2520action%2520lawsuits%26sour ce%3Dweb%26cd%3D11%26ved%3D0CC8QFjAAOAo%26url%3Dhttp%253A%252F%252Fdigitalcommons.lmu.edu%252Fcgi%252Fviewcontent.cgi%253Farticle%253D2626%2526context%253Dllr%26ei%3DajwhUc-IDImz2gXovICoCg%26usg%3DAFQjCNGj4a2wOtmk2AjNEFgmN_Oe1O5M1A%26bvm%3Dbv.42661473%2Cbs.1%2Cd.cGE#search=%22texas%20most%20difficult%20state%20file%20class%20action%20lawsuits%22.

9. Louise Story, "Lines Blur as Texas Gives Industries a Bonanza," *New York Times*, December 2, 2012, http://www.nytimes.com/2012/12/03/us/winners-and-losers-in-texas.html?pagewanted=all&_r=0.

10. Michael Gardner, "Is California the welfare capital?," *San Diego Union-Tribune*, "July 28, 2012, http://www.utsandiego.com/news/2012/jul/28/welfare-capital-of-the-us/?print&page=all.

11. Mark Lisheron, "Texas last in benefits for public employees – but government employees' packages still beat private sector in all but 6 states," Texas Watchdog, March 3, 2011, http://www.texaswatchdog.org/2011/03/texas-last-in-benefits-for-public-employees-but-government-benefits-beat-private-sector/1299184120.story.

12. Andrew Kirell, "O'Reilly Tells 'Tale Of Two Americas' Between Socialist California And Freedom-Loving Texas," Mediaite, November 26, 2012, http://www.mediaite.com/tv/oreilly-tells-tale-of-two-americas-between-socialist-california-and-freedom-loving-texas/.

13. Ibid.

14. Chuck Thompson, "Go Ahead and Secede, Texas. I Dare You.," *New Republic*, November 14, 2012, http://www.newrepublic.com/article/politics/110112/go-ahead-and-secede-texas-we-dare-you#.

15. Will Franklin, "Visualizing Texas' Job Dominance Since Before The Recession," willisms.com, July 12, 2012, http://www.willisms.com/archives/2012/07/visualizing_tex.html.

16. Ibid.

17. Will Franklin, "Trivia Tidbit of the Day: Part 847 — Our Broken Federal Fund Dispersal System," willisms.com, August 4, 2010, http://www.willisms.com/archives/2010/08/trivia_tidbit_o_845.html.

18. "FORTUNE 500," CNN, May 21, 2012, http://money.cnn.com/magazines/fortune/fortune500/2012/states/TX.html.

19. Chuck Thompson, "Go ahead and Secede, Texas. I Dare You.," New Republic, November 14, 2012, http://www.newrepublic.com/article/politics/110112/go-ahead-and-secede-texas-we-dare-you#.

20. Dennis Cauchon, "Texas wins in U.S. economy shift," USA TODAY, June 21, 2011, http://usatoday30.usatoday.com/money/economy/2011-06-20-state-gdp-growth_n.htm.

21. Steve Malanga, "How California Drives Away Jobs and Business," *Wall Street Journal*, October 15, 2011, http://online.wsj.com/article/SB10001424052970204422404576594890367486316.html.

22. David R. Baker, "Chevron moving 800 Bay Area jobs to Texas," *San Francisco Chronicle*, December 21, 2012, http://www.sfgate.com/bayarea/article/Chevron-moving-800-Bay-Area-jobs-to-Texas-4136930.php.

23. JP Donlon, "Another Triumph for Texas: Best/Worst States for Business 2012," Chief Executive Group, May 2, 2012, http://chiefexecutive.net/best-worst-states-for-business-2012.

24. Scott Cohn, "Texas Is America's Top State for Business 2012," CNBC, July 10, 2012, http://www.cnbc.com/id/47818860.

25. David Mildenberg, "Texas Starts Budget Debate Flush With Energy Boom Cash," Bloomberg, January 7, 2013, http://www.bloomberg.com/news/2013-01-07/texas-starts-budget-debate-flush-with-energy-boom-cash.html.

CHAPTER EIGHT

1. "Sustainable Business Practices," Small Business Administration, http://www.sba.gov/content/small-business-trends.

2. Tim Kane, "The Importance of Startups in Job Creation and Job Destruction," Kauffman Foundation, July 2010, http://www.kauffman.org/uploadedfiles/firm_formation_importance_of_startups.pdf.

3. "Sustainable Business Practices."

4. Janie Barrera, "Reflections on the Role of Small Businesses in the U.S.—and Why We Must Nurture Them," *THE BLOG, Huffington Post*, February 12, 2013, http://www.huffingtonpost.com/accion-and-opportunity-fund/reflections-on-the-role-o_b_2664974.html.

5. Ibid.

6. Ken Davenport, "What the financial reform bill means to Broadway investors and you.," *The Producer's Perspective* (blog), July 27, 2010, http://www.theproducersperspective.com/my_weblog/2010/07/what-the-financial-reform-bill-means-to-broadway-investors-and-you.html.

7. Emily Chasan, "Start-Ups Champ at the Bit for Fundraising Rule Change," *CFO Journal* (blog), *Wall Street Journal*, June 21, 2012, http://mobile.blogs.wsj.com/cfo/2012/06/21/start-ups-champ-at-the-bit-for-fundraisingrule-change/.

8. Elizabeth Harrington, "Escape From New York? High-Taxing Empire State Loses 3.4 Million Residents in 10 Years," CNS News, May 28, 2012, http://cnsnews.com/news/article/escape-new-york-high-taxing-empire-state-loses-34-million-residents-10-years.

9. Nathan Koppel, "Texas Legislature Approves 'Loser Pays'," *Law Blog, Wall Street Journal*, May 26, 2011, http://blogs.wsj.com/law/2011/05/26/texas-legislature-approves-loser-pays/.

10. Steve Gardner, "Texas Supreme Court: Putting the Squeeze on Class Actions?," *Public Citizen* (blog), March 5, 2007, http://pubcit.typepad.com/clpblog/2007/03/texas_supreme_c.html.

11. Elizabeth MacDonald, "Hate Your Boss? Call the Government," FOX Business, February 4, 2011, http://www.foxbusiness.com/markets/2011/02/04/white-house-launches-new-aba-hotline-labor-dept/.

12. Valerie Richardson, "Democrats Trying Again To Tax Internet," *Human Events*, August 9, 2010, http://www.humanevents.com/2010/08/09/democrats-trying-again-to-tax-internet/; Declan McCullagh, "Democrats push for new Internet sales taxes," CBS, July 2, 2010, http://news.cnet.com/8301-13578_3-20009603-38.html; Jason Mick, "Obama's FCC Looks to Tax the Internet," DailyTech, August 28, 2012, http://www.dailytech.com/Obamas+FCC+Looks+to+Tax+the+Internet/article25536.htm.

13. Curtis Dubay, "Senate Fails to Repeal Burdensome Obamacare Business Requirement," *The Foundry* (blog), The Heritage Foundation, September 14, 2010, http://blog.heritage.org/2010/09/14/senate-fails-to-repeal-burdensome-obamacare-business-requirement/.

14. Wayne Allyn Root, "Emergency Alert to Small Business: How One Clause of 'Jobs Bill' Could Wipe Out Small Business in America Tomorrow!," *ROOT for AMERICA!* (blog), June 15, 2010, http://www.rootforamerica.com/webroot/oldblog/index.php?entry=entry100615-120935.

15. Richard Rubin, "Obama Signs Law Repealing Business Tax Reporting Mandate," Bloomberg, April 14, 2011, http://www.bloomberg.com/news/2011-04-14/obama-signs-law-repealing-business-tax-reporting-mandate-1-.html.

16. Peter Eavis, "Mortgage Interest Deduction, Once a Sacred Cow, Is Under Scrutiny," DealBook, *New York Times*, November 26, 2012, http://dealbook.nytimes.com/2012/11/26/mortgage-interest-deduction-once-a-sacred-cow-is-seen-as-vulnerable/.

17. Carol Tice, "Does Your Small Business Have a Collateral Crisis?," *The Daily Dose* (blog), Entrepreneur, June 15, 2011, http://www.entrepreneur.com/blog/219768.

18. Sam Stein, "Obama Revives Social Security Idea: Raise Payroll Tax Cap To Replenish Fund," *Huffington Post*, September 21, 2012, http://www.huffingtonpost.com/2012/09/21/obama-social-security_n_1903773.html.

19. Jose Pagliery, "Obama's tax plan aims at rich, but catches small employers too," CNN, October 4, 2012, http://money.cnn.com/2012/10/04/small-business/obama-tax-employers/index.html.

20. John Kartch, "Five major ObamaCare taxes that will hit your wallet in 2013," FOX News, July 5, 2012, http://www.foxnews.com/opinion/2012/07/05/five-major-obamacare-taxes-that-will-hit-your-wallet-in-2013/; Betsy McCaughey, "Beware: ObamaCare's now reality," *New York Post*, November 13, 2012, http://www.nypost.com/p/news/opinion/opedcolumnists/beware_obamacare_now_reality_YT42eCrsbtZC3KbDONGm4O; Ashlea Ebeling, "ObamaCare's 7 Tax Hikes On Under $250,000-A-Year Earners," *Forbes*, June 28, 2012, http://www.forbes.com/sites/ashleaebeling/2012/06/28/obamacares-7-tax-hikes-on-under-250000-a-year-earners/.

21. Jeanne Sahadi, "Billionaires with 1% tax rates," CNN, December 7, 2011, http://money.cnn.com/2011/12/07/news/economy/obama_taxes/index.htm.

22. Ibid.

23. Linda McMahon, "How We can Revive The American Economy," *Hartford Courant*, January 25, 2013, http://articles.courant.com/2013-01-25/news/hc-op-mcmahon-focus-growth-small-business-limit-go-20130125_1_job-creators-small-business-american-economy.

24. "Obama: 'You didn't build that'," CBS News, December 19, 2012, http://www.cbsnews.com/video/watch/?id=50137457n.

CHAPTER NINE

1. "Charles Hugh Smith, "Wall Street's 'Recovery' Leaves Main Street Mugged in the Gutter," *Of Two Minds* (blog), November 17, 2010, http://www.oftwominds.com/blognov10/Main-St-mugged11-10.html; Charles Hugh Smith, "Why Main Street Doesn't Buy wall Street's 'Recovery'," DailyFinance, November 10, 2010, http://www.dailyfinance.com/2010/11/10/main-street-doesnt-buy-wall-streets-recovery/.

2. "The JOBS Act," *BLOG*, Committee on Financial Services, August 13, 2012, http://financialservices.house.gov/blog/default.aspx?postid=306306.

3. "Job Growth in U.S. Driven Entirely by Startups, According to Kauffman Foundation Study," Ewing Marion Kauffman Foundation, July 7, 2010, http://www.kauffman.org/newsroom/u-s-job-growth-driven-entirely-by-startups.aspx.

4. Timothy P. Carney, "The 'curious' case of HMOs liking Obamacare cash," *Washington Examiner*, March 1, 2012, http://washingtonexaminer.com/article/1154296; Ed Morrissey, "Study in crony capitalism: ObamaCare and Big Pharma," Hot Air, June 12, 2012, http://hotair.com/archives/2012/06/12/study-in-crony-capitalism-obamacare-and-big-pharma/.

5. Howard Gleckman, "Obama and Corporate Tax Rates: Talking the Talk," Tax Policy Center, March 24, 2009, http://taxvox.taxpolicycenter.org/2009/03/24/obama-and-corporate-tax-rates-talking-the-talk/; Kimberley A. Strassel, "Big Business Sells Out Small Business," *Wall Street Journal*, December 20, 2012, http://online.wsj.com/article/SB100014241278873244616045781899606332 66322.html.

6.   Strassel, "Big Business Sells Out Small Business," *Wall Street Journal*, December 20, 2012, http://online.wsj.com/article/SB100014241278873244 61604578189960633266322.html.

7.   "Crony Capitalist Blowout," *Wall Street Journal*, January 2, 2013, http://online.wsj.com/article/SB10001424127887323320404578216583921471560.html; Jared King, "Fiscal Cliff Deal Impact on Indian Country," Native News Network, January 5, 2013, http://www.nativenewsnetwork.com/fiscal-cliff-deal-impact-on-indian-country.html.

8.   "Crony Capitalist Blowout," *Wall Street Journal*, January 2, 2013, http://online.wsj.com/article/SB10001424127887323320404578216583921471560.html; King, "Fiscal Cliff Deal Impact on Indian Country," Native News Network, January 5, 2013, http://www.nativenewsnetwork.com/fiscal-cliff-deal-impact-on-indian-country.html.

9.   Strassel, "Big Business Sells Out Small Business," *Wall Street Journal*, December 20, 2012, http://online.wsj.com/article/SB100014241278873244 61604578189960633266322.html.

CHAPTER TEN

1.   "Ahmadinejad; outrage and controversy follow," CNN, September 24, 2007, http://www.cnn.com/2007/US/09/24/us.iran/index.html.

2.   Eliana Johnson, "At Columbia, Students Attack Minuteman Founder," *New York Sun*, October 5, 2006, http://www.nysun.com/new-york/at-columbia-students-attack-minuteman-founder/41020/.

3.   Lloyd Brown, "Seeing Things in Black and White Isn't Always Easy," *Sunshine State News*, October 2, 2012, http://www.sunshinestatenews.com/story/seeing-things-black-and-white-isnt-always-easy-task.

4.   Paul Mirengoff, "Obama Slandered America As Racist Using Dishonest Claims About The Response To Hurricane Katrina," *Power Line* (blog), October 2, 2012, http://www.powerlineblog.com/archives/2012/10/obama-slandered-american-as-racist-using-dishonest-claims-about-the-response-to-hurricane-katrina.php.

5.   Brad Johnson, "Exit Polls 2012: Hurricane Sandy Was A Deciding Factor For Millions Of Voters In The Election," ThinkProgress, November 6, 2012, http://thinkprogress.org/climate/2012/11/06/1152421/exit-polls-2012-hurricane-sandy-was-a-deciding-factor-in-the-election/.

6.   Eyder Peralta, "House Committee: Washington Denied More Security For Libyan Consulate," *the two-way* (blog), NPR, October 2, 2012, http://www.

npr.org/blogs/thetwo-way/2012/10/02/162160489/house-committee-washington-denied-more-security-for-libyan-consulate.

7. Kim Sengupta, "Revealed: inside story of US envoy's assassination," *The Independent*, September 14, 2012, http://www.independent.co.uk/news/world/politics/revealed-inside-story-of-us-envoys-assassination-8135797.html.

8. Jennifer Griffin, "EXCLUSIVE: CIA operators were denied request for help during Benghazi attack, sources say," FOX News, October 26, 2012, http://www.foxnews.com/politics/2012/10/26/cia-operators-were-denied-request-for-help-during-benghazi-attack-sources-say/.

9. James Risen, Mark Mazzetti, and Michael S. Schmidt, "U.S.-Approved Arms for Libya Rebels Fell Into Jihadis' Hands," *New York Times*, December 5, 2012, http://www.nytimes.com/2012/12/06/world/africa/weapons-sent-to-libyan-rebels-with-us-approval-fell-into-islamist-hands.html?pagewanted=all.

10. "Ex-CIA chief Petraeus testifies Benghazi attack was al Qaeda-linked terrorism," CNN, November 16, 2012, http://www.cnn.com/2012/11/16/politics/benghazi-hearings/index.html.

11. Katie Pavlich, "Unreal: State Department Now Saying They Never Blamed Video for Libya Attack," Townhall, October 10, 2012, http://townhall.com/tipsheet/katiepavlich/2012/10/10/unreal_state_department_now_saying_they_never_blamed_video_for_libya_attack.

12. "Work Still Wanted: 873,000 Jobs Added but 582,000 Were Part-Time," Newsmax Media, October 5, 2012, http://www.newsmax.com/Economy/Jobs-Part-Time-Positions-unemployment/2012/10/05/id/458819.

13. Michael Falcone, "Timing Is Everything: Unemployment Drops Below 8 Percent With One Month To Go (The Note)," *The Note* (blog), ABC News, October 5, 2012, http://abcnews.go.com/blogs/politics/2012/10/timing-is-everything-unemployment-drops-below-8-percent-with-one-month-to-go-the-note/.

14. Joel B. Pollack, "SURPRISE! JOBLESS CLAIMS UP 78,000 WEEK AFTER ELECTION: PA, OH WORST HIT," Breitbart, November 15, 2012, http://www.breitbart.com/Big-Government/2012/11/15/Surprise-Jobless-Claims-Up-Over-75000.

15. Sudeep Reddy and Scott Thurm, "Investment Falls Off a Cliff," *Wall Street Journal*, November 19, 2012, http://online.wsj.com/article/SB10001424127887324595904578123593211825394.html.

16. Daniel Halper, "Food Stamp Growth 75X Greater than Job Creation," *Weekly Standard* (blog), November 2, 2012, http://www.weeklystandard. com/blogs/food-stamp-growth-75x-greater-job-creation_660073.html.

17. "Obama Job Record worse than previous 11 presidents combined," *roccosphere.blogspot.com*, September 18, 2012, http://roccosphere.blogspot. com/2012/09/obama-job-record-worse-than-previous-11.html.

18. nick cruz, "Obama In 1998: 'I Actually Believe In Redistribution'," YouTube video, September 18, 2012, http://www.youtube.com/watch?v= ge3aGJfDSg4.

19. "Networks favor Romney '47%' 13-1 over Obama 'redistribution'," *Washington Examiner*, September 21, 2012, http://washingtonexaminer.com/ networks-favor-romney-47-13-1-over-obama-redistribution/ article/2508659#.UMu4IqVZ90c.

20. "Suicide at an All Time High," JD Journal, September 25, 2012, http://www. jdjournal.com/2012/09/25/suicide-at-an-all-time-high/.

21. Steven Reinberg, "Suicide now kills more Americans than car crashes: study," Medical Xpress, September 20, 2012, http://medicalxpress.com/ news/2012-09-suicide-americans-car.html.

22. Paul Klengor, "Reagan took a beating over homeless problem, but media ignore Obama's worse record," FOX News, October 16, 2012, http://www. foxnews.com/opinion/2012/10/16/reagan-took-beating-over-homeless- problem-but-media-ignore-obama-worse-record/.

23. "Graphic of the Day: Drilling Permits Down 36% Under Obama Administration," FOX News Insider, March 22, 2012, http://foxnewsinsider. com/2012/03/22/graphic-of-the-day-drilling-permits-down-36-under- obama-administration/.

24. Ibid.

25. "Champions of Change: Small Business," WhiteHouse.gov, http://www. whitehouse.gov/champions/small-business.

26. http://cnsnews.com/news/article/white-house-obama-has-strong-record- support-2nd-amendment-rights.

27. "EDITORIAL: Kagan's threat to gun owners," *Washington Times*, June 9, 2010, http://www.washingtontimes.com/news/2010/jun/9/kagans-threat- to-gun-owners/.

28. rightface1, "Senator Obama calls Bush 'unpatriotic' for adding trillions to debt www.RightFace.us," YouTube video, August 24, 2011, http://www. youtube.com/watch?v=DyLmru6no4U.

29. Amy Payne, "Morning Bell: $16,000,000,000,000," *The Foundry* (blog), The Heritage Foundation, September 5, 2012, http://blog.heritage. org/2012/09/05/morning-bell-16000000000000/.

30. Chris Chase, "Barack Obama played Election Day basketball game with Scottie Pippen," USA TODAY, November 6, 2012, http://www.usatoday. com/story/gameon/2012/11/06/barack-obama-scottie-pippen-election-day-pickup/1686751/; Chris Cillizza, "How many fundraisers is too many for President Obama?," *Washington Post*, June 12, 2012, http://www. washingtonpost.com/blogs/the-fix/post/president-obama-fundraiser-in-chief/2012/06/12/gJQAVAQ8XV_blog.html; Mark Landler, "Obama Formally Kicks Off Campaign in Ohio and Virginia," *New York Times*, May 5, 2012, http://www.nytimes.com/2012/05/06/us/politics/obama-holds-large-campaign-rallies-in-ohio-and-virginia.html; Kerry Picket, "Obama camp – Morning zoo radio 'equally important' for president to talk to," *Washington Times*, August 19, 2012, http://www.washingtontimes.com/ blog/watercooler/2012/aug/19/obama-camp-morning-zoo-radio-equally-important-oba/.

31. Molly Henneberg, "Obama's jobs council shutting down Thursday," FOX News, January 31, 2013, http://www.foxnews.com/politics/2013/01/31/ obama-jobs-council-shutting-down-thursday/.

CHAPTER ELEVEN

1. Awr Hawkins, "HOW SAUL ALINSKY TAUGHT BARACK OBAMA EVERYTHING HE KNOWS ABOUT CIVIC UPHEAVAL," Breitbart, March 14, 2012, http://www.breitbart.com/Big-Government/2012/03/14/ How%20Saul%20Alinsky%20Taught%20Barack%20Obama%20 Everything%20He%20Knows%20About%20Civic%20Upheaval.

2. "CLOWARD-PIVEN STRATEGY (CPS)," DiscoverTheNetworks.org, http://www.discoverthenetworks.org/groupProfile.asp?grpid=7522.

3. "Rules for Radicals: By Saul Alinsky – 1971," Crossroad.to, http://www. crossroad.to/Quotes/communism/alinsky.htm.

4. Terence P. Jeffrey, "Obama's Now Borrowed More Than All Presidents from Washington to W," CNS News, November 30, 2012, http://cnsnews.com/ news/article/obama-s-now-borrowed-more-all-presidents-washington-w.

5. Amy Payne, "Morning Bell: $16,000,000,000,000," *The Foundry* (blog), The Heritage Foundation, September 5, 2012, http://blog.heritage. org/2012/09/05/morning-bell-16000000000000.

6.   William J. Bennett, "The looming crisis of student loan debt," CNN, December 6, 2012, http://www.cnn.com/2012/12/06/opinion/bennett-student-debt/index.html.

7.   Joe Taylor Jr., "Credit Card Delinquencies Fall Below Student Loan Delinquencies for the First Time," FOX Business, December 18, 2012, http://www.foxbusiness.com/personal-finance/2012/12/11/credit-card-delinquencies-fall-below-student-loan-delinquencies-for-first-time/.

8.   Elizabeth Ecker, "Bloomberg: Will FHA Be the Next Government Bailout?," Reverse Mortgage Daily, July 27, 2011, http://reversemortgagedaily.com/2011/07/27/bloomberg-will-fha-be-the-next-government-bailout/.

9.   Jeff Swiatek, "Fed chairman Ben Bernanke tells Indianapolis audience inflation is under control," indystar.com, October 1, 2012, http://www.indystar.com/article/20121001/BUSINESS/121001030/Fed-chairman-Ben-Bernanke-tells-Indianapolis-audience-inflation-under-control.

10. Sheyna Steiner, "Is inflation higher than you think?," Bankrate, March 15, 2011, http://www.bankrate.com/finance/personal-finance/is-inflation-higher-than-you-think-1.aspx;

11. Liz Capo McCormick and Daniel Kruger, "Treasury Scarcity to Grow as Fed Buys 90% of New Bonds," Bloomberg, December 3, 2012, http://www.bloomberg.com/news/2012-12-03/treasury-scarcity-to-grow-as-fed-buys-90-of-new-bonds.html; Tyler Durden, "China Persists In Refusing To Buy US Paper As Foreign LTM Purchases Of Treasurys Plunge To Three Year Lows," Zero Hedge, November 17, 2012, http://www.zerohedge.com/news/2012-11-17/china-persists-refusing-buy-us-paper-foreign-ltm-purchases-treasurys-plunge-three-ye.

12. "Interest on the Debt Could Exceed Defense Budget," RealClearPolicy, April 6, 2012, http://www.realclearpolicy.com/data_lab/2012/04/06/interest_on_the_debt_could_exceed_defense_budget_106.html.

13. Stephen Gandel, "Bond King Bill Gross Exits US Debt: Good News?," Time, March 10, 2011, http://business.time.com/2011/03/10/the-worlds-largest-bond-fund-gets-out-of-us-debt-good-news/.

14. Max Jarman, "Robb & Stucky to close, liquidate," azcentral.com, March 8, 2011, http://www.azcentral.com/business/articles/2011/03/08/20110308arizona-robb-stucky-close-liquidate.html.

15. Brad Lendon, "Las Vegas' Sahara Hotel and Casino closing after more than 58 years," This Just In (blog), CNN, May 16, 2011, http://news.blogs.cnn.

com/2011/05/16/las-vegas-sahara-hotel-and-casino-closing-after-more-than-58-years/.

16. Glenn Collins and Florence Fabricant, "A Closing Ends an Era, and a Deli War," *New York Times*, December 1, 2012, http://www.nytimes.com/2012/12/01/dining/stage-delis-closing-ends-a-restaurant-war.html.

17. Ibid.

18. Rachel Feintzeig, Mike Spector, and Julia Jargon, "Twinkie Maker Hostess to Close," *Wall Street Journal*, November 16, 2012, http://online.wsj.com/article/SB10001424127887324556304578122632560842670.html.

19. James Sherk and Todd Zywicki, "Sherk and Zywicki: Obama's United Auto Workers Bailout," *Wall Street Journal*, June 13, 2012, http://online.wsj.com/article/SB10001424052702303836404577477003432140244.html.

20. Seton Motley, "AUTO BAILOUT LOSS COULD EXCEED $70 BILLION," Breitbart, December 11, 2012, http://www.breitbart.com/Big-Government/2012/12/10/Auto-Bailout-Loss-May-Soon-Exceed-70-Billion.

21. Wynton Hall, "DOCUMENTS: OBAMA ADMIN SLASHED 20,000 NON-UNION AUTOWORKER PENSIONS," Breitbart, October 29, 2012, http://www.breitbart.com/Big-Government/2012/10/29/Highly-Confidential-Documents-Reveal-Obama-Administration-Slashed-20-000-Non-Union-Autoworker-Pensions; John Berlau, "The great Obama auto dealer job shaft," Daily Caller, August, 9, 2012, http://dailycaller.com/2012/08/09/the-great-obama-auto-dealer-job-shaft/.

22. Jim McElhatton, "Solyndra investors could reap tax windfall," *Washington Times*, August 28, 2012, http://www.washingtontimes.com/news/2012/aug/28/solyndra-investors-could-reap-tax-windfall/.

23. Michael Bastasch, "As many as 50 Obama-backed green energy companies bankrupt or troubled," Daily Caller, October 30, 2012, http://dailycaller.com/2012/10/30/as-many-as-fifty-obama-backed-green-energy-companies-bankrupt-or-troubled/.

24. Dale Hurd, "Spain's Green Disaster a Lesson for America," CBN, December 26, 2011, http://www.cbn.com/cbnnews/finance/2011/november/spains-green-disaster-a-lesson-for-america/.

25. Jeff Cox, "US Housing Crisis Is Now Worse Than Great Depression," CNBC, June 14, 2011, http://www.cnbc.com/id/43395857/US_Housing_Crisis_Is_Now_Worse_Than_Great_Depression.

26. Peter Eavis, "Mortgage Interest Deduction, Once a Sacred Cow, Is Under Scrutiny," DealBook, *New York Times*, November 26, 2012, http://dealbook.

nytimes.com/2012/11/26/mortgage-interest-deduction-once-a-sacred-cow-is-seen-as-vulnerable/.

27.   "Keystone XL is coming back," *Washington Post*, January 23, 2012, http://www.washingtonpost.com/opinions/mr-obamas-second-chance-on-keystone-xl-pipeline/2013/01/23/3b6f709c-5b77-11e2-beee-6e38f5215402_story.html; Kerry Picket, "Flashback – Oil drilling permits down 36 percent under Obama," *Washington Times*, October 16, 2012, http://www.washingtontimes.com/blog/watercooler/2012/oct/16/picket-flashback-oil-drilling-permits-down-36-perc/; Michael Bastasch, "'Coal is toast' if Obama gains a second term," Daily Caller, November 6, 2012, http://dailycaller.com/2012/11/06/coal-is-toast-if-obama-gains-a-second-term/.

28.   Brian Merchant, "Obama to Automakers: Make Greener American Cars or Go Under," treehugger.com, March 30, 2009, http://www.treehugger.com/corporate-responsibility/obama-to-automakers-make-greener-american-cars-or-go-under.html.

29.   "New Senate Report Reveals Economic Pain of Obama-EPA Regulations Put on Hold Until After the Election," TeaParty.org, October 21, 2012, http://teapartyorg.ning.com/forum/topics/new-senate-report-reveals-economic-pain-of-obama-epa-regulations-?commentId=4301673%3AComment%3A1058905.

30.   "Coal," *New York Times*, December 20, 2012, http://topics.nytimes.com/top/news/business/energy-environment/coal/index.html.

31.   Judson Berger, "Attorney claims EPA chief resigned over alias email accounts," FOX News, December 27, 2012, http://www.foxnews.com/politics/2012/12/27/attorney-claims-epa-chief-resigned-over-alias-email-accounts/.

32.   Jim Efstathiou Jr., "Buffett's Burlington Northern Among Pipeline Winners," Bloomberg, January 23, 2012, http://www.bloomberg.com/news/2012-01-23/buffett-s-burlington-northern-among-winners-in-obama-rejection-of-pipeline.html.

33.   "Obama joins with Mexico in lawsuit against Arizona," Southern New Hampshire 9.12, July 23, 2011, http://www.southernnh912.com/content/obama-joins-mexico-lawsuit-against-arizona.

34.   Christine Armario, "Duncan: 82 Percent Of US Schools May Be Labeled 'Failing' Under No Child Left Behind Policies," *Huffington Post*, March 9, 2011, http://www.huffingtonpost.com/2011/03/09/failing-schools-82-percent_n_833653.html.

35. Janet Lorin, "SAT Reading, Writing Test Scores Drop to Lowest Levels," Bloomberg, September 24, 2012, http://www.bloomberg.com/news/2012-09-24/sat-reading-writing-test-scores-drop-to-lowest-levels.html.

36. Howard Blumenthal, "Infographic: US Education Spending vs. Results," *Digital Insider* (blog), July 22, 2012, http://diginsider.com/2012/07/22/infographic-us-education-spending-vs-results/.

37. "Little Change in Public's Response to 'Capitalism,' 'Socialism'," Pew Research Center, December 28, 2011, http://www.people-press.org/2011/12/28/little-change-in-publics-response-to-capitalism-socialism/.

38. Doug Mataconis, "Americans Don't Know The Difference Between James Madison and Karl Marx," *Outside the Beltway*, December 21, 2010, http://www.outsidethebeltway.com/americans-dont-know-the-difference-between-james-madison-and-karl-marx/.

39. Michael J. Totten, "Arab Spring or Islamist Winter?," *World Affairs Journal*, http://www.worldaffairsjournal.org/article/arab-spring-or-islamist-winter.

40. "'We will not tolerate it': U.S. talks tough with Iran over threat to close oil shipping lane following nuclear arms row," *Daily Mail*, December 29, 2011, http://www.dailymail.co.uk/news/article-2079287/Iran-threatens-close-key-oil-shipping-lane-Strait-Hormuz-US-sanctions.html.

41. Joanna Paraszczuk, "Ahmadinejad: World forces must annihilate Israel," *Jerusalem Post*, August 2, 2012, http://www.jpost.com/IranianThreat/News/Article.aspx?id=279864.

CHAPTER TWELVE

1. Scott Johnson, "A Nation Of Takers," *Power Line* (blog), January 25, 2013, http://www.powerlineblog.com/archives/2013/01/a-nation-of-takers.php.

2. Michael J. Boskin, "Get Ready for a 70% Marginal Tax Rate," *Wall Street Journal*, July 18, 2011, http://online.wsj.com/article/SB10001424052702304911104576443893352153776.html.

3. Daniel Halper, "Obama Pledges Only to Sign Deal that Includes Tax Hikes on the 2 Percent," *Weekly Standard* (blog), December 6, 2012, http://www.weeklystandard.com/blogs/obama-pledges-only-sign-deal-includes-tax-hikes-2-percent_665134.html.

4. Ibid.

5. Ryan Ellis, "How the Obama-Biden Plan raises Taxes on One Million Small Businesses," Americans for Tax Reform, October 16, 2012, http://atr.org/obama-biden-plan-raises-taxes-one-a7252.

6.   Robert Longley, "Why Small Business Fail: SBA," About.com, http://usgovinfo.about.com/od/smallbusiness/a/whybusfail.htm.

7.   Kimberly Amadeo, "The Auto Industry Bailout," About.com, January 12, 2013, http://useconomy.about.com/od/criticalssues/a/auto_bailout.htm; Tony Borroz, "Obama Tells GM Boss, 'You're Fired'," *Wired*, March 30, 2009, http://www.wired.com/autopia/2009/03/obama-to-wagone/; David Harsanyi, "President Obama's General Motors Hypocrisy," *Human Events*, September 17, 2012, http://www.humanevents.com/2012/09/17/obamas-broken-gm-promise/.

8.   Amadeo, "The Auto Industry Bailout."

9.   "Preventive Care," HealthCare.gov, July 1, 2010, http://www.healthcare.gov/law/features/rights/preventive-care/index.html; "The HHS Mandate Goes into Effect," National Review Online, August 1, 2012, http://www.nationalreview.com/articles/312809/hhs-mandate-goes-effect-editors.

10. "Federal Regulations Cost Reached $518 Billion in Obama's First Term," Flathead County Republican Women, January 22, 2013,

11. Ibid.

12. Rick Manning, "National Labor Relations Board says Boeing can't build plant in South Carolina," NetRightDaily, April 22, 2011, http://netrightdaily.com/2011/04/national-labor-relations-board-says-boeing-can%E2%80%99t-build-plant-in-south-carolina/.

13. Mark Modica and Hal John, "Model corruption," *New York Post*, August 13, 2010, http://www.nypost.com/p/news/opinion/opedcolumnists/model_corruption_ttyHIpNuoQRwVTkBZuhHeM.

14. "The HHS Mandate Goes into Effect."

15. Rob Barr, "Homeland Security continues to demonize conservatives and libertarians," Daily Caller, July 9, 2012, http://dailycaller.com/2012/07/09/homeland-security-continues-to-demonize-conservatives-and-libertarians/.

16. Jim Abrams, "Patriot Act Extension Signed By Obama," *Huffington Post*, May 26, 2011, http://www.huffingtonpost.com/2011/05/27/patriot-act-extension-signed-obama-autopen_n_867851.html.

17. Erik Kain, "President Obama Signed the National Defense Authorization Act – Now What?," *Forbes*, January 2, 2012, http://www.forbes.com/sites/erikkain/2012/01/02/president-obama-signed-the-national-defense-authorization-act-now-what/.

18. Chelsea Schilling, "Obamacare Prescriptions: 'Emergency Health Army,'" WND, March 25, 2010, http://www.wnd.com/2010/03/132001/.

19. Lachlan Markay, "By MSNBC Standards, GE's $16 Billion in Bailout Loans Compromises NBC News Coverage," NewsBusters, December 2, 2010, http://newsbusters.org/blogs/lachlan-markay/2010/12/02/msnbc-standards-ges-16-billion-bailout-loans-compromises-nbc-news-co.

20. "Did MSNBC Receive Taxpayer Money?," InvestorPlace, August 23, 2012, http://investorplace.com/investorpolitics/did-msnbc-receive-taxpayer-money.

21. Yael Bizouati and John Carney, "Obama: We Need To Bail Out Newspapers Or Blogs Will Run The World," *Business Insider*, September 21, 2009, http://articles.businessinsider.com/2009-09-21/tech/30038531_1_newspaper-owners-free-press-bailout.

22. Joe Newby, "Obama job council chairman Jeffrey Immelt: State run communism works in China," Examiner.com, December 11, 2012, http://www.examiner.com/article/obama-job-council-chairman-jeffrey-immelt-state-run-communism-works-china; Mark Felsenthal, "Obama Sells Fiscal Cliff Agenda To Jamie Dimon, Warren Buffett, And Other Major Business Leaders, *Huffington Post*, November 18, 2012, http://www.huffingtonpost.com/2012/11/18/obama-fiscal-cliff_n_2156666.html; Jocelyn Noveck, "Obama Is Hollywood's Man Once Again, But What Will Renewed Celeb Enthusiasm Cost Him?," *Huffington Post*, May 11, 2012, http://www.huffingtonpost.com/2012/05/12/obama-hollywood-gay-marriage_n_1510902.html.

CHAPTER THIRTEEN

1. Rick Manning, "National Labor Relations Board says Boeing can't build plant in South Carolina," NetRightDaily, April 22, 2011, http://netrightdaily.com/2011/04/national-labor-relations-board-says-boeing-can%E2%80%99t-build-plant-in-south-carolina/.

2. Shaila Dewan and Robert Gebeloff, "Among the Wealthiest 1 Percent, Many Variations," *New York Times*, January 14, 2012, http://www.nytimes.com/2012/01/15/business/the-1-percent-paint-a-more-nuanced-portrait-of-the-rich.html?pagewanted=all.

3. "If top 5% paid 40% of taxes, what is their 'fair' share?," *Washington Examiner*, November 22, 2012, http://washingtonexaminer.com/examiner-

editorial-if-top-5-paid-40-of-taxes-what-is-their-fair-share/
article/2513985#.UNx1NqVZ90c.

4. Mark J. Perry, "The Top 20% Paid 94.1% of income Taxes in 2009," Free
Republic, July 20, 2012, http://www.freerepublic.com/
focus/f-bloggers/2908641/posts.

5. Tami Luhby, "Fiscal cliff deal raises taxes on 77% of Americans," CNN,
January 3, 2013, http://money.cnn.com/2013/01/03/news/economy/fiscal-
cliff-taxes/index.html.

6. Peter Ferrara, "Is President Obama Really A Socialist? Let's Analyze Obam-
anomics," *Forbes*, December 20, 2012, http://www.forbes.com/sites/
peterferrara/2012/12/20is-president-obama-really-a-socialist-lets-analyze-
obamanomics/.

7. Peter Ferrara, "How President Obama Is Deceiving You On Tax Policy,"
Forbes, July 26, 2012, http://www.forbes.com/sites/peterferrara/2012/07/26/
how-president-obama-is-deceiving-you-on-tax-policy/.

8. Luhby, "Fiscal cliff deal raises taxes on 77%of Americans."

9. Stephanie Condon, "Obama meets with middle-class family on 'fiscal
cliff'," CBS News, December 6, 2012, http://www.cbsnews.com/8301-
250_162-57557628/obama-meets-with-middle-class-family-on-fiscal-cliff/.

10. Shaila Dewan and Robert Gebeloff, "Among the Wealthiest 1 Percent, Many
Variations," *New York Times*, January 14, 2012, http://www.nytimes.
com/2012/01/15/business/the-1-percent-paint-a-more-nuanced-portrait-
of-the-rich.html?pagewanted=all.

11. "The Politics of Small Business," National Small Business Association, 2012,
http://www.nsba.biz/vote/docs/NSBA-Politics-2012.pdf.

12. Chris Sieroty, "Nevada's wealthy households make 27 percent of charitable
donations," *Las Vegas Review-Journal*, December 27, 2012, http://www.lvrj.
com/business/nevada-s-wealthy-households-make-27-percent-of-
charitable-donations-184908341.html.

13. "The Charitable Deduction," Independent Sector, http://www.
independentsector.org/charitable_deduction.

14. George Landrith, "Clinton-era tax rates but not spending rates," *Washington
Times*, December 14, 2012, http://www.washingtontimes.com/news/2012/
dec/14/clinton-era-tax-rates-but-not-spending-rates/; Curtis S. Dubay,
"Fiscal Cliff Deal: Tax Increase Spoils Permanent Victory for Most
Taxpayers," The Heritage Foundation, January 9, 2013, http://www.

heritage.org/research/reports/2013/01/fiscal-cliff-deal-how-it-will-affect-taxpayers-and-the-economy.

15. Grace-Marie Turner, "As 2013 Begins, Get Ready For An ObamaCare Tax Onslaught," *Forbes*, January 2, 2013, http://www.forbes.com/sites/gracemarieturner/2013/01/02/as-2013-begins-get-ready-for-an-obamacare-tax-onslaught/.

16. "Tax Freedom Day ®," Tax Foundation, http://taxfoundation.org/tax-topics/tax-freedom-day.

17. Ibid.

18. Amity Shlaes, "Think Obama's Tax Hikes Are Low Compared With Rates Of The 1950s? Think Again," *Investor's Business Daily*, January 4, 2013, http://news.investors.com/ibd-editorials-perspective/010413-639424-obama-high-taxes-still-worse-than-1950s-tax-rates.htm?p=full.

19. "Social Security and Tax Reform," Boundless, https://www.boundless.com/history/new-deal-1933-1940/toward-welfare-state/social-security-and-tax-reform/.

20. "Peter Schiff, "The Fantasy of a 91% Top Income Tax Rate," *Wall Street Journal*, December 6, 2012, http://online.wsj.com/article/SB100014241278 87324705104578151601554982808.html.

21. Dubay, "Fiscal Cliff Deal: Tax Increase Spoils Permanent victory for Most Taxpayers," The Heritage Foundation, January 9, 2013, http://www.heritage.org/research/reports/2013/01/fiscal-cliff-deal-how-it-will-affect-taxpayers-and-the-economy; Ron Scherer, "Obama tax proposal: Who makes more than $250k, and are they rich? (+video)," *Christian Science Monitor*, July 10, 2012, http://www.csmonitor.com/USA/DC-Decoder/2012/0710/Obama-tax-proposal-Who-makes-more-than-250k-and-are-they-rich-video.

22. "Transcript of Obama on '60 Minutes'," FOX News, September 24, 2012, http://www.foxnews.com/politics/2012/09/24/transcript-obama-on-60-minutes/.

23. "Report: Buffett's Berkshire Owes $1 Billion In Back Taxes," Newsmax Media, September 1, 2011, http://www.newsmax.com/Headline/buffett-irs-back-taxes/2011/09/01/id/409520.

24. Lynnley Browning, "Denise Rich Renounces U.S. Citizenship, Will Save Tens Of Millions In Tax Dollars," *Huffington Post*, July 9, 2012, http://www.huffingtonpost.com/2012/07/09/denise-rich-us-citizenship_n_1658479.html.

25. Julie Halpert, "Michigan's next big blow: The film industry," CNN, March 21, 2011, http://money.cnn.com/2011/03/21/news/companies/michigan_film_industry.fortune/index.htm.

26. Paul Tharp, "Conn. Tax breaks lure NBC Sports from NYC," *New York Post*, October 22, 2011, http://www.nypost.com/p/news/business/nbc_men_in_motion_735ZKi6xWIhKY6etlbRKaN.

27. "Google parks $10 billion in Bermuda, avoiding $2 billion in taxes," Russia Today, December 10, 2012, http://rt.com/business/news/google-avoided-taxes-ireland-bermuda-742/.

28. "Nike Presses for 40-Year Tax Deal in Oregon," *Wall Street Journal*, December 14, 2012, http://online.wsj.com/article/SB100014241278873242966045781777771076945076.html.

29. Danielle Kucera, Sanat Vallikappen, and Crhistine Harper, "Facebook Co-Founder Saverin Gives Up U.S. Citizenship," Bloomberg, May 11, 2011, http://www.bloomberg.com/news/2012-05-11/facebook-co-founder-saverin-gives-up-u-s-citizenship-before-ipo.html.

30. Annie Linskey, "Health advocates want to increase cigarette tax," *Baltimore Sun*, November 14, 2012, http://articles.baltimoresun.com/2012-11-14/news/bal-health-advocates-want-to-increase-cigarette-tax-20121114_1_cigarette-tax-pack-tax-tax-revenue.

31. Blake Ellis, "Tanning salons burned by health care bill," CNN, March 24, 2010, http://money.cnn.com/2010/03/24/news/economy/tanning_tax/.

32. Jordan E. Otero, "Banking on sin: States profit as taxes rise on vice," *Washington Times*, October 26, 2011, http://www.washingtontimes.com/news/2011/oct/26/banking-on-sin-states-profit-as-taxes-rise-on-vice/?page=all.

33. "Raise the gas tax," *Washington Post*, May 25, 2012, http://articles.washingtonpost.com/2012-05-25/opinions/35454633_1_gas-tax-fuel-efficient-cars-higher-prices.

34. Wynton Hall, "OBAMA'S 'CASH FOR CLUNKERS' UNLEASHED 'ENVIRONMENTAL NIGHTMARE'," Breitbart, January 5, 2013, http://www.breitbart.com/Big-Government/2013/01/05/Obama-s-Cash-For-Clunkers-Unleashed-Environmental-Nightmare.

35. "First-Time Homebuyer Credit," Internal Revenue Service, January 3, 2013, http://www.irs.gov/uac/First-Time-Homebuyer-Credit-1.

36. "Add State and Local Incentives to the 30% Federal Tax Credit," Wholesale Solar, http://www.wholesalesolar.com/states.html.

37. David Martosko, "As UK millionaires flee country over tax hikes, British treasury loses billions," Daily Caller, November 28, 2012, http://dailycaller. com/2012/11/28/as-uk-millionaires-flee-country-over-tax-hikes-british-treasury-loses-billions/.

38. Guido Tabellini and Alberto Alesina, "US-Europe income gap: Is it for real?," VoxEU.org, June 8, 2007, http://www.voxeu.org/article/us-europe-income-gap-it-real.

39. Edward C. Prescott and Lee E. Ohanian, "Taxes Are Much Higher Than You Think." *Wall Street Journal*, December 11, 2012, http://online.wsj.com/ article/SB10001424127887324469304578142790851767144.html.

CHAPTER FOURTEEN

1. Jim Swift, "Rahm Emanuel: You never want a serious crisit to go to waste," YouTube video, February 9, 2009, http://www.youtube.com/watch?v=1yeA_ kHHLow.

2. Jeffrey M. Jones, "Majority of Americans Satisfied With Their Healthcare Plans," Gallup, November 29, 2007, http://www.gallup.com/poll/102934/ majority-americans-satisfied-their-own-healthcare.aspx.

3. Avik Roy, "Trustees: Medicare Will Go Broke in 2016, If You Exclude Obamacare's Double-Counting," *Forbes*, April 23, 2012, http://www.forbes. com/sites/aroy/2012/04/23/trustees-medicare-will-go-broke-in-2016-if-you-exclude-obamacares-double-counting/; Gerry W. Beyer, "Social Security Fund and Medicaid Fund Running Out," *Wills, Trusts & Estates Prof* (blog), April 23, 2012, http://lawprofessors.typepad.com/trusts_ estates_prof/2012/04/social-security-fund-and-medicaid-fund-running-out.html.

4. Chris Cox and Bill Archer, "Why $16 Trillion Only Hints at the True U.S. Debt," *Wall Street Journal*, November 26, 2012, http://online.wsj.com/ article/SB10001424127887323353204578127374039087636.html.

5. "The Federal Government's Financial Health," WhiteHouse.gov, http://m. whitehouse.gov/sites/default/files/omb/assets/omb/financial/reports/ citizens_guide.pdf.

6. "Obamacare's Medicaid time bomb," *Washington Times*, November 30, 2012, http://www.washingtontimes.com/news/2012/nov/30/obamacares-medicaid-time-bomb/.

7. Jan Norman, "Which states rank highest in health care costs?," blog, *Orange County Register,* January 31, 2011, http://jan.blog.ocregister.com/2011/01/31/which-states-rank-highest-in-health-care-costs/53810/.

8. Chris Edwards, "Government Cost Overruns," Cato Institute, March 2009, http://www.downsizinggovernment.org/government-cost-overruns; Robert Wenzel, "Selected Government Cost Overruns," *Economic Policy Journal* (blog), November 25, 2012, http://www.economicpolicyjournal.com/2012/11/selected-government-cost-overruns.html.

9. Hope Yen, "Postal Service Loss Of $15.9 Billion Sets Record," *Huffington Post,* November 15, 2012, http://www.huffingtonpost.com/2012/11/15/postal-service-loss-_n_2137033.html.

10. Alyene Senger, "Side Effects: Obamacare Adds $17 Trillion to Long-Term Unfunded Government Spending," *The Foundry* (blog), The Heritage Foundation, April 2, 2012, http://blog.heritage.org/2012/04/02/side-effects-obamacare-adds-17-trillion-to-long-term-unfunded-government-spending/.

11. Neil Munro, "Another $17 trillion surprise found in Obamacare," Daily Caller, March 30, 2012, http://dailycaller.com/2012/03/30/another-17-trillion-surprise-found-in-obamacare/.

12. Cal Thomas, "United Kingdom health horror stories should scare U.S. public," *Sun Journal,* June 27, 2012, http://www.sunjournal.com/news/columns-analysis/2012/06/27/cal-thomas-united-kingdom-health-horror-stories-sh/1215498.

CHAPTER FIFTEEN

1. Erin Hatton, "The Rise of the Permanent Temp Economy," *Opinionator* (blog), *New York Times,* January 26, 2013, http://opinionator.blogs.nytimes.com/2013/01/26/the-rise-of-the-permanent-temp-economy/?smid=tw-share.

2. Noel Sheppard, "8.5 Million Americans Left Labor Force In Obama's First Term," NewsBusters, February 1, 2013, http://newsbusters.org/blogs/noel-sheppard/2013/02/01/85-million-americans-left-labor-force-obamas-first-term#ixzz2Jehi6Wet.

3. "1 in 3 Illinoisans lives in or near poverty level: report," myFOXchicago, January 16, 2013, http://www.myfoxchicago.com/story/20601722/1-in-3-illinoisans-lives-in-or-near-poverty-level-report.

4. John Ostapkovich, "Survey: 40 Percent Of Americans Have $500 Or Less In Savings," CBS Philly, October 19, 2012, http://philadelphia.cbslocal. com/2012/10/19/survey-40-percent-of-americans-have-500-or-less-in-savings/.

5. Matt Cover, "IRS: Cheapest Obamacare Plan Will Be $20,000 Per Family," CNS News, January 31, 2013, http://cnsnews.com/news/article/irs-cheapest-obamacare-plan-will-be-20000-family; Todd Beamon, "Rules Issued for Obamacare's Individual Mandate," Newsmax Media, January 30, 2013, http://www.newsmax.com/Newsfront/individual-manage-regulations-issued/2013/01/30/id/488132.

6. "Classifying food allergies like celiac as disabilities could make restaurants more liable," *Daily News*, January 18, 2013, http://www.nydailynews.com/ life-style/health/food-allergies-disabilities-restaurants-liable-article-1.1242534.

7. Shannon Bream, "Supermarkets cry foul as FDA proposes new food labeling rule under ObamaCare," FOX News, February 6, 2013, http://www. foxnews.com/politics/2013/02/06/jail-time-for-food-labels/?test=latestnews.

8. "Despite court ruling, EPA raises biofuel estimate," FOX News, January 31, 2013, http://www.foxnews.com/politics/2013/01/31/despite-court-ruling-epa-raises-biofuel-estimate/.

9. "Greece Tax Rates," TaxRates.cc, http://www.taxrates.cc/html/greece-tax-rates.html.

10. "Report: Obama Administration Added 600 Regulations, $9.5 Billion in Red tape in July," *thecomingcrisis.blogspot.com* (blog), August 4, 2011, http:// thecomingcrisis.blogspot.com/2011/08/report-obama-administration-added-600.html; Wayne Allyn Root, "Atlast Shrugged: Is American Business Going on Strike?," Townhall, April 27, 2012, http://townhall.com/ columnists/wayneallynroot/2012/04/27/atlas_shrugged_is_american_ business_going_on_strike/page/full/.

11. "Obama's 4 Years Of Deficient Leadership: 47 Mistakes," *Investor's Business Daily*, November 2, 2012, http://news.investors.com/ibd-editorials/110212-632007-obama-legacy-is-four-years-deficient-leadership.htm?p=full.

12. Josh Lederman, "Obama's Jobs Council Shutting Down Thursday," *U.S. News & World Report*, January 31, 2013, http://www.usnews.com/news/ politics/articles/2013/01/31/obamas-jobs-council-shutting-down-thursday.

13.	Jason Koebler, "Study: Global Warming Can Be Slowed By Working Less," *U.S. News & World Report*, February 4, 2013, http://www.usnews.com/ news/articles/2013/02/04/-study-global-warming-can-be-slowed-by-working-less.

14.	Graham Ruddick, "France 'totally bankrupt', says labour minister Michel Sapin," *Telegraph*, January 28, 2013, http://www.telegraph.co.uk/finance/ financialcrisis/9832845/France-totally-bankrupt-says-labour-minister-Michel-Sapin.html.

15.	Andrew Grice, "Triple-dip recession looms as economy shrinks by 0.3%," *Independent*, January 25, 2013, http://www.independent.co.uk/news/ business/news/tripledip-recession-looms-as-economy-shrinks-by-03-8466471.html.

16.	"Bus service grinds to halt in Naples: no fuel," myfoxny.com, January 30, 2013, http://www.myfoxny.com/story/20811292/bus-service-grinds-to-halt-in-naples-no-fuel.

17.	Harold Heckle, "Details in Las Vegas 'EuroVegas' project unveiled," *Las Vegas Review-Journal*, February 8, 2013, http://www.lvrj.com/business/ details-to-las-vegas-sands-eurovegas-project-unveiled-190468771.html.

18.	Dan Alexander, "With Youth Unemployment At 55 Percent, Spanish Students Take To The Streets," *Forbes*, February 8, 2013, http://www.forbes. com/sites/danalexander/2013/02/08/with-youth-unemployment-at-55-percent-spanish-students-take-to-the-streets/.

CHAPTER SIXTEEN

1.	"S&P 500 Index Daily Price Gain Annualized," Congressional Effect Fund, http://www.ceffx.com/wp-content/uploads/2011/06/sandp65-09.pdf.

2.	Ashton Ellis, "Investment Fund Shows That Betting Against Congress is a Great Way to Make Money," Center for Individual Freedom, August 12, 2010, http://cfif.org/v/index.php/commentary/43-taxes-and-economy/709-investment-fund-shows-that-betting-against-congress-is-a-great-way-to-make-money.

3.	Azriel James Ralph, "Returning veterans encounter VA mental health meltdown," NBC News, May 28, 2011, http://www.msnbc.msn.com/ id/42995663/ns/health-health_care/t/returning-veterans-encounter-va-mental-health-meltdown/#.UOnWBKVZ90c; Lonny Shavelson, "Video: Veterans' disability benefits delayed," Bay Citizen, August 29, 2012, https:// www.baycitizen.org/news/veterans/video-veterans-disability-benefits/.

4. Angela Greiling Keane, "U.S. Postal Service on a 'Tightrope' Lost $15.9 Billion," Bloomberg, November 15, 2012, http://www.bloomberg.com/news/2012-11-15/u-s-postal-service-on-tightrope-loses-15-9-billion.html.

5. Conn Carroll, "Health Care Reform Cost Estimates: What is the Track Record?," *The Foundry* (blog), The Heritage Foundation, August 4, 2009, http://blog.heritage.org/2009/08/04/health-care-reform-cost-estimates-what-is-the-track-record/.

6. Rob Port, "The 'War On Poverty' Has Cost Three Times What All Of America's Actual Wars Have Cost," *Say Anything Blog*, August 10, 2012, http://sayanythingblog.com/entry/the-war-on-poverty-has-cost-three-times-what-all-of-americas-actual-wars-have-cost/.

7. "Criticism of the Space Shuttle program," *Wikipedia*, January 28, 2013, http://en.wikipedia.org/wiki/Criticism_of_the_Space_Shuttle_program.

8. Tom Schatz, "Amtrak: 40 Years, $40 Billion," National Review Online, May 6, 2011, http://www.nationalreview.com/articles/266575/amtrak-40-years-40-billion-tom-schatz#.

9. Bruce Watson, "Study shows that Amtrak loses $32 per passenger. How much do highways cost?," DailyFinance, October 29, 2009, http://www.dailyfinance.com/2009/10/29/study-shows-that-amtrak-costs-38-per-passenger-how-much-do-hig/.

10. Elizabeth Harrington, "Education Spending up 64% Under No Child Left Behind But Test Scores Improve Little," CNS News, September 26, 2011, cnsnews.com/news/article/education-spending-64-under-no-child-left-behind-test-scores-improve-little.

11. Lindsey Burke, "SAT Scores at Historical Low; Education Spending at Historical High," *The Foundry* (blog), The Heritage Foundation, September 25, 2012, http://blog.heritage.org/2012/09/25/sat-scores-at-historical-low-education-spending-at-historical-high/.

12. Matthew L. Wald, "Report Calls for Changes in the Energy Department," *New York Times*, November 15, 2011, http://www.nytimes.com/2011/11/16/science/earth/report-calls-for-broad-restructuring-of-energy-department.html?_r=0.

13. "AP Impact: After 40 years, $1 trillion, US War on Drugs has failed to meet any of its goals," FOX News, May 13, 2010, http://www.foxnews.com/world/2010/05/13/ap-impact-years-trillion-war-drugs-failed-meet-goals/.

14. Ibid.

15. "Prisons & Drug Offenders," DrugWarFacts.org, http://www.drugwarfacts. org/cms/Prisons_and_Drugs.

16. Simon Cox, "Why can't we stop drugs getting into prisons?," BBC News, April 10, 2008, http://news.bbc.co.uk/2/hi/uk_news/magazine/7340533. stm; Max Chambers, "The truth about drugs in prisons," *Guardian*, March 19, 2010, http://www.guardian.co.uk/commentisfree/2010/mar/19/prison-mandatory-drug-testing-figures.

17. Daniel Horowitz, "U.S. With Highest Corporate Tax Rate," *RedState*, October 10, 2012, http://www.redstate.com/2012/10/10/u-s-with-highest-corporate-tax-rate/.

18. Michael, "10 Facts About Corporate Taxes That Will Make Your Blood Boil," The American Dream, March 29, 2011, http:// endoftheamericandream.com/archives/10-facts-about-corporate-taxes-that-will-make-your-blood-boil.

19. "Predicted effects of the FairTax," *Wikipedia*, February 5, 2013, http:// en.wikipedia.org/wiki/Predicted_effects_of_the_FairTax.

20. Michael Snyder, "Show This To Anyone That Believes That Taxes Are 'Too Low'," *alt-market.com* (blog), December 9, 2012, http://www.alt-market. com/articles/1202-show-this-to-anyone-that-believes-that-taxes-are-qtoo-lowq.

21. "Dollar Devaluation since 1913," Compare Gold and Silver Prices, January 23, 2012, http://www.comparegoldandsilverprices.com/dollar-devaluation-since-1913/.

22. http://www.governing.com/blogs/bfc/pension-retirement-liability-shortfall-federal-employee-retirement-system.html.

23. Charles Chieppo, "The Worst Pension Gap," *Governing.com* (blog), October 12, 2011, http://www.ncpa.org/sub/dpd/index.php?Article_ID=19634.

24. Chriss Street, "CA Unfunded Pensions Triple to $884 Bil," Cal Watchdog, August 23, 2011, http://www.calwatchdog.com/2011/08/23/ca-admits-884-billion-unfunded-pensions/.

25. Mark Niquette, "$822,000 Worker Shows California Leads U.S. Pay Giveaway," Bloomberg, December 11, 2012, http://www.bloomberg.com/news/2012-12-11/-822-000-worker-shows-california-leads-u-s-pay-giveaway.html.

26. Bill Wilson, "165 Million Americans Are Dependents of the State: Is Tyranny Next?," *Forbes*, August 15, 2012, http://www.forbes.com/sites/

realspin/2012/08/15/165-million-americans-are-dependents-of-the-state-is-tyranny-next/.

27.   James Pethokoukis, "Is $100 trillion in future entitlements debt really no biggie?," *AEIdeas* (blog), American Enterprise Institute, February 8, 2013, http://www.aei-ideas.org/2012/11/is-100-trillion-in-future-entitlements-debt-really-no-biggie/.

28.   "Public Data," Google, January 17, 2013, https://www.google.com/publicdata/explore?ds=d5bncppjof8f9_&met_y=ny_gdp_mktp_cd&tdim=true&dl=en&hl=en&q=gdp%20of%20the%20world.

29.   Great Depression, "Great Depression Millionaires," HubPages, http://greatdepression.hubpages.com/hub/Great-Depression-Millionaires.

PART TWO

1.   "Obama To Travel To Chicago To Talk Gun Control," CBS DC, February 10, 2013, washington.cbslocal.com/2013/02/10/obama-to-travel-to-chicago-to-talk-gun-control/.

CHAPTER SEVENTEEN

1.   "Spain Drains Fund Backing Pensions," *Wall Street Journal*, January 3, 2013, http://online.wsj.com/article/SB10001424127887323374504578217384062120520.html.

2.   Dan Kadlec, "Fiscal Cliff: Why Congress Might Have to Mess with the 401(k)," *Time*, November 28, 2012, http://business.time.com/2012/11/28/fiscal-cliff-why-congress-might-have-to-mess-with-the-401k/.

3.   Carter Dougherty, "Retirement Savings Accounts Draw U.S. Consumer Bureau Attention," Bloomberg, January 18, 2013, http://www.bloomberg.com/news/2013-01-18/retirement-savings-accounts-draw-u-s-consumer-bureau-attention.html; Phil Kerpen, "Is your retirement account safe from our government?," FOX News, February 11, 2013, http://www.foxnews.com/opinion/2013/02/11/is-your-retirement-account-safe-from-our-government/.

4.   Chris Woolf, "Grading Obama's State of the Union Address on Education and Europe," The World, February 13, 2013, http://www.theworld.org/2013/02/grading-obamas-state-of-the-union-address-on-education-and-europe/.

5.   DK Matai, "Smuggled Cash, Gold & Silver Seizures Soar at Italy's Borders – Eurozone Crisis Escalates – Diamonds Are Forever?," dkmatai.tumblr.

com (blog), August 15, 2012, http://www.google.com/url?sa=t&rct=j&q
=&esrc=s&source=web&cd=1&ved=0CDAQFjAA&url=http%3A%2F%
2Fdkmatai.tumblr.com%2Fpost%2F29439864625%2Fsmuggled-cash-
gold-silver-seizures-soar-at-italys&ei=bA4dUcCAF6WZ0QHM0ICIDQ&
usg=AFQjCNGRouDfbDyhkCFdrS-YXVnNS7fSvQ&bvm=bv.42452523,d.
dmg.

6. "The European Finance Crisis & Potential Eurozone Collapse," Thriving
    Tools, http://www.thrivingtools.com/world-news/the-european-finance-
    crisis-potential-eurozone-collapse/2/.

7. Simon Black, "It starts: the government's plan to steal your money.,"
    Sovereign Man, June 12, 2012, http://www.sovereignman.com/expat/
    it-starts-the-governments-plan-to-steal-your-money-7137/.

8. "France Unveils Temporary 75 Percent Super-Rich Tax Rate," *Huffington
    Post*, September 28, 2012, http://www.huffingtonpost.com/2012/09/28/
    france-tax-rich-rate_n_1922089.html.

9. Wynton Hall, "IRS AUDITS OF SMALL BUSINESSES SOAR UNDER
    OBAMA," Breitbart, October 25, 2012, http://www.breitbart.com/Big-
    Government/2012/10/25/IRS-Audits-Of-Small-Businesses-Soar-Under-
    Obama.

10. "Owe The IRS? Bill Would Suspend Passport Rights For Delinquent
    Taxpayers," CBS Los Angeles, April 4, 2012, http://losangeles.cbslocal.
    com/2012/04/04/owe-the-irs-bill-would-suspend-passport-travel-rights-
    for-delinquent-taxpayers/.

11. Laura Saunders, "Should You Renounce Your U.S. Citizenship?," *Wall Street
    Journal*, May 18, 2012, http://online.wsj.com/article/SB1000142405270230
    3879604577410021186373802.html.

12. Laurence Kotlikoff, "The Treasury Has Already Minted Two Trillion Dollar
    Coins," *Forbes*, January 19, 2013, http://www.forbes.com/sites/
    kotlikoff/2013/01/19the-treasury-has-already-minted-two-trillion-dollar-
    coins/.

13. "Zimbabwe says public account stood at $217 last week," BBC, January 30,
    2013, http://www.bbc.co.uk/news/world-africa-21257765.

14. Tyler Durden, "Doug Casey: "We Are Living In The Middle Of The
    Biggest Bubble In History.," *Zero Hedge*, January 18, 2013, http://www.
    zerohedge.com/news/2013-01-18/doug-casey-we-are-living-middle-
    biggest-bubble-history.

15. Daniel Halper, "Text of Obama's Second Inaugural Address," *Weekly Standard* (blog), January 21, 2013, http://www.weeklystandard.com/blogs/text-obamas-second-inaugural-address_696599.html.

16. "Justice Department Charges Standard & Poor's Defrauded Investors," PBS, February 5, 2013, http://www.pbs.org/newshour/bb/business/jan-june13/sandp_02-05.html.

17. Kara Scannell, "Egan-Jones is given SEC ratings ban," *Financial Times*, January 22, 2013, http://www.ft.com/intl/cms/s/0/492473fe-64be-11e2-ac53-00144feab49a.html#axzz2K81Ix4x6.

18. Nouriel Roubini, "We Face up to a Decade, of Low Economic Growth," *nourielroubini.blogspot.com* (blog), September 10, 2012, http://nourielroubini.blogspot.com/2012/09/roubini-we-face-low-economic-growth.html.

19. Martin Crutsinger, "Fed commits extra $45 billion a month to bond-buying program," *San Jose Mercury News*, December 12, 2012, http://www.mercurynews.com/economy/ci_22176804/fed-commits-extra-45-billion-month-bond-buying.

20. Renee Dudley, "Wal-Mart Executives Sweat Slow February Start in E-Mails," Bloomberg, February 16, 2013, http://www.bloomberg.com/news/2013-02-15/wal-mart-executives-sweat-slow-february-start-in-e-mails.html.

CHAPTER EIGHTEEN

1. Advice from Michael Checkan of Assets Strategies International throughout this chapter is from interviews with the author between January 5 and January 20, 2012.

2. Tim Price, "Guest Post: What Warren Buffet Doesn't Understand About Investing," *Offshore, gold, anarchy, privacy anti-big-brother* (blog), February 19, 2013, http://www.one-admin.com/18389/guest-post-what-warren-buffett-doesnt-understand-about-investing/.

3. Chidanand Rajghatta and Prabhakar Sinha, "Full circle: India buys 200 tons gold from IMF," *India Times*, November 4, 2009, http://www.google.com/url?sa=t&rct=j&q=&esrc=s&source=web&cd=1&ved=0CDAQFjAA&url=http%3A%2F%2Ftimesofindia.indiatimes.com%2Fbusiness%2Findia-business%2FFull-circle-India-buys-200-tons-gold-from-IMF%2Farticleshow%2F5194338.cms&ei=QFgeUYuAMI6w0QHfvYCI

CA&usg=AFQjCNEBsJYoIQYpWUYyyuWnPQeHsmjvYw&bvm=bv.42 553238,d.dmQ.

4. "Putin Turns Black Gold to Bullion as Russia Outbuys World – Bloomberg 02-11-13," Investa Asset Management, February 11, 2013, http://investa. com/putin-turns-black-gold-to-bullion-as-russia-outbuys-world-bloomberg-02-11-13/.

5. Himanshu Pandey, "China world's top gold producer for 6th year," Indian Defence, February 11, 2013, http://www.indiandefence.com/forums/ chinese-defence-affairs/24041-china-worlds-top-gold-producer-6th-year. html; Joseph Boris, "China poised to become world's biggest gold consumer," China Daily USA, May 18, 2012, http://usa.chinadaily.com.cn/ business/2012-05/18/content_15325123.htm.

6. These figures were compiled by Michael and Rich Checkan of Asset Strategies International from publicly available data using ycharts.com. In analyzing the return on stocks, the Checkans took dividends as well as price increases into account; "iShares Barclays 20+ Year Treas Bond Chart," YCharts, http://ycharts.com/companies/TLT/chart#series=type%3Acompany%2Cid%3ATLT%2Ccalc%3Aprice&format=real&recessions=false &zoom=custom&startDate=7%2F26%2F2000&endDate=2%2F5 %2F2013; "Case-Shiller Home Price Index: National: 132.70 for Q3 2012," YCharts, http://ycharts.com/indicators/case_shiller_home_price_index_ national_.

7. Stefan Gleason, "Physical Gold Bullion vs. Gold Mining Stocks," Independent Living Bullion, http://www.independentlivingbullion.com/ precious_metals_buying_guide/physical-gold-bullion-vs-gold-mining-stocks.php; Rich Toscano, "GOLD REVISITED, PART II: TREMENDOUS POTENTIAL IN GOLD MINING STOCKS," Pacific Capital Associates, May 7, 2012, http://www.pcasd.com/gold_revisited_part_ii_tremendous_ potential_in_gold_mining_stocks.

8. Brett Arends, "In Gold Investing, Forget the Metal and focus on Stocks," Wall Street Journal, December 7, 2012, http://online.wsj.com/article/SB10 001424127887323316804578161230254371890.html.

9. Benny Johnson, "NOT JUST GAS! CHECK OUT THE DRASTIC PRICE INCREASES ON THESE 21 EVERYDAY ITEMS," TheBlaze, October 17, 2012, http://www.theblaze.com/stories/2012/10/17/not-just-gas-check-out-the-drastic-price-increases-on-these-21-everyday-items/; Jeff Rubin, "How High Oil Prices Will Permanently Cap Economic Growth," Bloomberg,

September 23, 2012, http://www.bloomberg.com/news/2012-09-23/how-high-oil-prices-will-permanently-cap-economic-growth.html; Michael, "Why Are Food Prices Rising So Fast?," *The Economic Collapse* (blog), June 24, 2011, http://theeconomiccollapseblog.com/archives/why-are-food-prices-rising-so-fast.

CHAPTER NINETEEN

1. "Centerplate Concludes 2012 Art Basel With Record Sales And Commendation From Host City, Miami Beach," PR Newswire, January 18, 2012, http://www.prnewswire.com/news-releases/centerplate-concludes-2012-art-basel-with-record-sales-and-commendation-from-host-city-miami-beach-187442301.html.

2. Jeremy Korzeniewski, "1960 Ferrari 250 GT sells for over $8 million in record-setting RM auction weekend," *Autoblog*, AOL, January 22, 2013, http://www.autoblog.com/2013/01/22/1960-ferrari-250-gt-sells-for-over-8-million-in-record-setting/; Scott Reyburn, "Batmobile Zaps Auction, Ferraris Boost $100 Million Total," Bloomberg, January 21, 2013, http://www.bloomberg.com/news/2013-01-19/batmobile-to-follow-8-million-ferraris-in-car-auctions.html; Matthew Hendley, "Ferraris Sold at Arizona Auctions for More Than $8 Million — Millions More Than the Batmobile," blog, *Phoenix News Times*, January 22, 2013, http://blogs.phoenixnewtimes.com/valleyfever/2013/01/ferraris_sold_at_arizona_aucti.php.

3. This quotation and all quotations of Richard Spring throughout this chapter are from the author's interviews with Richard Spring, January 30–February 1, 2013.

4. Thomas Martinez, "Irvine broker sells 1794 silver dollar for $10 million," *Orange County Register*, January 25, 2013, http://www.ocregister.com/articles/coin-409350-silver-first.html.

5. dirtyoldcoins.com, http://www.dirtyoldcoins.com/shop/Uncleaned-Roman-Coins.html.

6. "US Coins Buying Guide : eBay Guides," eBay, December 18, 2012, http://reviews.ebay.com/US-Coins-Buying-Guide?ugid=143.

7. "Find a Reputable, Knowledgeable Coin Dealer From the Professional Numismatists Guild (PNG)," Professional Numismatists Guild, http://www.pngdealers.com.

8. James Bucki, "Top 5 Famous Coin Collections of All Time," About.com, http://coins.about.com/od/Start-Collecting-Coins/a/Top-5-Famous-Coin-Collections-Of-All-Time.htm.

9. The details of the trades of all three coins described below are available at Professional Coin Grading Service, http://www.pcgs.com.

CHAPTER TWENTY

1. "Energy," yorkcommunitymain.org, http://www.yorkcommunitymaine.org/energy.html; "Total Primary Energy Consumption per Capita," gailtheactuary.files.wordpress.com (blog), http://gailtheactuary.files.wordpress.com/2013/02/total-primary-energy-consumption-per-capita.png.

2. "Non Renewable Energy," All-recycling-facts.com, http://www.all-recycling-facts.com/non-renewable-energy.html.

3. "U.S. Crude Oil Production versus Hubbert Curve," *Wikipedia*, http://upload.wikimedia.org/wikipedia/commons/7/79/US_Crude_Oil_Production_versus_Hubbert_Curve.png; "Peak oil," *Wikipedia*, February 20, 2013, http://en.wikipedia.org/wiki/Peak_oil.

4. "U.S. Crude Oil Production versus Hubbert Curve," *Wikipedia*, http://upload.wikimedia.org/wikipedia/commons/7/79/US_Crude_Oil_Production_versus_Hubbert_Curve.png.

5. "Gold to Oil Ratio Historical Chart," macrotrends.org, http://www.macrotrends.org/1380/gold-to-oil-ratio-historical-chart; "The Gold-Oil Ratio," incrediblecharts.com, http://www.incrediblecharts.com/economy/gold_oil_ratio.php.

6. "SHORT-TERM ENERGY OUTLOOK," U.S. Energy Information Administration, February 12, 2013, http://www.eia.gov/forecasts/steo/.

7. "Gasoline price hike biggest since 2009," United Press International, February 21, 2013, http://www.upi.com/Business_News/2013/02/21/Gasoline-price-hike-biggest-since-2009/UPI-45311361431800/.

8. Rob Bluey, "Chart of the Week: Winter Gas Prices Reach All-Time High," *The Foundry* (blog), The Heritage Foundation, February 26, 2012, http://blog.heritage.org/2012/02/26/chart-of-the-week-winter-gas-prices-reach-all-time-high/.

9. Global Macro Monitor, "Chart of the Day: Price Divergence between Oil and Natural Gas," Credit Writedowns, April 5, 2012, http://www.

creditwritedowns.com/2012/04/chart-of-the-day-price-divergence-between-oil-and-natural-gas.html.

10. Benjamin Preston, "Why We Aren't Driving Natural Gas Powered Cars," Jalopnik, May 18, 2012, http://jalopnik.com/5911513/why-we-arent-driving-natural-gas-powered-cars.

11. Maria Sudekum, "JJ's, Kansas City Restaurant, Destroyed By Gas Explosion (PHOTOS)," February 21, 2013, http://www.huffingtonpost.com/2013/02/21/jjs-kansas-city-restaurant-destroyed_n_2732756.html;

12. James Delingpole, "Man-made global warming: even the IPCC admits the jig is up," December 13, 2012, Telegraph, http://blogs.telegraph.co.uk/news/jamesdelingpole/100194166/man-made-global-warming-even-the-ipcc-admits-the-jig-is-up/; Joseph L. Bast, "IPCC Admits Its Past Reports Were Junk," July 16, 2012, http://www.americanthinker.com/2012/07/ipcc_admits_its_past_reports_were_junk.html.

CHAPTER TWENTY-ONE

1. Don Miller, "Why Jim Rogers is Investing in Farmland," Money Morning, July 12, 2012, http://moneymorning.com/2012/07/12/why-jim-rogers-is-investing-in-farmland/.

2. Ibid.

3. Ibid.

4. Ibid.

5. Ibid.

6. Ibid.

7. Ibid.

8. Matthew Cranston, "Rogers in town to buy the farm," Australian Financial Review, November 10, 2011, http://afr.com/p/markets/rogers_in_town_to_buy_the_farm_vkylvEiMobqYEh2aCLECyO.

CHAPTER TWENTY-TWO

1. Ann W., "Cook taxpayers owe $108 billion, county Treasurer Pappas says: Gre Hinz [Chicago, Ill County]," FreeRepublic, June 21, 2011, http://www.freerepublic.com/focus/f-news/2737919/posts.

2. "City of Baltimore is on path to financial ruin, report says," FOX News, February 6, 2013, http://www.foxnews.com/politics/2013/02/06/city-baltimore-is-on-path-to-financial-ruin-report-says/.

3.   Brian Keegan, "A Widening Gap in Cities," The Pew Charitable Trusts, January 16, 2013, http://www.pewstates.org/research/reports/a-widening-gap-in-cities-85899442341.

4.   Trevon Milliard, "Health trust for Clark County teachers in trouble," *Las Vegas Review-Journal*, February 1, 2013, http://www.lvrj.com/news/health-trust-for-clark-county-teachers-founders-189471191.html.

5.   "Bailed out banks," CNN, http://money.cnn.com/news/specials/storysupplement/bankbailout/; "Why are interest rates being kept at a low level?," Board of Governors of the Federal Reserve System, December 12, 2012, http://www.federalreserve.gov/faqs/money_12849.htm.

6.   Cliff Küle, "What are Banks doing with the Bailout Money? Lending? No! Buying Government Bonds? Yes!," Financial Sense, December 5, 2008, http://www.financialsensearchive.com/editorials/cliffkule/2008/1205.html.

7.   Andrew Barry, "State of the States," *Barron's*, August 27, 2012, http://online.barrons.com/article/SB50001424053111904881404577603301566976464.html#articleTabs_article%3D1.

8.   Duff McDonald, "Meredith Whitney was right," CNN, March 12, 2012, http://finance.fortune.cnn.com/2012/03/12/meredith-whitney-was-right/.

9.   metroebukmetro, "Greece: Riots erupt over knife edge ballot for more cuts," *Metro*, November 7, 2012, http://metro.co.uk/2012/11/07/greece-riots-erupt-over-knife-edge-ballot-for-more-cuts-615263/.

10.   Liz Capo McCormick and Daniel Kruger, "Treasury Scarcity to Grow as Fed Buys 90% of New Bonds," Bloomberg, December 3, 2012, http://www.bloomberg.com/news/2012-12-03/treasury-scarcity-to-grow-as-fed-buys-90-of-new-bonds.html.

11.   Catherine Boyle, "Debt Crisis Could Be Turning Point for US-China," CNBC, August 16, 2011, http://www.cnbc.com/id/44142438/Debt_Crisis_Could_Be_Turning_Point_for_USChina.

12.   Detlev Schlichter, "'When they stop buying bonds, the game is over.'," detlevschlichter.com, January 6, 2012, http://detlevschlichter.com/2012/01/"when-they-stop-buying-bonds-the-game-is-over-"/.

13.   "Rogers: Fed-created bond bubble could pop soon – Fast Forward (6:46)," Reuters, September 12, 2012, http://in.reuters.com/video/2012/09/12/rogers-fed-created-bond-bubble-could-pop?videoId=237677061.

14.   John Carney, "How to Profit From a Muni Bond Crisis," CNBC, February 10, 2011, http://www.cnbc.com/id/41513958/How_to_Profit_From_a_Muni_Bond_Crisis.

CHAPTER TWENTY-THREE

1.   Angela Banks, "Obamacare adds 30 million more people to a broken healthcare system," Examiner.com, July 1, 2012, http://www.examiner.com/article/obamacare-adds-30-million-more-people-to-a-broken-healthcare-system.

2.   Joshua M Brown, "79 million baby boomers enter retirement: What it could mean for the market," *Christian Science Monitor,* July 6, 2010, http://www.csmonitor.com/Business/The-Reformed-Broker/2010/0706/79-million-baby-boomers-enter-retirement-What-it-could-mean-for-the-market.

3.   Hubble Smith, "Medical real estate development expected to boom soon in valley," *Las Vegas Review-Journal,* December 27, 2012, http://www.lvrj.com/business/medical-real-estate-development-expected-to-boom-soon-in-valley-184908261.html.

CHAPTER TWENTY-FOUR

1.   Chrystia Freedman, "What Toronto can teach New York and London," *Financial Times,* January 29, 2010, http://www.ft.com/intl/cms/s/0/db2b340a-0a1b-11df-8b23-00144feabdc0.html#axzz2LZltMBzf; Kurt Badenhausen, "New Zealand Tops Our List Of The Best Countries For Business," *Forbes,* November 14, 2012, http://www.forbes.com/sites/kurtbadenhausen/2012/11/14/new-zealand-tops-list-of-the-best-countries-for-business/.

2.   2013 Index of Economic Freedom, The Heritage Foundation, http://www.heritage.org/index/.

3.   Ansuya Harjani, "India's Secret Weapon: Its Young Population," CNBC, October 24, 2012, http://www.cnbc.com/id/49472962/Indiarsquos_Secret_Weapon_Its_Young_Population; Graeme Hugo, "DEMOGRAPHIC AGEING IN EAST AND SOUTHEAST ASIA AND IMPLICATIONS FOR THE FUTURE," Pacific Economic Cooperation Council, October 18–22, 2010, http://www.pecc.org/resources/doc_view/1518-demographic-ageing-in-east-and-southeast-asia-and-implications-for-the-future; "Age Structure," siakhenn.tripod.com, http://siakhenn.tripod.com/age.html.

4.   "How to Finance a Car," autobytel, http://www.autobytel.com/car-
        financing/how-to-finance-a-car-100492/; Jeffrey Hays, "DRIVING AND
        OWNING A CAR IN CHINA," factsanddetails.com, July 2012, http://
        factsanddetails.com/china.php?itemid=409&.

5.   Matt Welch, "Economic Freedom: China Up, U.S. Down," Reason, May
        2012, http://reason.com/archives/2012/05/03/economic-freedom-china-
        up-us-down.

6.   "Trade at a Glance 2011," Australian Government: Department of Foreign
        Affairs and Trade, October 2011, http://www.dfat.gov.au/publications/
        trade/trade-at-a-glance-2011.html; Justin Kuepper, "The 3 Countries With
        the Most Growth Potential," About.com, http://internationalinvest.about.
        com/od/globalmarkets101/a/The-3-Countries-With-The-Most-Growth-
        Potential.htm.

7.   "Agriculture And Food," hollandtrade.com, January 2011, http://www.
        hollandtrade.com/sector-information/agriculture-and-food/.

CHAPTER TWENTY-FIVE

1.   "Deducting Health Insurance Premiums If You're Self-Employed,"
        TurboTax, http://turbotax.intuit.com/tax-tools/tax-tips/Self-Employment-
        Taxes/Deducting-Health-Insurance-Premiums-If-You-re-Self-Employed/
        INF12128.html.

2.   Laura Saunders, "A Tax Man Takes Account Of His Life," Wall Street
        Journal, April 5, 2011, http://online.wsj.com/article/SB1000142405274870
        36967045762225902532912663.html.

3.   Jeff Haden, "How the Rich Got Rich," Inc., June 20, 2012, http://www.inc.
        com/jeff-haden/how-the-rich-got-rich.html.

4.   Joshua Kennon, "10 Secrets of the Capitalist Class," About.com, http://
        beginnersinvest.about.com/od/wealthmanagement1/ss/capitalist-class_11.
        htm.

CHAPTER TWENTY-SIX

1.   Joseph R. Szczesny, "GM's Pension: A Ticking Time Bomb for Taxpayers?,"
        Time, April 15, 2010, http://www.time.com/time/business/
        article/0,8599,1981958,00.html; Mark Miller, "American Airlines pension
        default Q&A," Reuters, February 8, 2012, http://www.reuters.com/
        article/2012/02/08/us-column-miller-idUSTRE81718S20120208.

2.   Advice in this chapter was provided by David Bray to the author, who interviewed him January 20-21, 2013.

CHAPTER TWENTY-SEVEN

1.   Lauren Fox, ""NRA: Membership Has Grown by 250,000 in One Month," *U.S. News & World Report*, January 15, 2013, http://www.usnews.com/news/articles/2013/01/15/nra-membership-has-grown-by-250000-in-one-month.

2.   Monica Davey, "Strict Gun Laws in Chicago Can't Stem Fatal Shots," *New York Times*, January 29, 2013, http://www.nytimes.com/2013/01/30/us/strict-chicago-gun-laws-cant-stem-fatal-shots.html?pagewanted=all&_r=0.

3.   Aaron Blake, "Connecticut gun laws among the nation's strictest," *The Fix* (blog), *Washington Post*, December 17, 2012, http://www.washingtonpost.com/blogs/the-fix/wp/2012/12/17/connecticut-gun-laws-among-the-nations-strictest/.

4.   Joyce Lee Malcolm, "Two cautionary Tales of Gun Control," *Wall Street Journal*, December 26, 2012, http://online.wsj.com/article/SB10001424127887323777204578195470446855466.html.

5.   James Slack, "The most violent country in Europe, "Britain is also worse than South Africa and U.S.," *Daily Mail*, July 2, 2009, http://www.dailymail.co.uk/news/article-1196941/The-violent-country-Europe-Britain-worse-South-Africa-U-S.html#ixzz2HQDkC3re.

6.   Scott Rasmussen, "Following School Shooting, 86% Want More Action to Identify and Treat Mental Illness," Rasmussen Reports, December 19, 2012, http://www.rasmussenreports.com/public_content/politics/general_politics/december_2012/following_school_shooting_86_want_more_action_to_identify_and_treat_mental_illness.

7.   Tyler Durden, "Newton Shooter Had Asperger Syndrome, And Some US Gun Facts," *Zero Hedge*, December 15, 2012, http://www.zerohedge.com/news/2012-12-15/newtown-shooter-had-asperger-syndrome-and-some-us-gun-facts.

8.   "Gun Control Fact-Sheet 2004," Gun Owners of America, September 19, 2008, http://gunowners.org/fs0404.htm.

9.   "Fact Sheet: Guns Save Lives," Gun Owners of America, September 29, 2008, https://www.gunowners.org/sk0802htm.htm.

10.   "Gun Control Fact-Sheet 2004."

11. "Fact Sheet: Guns Save Lives."

12. Victor Medina, "Anti-gun crusader Michael Moore has an armed bodyguard," Examiner.com, December 22, 2012, http://www.examiner.com/article/anti-gun-crusader-michael-moore-s-bodyguard-carries-a-gun.

13. Jacque Fresco, "Mayor Bloomberg has armed guards but wants the people disarmed," Hang The Bankers, January 29, 2013, http://www.hangthebankers.com/mayor-bloomberg-has-armed-guards-but-wants-the-people-disarmed/.

14. "Hitler was a Leftist: Nazi Gun Control," constitutionalistnc.tripod.com, http://constitutionalistnc.tripod.com/hitler-leftist/id14.html.

15. "Death by 'Gun Control'," Jews for the Preservation of Firearms Ownership, http://jpfo.org/filegen-a-m/deathgc.htm.

16. Gregory Gwyn-Williams, Jr., "65.4 Million Gun Purchases Since Obama Took Office, 91% More Than Bush's First-Term Total," (blog), CNS News, February 11, 2013, http://cnsnews.com/blog/gregory-gwyn-williams-jr/654-million-gun-purchases-obama-took-office-91-more-bushs-first-term.

17. Gregory Gwyn-Williams, "Gun Maker's Annual Earnings Skyrocket 77.7%," CNS News, February 27, 2013, http://cnsnews.com/blog/gregory-gwyn-williams-jr/gun-makers-annual-earnings-skyrocket-777#.

CHAPTER TWENTY-EIGHT

1. "Mickelson plans 'drastic changes' over taxes," MSN, January 21, 2013, http://news.msn.com/pop-culture/mickelson-plans-drastic-changes-over-taxes.

2. Robert W. Wood, "Tiger Woods Moved Too, Says Mickelson Was Right About Taxes," Forbes, January 23, 2013, http://www.forbes.com/sites/robertwood/2013/01/23/tiger-woods-moved-too-says-mickelson-was-right-about-taxes/.

3. Chris Williams, "Arum: Pacquiao doesn't want to fight in U.S because the taxes are too high," boxingnews24.com, January 22, 2013, http://www.boxingnews24.com/2013/01/arum-pacquiao-doesnt-want-to-fight-in-u-s-because-the-taxes-are-too-high/.

4. Bruce Baker, "Tina Turner renounces American citizenship, becomes Swiss," Examiner.com, January 26, 2013, http://www.examiner.com/article/tina-turner-renounces-american-citizenship-becomes-swiss.

5. NAR Research, "Fastest Growing States: 2000 to 2010," Facebook, February 9, 2011, http://www.facebook.com/note.php?note_id=10150130579902069.

6. Tonya Moreno, "States Without an Income Tax," About.com, http://taxes.about.com/od/statetaxes/a/tax-free-states.htm.

7. Dan Mitchell, "Do Taxes Make People Unhappy?," danieljmitchell.wordpress.com (blog), January 1, 2010, http://danieljmitchell.wordpress.com/2010/01/01/do-taxes-make-people-unhappy/.

8. "States that Spend Less, Tax Less—-and Grow More," *Wall Street Journal*, December 14, 2012, http://professional.wsj.com/article/SB1000142405297 0204349404578099233101373940.html.

9. Elizabeth Harrington, "Escape From New York? High-Taxing Empire State Loses 3.4 Million Residents in 10 Years," CNS News, May 28, 2012, http://cnsnews.com/news/article/escape-new-york-high-taxing-empire-state-loses-34-million-residents-10-years.

10. Emily Hatton and Elizabeth Sallie, "Marylanders move in droves to Virginia," *Washington Times*, July 3, 2012, http://www.washingtontimes.com/news/2012/jul/3/marylanders-move-in-droves-to-virginia/?page=all.

11. Harrington, "Escape From New York?"

12. Dan Mitchell, "Connecticut's Fiscal Suicide," danieljmitchell.wordpress.com (blog), September 2, 2009, http://danieljmitchell.wordpress.com/2009/09/02/connecticuts-fiscal-suicide/.

13. "California Scheming: What One-Party Rule Is Doing To Once-Golden State," *Investor's Business Daily*, December 22, 2008, http://news.investors.com/122208-453857-california-scheming-what-one-party-rule-is-doing-to-once-golden-state.aspx?p=full#axzz2JzM0SPln.

14. Mitchell, "Connecticut's Fiscal Suicide."

15. "89,240 JOBS LOST SINCE THE 66% TAX HIKE ... AND COUNTING," Illinois Review, August 23, 2011, http://illinoisreview.typepad.com/illinoisreview/2011/08/89240-jobs-lost-since-the-66-tax-hikeand-counting.html.

16. Brian Solomon, "Eduardo Saverin Renounces U.S. Citizenship Ahead Of Mega Facebook IPO," *Forbes*, May 11, 2012, http://www.forbes.com/sites/briansolomon/2012/05/11/eduardo-saverin-renounces-u-s-citizenship-ahead-of-mega-facebook-ipo/.

17. "Denise Rich gives up a U.S. citizenship, will save millions in U.S. taxes, report says," FOX News, July 9, 2012, http://www.foxnews.com/

entertainment/2012/07/09/denis-rich-gives-up-us-citizenship-will-save-
millions-in-us-taxes-report-says/.

18. "Record number of Americans renouncing their citizenship to avoid paying
     taxes," *Daily Mail*, April 17, 2012, http://www.dailymail.co.uk/news/
     article-2131225/Record-number-American-citizens-renouncing-
     citizenship-avoid-paying-taxes.html.

19. "Two-thirds of British millionaires disappeared after income tax increase
     on the rich," winterknight.wordpress.com (blog), November 28, 2012,
     http://winteryknight.wordpress.com/2012/11/28/two-thirds-of-british-
     millionaires-disappeared-after-income-tax-increase-on-the-rich/.

20. Henry Blodget, "Gerard Depardieu Quits France Because of High Taxes,"
     Yahoo!, January 7, 2013, http://finance.yahoo.com/blogs/daily-ticker/
     gerard-depardieu-quits-france-because-high-taxes-173222852.html.

21. Jean-Philippe Delsol, "Can The Last Taxpayer Leaving France Please Turn
     Out The Lights?," *Forbes*, December 18, 2012, http://www.forbes.com/sites/
     realspin/2012/12/18/can-the-last-taxpayer-leaving-france-please-turn-out-
     the-lights/.

22. "Former French President Sarkozy may leave country to avoid high taxes,"
     FOX News, January 22, 2013, http://www.foxnews.com/world/2013/01/22/
     former-french-president-sarkozy-may-leave-country-to-avoid-high-taxes/.

23. Harrington, "Escape From New York?"

24. David Martosko, "As UK millionaires flee country over tax hikes, British
     treasury loses billions," Daily Caller, November 28, 2012, http://dailycaller.
     com/2012/11/28/as-uk-millionaires-flee-country-over-tax-hikes-british-
     treasury-loses-billions/; "France's proposed tax hikes spark 'exodus' of
     wealthy," *Telegraph*, July 16, 2012, http://www.telegraph.co.uk/news/
     worldnews/europe/france/9404209/Frances-proposed-tax-hikes-spark-
     exodus-of-wealthy.html; Bob Adelmann, "Rich French Citizens are Leaving
     France," New American, August 9, 2012, http://www.thenewamerican.
     com/world-news/europe/item/12408-rich-french-citizens-are-leaving-
     france.

25. Betsy Woodruff, "Reid's Glass House," *National Review*, August 24, 2012,
     http://www.nationalreview.com/articles/314851/reid-s-glass-house-betsy-
     woodruff; Talesha Reynolds and Rich Gardella, " Jack Lew's investment in
     Cayman Islands flagged by Senate Finance Committee," NBC News,
     February 9, 2013, http://www.nbcnews.com/business/jack-lews-
     investment-cayman-islands-flagged-senate-finance-

committee-1B8309826; Michael, "The Global Elite Are Hiding 18 Trillion Dollars In Offshore Banks," *The Economic Collapse* (blog), January 20, 2012, http://theeconomiccollapseblog.com/archives/the-global-elite-are-hiding-18-trillion-dollars-in-offshore-banks; Merrill Bender, "Wealthy Democrats don't pay their Fair Share of Tax," FreeRepublic, December 13, 2005, http://www.freerepublic.com/focus/f-news/1539821/posts.

26. Doug Mataconis, "Mitt Romney's Offshore Bank Accounts," Outside the Beltway, January 19, 2012, http://www.outsidethebeltway.com/mitt-romneys-offshore-bank-accounts/.

CHAPTER TWENTY-NINE

1. "SAT Reading Scores Fall to Lowest Level on Record," FOX News, September 14, 2011, http://www.foxnews.com/us/2011/09/14/sat-reading-scores-fall-to-lowest-level-on-record/.

2. William J. Bennett, "Record-low SAT scores a wake-up call," CNN, September 21, 2011, http://www.cnn.com/2011/09/21/opinion/bennett-education.

3. "Federal Spending on Education up 375% Learning Scores Down!," The Report Card, July 24, 2012, http://education-curriculum-reform-government-schools.org/w/2012/07/federal-spending-on-education-up-375-learning-scores-down/.

4. "25 American History Facts Most Students Don't Know," CollegeStats, http://collegestats.org/articles/2012/07/25-american-history-facts-most-students-dont-know/.

5. Libby Quaid, "Report: U.S. kids less likely to graduate than parents," ceep.indiana.edu, October 23, 2008, http://ceep.indiana.edu/hssse/pdfs/Chron.com%20—U.S.%20Kids%20Less%20Likely%20to%20Graduate%20than%20Parents%20—%2023%20Oct%2008.pdf.

6. "Cities in Crisis," America's Promise Alliance, 2008, http://www.americaspromise.org/Our-Work/Dropout-Prevention/Cities-in-Crisis.aspx#.URMG2KXEVk4.

7. Sam Dillon, "Study Finds High Rate of Imprisonment Among Dropouts," *New York Times*, October 8, 2009, http://www.nytimes.com/2009/10/09/education/09dropout.html.

8. Ibid.

9. "Fighting Against Merit Pay," Teachers Union Exposed, http://www.teachersunionsexposed.com/meritpay.cfm.

10. Elizabeth Harrington, "Education Spending Up 64% Under No Child Left Behind But Test Scores Improve Little," CNS News, September 26, 2011, http://cnsnews.com/news/article/education-spending-64-under-no-child-left-behind-test-scores-improve-little.

11. M. Alex Johnson, "US turns down No Child Left Behind waiver for California," December 26, 2012, http://usnews.nbcnews.com/_news/2012/12/26/16171331-us-turns-down-no-child-left-behind-waiver-for-california?lite.

12. Lindsey Burke, "Homeschooling Sees Dramatic Rise in Popularity," The Heritage Foundation, January 28, 2009, http://www.heritage.org/research/reports/2009/01/homeschooling-sees-dramatic-rise-in-popularity.

13. "World University Rankings 2011-2012," timeshighereducation.co.uk, http://www.timeshighereducation.co.uk/world-university-rankings/2011-12/world-ranking.

14. Phil Cooke, "Bloomberg: The US Postal Service lost $15.9 billion last year. That's more than Wal-Mart MADE ($15.8 billion).," Twitter, December 28, 2012, billhttps://twitter.com/PhilCooke/status/284718247784349697.

15. "Do Homeschool Kids Really Rate Better on Standardized Tests?," HubPages, http://learnthingsweb.hubpages.com/hub/Do-Homeschoolers-Really-Do-Better-on-Tests.

16. "15 Key Facts About Homeschooled Kids in College," Online Colleges, September 13, 2011, http://www.onlinecollege.org/2011/09/13/15-key-facts-about-homeschooled-kids-in-college/.

17. Chris Klicka, "The Facts Are In: Homeschoolers Excel," Homeschool World, 2004, http://www.home-school.com/Articles/the-facts-are-in-homeschoolers-excel.php.

18. Chris Klicka, "Socialization: Homeschoolers Are in the Real World," Home School Legal Defense Association, March 2007, http://www.hslda.org/docs/nche/000000/00000068.asp.

CHAPTER THIRTY

1. AnnaMaria Andriotis, "5 Housing Markets Where Renting Beats Owning," REAL-TIME ADVICE (blog), Smart Money, June 21, 2012, http://blogs.smartmoney.com/advice/2012/06/21/5-housing-markets-where-renting-beats-owning/.

2.   Chris Edwards, "Overpaid Federal Workers," Cato Institute, February 2012, http://www.downsizinggovernment.org/overpaid-federal-workers; Andrew Biggs, "How Generous Are Federal Employee Pensions?," *AEIdeas* (blog), American Enterprise Institute, September 30, 2011, http://www. aei-ideas.org/2011/09/how-generous-are-federal-employee-pensions/; Dennis Cauchon, "Federal workers earning double their private counterparts," USA TODAY, August 13, 2010, http://usatoday30.usatoday. com/money/economy/income/2010-08-10-1Afedpay10_ST_N.htm.

CHAPTER THIRTY-TWO

1.   Charles Crumm, "Billboard pokes at Michigan Gov. Rick Snyder in advance of Democrats' state convention," *Oakland Press*, February 21, 2013, http:// www.theoaklandpress.com/articles/2013/02/21/news/doc5126474f0ee 7b282947976.txt; "Gov. Christie: 'They believe in teacher's unions, we believe in teachers'," CBS News, August 28, 2012, http://www.cbsnews.com/ video/watch/?id=7419706n; Bonnie Kavoussi, "Scott Walker Rejects Obamacare Medicaid Expansion in Wisconsin," *Huffington Post*, February 13, 2013, http://www.huffingtonpost.com/2013/02/13/scott-walker-obamacare_n_2680430.html.

2.   Mark Guarino, "Gov. Scott Walker makes history, survives Wisconsin recall election (+ video)," *Christian Science Monitor*, Jnue 6, 2012, http://www. csmonitor.com/USA/Elections/Governors/2012/0606/Gov.-Scott-Walker-makes-history-survives-Wisconsin-recall-election-video; Christian Schneider, "It's Working in Walker's Wisconsin," *City Journal* 22, no. 1 (Winter 2012), http://www.city-journal.org/2012/22_1_scott-walker.html.

CHAPTER THIRTY-THREE

1.   Marc Faber, *Gloom Boom & Doom Report*, http://new.gloomboomdoom. com/portalgbd/homegbd.cfm; Marc Faber, *Tomorrow's Gold: Asia's age of Discovery* (New York: CLSA, 2008); Nury Vittachi, *Riding the Millennial Storm: Marc Faber's Path to Profit in the Financial Markets* (Singapore: John Wiley & Sons, 1998).

2.   "Government," Bastiat.org, http://bastiat.org/en/government.html.

3.   "TV Interview for Thames TV *This Week*," Margaret Thatcher Foundation, http://www.margaretthatcher.org/document/102953.

4. Harold J. Laski, *Studies in Law and Politics* (Piscataway, New Jersey: Transaction Publishers, 2009).

5. Will Durant and Ariel Durant, The Lessons of History (New York Simon and Schuster, 2012).

6. "ERNEST HEMINGWAY QUOTES," notable-quotes.com, http://www.notable-quotes.com/h/hemingway_ernest.html.

7. Ben Duronio, "9 Unforgettable Quotes From Milton Friedman," Business Insider, July 31, 2012, http://www.businessinsider.com/milton-friedman-quotes-2012-7.

CHAPTER THIRTY-SEVEN

1. Charlie Spiering, "Obama to Leno: I struggle with math above the 7th grade level," *Washington Examiner,* October 25, 2012, http://washingtonexaminer.com/obama-to-leno-i-struggle-with-math-above-the-7th-grade-level/article/2511708.

CHAPTER THIRTY-EIGHT

1. William Baldwin, "Do You Live in a Death Spiral State?," Forbes, November 25, 2012, www.forbes.com/sites/baldwin/2012/11/25/do-you-live-in-a-death-spiral-state.

CHAPTER FORTY-ONE

1. Listen to his speech on YouTube, http://www.youtube.com/watch?v=SDouNtnR_IA.

CHAPTER FORTY-TWO

1. SuperScholar.org, www.superscholar.org.

2. Adam Smith, *The Wealth of Nations* (New York: Oxford University Press, 1998).

3. Ibid.

4. Free the World.com, www.freetheworld.com.

5. "'Are We Rome?,'" FreedomFest, www.freedomfest.com.

6. Harold Bloom, *The Anatomy of Influence: Literature as a Way of Life* (New Haven: Yale University Press, 2011).

CHAPTER FORTY-NINE

1. "Pelosi: 'We Have to Pass the Bill So That You Can Find Out What Is In It,'" YouTube, http://www.youtube.com/watch?v=hV-05TLiiLU.

CHAPTER FIFTY-ONE

1. Arthur C. Brooks, "Why Conservatives Are Happier Than Liberals," *New York Times*, July 7, 2012, http://www.nytimes.com/2012/07/08/opinion/sunday/conservatives-are-happier-and-extremists-are-happiest-of-all.html?_r=1&ref=opinion.
2. Jaime L. Napier and John T. Jost, "Why Are Conservatives Happier Than Liberals?," Harvard.edu, 2008, http://isites.harvard.edu/fs/docs/icb.topic895260.files/Napier%20Jost%20Why%20Are%20Conservatives%20Happier.pdf.
3. "Pew Survey: Republicans Are Happier," NewsMax.com, February 24, 2006, http://archive.newsmax.com/archives/ic/2006/2/24/134013.shtml.
4. David Montgomery, "A Happiness Gap: Doomacrats And Republigrins," *Washington Post*, October 24, 2008, http://articles.washingtonpost.com/2008-10-24/news/36866515_1_republicans-democrats-happiness-gap.
5. David Zurawik, "SUPER BOWL XLVII Sunday's Super Bowl most watched TV show in U.S. history, CBS says," *Baltimore Sun*, February 4, 2013, http://articles.baltimoresun.com/2013-02-04/entertainment/bal-super-bowl-most-watched-tv-show-ever-20130204_1_total-viewers-audience-nielsen-figures.
6. "NFL Network: The Harbaughs," Forty Niners Football Company, November 22, 2011, http://www.49ers.com/media-gallery/videos/NFL-Network-The-Harbaughs/a266284a-ae84-4fb6-898f-8c7280087906.

INDEX